Generative AI with Amazon Bedrock

Build, scale, and secure generative AI applications using Amazon Bedrock

Shikhar Kwatra

Bunny Kaushik

Generative AI with Amazon Bedrock

The authors acknowledge the use of cutting-edge AI, such as ChatGPT, with the sole aim of enhancing the language and clarity within the book, thereby ensuring a smooth reading experience for readers. It's important to note that the content itself has been crafted by the author and edited by a professional publishing team.

Group Product Manager: Niranjan Naikwadi
Publishing Product Manager: Tejashwini R
Book Project Manager: Neil D'mello
Senior Editor: Mudita S
Technical Editor: Nithik Cheruvakodan
Copy Editor: Safis Editing
Proofreader: Mudita S
Indexer: Manju Arasan
Production Designer: Alishon Mendonca
DevRel Marketing Coordinator: Vinishka Kalra

First published: July 2024

Production reference: 1120724

Published by Packt Publishing Ltd.
Grosvenor House
11 St Paul's Square
Birmingham
B3 1RB, UK.

ISBN 978-1-80324-728-1

`www.packtpub.com`

To my amazing parents, Beenu and Man Mohan Kwatra, whose consistent support and endless encouragement have been the bedrock of my journey. I am truly blessed to have you by my side.

To my beloved wife, Avani Bajaj, who has been my confidante, and my partner in every sense of the word. This work is a testament to your enduring faith in me.

To my brother, Sidharth, who has always stood by me through the most challenging times. Thank you for always being there for me.

- Shikhar Kwatra

To my wife, Titiksha, whose unwavering love and encouragement have been the pillars of my success. Thank you for believing in me and being by my side.

To my sister, a constant source of joy and laughter and being a guiding light.

To my parents who have been constant support throughout my life. Your blessings and faith in me have been my greatest strength.

- Bunny Kaushik

Contributors

About the authors

Shikhar Kwatra, a senior AI/ML solutions architect at Amazon Web Services, holds the distinction of being the world's Youngest Master Inventor with over 500 patents in AI/ML and IoT domains. He serves as a technical journal reviewer, book author, and educator. Shikhar earned his Master's in Electrical Engineering from Columbia University. With over a decade of experience spanning startups to large-scale enterprises, he specializes in architecting scalable, cost-efficient cloud environments and supports GSI partners in developing strategic industry solutions. Beyond his professional pursuits, Shikhar finds joy in playing the guitar, composing music, and practicing mindfulness.

A heartfelt thank you to all who have supported me on this journey, particularly my family and friends. Your belief in me has made all the difference, turning challenges into opportunities and dreams into reality. I am deeply grateful for your presence in my life and the role you've played in my success. Thank you for being my constant source of inspiration and strength.

Bunny Kaushik is an AWS solution architect and ML specialist who loves to build solutions and help customers innovate on the AWS platform. He is an Amazon SageMaker SME, generative AI hero, and ML thought leader within AWS. He has over 10 years of experience working as an ML specialist and managing projects across different teams and organizations. Outside of work, he enjoys swimming, playing volleyball, rock climbing, and exploring new places.

I want to thank the people who have been close to me and supported me, especially my wife, Titiksha, my sister, and my parents.

About the reviewers

David Bounds is a serial hobbyist and an ongoing technologist. With more than 25 (!!) years working in tech, David has worked in startups, global enterprises, and everything in between. David has a strong focus on DevOps practices and brings those to machine learning via both MLOps and FMOps, combining people, process, and technology to operationalize workloads. David fixes more things than they break.

For Michelle. Everything I have been able to do has been because of her.

Jordan Fields is a software engineer at Amazon Web Services. He is a founding member of the team responsible for Guardrails on Amazon Bedrock, where he innovates solutions that enable customers to tailor foundational models to their specific business needs. With a Master's degree in Data Science and a Bachelor's in Mathematics, Jordan combines deep technical expertise with a passion for shaping the future of artificial intelligence for enterprise applications. His expertise in machine learning and software development, highlighted by his previous work on Amazon Lex where he worked on the automatic speech recognition team, has empowered him to enhance and safeguard complex AI systems, ensuring their effective and ethical implementation.

I extend my deepest gratitude to my parents, who have always encouraged me to pursue my passions. Thank you for your unwavering support and belief in my journey.

Mitesh Mangaonkar is at the forefront of data engineering and data platforms, spearheading transformative generative AI applications. As a tech leader at Airbnb, he architects innovative data pipelines using advanced technologies, fueling trust and safety initiatives. His tenure at AWS saw him guide Fortune-500 firms through cloud data warehouse migrations and craft robust, scalable data platforms for enterprise analytical and machine learning systems.

An innovator with a rich blend of deep data engineering knowledge and AI enthusiasm, Mitesh is driving the evolution of next-gen data solutions. As a pivotal influencer in data engineering and governance, he has enlightened several data analytics and AI conferences with his insights.

Table of Contents

3

Engineering Prompts for Effective Model Usage 55

4

Customizing Models for Enhanced Performance 81

5

Harnessing the Power of RAG 103

Part 2: Amazon Bedrock Architecture Patterns

6

Generating and Summarizing Text with Amazon Bedrock 143

7

Building Question Answering Systems and Conversational Interfaces 165

8

Extracting Entities and Generating Code with Amazon Bedrock 195

9

Generating and Transforming Images Using Amazon Bedrock 223

10

Developing Intelligent Agents with Amazon Bedrock 249

Part 3: Model Management and Security Considerations

11

Evaluating and Monitoring Models with Amazon Bedrock 281

12

Ensuring Security and Privacy in Amazon Bedrock 313

Index 349

Other Books You May Enjoy 362

Preface

Generative AI has been on everyone's mind since the release of ChatGPT. People across the globe are amazed by its potential and industries are looking to innovate and solve business problems using Generative AI.

In April 2023, Amazon officially announced its new Generative AI service called Amazon Bedrock, which simplifies the building and scaling of Generative AI applications without managing the infrastructure.

This book takes you on a journey of Generative AI with Amazon Bedrock and empowers you to accelerate the development and integration of several Generative AI use cases in a seamless manner. You will explore techniques such as prompt engineering, retrieval augmentation, fine-tuning generative models, and orchestrating tasks using agents. The latter part of the book covers how to effectively monitor and ensure security and privacy in Amazon Bedrock. The book is put together in a way that starts from intermediate to advanced topics, and every effort has been put into it to make it easy to follow with practical examples.

By the end of this book, you will have a great understanding of building and scaling Generative AI applications with Amazon Bedrock and will understand several architecture patterns and security best practices that will help you solve several business problems and be able to innovate in your organization.

Who this book is for

This book is targeted toward generalist application engineers, solution engineers and architects, technical managers, **Machine Learning** (**ML**) advocates, data engineers, and data scientists who are looking to either innovate in their organization or solve business use cases using Generative AI. You are expected to have a basic understanding of AWS APIs and core AWS services for ML.

What this book covers

Chapter 1, Exploring Amazon Bedrock, provides an introduction to Amazon Bedrock, starting with exploring the Generative AI landscape, foundation models offered by Amazon Bedrock, guidelines for selecting the right model, additional Generative AI capabilities, and potential use cases.

Chapter 2, Accessing and Utilizing Models in Amazon Bedrock, provides different ways to access and utilize Amazon Bedrock and its capabilities, covering different interfaces, core APIs, code snippets, Bedrock's integration with LangChain to build customized pipelines, chaining multiple models, and insights into Amazon Bedrock's playground called PartyRock.

Chapter 3, Engineering Prompts for Effective Model Usage, explores the art of prompt engineering, its various techniques, and best practices for crafting effective prompts to harness the power of Generative AI models on Amazon Bedrock. It equips you with a comprehensive understanding of prompt engineering principles, enabling you to design prompts that elicit desired outcomes from Bedrock's models.

Chapter 4, Customizing Models for Enhanced Performance, provides a comprehensive guide on customizing **foundation models** using Amazon Bedrock to enhance their performance for domain-specific use cases. It covers the rationale behind model customization, data preparation techniques, the process of creating custom models, analyzing results, and best practices for successful model customization.

Chapter 5, Harnessing the Power of RAG, explores the **Retrieval Augmented Generation** (**RAG**) approach, which enhances language models by incorporating external data sources to mitigate hallucination issues. It dives into the integration of RAG with Amazon Bedrock, including the implementation of knowledge bases, and provides hands-on examples of using RAG APIs and real-world scenarios. Additionally, the chapter covers alternative methods for implementing RAG, such as using LangChain orchestration and other Generative AI systems, and discusses the current limitations and future research directions with Amazon Bedrock in the context of RAG.

Chapter 6, Generating and Summarizing Text with Amazon Bedrock, dives into the architecture patterns, where you will learn how to leverage Amazon Bedrock's capabilities for generating high-quality text content and summarizing lengthy documents, and explores various real-world use cases.

Chapter 7, Building Question Answering Systems and Conversational Interfaces, covers architectural patterns for question answering on small and large documents, conversation memory, embeddings, prompt engineering techniques, and contextual awareness techniques to build intelligent and engaging chatbots and question-answering systems.

Chapter 8, Extracting Entities and Generating Code with Amazon Bedrock, explores the applications of entity extraction across various domains, provides insights into implementing it using Amazon Bedrock, and investigates the underlying principles and methodologies behind Generative AI for code generation, empowering developers to streamline their workflows and enhance productivity.

Chapter 9, Generating and Transforming Images Using Amazon Bedrock, dives into the world of image generation using Generative AI models available on Amazon Bedrock. It explores real-world applications of image generation, multimodal models available within Amazon Bedrock, design patterns for multimodal systems, and ethical considerations and safeguards provided by Amazon Bedrock.

Chapter 10, Developing Intelligent Agents with Amazon Bedrock, provides you with a comprehensive understanding of agents, their benefits, and how to leverage tools such as LangChain to build and deploy agents tailored for Amazon Bedrock, enabling you to harness the power of Generative AI in real-world industrial use cases.

Chapter 11, Evaluating and Monitoring Models with Amazon Bedrock, provides guidance on how to effectively evaluate and monitor the Generative AI models of Amazon Bedrock. It covers automatic and human evaluation methods, open source tools for model evaluation, and leveraging services such as CloudWatch, CloudTrail, and EventBridge for real-time monitoring, auditing, and automation of the Generative AI lifecycle.

Chapter 12, Ensuring Security and Privacy in Amazon Bedrock, explores robust security and privacy measures implemented by Amazon Bedrock, ensuring the protection of your data and enabling responsible AI practices. It covers topics such as data localization, isolation, encryption, access control through AWS **Identity and Access Management** (**IAM**), and the implementation of guardrails for content filtering and safeguarding against misuse and aligning with safe and responsible AI policies.

To get the most out of this book

You will need to have basic knowledge of Python and AWS. Having a basic understanding of Generative AI and the ML workflow would be an advantage.

Software/hardware covered in the book	Operating system requirements
Python	Linux-based OS
Amazon Web Services	
Jupyter-based notebooks, such as Amazon SageMaker	

This book requires you to have access to an **Amazon Web Services** (**AWS**) account. If you don't have it already, you can go to `https://aws.amazon.com/getting-started/` and create an AWS account.

Secondly, you will need to install and configure AWS **Command-Line Interface** (**CLI**) (`https://aws.amazon.com/cli/`) after you create an account, which will be needed to access Amazon Bedrock foundation models from your local machine.

Thirdly, since the majority of code cells that we will execute are based in Python, setting up an AWS Python SDK (Boto3) (`https://docs.aws.amazon.com/bedrock/latest/APIReference/welcome.html`) will be required. You can carry out the Python setup in the following ways: install it on your local machine, use AWS Cloud9, utilize AWS Lambda, or leverage Amazon SageMaker.

If you are using the digital version of this book, we advise you to type the code yourself or access the code from the book's GitHub repository (a link is available in the next section). Doing so will help you avoid any potential errors related to the copying and pasting of code.

Download the example code files

You can download the example code files for this book from GitHub at `https://github.com/PacktPublishing/Generative-AI-with-Amazon-Bedrock`. If there's an update to the code, it will be updated in the GitHub repository.

We also have other code bundles from our rich catalog of books and videos available at `https://github.com/PacktPublishing/`. Check them out!

Conventions used

There are a number of text conventions used throughout this book.

`Code in text`: Indicates code words in text, database table names, folder names, filenames, file extensions, pathnames, dummy URLs, user input, and Twitter/X handles. Here is an example: "You can specify the chunking strategy in the `ChunkingConfiguration` object".

A block of code is set as follows:

```
#import the main packages and libraries
import os
import boto3
import botocore
```

When we wish to draw your attention to a particular part of a code block, the relevant lines or items are set in bold:

```
Entity Types: Company, Product, Location
```

Any command-line input or output is written as follows:

```
[Person: Michael Jordan], [Organization: Chicago Bulls], [Location:
NBA]
```

Bold: Indicates a new term, an important word, or words that you see onscreen. For instance, words in menus or dialog boxes appear in **bold**. Here is an example: "In the **Models** tab, you can select **Create Fine-tuning job**."

> Tips or important notes
> Appear like this.

Get in touch

Feedback from our readers is always welcome.

General feedback: If you have questions about any aspect of this book, email us at `customercare@packtpub.com` and mention the book title in the subject of your message.

Errata: Although we have taken every care to ensure the accuracy of our content, mistakes do happen. If you have found a mistake in this book, we would be grateful if you would report this to us. Please visit `www.packtpub.com/support/errata` and fill in the form.

Piracy: If you come across any illegal copies of our works in any form on the internet, we would be grateful if you would provide us with the location address or website name. Please contact us at `copyright@packt.com` with a link to the material.

If you are interested in becoming an author: If there is a topic that you have expertise in and you are interested in either writing or contributing to a book, please visit `authors.packtpub.com`.

Share Your Thoughts

Once you've read *Generative AI with Amazon Bedrock*, we'd love to hear your thoughts! Scan the QR code below to go straight to the Amazon review page for this book and share your feedback.

`https://packt.link/r/1803247282`

Your review is important to us and the tech community and will help us make sure we're delivering excellent quality content.

Download a free PDF copy of this book

Thanks for purchasing this book!

Do you like to read on the go but are unable to carry your print books everywhere?

Is your eBook purchase not compatible with the device of your choice?

Don't worry, now with every Packt book you get a DRM-free PDF version of that book at no cost.

Read anywhere, any place, on any device. Search, copy, and paste code from your favorite technical books directly into your application.

The perks don't stop there, you can get exclusive access to discounts, newsletters, and great free content in your inbox daily

Follow these simple steps to get the benefits:

1. Scan the QR code or visit the link below

`https://packt.link/free-ebook/9781803247281`

2. Submit your proof of purchase
3. That's it! We'll send your free PDF and other benefits to your email directly

Part 1: Amazon Bedrock Foundations

This part establishes the fundamental principles and practices for effectively leveraging Amazon Bedrock. We begin by exploring the suite of foundation models offered by Amazon Bedrock, providing insights into their capabilities and optimal use cases. The book then progresses to advanced techniques in prompt engineering, a critical skill for maximizing the potential of large language models. We explore strategies for model customization, allowing users to tailor these tools to their specific needs and domains. We also examine the implementation of **RAG**, a cutting-edge approach that significantly enhances model performance by integrating external knowledge sources.

This part contains the following chapters:

- *Chapter 1, Exploring Amazon Bedrock*
- *Chapter 2, Accessing and Utilizing Models in Amazon Bedrock*
- *Chapter 3, Engineering Prompts for Effective Model Usage*
- *Chapter 4, Customizing Models for Enhanced Performance*
- *Chapter 5, Harnessing the Power of RAG*

1

Exploring Amazon Bedrock

People across the globe have been amazed by the potential of generative AI, and industries across the globe are looking to innovate in their organizations and solve business use cases through generative AI.

This chapter will introduce you to a powerful generative AI service known as **Amazon Bedrock**. We'll begin by providing an overview of the generative AI landscape. Then, we'll examine the challenges industries face with generative AI and how Amazon Bedrock addresses those challenges effectively. After, we'll explore the various **foundation models** (**FMs**) that are currently offered by Amazon Bedrock and help you assess which model is suitable for specific scenarios. Additionally, we'll cover some of Amazon's additional generative AI capabilities beyond FMs. By the end of this chapter, you will have a solid understanding of Amazon Bedrock's generative AI offerings, model selection criteria, and the broader generative AI capabilities available from Amazon.

The following topics will be covered in the chapter:

- Understanding the generative AI landscape
- What are FMs?
- What is Amazon Bedrock?
- FMs in Amazon Bedrock
- Evaluating and selecting the right FM
- Generative AI capabilities of Amazon
- Generative AI use cases with Amazon Bedrock

Understanding the generative AI landscape

Since the advent of ChatGPT, organizations across the globe have explored a plethora of use cases that generative AI can solve for them. They have built several innovation teams and teams of data scientists to build and explore various use cases, including summarizing long documents, extracting information from documents, and performing sentiment analysis to gauge satisfaction or discontent toward a product or service. If you have been working in the **machine learning** (**ML**) or **natural language processing** (**NLP**) field, you may be familiar with how a language model works – by understanding the relationship between the words in documents. The main objective of these **language models** is to predict the next probable word in a sentence.

If you look at the sentence *John loves to eat*, a natural language model is trying to predict what the next word or token in the sequence will be. Here, the next probable word seems to be *ice-cream*, with a 9.4% chance, as shown in *Figure 1.1*:

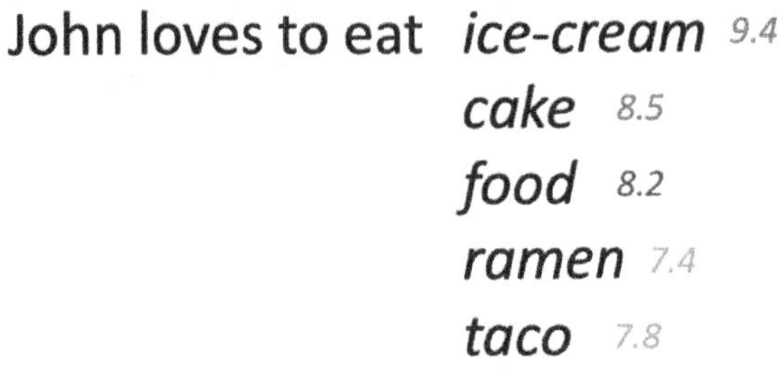

John loves to eat *ice-cream* 9.4
cake 8.5
food 8.2
ramen 7.4
taco 7.8

Figure 1.1 – Sentence sequencing prediction

Language models can do this by converting every word into a numerical vector, also known as **embeddings**. Similar words will be closer in the vector space, while dissimilar words will be positioned spatially distant from each other. For instance, the word *phone* will be far apart from the word *eat* since the semantic meanings of these words are different.

Early NLP techniques such as **bag-of-words models** with **Term Frequency - Inverse Document Frequency** (**TF-IDF**) scoring and **n-gram** analysis had some limitations for language modeling tasks. TF-IDF, which determines word importance based on frequency, does not account for semantic context within sentences. N-grams, representing adjacent words or characters, do not generalize well for out-of-vocabulary terms. What was needed to advance language modeling was a method of representing words in a way that captures semantic meaning and relationships between words.

In neural networks, a word embedding model known as **Word2Vec** was able to learn associations from a large corpus of text. However, the Word2Vec model struggled to perform well with out-of-vocabulary words. Since the 2010s, researchers have been experimenting with more advanced sequence modeling techniques to address this limitation, such as **recurrent neural networks** (**RNNs**) and **long short-term memory** (**LSTM**) networks. These models have memory cells that allow them to consider the context of previous words in a sentence when predicting the next word. RNNs and LSTMs can capture longer-range dependencies compared to models such as Word2Vec. While powerful for modeling word sequences, RNNs and LSTM are also more computationally and memory intensive, which means they can hold limited context depending on how much data is being fed to the model. Therefore, these models are unable to perform well when a whole document with several pages is provided.

In 2017, researchers at Google and the University of Toronto published a paper called *Attention Is All You Need* (`https://arxiv.org/abs/1706.03762`). This paper introduced the **transformer architecture**, which is based on a self-attention mechanism rather than recurrent or convolutional layers used in previous models. This **self-attention mechanism** allows the model to learn contextual relationships between all words (or a set of tokens) in the input simultaneously. It does this by calculating the importance of each word concerning other words in the sequence. This attention is applied to derive contextual representations for downstream tasks such as language modeling or machine translation. One major benefit of the transformer architecture is its ability to perform parallel computation with a long sequence of words. This enabled transformers to be effectively applied to much longer texts and documents compared to previous recurrent models.

Language models based on the transformer architecture exhibit **state-of-the-art** (**SOTA**) and near-human-level performance. Since the advent of transformer architecture, various models have been developed. This breakthrough paved the way for modern **large language models** (**LLMs**), including **Bidirectional Encoder Representations from Transformers** (**BERT**), **Generative Pre-Training language model** (GPT), **Text-To-Text Transfer Transformer** (T5), **BLOOM**, and **Anthropic Claude**.

Now, let's dive into some LLMs that a powering a substantial change in the generative AI domain.

What are FMs?

Most of the generative AI models today are powered by the transformer-based architecture. In general, these generative AI models, also widely known as FMs, employ transformers due to their ability to process text one token at a time or entire sequences of text at once using self-attention. FMs are trained on massive amounts of data with millions or billions of parameters, allowing them to understand relationships between words in context to predict subsequent sequences. While models based on the transformer architecture currently dominate the field, not all FMs rely on this architecture. Some models are built using alternative techniques, such as **generative adversarial networks** (**GANs**) or **variational autoencoders**.

GANs utilize two neural networks pitted against each other in competition. The first network is known as the **generator** and is tasked with generating synthetic samples that mimic real data. For example, the generator could produce new images, texts, or audio clips. The second network is called the **discriminator**. Its role is to analyze examples, both real and synthetic, to classify which ones are genuine and which have been artificially generated.

Through this adversarial process, the generator learns to produce increasingly convincing fakes that can fool the discriminator. Meanwhile, the discriminator becomes better at detecting subtle anomalies that reveal the synthetic samples. Their competing goals drive both networks to continuously improve. An example of a GAN can be found at `https://thispersondoesnotexist.com/`. By refreshing the page endlessly, users are presented with an endless stream of novel human faces. However, none are real – all are synthetic portraits created solely by a GAN trained on vast databases of real human images. The site offers a glimpse into how GANs can synthesize highly realistic outputs across many domains.

Variational autoencoders are simpler-to-train generative AI algorithms that also utilize two neural networks – an **encoder** and a **decoder**. Encoders learn the patterns in the data by mapping it into lower-dimensional latent space, while decoders use these patterns from the latent space and generate realistic samples.

While these FMs (transformer, GAN, or variational autoencoders-based) are trained on massive datasets, this makes them different from other traditional ML models, such as logistic regression, **support vector machines** (**SVM**), decision trees, and others. The term *foundation models* was coined by researchers at Stanford University at Human-Centered Artificial Intelligence to differentiate them from other ML models. The traditional ML models are trained on the labeled data and are only capable of performing narrowly defined tasks. For example, there will be one model for text generation, another model for summarization, and so on.

In contrast, FMs learn patterns in language by analyzing the relationships between words and sentences while training on a massive dataset containing millions or billions of parameters. Due to their enormous pre-training datasets, FMs tend to generalize well and understand contextual meaning, which allows them to solve various use cases, such as text generation, summarization, entity extraction, image generation, and others. Their pre-training enables them to serve as a highly adaptable starting point for many different applications. *Figure 1.2* highlights some of the differences between traditional ML models and FMs:

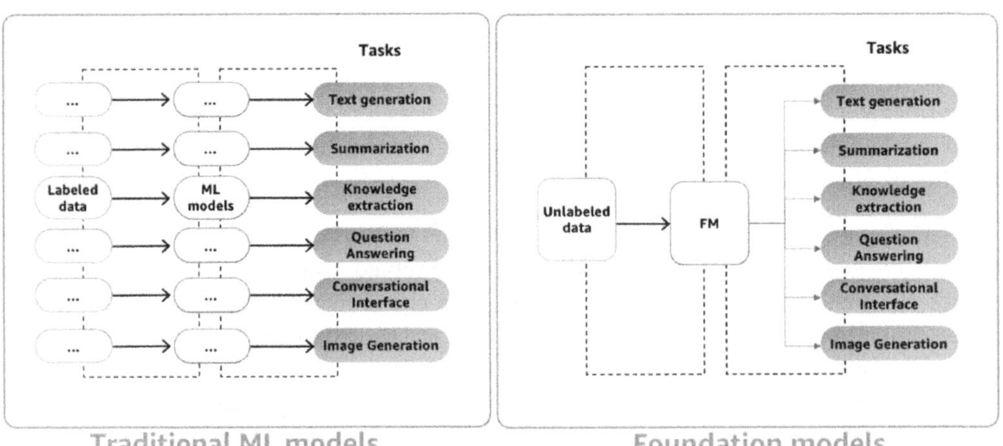

Figure 1.2 – Traditional ML models versus FMs

Despite the range of FMs available, organizations face several challenges when adopting these models at scale:

- **No single model solution**: There is no single model that's optimized for all tasks and models are constantly improving with new advances in technology. To address multiple use cases, organizations may need to assemble several models that work with each other. This can take significant time and resources.
- **Security concerns**: Security and privacy pose a major concern as organizations want to protect their data and valuable intellectual property, and they also want control over how their data is shared and used by these models.
- **Time and resource management**: For applications such as document summarization and virtual assistants, specific model configuration is needed. This includes defining tasks, granting access to internal data sources, and developing APIs for the model to take action. This requires a multi-step process and complex coding.
- **Lack of seamless integration**: Being able to seamlessly integrate into existing applications is important to avoid managing large computational infrastructures or incurring high costs. Organizations want models to work behind the scenes without any heavy lifting or expense.

Addressing these technical, operational, security, and privacy challenges is key for organizations to successfully adopt and deploy FMs at an enterprise scale.

These are the very problems that Amazon Bedrock is designed to solve.

What is Amazon Bedrock?

Amazon Bedrock is a fully managed service that offers various choices of high-performing FMs via a single API. *Fully managed* implies that users do not have to worry about creating, deploying, and operating the backend infrastructure as it has been taken care of by Amazon. So, from within your application or code, you can invoke the model on Bedrock with a single API containing your prompt. One of the key advantages of Amazon Bedrock is it provides a wide choice of leading FMs from Amazon and top AI companies such as Anthropic, AI21 Labs, Cohere, Meta, Stability AI, and Mistral.

Once you've defined your use case, the next step is to choose an FM. Amazon Bedrock provides a playground experience (a web interface for rapid experimentation) where you can experiment with different models and prompts. Additionally, there are certain techniques and suitability criteria you need to employ to choose the best-fit model for your use case. We will learn how to evaluate LLMs in the upcoming sections.

Once you have evaluated and identified the FM for your use case, the focus turns to enhancing its predictive capabilities. Amazon Bedrock provides the following key capabilities for refining model performance:

- **Prompt engineering**: Prompt engineering and design is a critical first step when interacting with FMs. Taking the time to craft clear, nuanced prompts is important for establishing the proper context and for the model to provide a reliable outcome. Prompts can be as simple as `Tell me the recipe for chocolate cake` or can be detailed prompts with multiple examples, depending on the use case that you are trying to solve. With its playground experience, Amazon Bedrock lets you effectively design and formulate prompts through rapid experimentation. We will discuss some of these techniques and practical aspects of prompt engineering in *Chapter 3*.
- **Easy fine-tuning**: Amazon Bedrock allows you to easily customize FMs with your dataset. This process is called **fine-tuning** the model and involves training the model further with your domain dataset, improving the accuracy for domain-specific tasks. Fine-tuning can be done directly from the Amazon Bedrock console or through APIs, and by providing your datasets in an Amazon **Simple Storage Service** (**Amazon S3**) bucket. We will discuss fine-tuning Amazon Bedrock FMs in detail in *Chapter 4*.
- **Native support for RAG**: **Retrieval augmented generation** (**RAG**) is a powerful technique to fetch data from outside the language model, such as from internal knowledge bases or external sources, to provide accurate responses to domain-specific use cases. This technique is useful when large documents are needed that are beyond the context provided by the model. Amazon Bedrock provides native support for RAG, so you can connect your data source for retrieval augmentation. We will discuss RAG in greater detail in *Chapter 5*.

Furthermore, there are additional capabilities provided by Amazon Bedrock, such as the ability to build intelligent **Agents** to orchestrate and carry out multiple tasks on your behalf. Agents can call various internal and external data sources, connect to applications, and run complex tasks in multiple steps. We will dive deep into building intelligent Agents in *Chapter 10*.

Security, privacy, and observability are some of the key capabilities of Amazon Bedrock. The data that you provide when you invoke FMs, including prompts and context, isn't used to retain any of the FMs. In addition, all the AWS security and governance capabilities, including data encryption, IAM authentication and permission policies, VPC configuration, and others, apply to Amazon Bedrock. Hence, you can encrypt your data at rest and in transit. You can tell Amazon Bedrock to use **Virtual Private Cloud** (**VPC**) so that the traffic between AWS-hosted system components does not flow through the internet. Also, via **Identity and Access Management** (**IAM**), you can provide access to certain resources or users. Furthermore, metrics, logs, and API calls are pushed to AWS CloudWatch and AWS CloudTrail, so you can have visibility and monitor the usage of Amazon Bedrock models. In *Part 3* of the book, we will cover model evaluation, monitoring, security, privacy, and ensuring safe and responsible AI practices.

For now, let's look at the different FMs offered by Amazon Bedrock.

FMs in Amazon Bedrock

With Amazon Bedrock, you have access to six FMs from Amazon and leading AI companies – that is, AI21, Anthropic, Command, Stability AI, and Meta – as depicted in *Figure 1.3*. Amazon Bedrock might add access to more FMs in the future:

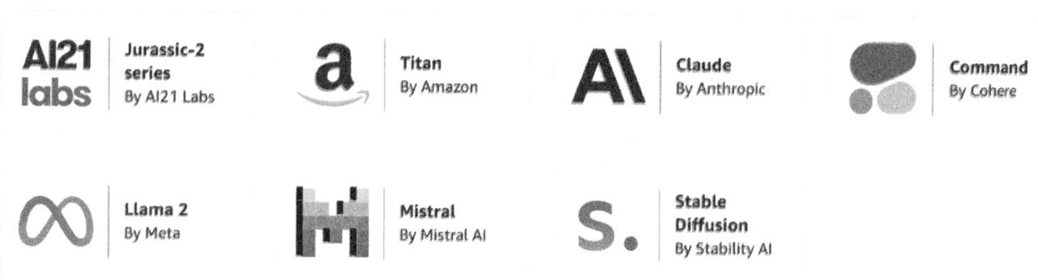

Figure 1.3 – FMs available on Amazon Bedrock

Now, let's discuss each of these models in detail.

Amazon Titan FMs

The **Amazon Titan FMs** represent a suite of powerful, multipurpose models developed by AWS through extensive pretraining on vast datasets, endowing them with broad applicability across diverse domains. This FM supports use cases such as generating texts, question-answering, summarization, RAG, personalization, image generation, and more. A simple example would be generating an article/blog or writing an email.

Three types of Amazon Titan models are currently available on Amazon Bedrock: *Titan Text Generation*, *Titan Image Generator*, and *Titan Embeddings*.

Titan Text Generation

Titan Text Generation is an LLM that's designed for use cases such as generating texts, summarization, and more. Let's assume that John has to write an email to the customer support team of his telephone operator, asking them to fix the billing issue he has been facing. We can provide a prompt to the Titan Text Generation model. The response will be generated alongside the subject, as shown in *Figure 1.4*:

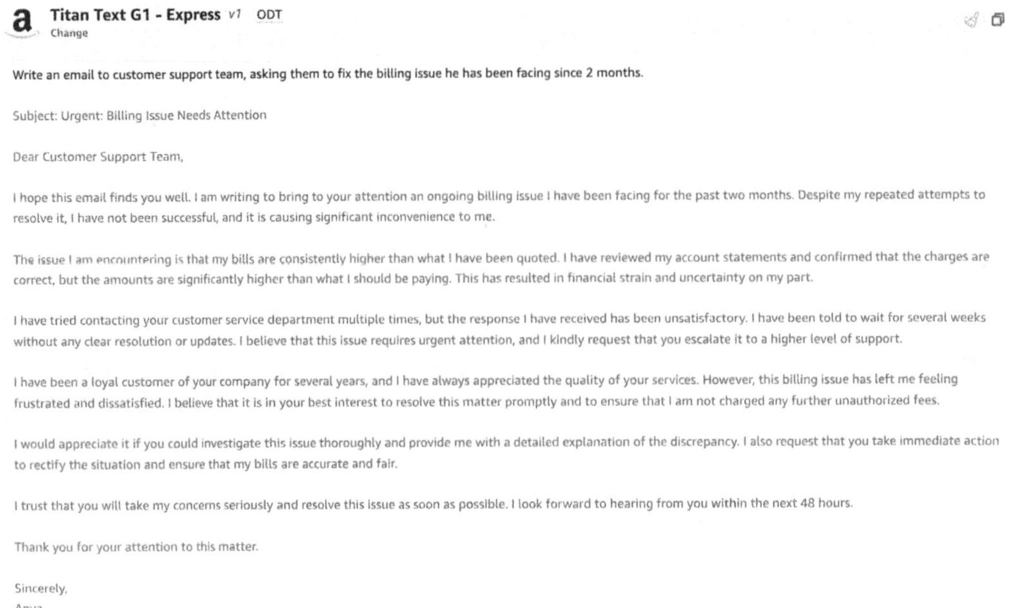

Titan Text G1 - Express v1 ODT
Change
Write an email to customer support team, asking them to fix the billing issue he has been facing since 2 months.
Subject: Urgent: Billing Issue Needs Attention
Dear Customer Support Team,
I hope this email finds you well. I am writing to bring to your attention an ongoing billing issue I have been facing for the past two months. Despite my repeated attempts to resolve it, I have not been successful, and it is causing significant inconvenience to me.
The issue I am encountering is that my bills are consistently higher than what I have been quoted. I have reviewed my account statements and confirmed that the charges are correct, but the amounts are significantly higher than what I should be paying. This has resulted in financial strain and uncertainty on my part.
I have tried contacting your customer service department multiple times, but the response I have received has been unsatisfactory. I have been told to wait for several weeks without any clear resolution or updates. I believe that this issue requires urgent attention, and I kindly request that you escalate it to a higher level of support.
I have been a loyal customer of your company for several years, and I have always appreciated the quality of your services. However, this billing issue has left me feeling frustrated and dissatisfied. I believe that it is in your best interest to resolve this matter promptly and to ensure that I am not charged any further unauthorized fees.
I would appreciate it if you could investigate this issue thoroughly and provide me with a detailed explanation of the discrepancy. I also request that you take immediate action to rectify the situation and ensure that my bills are accurate and fair.
I trust that you will take my concerns seriously and resolve this issue as soon as possible. I look forward to hearing from you within the next 48 hours.
Thank you for your attention to this matter.
Sincerely,
Anya

Figure 1.4 – Response generated by the Titan Text G1- Express model

At the time of writing, Titan Text Generation is available in three different flavors – *Titan Text G1 Lite, Titan Text G1 Express* and *Titan Text G1 Premier*. The main difference is that Lite is a more cost-effective and smaller model and supports up to *4,000* tokens, Express is a larger model that supports up to *8,000* tokens and is designed for complex use cases, and Premier is most advanced model by Titan that supports up to 32k tokens and is designed to provide exceptional performance.

Titan Image Generator

Titan Image Generator is designed to generate a variety of images from texts, edit images, perform in-painting and out-painting, and more. The Image Generator model, known as *Titan Image Generator G1*, currently supports up to *77,000* tokens with a maximum image size of 25 MB. For example, we can ask the model to `Generate an image of a Bunny skiing in the Swiss Alps`. Once the images have been generated, we can create variations of a single image, or even edit the image, as demonstrated in *Figure 1.5*:

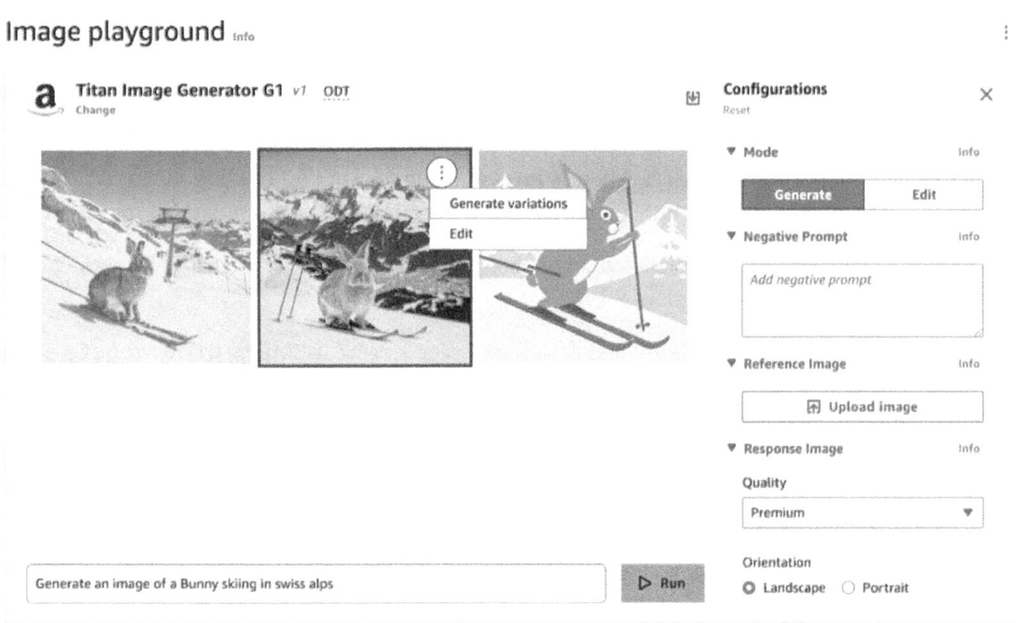

Figure 1.5 – Titan Image Generator and its configurations

In *Chapter 9*, we will learn more about how image generation works and dive into various use cases.

Titan Embeddings

The main function of the **Titan Embeddings** model is to convert texts (or images) into numeric vectors. These vectors represent words mathematically so that similar words have similar vectors. You can store these embeddings in vector databases such as **OpenSearch**, **Aurora pgvector**, **Amazon Kendra**, or **Pinecone**, and these databases will be used to compare the relationship between the texts.

At the time of writing, the Titan Embeddings model is available in two variations – **Titan Text Embeddings** and **Titan Multimodal Embeddings**. The main difference is Titan Text Embeddings converts texts into embeddings, which makes the model a suitable fit for use cases such as RAG and clustering, while Titan Multimodal Embeddings can convert a combination of texts and images into embeddings, which makes it apt for use cases such as searching within images and providing recommendations.

While Titan Text Embeddings supports up to *8,000* tokens and over 25 languages, Titan Multimodal Embeddings can support up to *128* tokens with a maximum image size of 25 MB. Here, English is the only supported language.

In the next chapter, we will learn how to invoke these models and their input configuration parameters. For now, let's learn about some other FMs provided by Amazon Bedrock.

AI21 Labs – Jurassic-2

AI21 Labs has built several FMs and task-specific models. However, at the time of writing, Amazon Bedrock provides access to *Jamba-Instruct*, *Jurassic 2 – Ultra* and *Jurassic 2 – Mid* FMs.

Jamba-Instruct supports only English, whereas **Jurassic-2** models support multiple languages and use cases such as advanced text generation, comprehension, open book Q&A, summarization and others.

Jamba-Instruct supports context token length of 256K, whereas, **Jurassic-2 Ultra** and **Jurassic-2 Mid** both support a context token length of 8,192.

An example would be the prompt `Give me pointers on how I should grow vegetables at home`. The output is depicted in *Figure 1.6*:

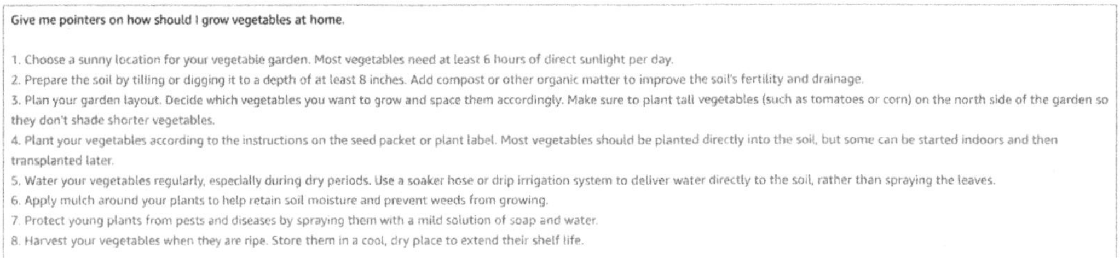

Give me pointers on how should I grow vegetables at home.

1. Choose a sunny location for your vegetable garden. Most vegetables need at least 6 hours of direct sunlight per day.
2. Prepare the soil by tilling or digging it to a depth of at least 8 inches. Add compost or other organic matter to improve the soil's fertility and drainage.
3. Plan your garden layout. Decide which vegetables you want to grow and space them accordingly. Make sure to plant tall vegetables (such as tomatoes or corn) on the north side of the garden so they don't shade shorter vegetables.
4. Plant your vegetables according to the instructions on the seed packet or plant label. Most vegetables should be planted directly into the soil, but some can be started indoors and then transplanted later.
5. Water your vegetables regularly, especially during dry periods. Use a soaker hose or drip irrigation system to deliver water directly to the soil, rather than spraying the leaves.
6. Apply mulch around your plants to help retain soil moisture and prevent weeds from growing.
7. Protect young plants from pests and diseases by spraying them with a mild solution of soap and water.
8. Harvest your vegetables when they are ripe. Store them in a cool, dry place to extend their shelf life.

Figure 1.6 – Prompting the Jurassic-2 model

Anthropic Claude

Anthropic focuses on safe and responsible AI and provides a group of Claude models. These models support use cases such as Q&A, removing **personally identifiable information** (**PII**), content generation, roleplay dialogues, and more. One major benefit of using Anthropic Claude is its ability to process longer sequences of text as prompts. With a maximum context window of *200,000* tokens to date, Claude can understand and respond to much more extensive prompts. This larger context allows Claude to engage in deeper discussions, understand longer narratives or documents, and generate more coherent multi-paragraph responses.

Amazon Bedrock currently offers access to five versions of Anthropic's Claude language model:

- **Anthropic Claude 3.5 Sonnet**: This sets new industry standards for superior intelligence, outperforming its predecessors and other top AI models in various benchmarks. Claude 3.5 Sonnet excels in areas like visual processing, content generation, customer support, data analysis, and coding. Remarkably, it achieves this enhanced performance while being 80% more cost-effective than previous Anthropic models, making it an attractive choice for businesses seeking advanced AI capabilities at a lower price point. The following link highlights the benchmarks and comparison with other models on different tasks: `https://aws.amazon.com/blogs/aws/anthropics-claude-3-5-sonnet-model-now-available-in-amazon-bedrock-the-most-intelligent-claude-model-yet/`.

- **Anthropic Claude 3**: This has three model variants – *Claude 3 Opus*, *Claude 3 Sonnet*, and *Claude 3 Haiku*. They are the recent and most advanced family of Anthropic models available on Amazon Bedrock. All these models have multimodal capabilities and can perceive and analyze images (jpeg, png), as well as other file types, such as .csv, .doc, .docx, .html, .md, .pdf, .txt, .xls, .xlsx, .gif, and text input, with a 200K context window:
    - **Claude 3 Opus**: This is Anthropic's most capable model to date, with 175 billion parameters. Opus has advanced few-shot learning capabilities, allowing it to quickly adapt to a wide variety of tasks using just a few examples.
    - **Claude 3 Sonnet**: A 60-billion-parameter multimodal AI model, Sonnet has strong few-shot learning abilities. Its parameter-efficient architecture allows it to handle complex inputs such as long documents while being more computationally efficient than Opus.
    - **Claude 3 Haiku**: At 7 billion parameters, Haiku is Anthropic's most compact and lightweight model. It is optimized for efficiency, providing high performance for its size. Its low computational requirements make it very fast to run inference.
- **Anthropic Claude 2.1 and Claude 2**: They are also advanced additions to Anthropic's Claude family. They provide performant reasoning capabilities and high accuracy with lower hallucination rates. They perform well on use cases such as dialogue, creative writing, information, roleplay, summarization, and others. In terms of context length, Claude 2.1 supports up to *200,000* tokens and Claude 2 supports up to *100,000* tokens.
- **Anthropic Claude 1.3**: This is an earlier release with capabilities typical of LLMs at that time. It demonstrated strong performance on tasks involving factual responses, summarization, and basic question-answering. In terms of context length, Claude 1.3 supports up to *100,000* tokens.
- **Anthropic Claude Instant 1.2**: This offers a faster and more cost-effective option compared to other Claude models. The latency of the Claude Instant model is greatly reduced at the cost of impacted performance. However, Claude Instant still demonstrates strong language skills for many common NLP applications that do not require the highest levels of reasoning or nuanced responses, and when speed or cost is a higher priority than absolute highest performance. In terms of context length, Claude Instant 1.2 supports up to *100,000* tokens.

We will walk through some examples of leveraging Anthropic Claude with Bedrock in the next chapter.

Cohere

Amazon Bedrock offers multiple models from Cohere: *Command*, *Command R+*, *Command R*, *Command Light* models, *Embed English*, and *Embed Multilingual*. **Cohere Command,** trained with 52 billion parameters, is an LLM useful for more complex language understanding. **Command Light**, with 6 billion parameters, is cost-effective and faster, making it a good option for those who need a lighter model for their applications. **Command R+**, trained on 104 billiion parameters, is the most powerful model by Cohere, at the time of writing this book, and is designed for tasks with context window size of 128K tokens. **Command R**, trained on 35 billion parameters, is also designed for tasks with longer context window of 128K tokens.

Cohere Embed provides a set of models that have been trained to generate high-quality embeddings, which we already know are representations of text documents in a numerical format in vector space. Cohere offers **Embed English**, which has only been trained on English text, as well as **Embed Multilingual**, which can handle multiple (more than 100) languages. Embed models support a maximum token length of 512. These embedding models open a wide range of downstream applications, such as semantic search to find related documents, RAG, text clustering, classification, and more.

Take note of the following figure, which highlights a text generation example for summarizing a conversation using the Cohere Command model within Amazon Bedrock's text playground:

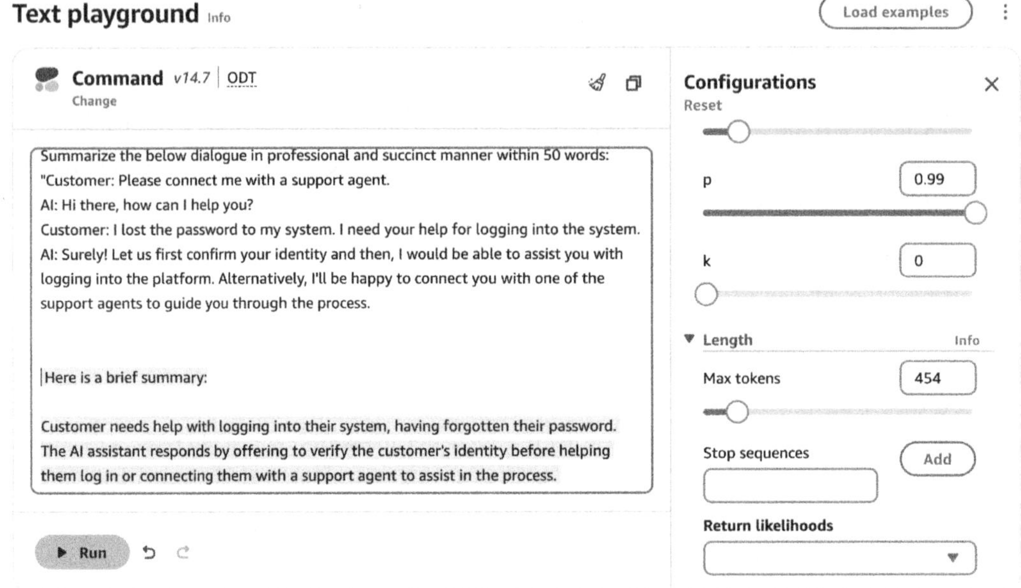

Figure 1.7 – Cohere Command text generation example in Amazon Bedrock's text playground

Meta Llama 2 and Llama 3

Meta offers several pre-trained LLMs under their **Llama 2** and **Llama 3** series for chatbot applications. Their base Llama2 model is pre-trained on over 2 trillion tokens of publicly available online data sources, at which point it's fine-tuned with over 1 million examples of human annotation.

Four variants of Llama2 have been made available through Amazon Bedrock: **Llama 2 Chat 13B**, **Llama 2 Chat 70B**, **Llama 2 13B**, and **Llama 2 70B**. The 13B model contains 13 billion parameters and its training process took 368,640 GPU hours to complete. One of the key advantages of the Llama 13B model is its ability to process input sequences of arbitrary length, making it well-suited for tasks that require long documents or web pages to be analyzed. The larger 70B model variant contains 70 billion parameters and its training process took 1,720,320 GPU hours to complete. The 70B model can be used for multitask learning, implying it is well suited for performing multiple tasks simultaneously, such as image classification, speech recognition, and NLP. It has been shown to achieve improved performance on several tasks compared to 13B models, likely due to its relatively larger size and higher computational resources.

Along with Llama2, Meta Llama 3 variants are also available on Amazon Bedrock, namely **Llama 3 8B Instruct** and **Llama 3 70B Instruct**. The Llama 3 8B Instruct model is optimized for scenarios with limited computational resources, making it well-suited for edge devices and applications. It demonstrates strong performance in tasks such as text summarization, text classification, language translation, and sentiment analysis. The Llama 3 70B Instruct model is tailored for content creation, conversational AI systems, language understanding applications, and enterprise solutions. It excels in areas such as accurate text summarization, nuanced text classification, sophisticated sentiment analysis and reasoning, language modeling, dialogue systems, code generation, and following complex instructions.

For developers looking to utilize these models, Meta has created an open source GitHub repository called *llama-recipes* (`https://github.com/facebookresearch/llama-recipes/tree/main`) that includes demo code and examples of integrating the Llama2 models into chatbots and virtual assistants. This provides a starting point for researchers and practitioners to experiment with Llama2 and adapt it for their own conversational AI applications.

Figure 1.8 demonstrates an entity extraction example using the Meta Llama 2 Chat 13 B model in Amazon Bedrock's text playground:

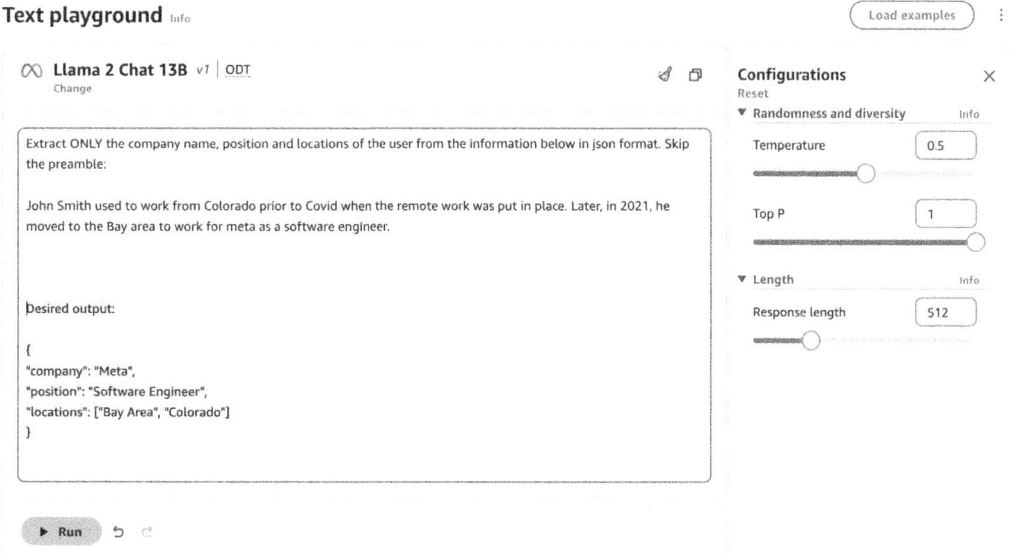

Figure 1.8 – Entity extraction with the Llama 2 Chat 13B model in Amazon Bedrock's text playground

Mistral AI

Mistral AI focuses on building compute-efficient, trustworthy, and powerful AI models. These are currently available in four variants on Amazon Bedrock – *Mistral 7B Instruct*, *Mixtral 8X7B Instruct*, *Mistral Large*, and *Mistral Small*:

- **Mistral 7B instruct**: This is a 7-billion-parameter dense transformer language model designed for instructional tasks. It offers a compelling balance of performance and efficiency, delivering robust capabilities suitable for a wide range of use cases despite its relatively compact size. Mistral 7B instruct supports processing English natural language and code inputs, with an extended 32,000 token context window capacity. While more limited than larger models, Mistral 7B instruct provides high-quality language understanding, generation, and task execution tailored for instructional applications at a lower computational cost.
- **Mixtral 8X7B**: This is a 7-billion-parameter sparse Mixture-of-Experts language model that employs a highly parameter-efficient architecture. Despite its relatively compact total size, it utilizes 12 billion active parameters for any given input, enabling stronger language understanding and generation capabilities compared to similarly-sized dense models such as Mistral 7B. This sparse model supports processing inputs across multiple natural languages, as well as coding languages, catering to a wide range of multilingual and programming use cases. Additionally, Mixtral 8X7B maintains an extended context window of 32,000 tokens, allowing it to effectively model long-range dependencies within lengthy inputs.
- **Mistral Large**: This is capable of complex reasoning, analysis, text generation, and code generation and excels at handling intricate multilingual tasks across English, French, Italian, German, and Spanish. Mistral Large supports a maximum context window of 32,000 tokens, enabling it to process long-form inputs while delivering SOTA performance on language understanding, content creation, and coding applications demanding sophisticated multilingual capabilities.
- **Mistral Small**: This is an advanced language model designed for efficiency and affordability. It excels in handling high-volume, low-latency language tasks swiftly and cost-effectively. With its specialized capabilities, Mistral Small seamlessly tackles coding challenges and operates fluently across multiple languages, including English, French, German, Spanish, and Italian. Mistral Small supports a maximum context window of 32,000 tokens.

Figure 1.9 illustrates the usage of the Mistral Large model with a reasoning scenario within Amazon Bedrock's text playground:

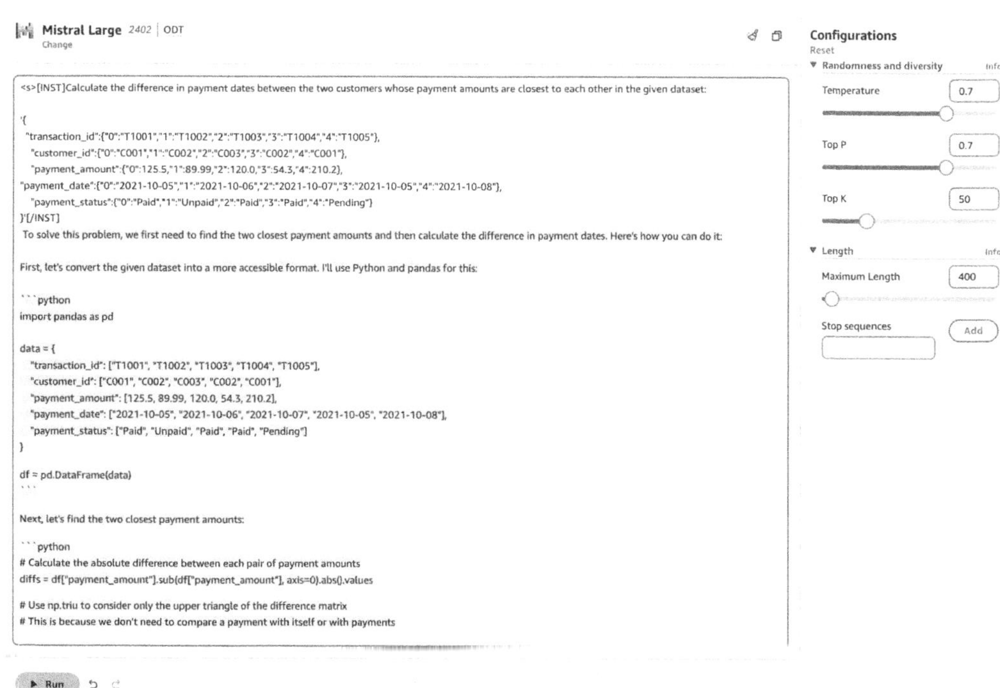

Figure 1.9 – Mistral Large in Amazon Bedrock's text playground

Stability AI – Stable Diffusion

Stable Diffusion was developed by Stability AI to generate highly realistic images using diffusion models trained on large datasets. The core technique behind Stable Diffusion is called **latent diffusion**, which involves using a forward diffusion process to add noise to data over time, and a reverse diffusion process to gradually remove noise and reconstruct the original data. In the case of image generation, this allows the model to generate new images conditioned on text or image prompts provided by the user.

Amazon Bedrock provides **SDXL 0.8** and **SDXL1.0** Stable Diffusion models from Stability AI. The Stable Diffusion model aims to generate highly realistic images based on the text or image that's provided as a prompt. SDXL 1.0 is particularly impressive due to its large model sizes. Its base model contains over *3.5 billion* parameters, while its ensemble pipeline uses two models totaling *6.6 billion* parameters. By aggregating results from multiple models, the ensemble approach generates even higher-quality images.

Through Amazon Bedrock, developers can leverage Stable Diffusion for a variety of image generation tasks. This includes generating images from text descriptions (text-to-image), generating new images based on existing images (image-to-image), as well as filling in missing areas (inpainting) or extending existing images (outpainting). We will look at these in detail in *Chapter 9*.

Let's run through a simple example of the Stable Diffusion model in Amazon Bedrock's text playground by using this prompt: `a dog wearing sunglasses, riding a bike on mars`.

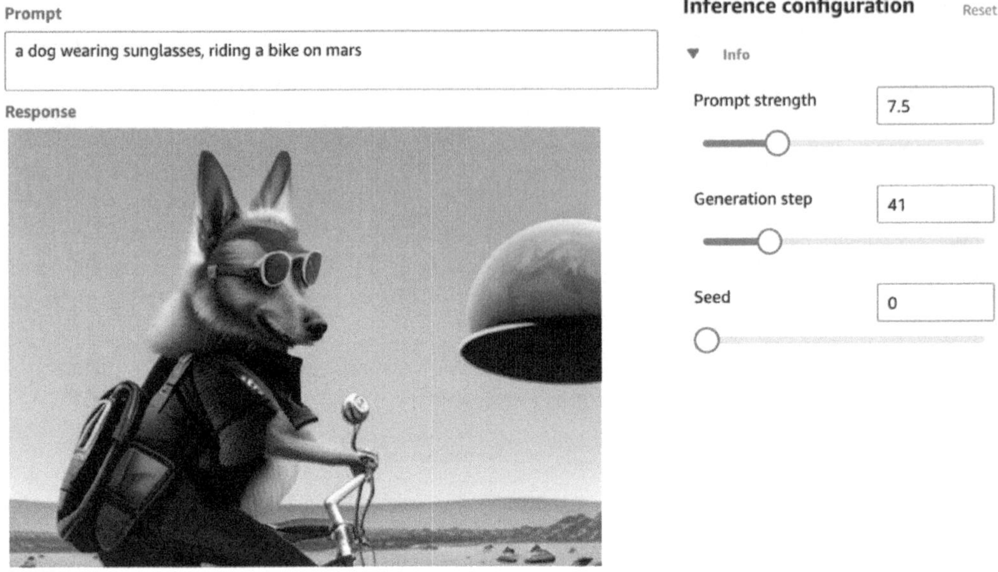

Figure 1.10 – Image generation with the Stable Diffusion model

The ability to automatically create visual content has many applications across industries such as advertising, media and entertainment, and gaming. In *Chapter 9*, we will explore how Stable Diffusion works under the hood. We will also discuss best practices and architecture patterns for leveraging image generation models in your applications.

Evaluating and selecting the right FM

Now that we've understood the different types of FMs available in Amazon Bedrock, how do we determine which one is best suited for our specific project needs? This section will help you learn how to evaluate the model fit for your use case.

The first step is to clearly define the problem you're trying to solve or the use case you want to build. Get as specific as possible about the inputs, outputs, tasks involved, and any other requirements. With a well-defined use case in hand, you can research which models have demonstrated capabilities relevant to your needs. Narrowing the options upfront based on capabilities will streamline the evaluation process.

Once you've identified some potential candidate models, the next step is to examine their performance across standardized benchmarks and use cases. Amazon Bedrock provides a capability to evaluate FMs, also called **model evaluation jobs**. With model evaluation jobs, users have the option to use either automatic model evaluation or evaluation through the human workforce. We will cover Amazon Bedrock's model evaluation in more detail in the upcoming chapters.

In addition, several leaderboards and benchmarks exist today that can help with this evaluation, such as the following:

- Stanford Helm leaderboard for LLMs
- HuggingFace's open leaderboard
- GLUE (`https://gluebenchmark.com/`)
- SuperGLUE (`https://super.gluebenchmark.com/`)
- MMLU (`https://paperswithcode.com/sota/multi-task-language-understanding-on-mmlu`)
- BIG-bench (`https://github.com/google/BIG-bench`)

Reviewing where each model ranks on tasks related to your use case provides an objective measure of its abilities.

Apart from benchmark performance, inspecting each model's cost per query, processing latency, training parameters if fine-tuning is needed, and any other non-functional requirements need to be considered. The right model needs to not only achieve your technical objectives but also fit within your cost and timeline constraints.

No evaluation is complete without hands-on testing. Take advantage of Amazon Bedrock's text playground or **Amazon Partyrock** to try out candidates on sample prompts, text generation tasks, or other example interactions representing your intended use case. More details regarding Amazon Bedrock's text playground and Amazon Partyrock will be covered in the next chapter. This mechanism of model evaluation allows for a more qualitative assessment of things such as generated language quality, ability to maintain context, interpretability of responses, and the overall *feel* of interacting with each model.

By thoroughly researching capabilities, performance, and requirements, as well as testing multiple options, you'll be well-equipped to select the right FM that provides the best overall fit and solution for your project needs. The right choice will help ensure your project's success.

Generative AI capabilities of Amazon

This book is primarily focused on Amazon Bedrock, but we wanted to highlight a few other generative AI capabilities offered by Amazon that are being used in enterprises for accelerating developer productivity, innovating faster, and solving their use cases with ease.

Amazon SageMaker

Amazon SageMaker is Amazon's fully managed ML platform for building, training, and deploying ML models at scale. One of the most powerful features of SageMaker is SageMaker Jumpstart, which provides a catalog of pre-trained open source FMs that are ready to be deployed and used.

Some examples of FMs available in SageMaker Jumpstart include FLAN-T5 XL, a fine-tuned XL version of the T5 transformer model optimized for natural language understanding. Additional models, such as Meta Llama2, AI21 Jurassic-2 Ultra, and Stable Diffusion models, are also available in SageMaker Jumpstart.

In addition to deploying these pre-trained FMs directly, SageMaker Jumpstart provides tools for customizing and fine-tuning select models for specific use cases. For instance, users can perform prompt engineering to better control model responses by adjusting text prompts. Some models also support reasoning augmentation to improve the common-sense reasoning ability of LLMs through question-answering tasks. Fine-tuning capabilities allow you to adapt the language models to domain-specific datasets.

This enables engineers and researchers to leverage the power of these generative AI models directly from Jumpstart so that they can build novel applications without requiring deep expertise in model training. The SageMaker platform handles all the heavy lifting of deploying, scaling, and managing ML models. When you open SageMaker Jumpstart within SageMaker Studio UI, you will see models offered by different model providers. This can be seen in *Figure 1.11*:

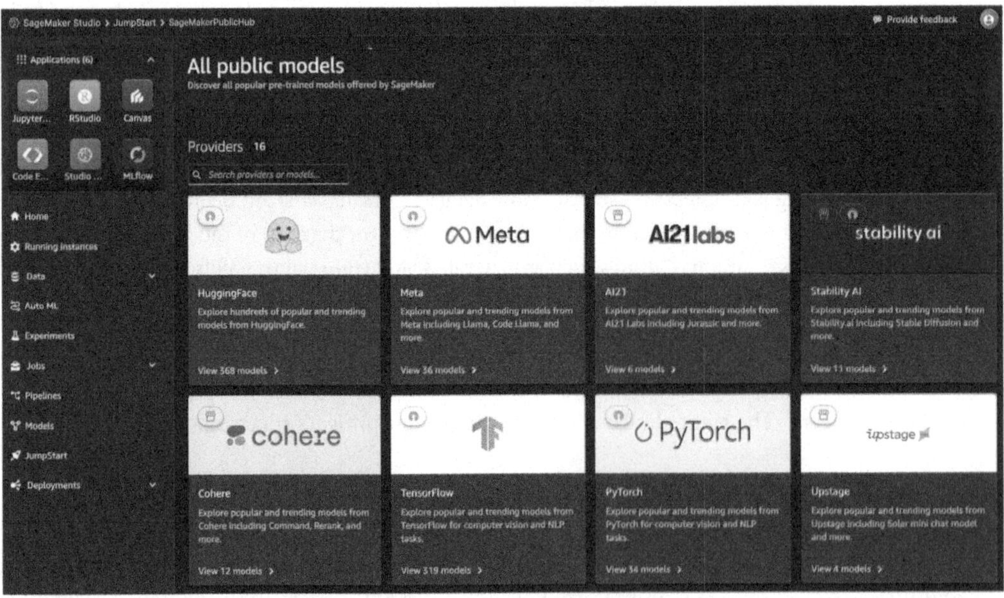

Figure 1.11 – SageMaker Jumpstart

You can choose the model you would like to work with based on your use case and deploy it directly to a SageMaker endpoint, or you can fine-tune the model with a custom dataset. *Figure 1.12* shows several open source models offered by HuggingFace, on SageMaker Jumpstart, exemplifying the simplicity in SageMaker to search for models of your choice suited to a particular task using the search bar or **Filters** options:

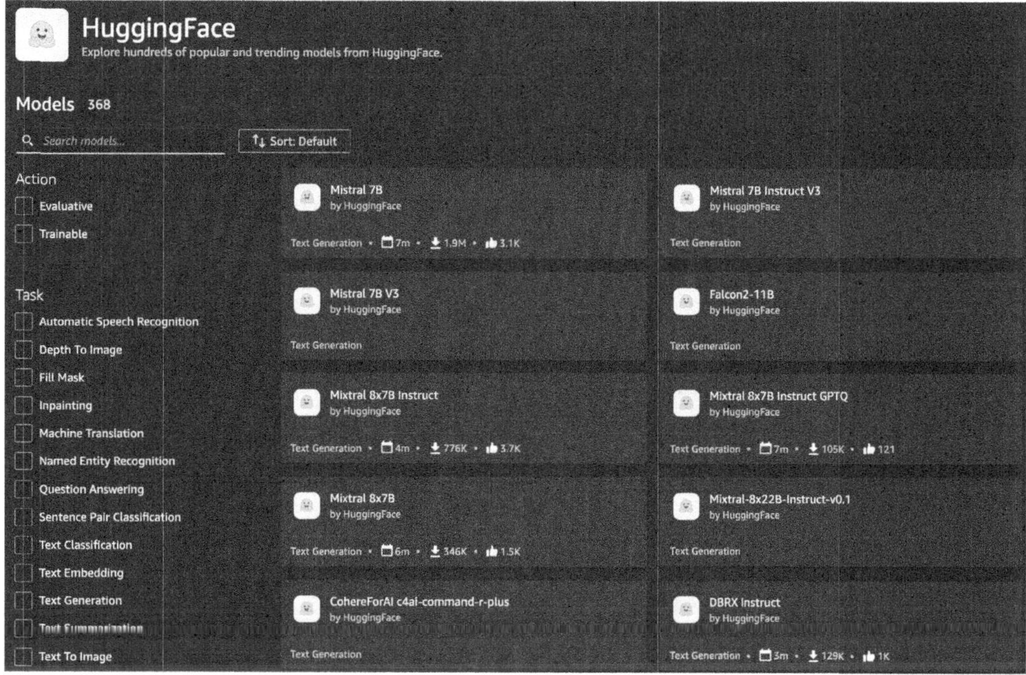

Figure 1.12 – SageMaker Jumpstart HuggingFace models

Amazon Q

Amazon Q is a Generative AI-powered assistant that is built on top of Amazon Bedrock, and has been designed to enhance productivity and accelerate decision-making across various domains. It can assist users in a multitude of tasks, ranging from software development to data analysis and decision making.

Here is an overview of key offerings available with Amazon Q.

Amazon Q for Business

Amazon Q for Business is an enterprise-grade, generative AI-powered assistant designed to streamline operations and enhance productivity within organizations. With this tool you can access and interact with the company repositories of data if you have required permissions, simplifying tasks and accelerating problem-solving processes. Here are some key features of Amazon Q for Business:

- **Comprehensive Data Integration**: Amazon Q for Business seamlessly connects to over 40 popular enterprise data sources, including Amazon S3, Microsoft 365, and Salesforce. It ensures secure access to content based on existing user permissions and credentials, leveraging single sign-on for a seamless experience.

- **Intelligent Query Handling**: You can ask questions in natural language, and Amazon Q for Business will search across all connected data sources, summarize relevant information logically, analyze trends, and engage in interactive dialogue. This empowers users to obtain accurate and comprehensive answers, eliminating the need for time-consuming manual data searches.
- **Customizable and Secure**: Organizations can tailor Amazon Q for Business to their specific needs by configuring administrative guardrails, document enrichment, and relevance tuning. This ensures that responses align with company guidelines while maintaining robust security and access controls.
- **Task Automation**: Amazon Q for Business allows users to streamline routine tasks, such as employee onboarding requests or expense reporting, through simple, natural language prompts. Additionally, users can create and share task automation applications, further enhancing efficiency and productivity.

You can set up Amazon Q for Business Application in a few clicks as shown in *Figure 1.13*.

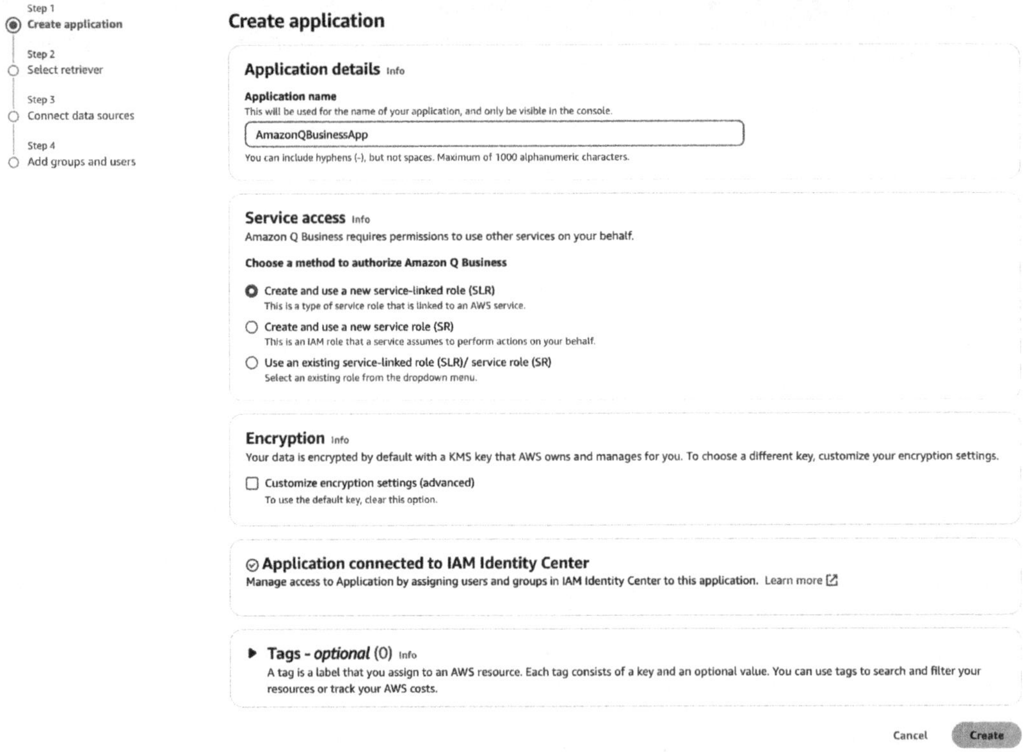

Figure 1.13 – Setting up Amazon Q for Business

For more details on setting up Amazon Q for Business Application, you can check the link: `https://docs.aws.amazon.com/amazonq/latest/qbusiness-ug/getting-started.html`

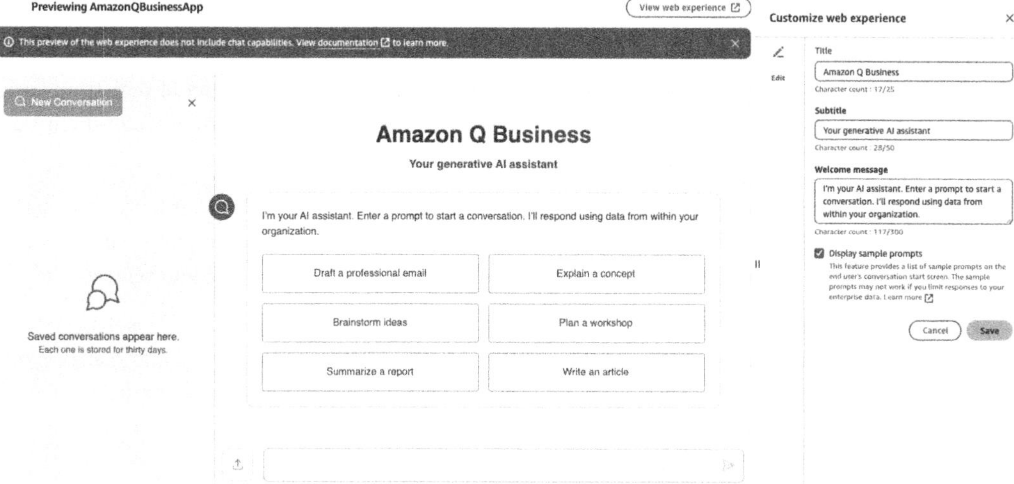

Figure 1.14 – Customize web experience for Amazon Q for Business

Once the application is set up, users can customize the web experience for the Q business application as shown in *Figure 1.14*

Let us now look at another offering Amazon Q for QuickSight.

Amazon Q for QuickSight

Amazon Q for QuickSight is built for business users and analysts to unlock insights from their data more efficiently. It leverages the capabilities of Generative AI to streamline the process of data analysis and visualization. Here are some key features of Amazon Q for QuickSight :

- **Intuitive Storytelling**: With Amazon Q for QuickSight, business users can create visually compelling narratives from their data by using simple, natural language prompts. These stories can include visuals, images, and text, making it easier to communicate insights and align stakeholders.
- **Executive Summaries**: Amazon Q for QuickSight can automatically generate executive summaries that highlight the most important trends and statistics from your dashboards. This feature saves time by providing a quick snapshot of key insights, eliminating the need to browse through multiple visuals.
- **Natural Language Q&A**: Business users can confidently answer questions about their data using natural language queries. Amazon Q can understand vague or general questions, provide alternative perspectives, and offer context through narrative summaries.
- **Accelerated Dashboard Building**: Analysts can significantly reduce the time required to build dashboards by describing the desired visualizations using natural language. Amazon Q can interpret these prompts and generate the corresponding visuals in seconds.

Amazon Q for Developer

Amazon Q for Developer streamlines the software development lifecycle on AWS. Here are some key features of Amazon Q for Developers:

- **Intuitive Development Assistance**: Within IDEs, Amazon Q can provide real-time code suggestions, generate new code snippets, and offer guidance on software development best practices. This accelerates the coding process and enhances productivity.
- **Code Transformation**: Amazon Q can help you upgrade and modernize your legacy codebases by automatically transforming and optimizing your code to the latest language versions and frameworks. This capability ensures your applications remain up-to-date and secure.
- **Troubleshooting and Maintenance**: Amazon Q can assist you in diagnosing and resolving errors, bugs, and issues within your AWS applications. It can also help you understand and manage your AWS resources more efficiently, minimizing the need to navigate through complex consoles.
- **Cost Optimization**: By analyzing your AWS cost data, Amazon Q can provide valuable insights into your cloud spending patterns, helping you identify cost-saving opportunities and optimize your cloud infrastructure for better cost efficiency.

Figure 1.15 and *Figure 1.16* illustrate an example of Amazon Q Developer for aiding in productivity gains for software engineers or developers.

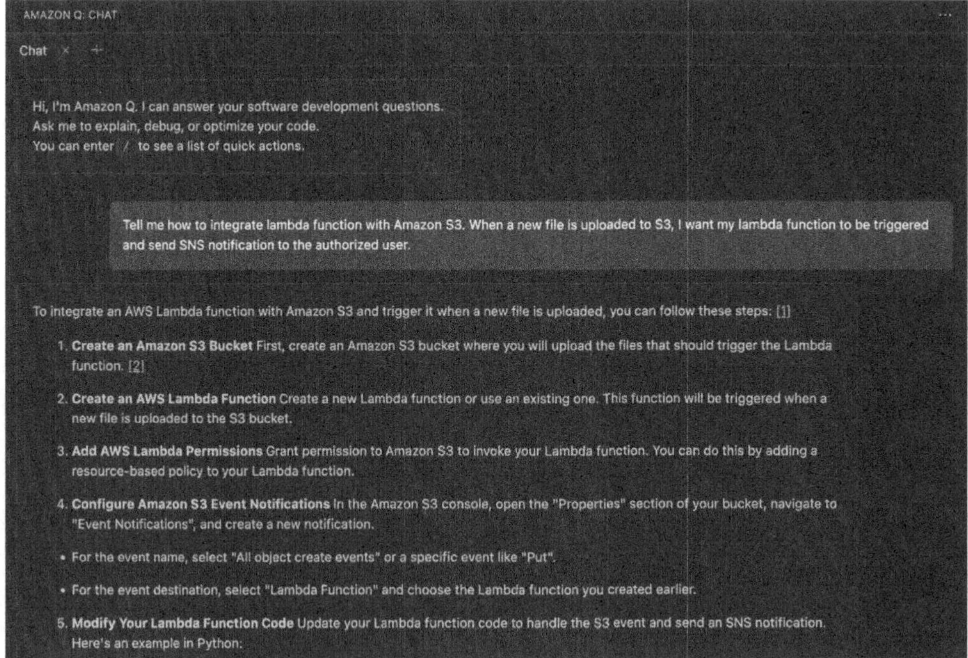

Figure 1.15 – Amazon Q Developer

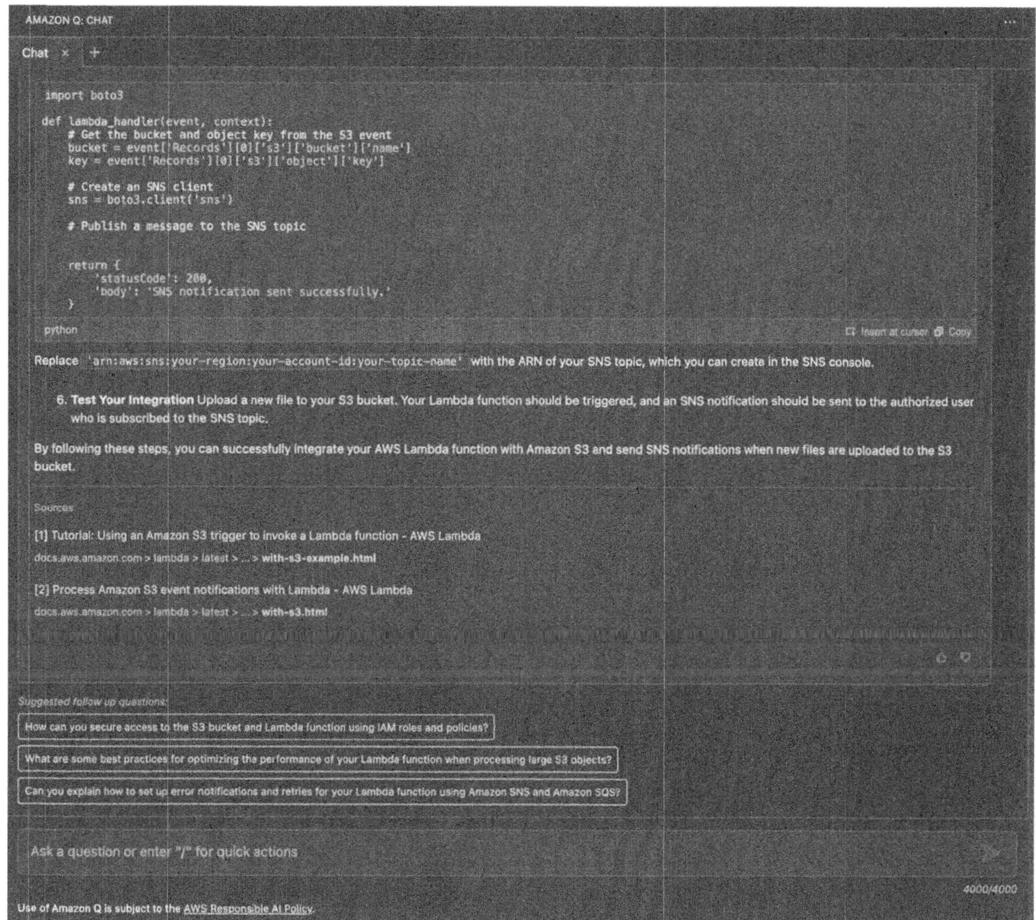

Figure 1.16 – Amazon Q Developer Lambda function

With Amazon Q, developers can streamline their workflows, from planning and development to testing, deployment, and maintenance, ultimately enabling them to deliver high-quality applications faster and with greater confidence.

Generative AI use cases with Amazon Bedrock

Since the advent of generative AI, numerous organizations have benefited from the potential applications of this transformative technology in achieving their business objectives. Many of these organizations, which include Accenture, Adidas, Intuit, and Salesforce, have successfully developed prototypes and even have deployed production-ready generative AI systems using Amazon Bedrock. Across various industries, we have seen numerous compelling use cases for generative AI with Amazon Bedrock. Let's learn more about some of these industries in detail:

- **Finance**: In the financial services sector, organizations have been working on use cases such as classifying and categorizing huge corpus of legal documents, developing systems to select optimal funding and investment plans for customers, providing insights and simplified summaries and Q&As of complex financial documents, as well as detecting fraudulent activities such as forged signatures and tampered invoices. Additionally, organizations are utilizing Amazon Bedrock to understand market trends and customer behavior, aiding in informed decision-making processes.
- **Healthcare**: The healthcare industry has witnessed significant investment in developing generative AI applications with Amazon Bedrock. At the time of writing, AWS HealthScribe has been announced, which is powered by Amazon Bedrock (`https://aws.amazon.com/healthscribe/`). These applications address a wide range of use cases, such as automating medical claims and adjudication processes, extracting valuable insights from health documents and medical research papers, and generating summaries of patient-doctor interactions. By leveraging Amazon Bedrock, healthcare providers are aiming to enhance patient care and drive innovation in the field.
- **Media and entertainment**: In the media and entertainment industry, organizations are actively exploring the diverse applications with Amazon Bedrock. These include generating narratives and storylines in sports and broadcasting, creating captions, images, and animations for storytelling, as well as providing personalized recommendations for TV shows, movies, and other forms of entertainment. By harnessing the capabilities of generative AI with Amazon Bedrock, media and entertainment companies aim to enhance the user experience, create engaging content, and stay ahead of the competition.

These are just a few examples of the numerous use cases that various industries are working on. In later chapters, we will understand architectural patterns in building industry-specific use cases through Amazon Bedrock.

Summary

In this chapter, we explored the various facets of the generative AI landscape: from understanding language models and the development of various NLP techniques to the invention of current SOTA transformer models. Then, we covered industrial challenges in building generative AI applications at scale and how Amazon Bedrock is seamlessly tackling those challenges.

Furthermore, we explored various FMs offered by Amazon Bedrock and provided insights into how you can take advantage of various frameworks and tools to evaluate and select the right FM for your use case. We also looked at alternative generative AI capabilities offered by Amazon, including Amazon SageMaker and Amazon Q. We concluded this chapter by uncovering a few generative AI use cases with Amazon Bedrock in financial services, healthcare, and media and entertainment.

In the next chapter, we will discover several techniques to access Amazon Bedrock and dive into various APIs via serverless services. Furthermore, we will learn about a hands-on approach toward invoking Bedrock FMs that can be integrated into enterprise-grade applications.

2

Accessing and Utilizing Models in Amazon Bedrock

This chapter provides a practical guide to accessing Amazon Bedrock and uncovering its generative AI capabilities. We will start with an overview of the different interfaces for invoking Bedrock models, including the console playground, **command-line interface** (**CLI**), and **software development kit** (**SDK**). Then, we will unveil some of the core Bedrock APIs, along with the code snippets that you can run in your environment. Finally, we'll demonstrate how to leverage Bedrock within the LangChain Python framework to build customized pipelines that chain multiple models and provide insight into PartyRock, a powerful playground for Amazon Bedrock.

By the end of this chapter, you will be able to run and execute applications by leveraging SOTA FMs available from Amazon Bedrock as you gain a deeper understanding of each of the FMs available and how to utilize them for your needs. You will also be able to accelerate your creative thinking regarding building new generative AI applications as we dive into building cool apps with PartyRock and learn how to integrate Amazon Bedrock into different use cases.

The following key topics will be covered in this chapter:

- Accessing Amazon Bedrock
- Using Amazon Bedrock APIs
- Amazon Bedrock integration points

Technical requirements

For this chapter, you'll need to have access to an **Amazon Web Services** (**AWS**) account. If you don't have one already, you can go to `https://aws.amazon.com/getting-started/` and create one.

Once you've done this, you'll need to install and configure the AWS CLI (`https://aws.amazon.com/cli/`) as you'll need this to access Amazon Bedrock FMs from your local machine. Since the majority of the code blocks that we will execute are based on Python, setting up an AWS Python SDK (Boto3) (`https://docs.aws.amazon.com/bedrock/latest/APIReference/welcome.html`) would be beneficial. You can set up Python by installing it on your local machine, or using AWS Cloud9, or utilizing AWS Lambda, or leveraging Amazon SageMaker.

> **Note**
>
> There will be a charge associated with invocating and customizing the FMs of Amazon Bedrock. Please refer to `https://aws.amazon.com/bedrock/pricing/` to learn more.

Accessing Amazon Bedrock

When building a generative AI application, you're faced with a dizzying array of choices. Which FM should you use? How will you ensure security and privacy? Do you have the infrastructure to support large-scale deployment? Enter Amazon Bedrock.

As you know by now, Amazon Bedrock provides access to a selection of SOTA FMs from leading AI companies in the space, including AI21 Labs, Anthropic, Cohere, Meta, Stability AI, Amazon, and Mistral. With a single API, you can tap into cutting-edge generative AI across modalities such as text, embeddings, and images. You have the flexibility to mix and match models to find the perfect fit for your needs. Bedrock handles provisioning, scalability, and governance behind the scenes. Hence, you can choose the best model suited to your needs and simply invoke the Bedrock serverless API to plug those models into your application.

So, let's jump onto the AWS console and see Amazon Bedrock in action.

When you open Amazon Bedrock in the AWS console by navigating to `https://console.aws.amazon.com/` and choosing Bedrock from the search bar, you can explore different FMs, as well as a few learning tools, as depicted in *Figure 2.1*:

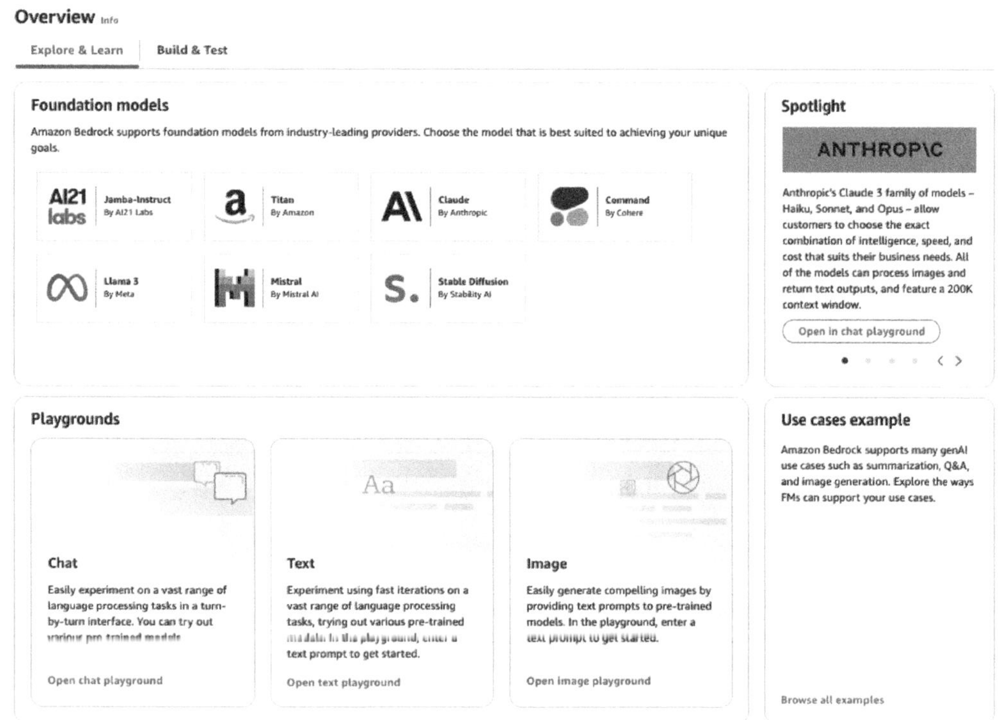

Figure 2.1 – Amazon Bedrock – Overview

Amazon Bedrock provides users with the flexibility to experiment with various models through its playground interface. Users can access the Bedrock playground from the AWS console by navigating to the Amazon Bedrock landing page and clicking **Examples** to open the playground environment.

> **Note**
>
> At the time of writing this book, users will have to initially enable access to the models by navigating to the **Model access** link in the left panel within the Bedrock console (as shown in *Figure 2.2*). Once you've landed on the **Model access** page view, you can click on **Manage model access**, select the list of base models you want to leverage for your use cases, and click **Save changes**. Instantly, the users will be given access to those models. Users can also review the EULA agreement next to the respective base models to view their terms of service.

Within the playground, you can explore the different examples of generative AI models available in Bedrock. This allows you to test out and interact with the models without needing to configure resources or write any code. Overall, the playground provides a convenient way for users to try out the capabilities of Bedrock's generative models. *Figure 2.2* depicts some of the capabilities available within the Amazon Bedrock console:

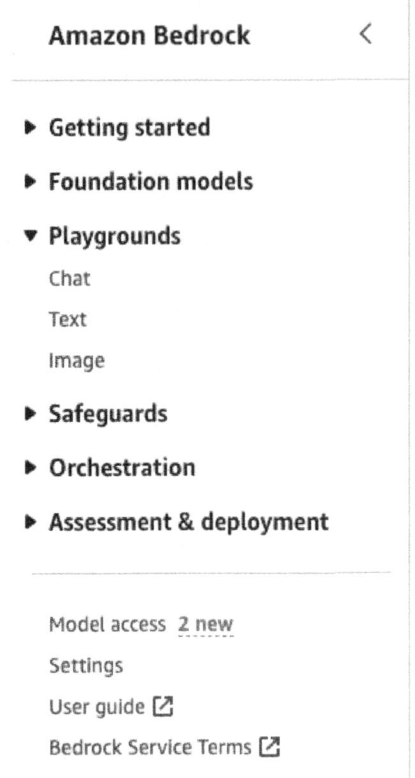

Figure 2.2 – Amazon Bedrock's capabilities

Within the playground, you are given the option to start exploring examples based on **Text**, **Chat**, and **Image**. This enables hands-on experimentation with the latest generative AI models in a convenient sandbox environment. The breadth of options, from conversational chatbots to text and image generation, gives you the flexibility to test diverse AI functions firsthand. By providing accessible entry points, emerging generative AI becomes more tangible and approachable for users to understand. Now, let's learn about each of these in greater detail.

Chat playground

Amazon Bedrock gives you access to chat models, which you can experiment with in the **Chat playground**.

The **Chat playground** is an experimental interface that allows you to test the conversational AI models available through Amazon Bedrock. You can enter sample prompts and view the responses that are generated by a selected model. Usage metrics are also displayed to evaluate the model's performance. A compare mode is available to contrast the outputs of up to three different models side by side.

As shown in the following figures, users can select which model they want to use (*Figure 2.3*):

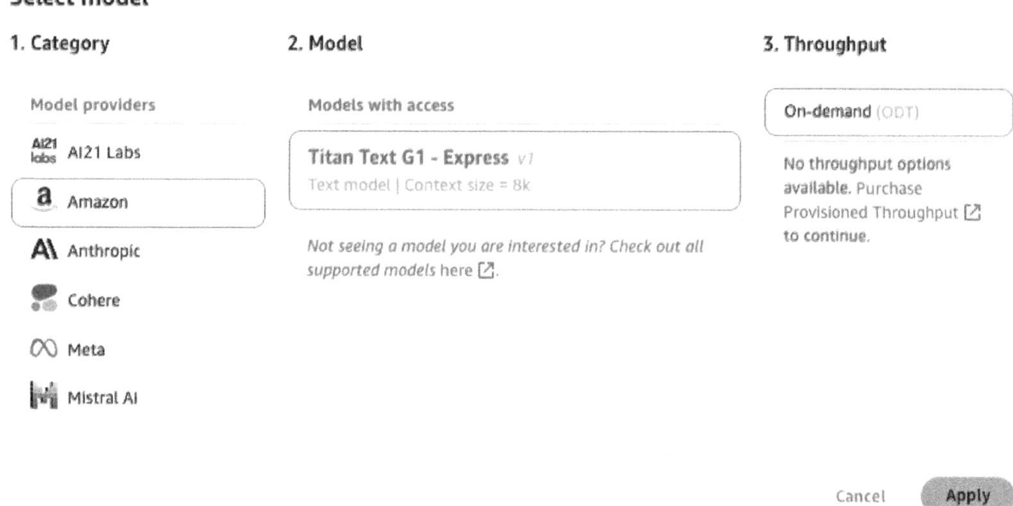

Figure 2.3 – Selecting a model

Thereafter, users can enter a query in the chat box (*Figure 2.4*):

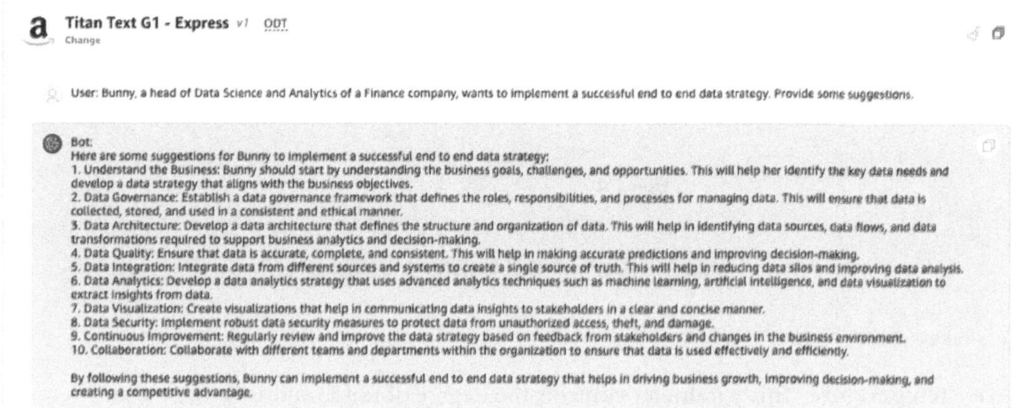

Figure 2.4 – Querying the chat model in the Chat playground

Running a query fetches information from the chosen model. This allows you to evaluate factors such as accuracy, response length, latency, and suitability for your use case. Selecting the optimal model depends on weighing these factors against individual needs.

While invoking the FMs, you will see the option to modify the **inference parameters** so that you can influence the model's response in a certain way. While some inference parameters are common among LLMs, image models have a separate set of parameters that can be tuned by users.

Let's look at some of these common parameters.

LLM inference parameters

Temperature, *Top P*, *Top K*, *Response length*, *Stop sequences*, and *Max tokens* are the inference parameters that we will learn about in detail in this section. *Figure 2.5* shows them on the Amazon Bedrock **Chat playground** screen; they can be found in the **Configurations** window:

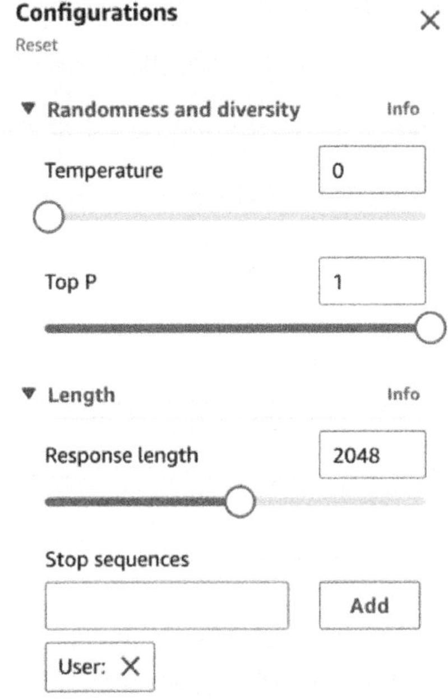

Figure 2.5 – Common LLM inference parameters

Let's take a closer look:

- **Temperature**: This parameter controls the degree of randomness in the output. A lower temperature results in more deterministic output, favoring the most likely option. On the other hand, a higher temperature promotes randomness, leading to a wider range of diverse and creative outputs. For example, in QA tasks, a lower temperature ensures more factual and concise responses, whereas if your use case revolves around generating creative and diverse output, such as in creative writing or advertisement generation, it might be worthwhile to increase the temperature value.

- **Top K and Top P**: Sampling techniques such as **Top K** and **Top P** can be employed to enhance the coherence and sense of the output. **Top K** limits the number of options to a specified number, ensuring a balance between randomness and coherence. **Top P**, on the other hand, restricts the predictions with combined probabilities below a specified threshold, preventing highly improbable options from being selected. These techniques help strike a balance between generating coherent text and maintaining a certain level of randomness, making the text generation process more natural and engaging for the reader.

  Using these together balances novelty and fluency. For example, you could set **Top K** to 70 and **Top P** to 0.8. This allows some uncommon but still relevant words via the **Top P** setting, while **Top K** retains focus on more common words. The result is text that is fairly fluent with occasional novel words mixed in. You can experiment with different values for **Top K** and **Top P** to achieve the novelty versus fluency balance you want for a particular generative AI application. Start with a **Top K** value around 50 to 100 and a **Top P** value around 0.7 to 0.9 as reasonable initial settings. The optimal values depend on factors such as model size, dataset, and use case.

- **Stop sequences**: This refers to a set of characters that the FM uses to determine when to stop generating output. The stop sequence can be any character or sequence of characters that you specify. For example, if you set the stop sequence to `bedrock`, the model will stop generating output as soon as it encounters the word *bedrock* in the generated text.

- **Max tokens**: Also known as **Length** or **Response Length** in some models, this is the maximum length of the generated response in the form of tokens. Setting a lower **Max tokens** value results in shorter generated text, while higher values allow for longer, more detailed responses from the FM. Hence, this parameter provides a useful way to specify the desired text length. For instance, if you are generating sample text for a book description, you may set **Max tokens** to 100 so that the FM generates a concise blurb within a tight word limit. In addition, you can also mention the word limit in the prompt by adding a simple instruction such as `Write a sentence in 100 words`.

Image model inference parameters

When performing image generation with FMs, several key parameters affect the inference process. For instance, in the case of Stable Diffusion models, the model takes in a text prompt and random noise vector to produce an image. Several configuration settings for the model can influence the final generated image, as depicted in *Figure 2.6*:

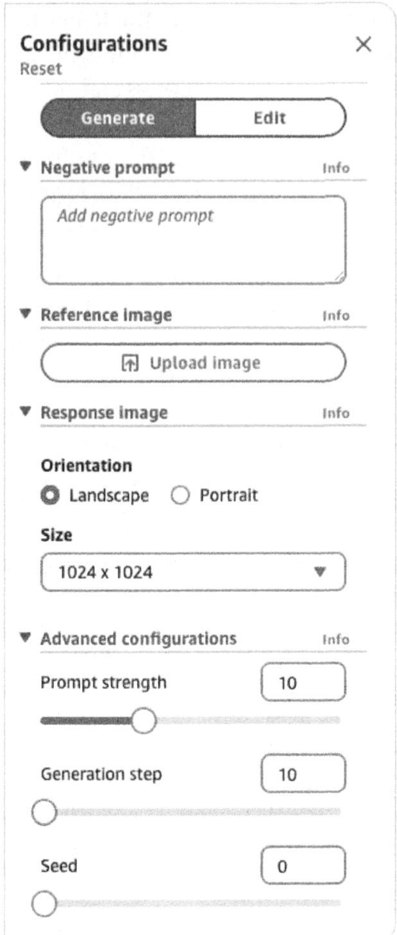

Figure 2.6 – Image model inference parameters

Let's take a closer look at these parameters:

- **Prompt strength**: This controls the degree of randomness. Lowering the **Prompt strength** value generates a more random image while increasing it generates a more accurate representation of the prompt.
- **Generation step**: Similar to **Prompt strength**, increasing the **Generation step** value generates a more intricate and detailed image while decreasing it generates a simpler image.
- **Seed**: The **Seed** parameter controls the initial state of the random number generator, which affects the overall randomness of the generated image. It is important to note that the precise values of these parameters can vary depending on the specific use case and the desired trade-off between image fidelity and randomness.

For a more detailed description of these parameters, take a look at the Stable Diffusion documentation: `https://platform.stability.ai/docs/api-reference#tag/Image-to-Image`.

If you're using Amazon Titan Image Generator, there are various parameters you can use. You can find a full list at `https://docs.aws.amazon.com/bedrock/latest/userguide/model-parameters-titan-image.html`.

Text playground

The **Text playground** serves a similar function for evaluating generative text models from Amazon Bedrock. You may enter text prompts that the selected model will then expand upon or continue as a longer passage of generated text reflecting that prompt. The expanded text from the model is shown in the playground's interface.

However, the **Text playground** doesn't manage conversational context. Essentially, it generates a sequence of most likely tokens from the end of the text placed in the **Text playground** window. The behavior demonstrated in the **Text playground** is a fundamental building block of the chat behavior, and when chained together over multiple turns, it can create a chat experience.

Hence, similar to the **Chat playground**, users can also navigate to the text playground, select another model (for instance, Anthropic Claude 3 Sonnet, as shown in *Figure 2.7*), update the inference configuration, and prompt the model to generate a response for their use case:

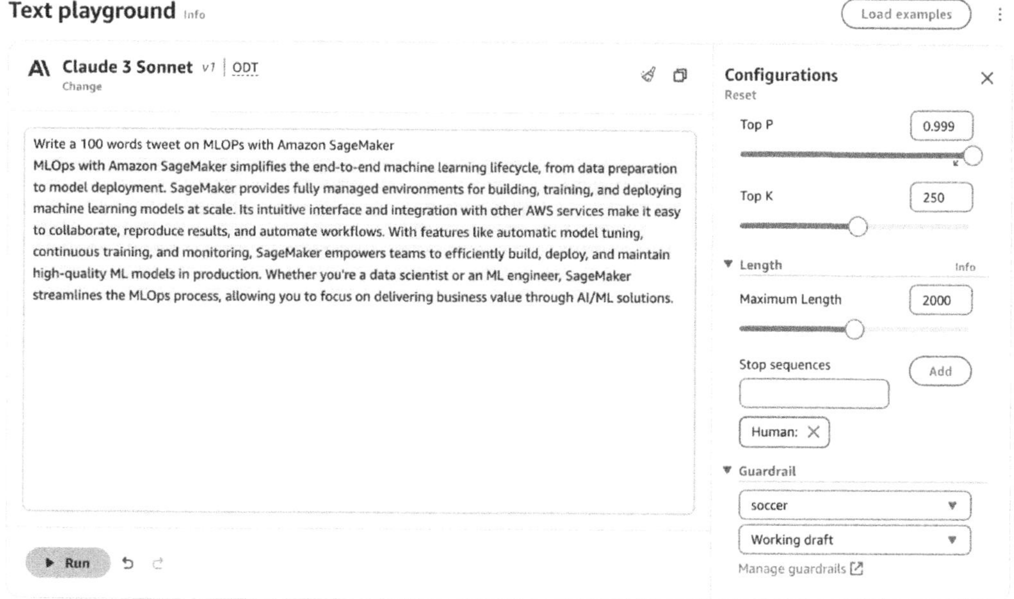

Figure 2.7 – Adding a prompt in the text playground

Image playground

In **Image playground**, you can try out two different image models: Amazon Titan Image Generator and Stability AI's Stable Diffusion. If these sound new to you, please refer to their eponymous sub-sections in *Chapter 1*. These models generate images through text or images and also perform in-painting, image editing, and more. Let's see an example:

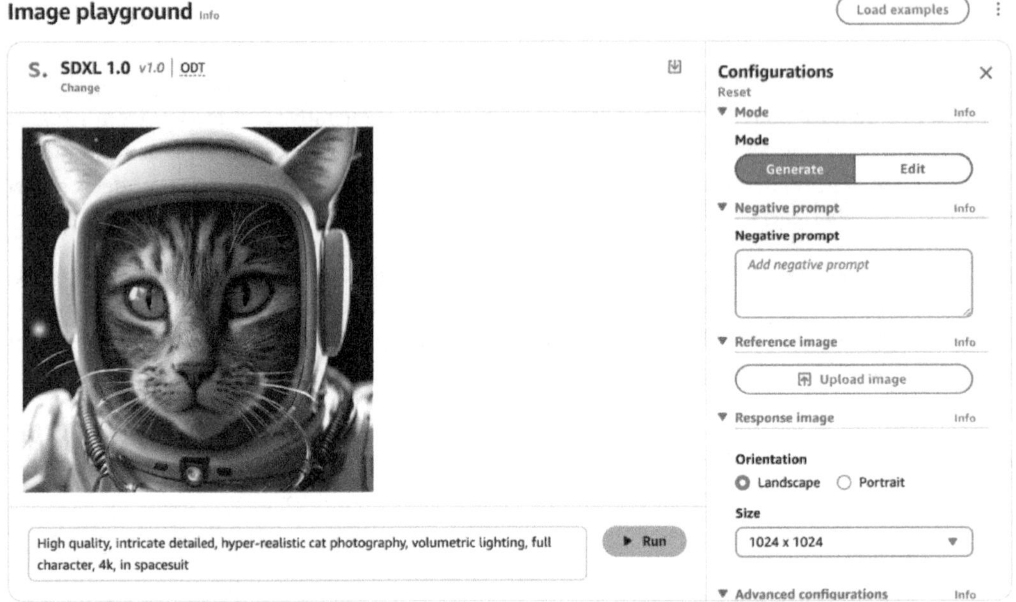

Figure 2.8 – Adding a prompt in the image playground

As shown in *Figure 2.8*, when we provide `High quality, intricate detailed, hyper-realistic cat photography, volumetric lighting, full character, 4k, in spacesuit` as a prompt, the model generates an image conditioned on the text that was provided. Within the configuration, you also have the option to provide a **Negative prompt** value, which tells the model what it shouldn't generate. In addition, you can provide a **Reference image** value, which the model will use as a reference to generate the image. In *Chapter 9*, we will explore how image generation and editing work with Amazon Bedrock.

API-based approach

One of the major benefits of using a unified API for inference is that it allows you to easily experiment with different models from various providers using the same interface. Even as new model versions are released, you can swap them in with minimal code changes required on your end.

The single API abstraction acts as an insulation layer, shielding your application code from underlying model implementation details. This frees you from vendor lock-in and grants flexibility to adopt cutting-edge models as they become available. With a consistent API shielding this complexity, you can focus on product innovation rather than engineering logistics.

Amazon Bedrock provides a set of APIs that can be directly accessed and utilized via the *AWS CLI* or *AWS SDK*.

AWS CLI

The **AWS CLI** allows you to make Bedrock API calls directly from the terminal of your machine, EC2 instance shell, and so on. Once you've configured the AWS CLI for your account, you can manage a range of AWS services, including Amazon Bedrock. For example, you can list the FMs available within Bedrock using the `list-foundation-models` API:

```
$ aws bedrock list-foundation-models
```

Similarly, to invoke a model (for example, the Mistral 7B Instruct model), you can call the `invoke-model` API of `bedrock-runtime`. At the time of writing, users have to request model access from the console. Once granted in the system, the following code can be used to invoke the respective model:

```
$ aws bedrock-runtime invoke-model \
  --model-id mistral.mistral-7b-instruct-v0:2 \
  --body "{\"prompt\":\"<s>[INST]100 words tweet on MLOps with
Amazon SageMaker [/INST]\", \"max_tokens\":200, \"temperature\":0.5}" \
  --cli-binary-format raw-in-base64-out \
  output.txt
```

In the `body` parameter of the `invoke-model` API call, you can see it is written in a particular format (`"{\"prompt\":\"<s>[INST]text [/INST]\"`). Different models may require a different structure of prompt while invoking the model. If you search for Amazon Bedrock in the AWS console, you can view the actual API request that's sent to the model. Follow these steps to view the API requests:

1. Open Amazon Bedrock in the AWS console by navigating to `https://console.aws.amazon.com/` and choosing **Bedrock** from the search bar.
2. Select **Providers** under **Getting started**.
3. Choose any provider and model of your choice.
4. Scroll down to the **Model** section and expand **API request**.

In *Figure 2.9*, you can see the API request in JSON from the *Mistral 7B Instruct* model. In the `body` parameter of the API request, we can see the format of the prompt needed by the model, along with the inference parameters:

▼ API request　　Copy code

```
{
 "modelId": "mistral.mistral-7b-instruct-v0:2",
 "contentType": "application/json",
 "accept": "application/json",
 "body": "{\"prompt\":\"<s>[INST] this is where you place your input text [/INST]\", \"max_tokens\":200, \"temperature\":0.5, \"top_p\":0.9, \"top_k\":50}"
}
```

Figure 2.9 – Mistral 7B Instruct API request

This enables transparency regarding how the user's input gets formatted and passed to the underlying AI system. Overall, the playground allows users to not only test prompts but also inspect the API requests that are made to generate the AI responses.

AWS SDK

AWS provides SDKs for various programming languages, such as JavaScript, Python, Java, and more. These SDKs provide wrapper libraries that make it easy to integrate Bedrock API calls into your code. It is often beneficial to use an SDK tailored to your programming language of choice. Consulting the SDK documentation for your chosen language can provide helpful code samples, usage guidelines, and other resources to ensure the integration process goes smoothly (`https://docs.aws.amazon.com/bedrock/latest/APIReference/welcome.html`).

You can call these Bedrock APIs through AWS SDKs from your local machines or use AWS services such as AWS Lambda, Amazon SageMaker Studio notebooks, AWS Cloud9, and others. Using the AWS SDK for Python (Boto3), you can call Bedrock APIs to build ML workflows. Let's look at some of the APIs provided by Amazon Bedrock and examples of their usage in the **AWS SDK** for Python (Boto3).

Thus far, we have explored the array of FMs that are offered through Amazon Bedrock, experimenting with various prompts and tuning inference configurations to produce preferred outputs. We've tapped into models directly via the Amazon Bedrock playground and examined leveraging the AWS CLI and various SDKs to invoke FMs programmatically.

Having established this foundation of working knowledge, we'll pivot to investigating Amazon Bedrock's APIs more deeply. The next section will help us leverage these APIs in custom generative AI applications that harness the power of FMs while providing developers with more control and customization. We will map out an end-to-end workflow – from initializing a client to generating outputs – that will empower you to build robust, reliable generative apps powered by industrial-grade FMs.

Using Amazon Bedrock APIs

Like other AWS services, Amazon Bedrock provides several APIs. These APIs can be placed under the Control Plane API for managing, training, and deploying FMs and the Runtime Plane API for making invocations or inference requests to the FMs. Some of the common Control Plane Bedrock APIs include **ListFoundationModels**, **GetFoundationModels**, and **CreateModelCustomizationJob**. On the other hand, the Runtime Plane API has two APIs: **InvokeModel** and **InvokeModelWithResponseStream**.

In addition, there are separate APIs associated with Agents for Amazon Bedrock, something we'll cover in more detail in *Chapter 10*.

You can find the complete list of API calls supported by Amazon Bedrock, including all the data types and actions you can perform, at `https://docs.aws.amazon.com/bedrock/latest/APIReference/`. Let's look at some of the commonly used Bedrock API calls.

ListFoundationModels

To utilize the generative capabilities of Bedrock, the first step is to discover which FMs are available via the service. The **ListFoundationModels** API retrieves metadata about the base models, including the unique model ID required to generate content using that model.

The following Python code sample demonstrates how to call the ListFoundationModels API to enumerate the available base models:

```
import boto3
bedrock_client = boto3.client(service_name='bedrock')
bedrock_client.list_foundation_models()
```

Let's consider some of the currently available base models and their respective model IDs provided via Amazon Bedrock. You use a model ID as a means to indicate the base model when users intend to leverage any of the existing models using InvokeModel (`https://docs.aws.amazon.com/bedrock/latest/APIReference/API_runtime_InvokeModel.html`) or InvokeModelWithResponseStream (`https://docs.aws.amazon.com/bedrock/latest/APIReference/API_runtime_InvokeModelWithResponseStream.html`). With this information, the desired model can be selected and its ID can be used to call other Bedrock operations, such as InvokeModel, to generate content tailored to your application's needs.

GetFoundationModel

Utilizing Amazon Bedrock, developers can access SOTA generative AI models through the **GetFoundationModel** API call. This operation retrieves comprehensive information on a specified base model. For example, to return details on Meta's Llama 3 70B Instruct model in Python, you can run the following code:

```
import boto3
bedrock_client = boto3.client(service_name='bedrock')
```

```
bedrock_client.get_foundation_model(modelIdentifier='meta.llama3-70b-instruct-v1:0')
```

InvokeModel

The **InvokeModel** API simplifies the deployment of ML models. With just a few API calls, you can deploy your trained models onto the AWS infrastructure securely. This eliminates the need for managing complex deployment processes, allowing you to focus on the core of your AI application.

You can invoke specified Bedrock models to perform inference using inputs provided in the request body. The InvokeModel API allows you to run inference for various model types, including text, embedding, and image models. This allows users to leverage pretrained models available via Amazon Bedrock to generate predictions and insights by passing data into the model and receiving the desired output.

Here's an example of an API request for sending text to Meta's Llama 3 70 B model. Inference parameters depend on the model that you are going to use.

```
import boto3
import json

model_id = 'meta.llama3-70b-instruct-v1:0' # change this to use a different version from the model provider

prompt_data = "What is the significance of the number 42?"

# Following the request syntax of invoke_model, you can create request body with the below prompt and respective inference parameters.
payload = json.dumps({
    'prompt': prompt_data,
    'max_gen_len': 512,
    'top_p': 0.5,
    'temperature': 0.5,
})

bedrock_runtime = boto3.client(
    service_name='bedrock-runtime',
    region_name='us-east-1'
)

response = bedrock_runtime.invoke_model(
    body=payload,
    modelId=model_id,
    accept='application/json',
    contentType='application/json'
)
```

```
response_body = json.loads(response.get('body').read())
print(response_body.get('generation'))
```

As shown in the preceding code block, the `InvokeModel` operation allows you to perform inference on models. The `modelId` field specifies the desired model to utilize. The process of obtaining `modelId` varies based on the model type. By leveraging the `InvokeModel` operation and specifying the appropriate `modelId` value, users can harness the power of a plethora of generative AI models to draw relevant insights.

If you are using Anthropic Claude models, you can use the Messages API to create conversational interfaces to manage the chat between the user and the model. Here's an example of an API request that could be sent to the Anthropic Claude Sonnet 3 model:

```
import boto3
import json

bedrock_client = boto3.client('bedrock-runtime',region_name='us-
east-1')

prompt = """
Task: Compose an email to customer support team.

Output:
"""

messages = [{ "role":'user', "content":[{'type':'text','text':
prompt}]}]
max_tokens=512
top_p=1
temp=0.5
system = "You are an AI Assistant"

body=json.dumps(
        {
            "anthropic_version": "bedrock-2023-05-31",
            "max_tokens": max_tokens,
            "messages": messages,
            "temperature": temp,
            "top_p": top_p,
            "system": system
        }
    )

modelId = "anthropic.claude-3-sonnet-20240229-v1:0"
```

```
accept = "application/json"
contentType = "application/json"

response = bedrock_client.invoke_model(body=body, modelId=modelId,
accept=accept, contentType=contentType)
response_body = json.loads(response.get('body').read())
print(response_body)
```

The API manages the back-and-forth flow of dialogue by accepting a series of messages with alternating *user* and *assistant* roles as input. To learn more about the Messages API, you can look at the documentation: `https://docs.anthropic.com/claude/reference/messages_post`.

Amazon Bedrock also allows you to precisely configure the throughput your models need to deliver responsive performance for your applications. With **Provisioned Throughput**, you can choose the compute capacity your models require to meet your workload demands and latency requirements. Hence, in the case of Amazon and third-party base models, and with customized models, users can purchase Provisioned Throughput before running inferences. This capability ensures that you get the guaranteed throughput your models require for optimal cost and performance. More details on Provisioned Throughput can be found here: `https://docs.aws.amazon.com/bedrock/latest/userguide/prov-throughput.html`.

InvokeModelWithResponseStream

This streaming inference method that's available via Amazon Bedrock allows FMs to produce long, coherent content on demand. Rather than waiting for generation to complete, applications can stream results. This allows you to send responses from the model in faster chunks rather than having to wait for a complete response.

To run inference with streaming, you can simply invoke the **InvokeModelWithResponseStream** operation. For instance, to leverage Claude V2's streaming capabilities, you would use the `InvokeModelWithResponseStream` operation provided by Amazon Bedrock. This runs inference on the model with the given input and returns the generated content progressively in a stream.

Let's look at how the Claude V2 model can generate a 500-word blog on quantum computing.

> **Note**
>
> The following code snippet works when run in a Jupyter Notebook environment. Jupyter Notebook provides additional functionality and initialization that allows this code to operate correctly. Attempting to run this snippet directly in a terminal without the Jupyter environment may result in errors. For the best results, run this code in Jupyter Notebook rather than directly in a terminal.

```
from IPython.display import clear_output, display, display_markdown,
Markdown
import boto3, json
```

```
brt = boto3.client(service_name='bedrock-runtime', region_name='us-
east-1'
)

payload = json.dumps({
    'prompt': '\n\nHuman: write a blog on quantum computing in 500
words.\n\nAssistant:',
    'max_tokens_to_sample': 4096
})

response = brt.invoke_model_with_response_stream(
    modelId='anthropic.claude-v2',
    body=payload,
    accept='application/json',
    contentType='application/json'
)

streaming = response.get('body')
output = []

if streaming:
    for event in streaming:
        chunk = event.get('chunk')
        if chunk:
            chunk_object = json.loads(chunk.get('bytes').decode())
            text = chunk_object['completion']
            clear_output(wait=True)
            output.append(text)
            display_markdown(Markdown(''.join(output)))
```

This will print out the generated blog text continuously as it is produced by the model. This stream-based approach allows the output to be displayed live while Claude V2 is *writing* the blog content. Hence, streaming inference unlocks new real-time and interactive use cases for large generative models.

In this section, we explored Amazon Bedrock's key APIs, all of which allow us to build generative AI applications. We reviewed how to list the FMs that are available through Amazon Bedrock and detailed how to invoke these models to produce customized outputs. Next, we will uncover how Amazon Bedrock integrates with LangChain to choreograph and address intricate use cases. By leveraging Bedrock's API and LangChain's orchestration, developers can assemble sophisticated generative solutions.

Converse API

The Amazon Bedrock **Converse API** offers a standardized method to interact with LLMs available via Amazon Bedrock. It facilitates turn-based communication between users and generative AI models and ensures consistent tool definitions for models that support functions (referred to as **function calling**).

The significance of the `Converse` API lies in its ability to streamline integration. Previously, using the `InvokeModel` API required adapting to varying JSON request and response structures from different model providers. With the `Converse` API, a uniform format for requests and responses is implemented across all LLMs on Amazon Bedrock, simplifying development and ensuring consistent interaction protocols.

Let us walk through an example of using `Converse` API for text generation scenario by leveraging Anthropic Claude 3 Sonnet model. Please ensure you have the required permission for you require permission for `bedrock:InvokeModel` operation in order to call `Converse` API.

```
# Install the latest version for boto3 to leverage Converse API. We
start with uninstalling the previous version
%pip install boto3==1.34.131
# Import the respective libraries
import boto3
import botocore
import os
import json
import sys

#Ensure you have the latest version of boto3 to invoke Converse API
print(boto3.__version__)

#Create client side Amazon Bedrock connection with Boto3 library
region = os.environ.get("AWS_REGION")
bedrock_client = boto3.client(service_name='bedrock-runtime',region_
name=region)

model_id = "anthropic.claude-3-sonnet-20240229-v1:0"

# Inference parameters
top_k = 100
temp = 0.3

# inference model request fields
model_fields = {"top_k": top_k}

# Base inference parameters
inference_configuration = {"temperature": temp}
```

```
# Setup the system prompts and messages to send to the model.
system_prompts = [{"text": "You are an expert stylist that recommends
different attire for the user based on the occasion."}]

message_1 = {
    "role": "user",
    "content": [{"text": "Give me top 3 trending style and attire
recommendations for my son's graduation party"}]
  }

messages = []
# Start the conversation with the 1st message.

messages.append(message_1)

# Send the message.
response = bedrock_client.converse(
        modelId=model_id,
        messages=messages,
        system=system_prompts,
        inferenceConfig=inference_configuration,
        additionalModelRequestFields=model_fields
    )

# Add the response message to the conversation.
output_message = response['output']['message']

print(output_message['content'][0]['text'])
```

Please note that switching the model ID to another text generation FM available on Amazon Bedrock allows it to run using the `Converse` API. The code example above, along with other `Converse` API examples, has been added to the GitHub repository for readers to experiment with in their own accounts.

The `Converse` API can also process documents and images. For instance, you can send an image or document in a message and use `Converse` API to have the model describe its contents. For more details on supported models and model features with `Converse` API, visit `https://docs.aws.amazon.com/bedrock/latest/userguide/conversation-inference.html#conversation-inference-call`

Similarly, the **ConverseStream API** makes it easy to send messages to specific Amazon Bedrock models and receive responses in a continuous stream. It provides a unified interface that works across all foundational models supported by Amazon Bedrock for messaging.

To use the `ConverseStream` API, you can invoke it with the **converse_stream** call, replacing the same code as used in the `Converse` API. Note that you need the `bedrock:InvokeModelWithResponseStream` operation permission to use `ConverseStream`.

```
# Send the message.
model_response = bedrock_client.converse_stream(
        modelId=model_id,
        messages=messages,
        system=system_prompts,
        inferenceConfig=inference_config,
        additionalModelRequestFields=additional_model_fields
    )

# # Add the response message to the conversation.
stream = model_response.get('stream')

if stream:
    for event in stream:
        if 'contentBlockDelta' in event:
print(event['contentBlockDelta']['delta']['text'], end="")
```

When you run the code sample above, it streams the response output. For more information on `ConverseStream`, you can refer to the documentation at `https://docs.aws.amazon.com/bedrock/latest/APIReference/API_runtime_ConverseStream.html`.

Amazon Bedrock integration points

When building end-to-end generative AI applications, architects must follow best practices for security, performance, cost optimization, and latency reduction, as outlined in the AWS Well-Architected Framework pillars. They aid developers in weighing different choices and optimizations when creating end-to-end systems on AWS. More information on the AWS Well-Architected Framework can be found here: `https://docs.aws.amazon.com/wellarchitected/latest/framework/welcome.html`.

Many customers looking to build conversational interfaces such as chatbots, virtual assistants, or summarization systems integrate Amazon Bedrock's serverless API with other services. Useful integration points include orchestration frameworks such as LangChain and AWS Step Functions for invoking Amazon Bedrock models via AWS Lambda.

As customers adopt LLMOps approaches to optimize building, scaling, and deploying LLMs for enterprise applications, these integration tools and frameworks are becoming more widely adopted. The serverless API, orchestration layer, and Lambda functions create a robust and scalable pipeline for delivering performant and cost-effective generative AI services.

Amazon Bedrock with LangChain

Now, let's take our understanding of Amazon Bedrock and generative AI applications to the next level by introducing LangChain integration with Amazon Bedrock!

LangChain is a revolutionary framework that empowers developers to build advanced language models and generate human-like text. By chaining together various components, you can create sophisticated use cases that were previously unimaginable. For example, if you work in the financial services industry, you can create an application that can provide insights, a simplified summary, and a Q&A of complex financial documents, and by using the LangChain framework, you can abstract the API complexities. By bringing Bedrock and LangChain together, developers gain the best of both worlds. Need an AI assistant, search engine, or content generator? Spin up a capable model with Bedrock, then use LangChain's templates and pipelines to craft the perfect prompt and handle the output. This modular approach allows for immense flexibility, adapting as your needs change. By creating a custom prompt template via LangChain, you can pass in different input variables on every run. This allows you to generate content that's tailored to your specific use case, whether it's responding to customer feedback or crafting personalized marketing messages.

And it's easy to get started! LangChain's Bedrock API component provides a simple way to invoke Bedrock APIs from within a LangChain pipeline. Just a few lines of code can kick off a request, feeding your input to a beefy model and returning the goods. From there, your app has a robust, scalable AI backend ready to go.

The following piece of code showcases the ease with which you can leverage Amazon Bedrock with LangChain.

> **Note**
>
> Before running the following code, make sure you have the latest version of the LangChain package installed. If not, run the package installation cell provided next to install LangChain in your environment. Alternatively, you can download the package from `https://pypi.org/project/langchain/`

```
# Installing LangChain
!pip install langchain

#import the respective libraries and packages
import os
import sys
import json
import boto3
import botocore

# You need to specify LLM for LangChain Bedrock class, and can pass
```

```
arguments for inference.
from langchain.llms.bedrock import Bedrock

#Create boto3 client for Amazon Bedrock-runtime
bedrock_client = boto3.client(service_name="bedrock-runtime", region_
name='us-east-1')

#Provide the respective model ID of the FM you want to use
modelId="amazon.titan-tg1-large"

#Pass the Model ID and respective arguments to the LangChain Bedrock
Class
llm = Bedrock(
    model_id=modelId,
    model_kwargs={
        "maxTokenCount": 4096,
        "stopSequences": [],
        "temperature": 0,
        "topP": 1,
    },
    client=bedrock_client,
)

#Provide Sample prompt data
prompt_data = "Tell me about LangChain"

#Invoke the LLM
response = llm(prompt_data)
print(response)
```

As shown in the preceding code snippet, users can invoke a particular model using a simple prompt by easily leveraging the LLM for the LangChain Bedrock class and passing the respective FM's arguments for inference.

Creating a LangChain custom prompt template

By creating a template for a prompt, you can pass different input variables to it on every run. This is useful when you have to generate content with different input variables that you may be fetching from a database:

```
#import the respective libraries and packages
import os
import sys
import boto3
```

```
import json
import botocore

# You need to specify LLM for LangChain Bedrock class, and can pass
arguments for inference.
from langchain_aws import BedrockLLM

#Create boto3 client for Amazon Bedrock-runtime
bedrock_client = boto3.client(service_name="bedrock-runtime", region_
name='us-east-1')

from langchain.prompts import PromptTemplate
# Create a prompt template that has multiple input variables
multi_var_prompt = PromptTemplate(
    input_variables=["leasingAgent", "tenantName",
"feedbackFromTenant"],
    template="""
<s>[INST] Write an email from the Leasing Agent {leasingAgent} to
{tenantName} in response to the following feedback that was received
from the customer:
<customer_feedback>
{feedbackFromTenant}
</customer_feedback> [/INST]\
"""
)
# Pass in values to the input variables
prompt_data = multi_var_prompt.format(leasingAgent="Jane",
                                     tenantName="Isabella",
                                     feedbackFromTenant="""Hi Jane,
     I have been living in this apartment for 2 years now, and
I wanted to appreciate how lucky I am to be living here. I have
hardly faced any issues in my apartment, but when any issue occurs,
administration staff is always there to fix the problem, and are very
polite. They also run multiple events throughout the year for all the
tenants which helps us socialize. The best part of the apartment is
it's location and it is very much affordable.
     """)

#Provide the respective model ID of the FM you want to use
modelId = 'mistral.mistral-large-2402-v1:0' # change this to use a
different version from the model provider

#Pass the Model ID and respective parameters to the Langchain Bedrock
Class
llm = BedrockLLM(
    model_id=modelId,
```

```
    model_kwargs={
        "max_tokens": 4096,
        "temperature": 0.5,
        "top_p": 0.5,
        "top_k":50,
    },
    client=bedrock_client,
)
```

Now, we can invoke Bedrock using the prompt template to see a curated response:

```
response = llm(prompt_data)
email = response[response.index('\n')+1:]
print(email)
```

This integration exemplifies how LangChain's framework facilitates the creation of complex language-based tasks. In this instance, the Bedrock API acts as a bridge between the LangChain components and the underlying language model.

Hence, by integrating LangChain and Amazon Bedrock, developers can leverage the advanced functionalities of LangChain, such as prompt templates, pipelines, and orchestration capabilities with other AI services, to create dynamic and adaptive applications.

PartyRock

Now that we've discussed how to access and explore Amazon Bedrock for your applications using different techniques, let's look at another interesting feature. Amazon also has a mechanism to quickly build and deploy a fun and intuitive application for experimentalists and hobbyists through **PartyRock**, a powerful playground for Amazon Bedrock. Within PartyRock, you can create multiple applications and experiment with Amazon Bedrock. For example, you can create an optimized party plan and budgeting tool for your 5-year-old.

In *Figure 2.10*, we have created a sample application that can list different Grammy award winners based on the year(s) that users can input in the app. Users can simply click on the link provided next and enter a particular year (or years in each line) in the left pane. On entering a particular year or a few years, the system will generate the Grammy award winners in the right pane. You can check out the app at `https://partyrock.aws/u/shikharkwtra/jAJQre8A0/Grammy-Celebrity-Namer`.

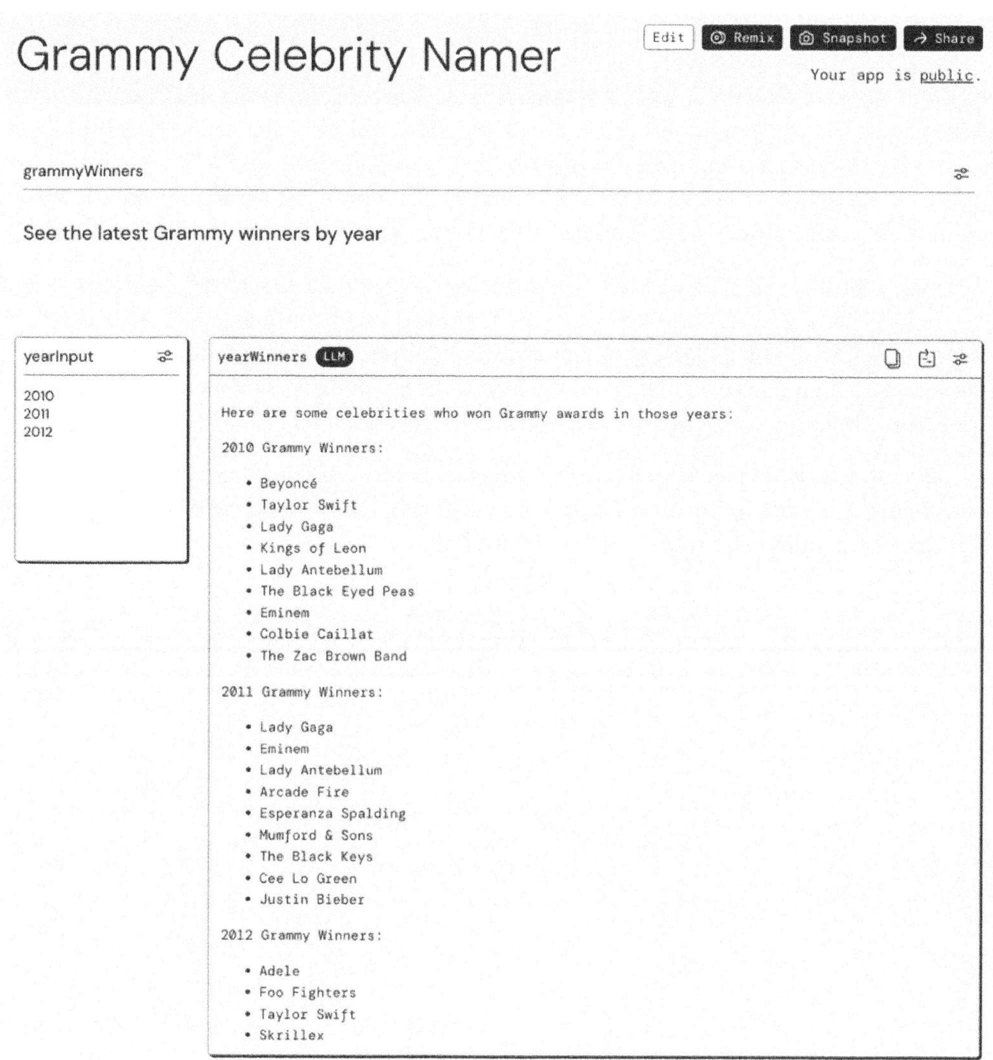

Figure 2.10 – PartyRock example – Grammy Celebrity Namer

PartyRock provides builders with access to FMs from Amazon Bedrock to learn the fundamentals of prompt engineering and generative AI. Users are encouraged to build some cool apps with PartyRock and go a step further to understand Amazon Bedrock. Simply navigate to `https://partyrock.aws/`, click on **Build your own app**, and get started with your journey to becoming a generative AI application developer on PartyRock!

Summary

Before moving on to the next chapter, let's quickly recap what we covered in this chapter. First, we looked at how to access Amazon Bedrock through the AWS console. Utilizing the Bedrock console, we queried the **Text**, **Chat**, and **Image playground** APIs and experimented with various inference parameters to analyze their impact on model outputs. In addition to interacting with the models through the Bedrock console, we investigated accessing the FMs via the AWS CLI and AWS SDK.

By leveraging the CLI and SDK, we were able to uncover some of the underlying Bedrock APIs that can be used to list available FMs, retrieve detailed information about them, and invoke them. We concluded this chapter by looking at some integration points of Amazon Bedrock, including the popular LangChain framework, and provided a brief overview of PartyRock, a powerful playground in Amazon Bedrock for testing prompts and building fun applications.

Now that we have a good conceptual understanding of Amazon Bedrock and the ability to access various Bedrock models, in the next chapter, we will explore some effective prompt engineering techniques we can implement when we use Amazon Bedrock.

3

Engineering Prompts for Effective Model Usage

This chapter begins with an overview of prompt engineering and its importance. We will walk through various prompt engineering techniques and the ability to incorporate them while prompting any model on Amazon Bedrock, primarily focusing on designing and analyzing effective prompt techniques to get the desired outcome from the Bedrock models. This chapter also entails some of the best practices associated with prompt engineering.

By the end of this chapter, you will have developed a clear understanding of the practical aspects of prompt engineering and be able to craft effective prompts while following the best practices to get the desired outcome from the models available on Amazon Bedrock.

In this chapter, we're going to cover the following main topics:

- What is prompt engineering?
- Unlocking prompt engineering techniques
- Designing prompts for Amazon Bedrock models
- Understanding best practices in prompt engineering

Technical requirements

To complete this chapter, you need to have access to the *AWS* console so that you can navigate to Amazon Bedrock Playground to execute prompt engineering techniques. Here's the web page to access the console: `https://console.aws.amazon.com/`.

Secondly, you need to have the right permissions to invoke Amazon Bedrock models from your local machine using *Amazon Bedrock APIs* or *Bedrock Python SDK* so that you can execute the prompts. To learn more, go to `https://docs.aws.amazon.com/bedrock/latest/userguide/security-iam.html`.

What is prompt engineering?

Since we have been discussing Amazon Bedrock models and how to invoke them, we need to dive into prompt engineering. Essentially, in a way that a particular child asks their parents questions about anything and everything, we can also ask an LLM anything under the Sun! However, to get the best and most precise outputs possible, we must train ourselves to ask the model the right questions in the right manner.

With the increasing popularity of LLMs, users are actively striving to refine their way of asking the model different kinds of questions to attain a desired response. For instance, we can simply ask an LLM questions such as `Who was the first person to land on the Moon?` or `How many moons does Jupiter have?`. Based on these questions, the language model can respond to the user's queries either factually or provide an inadequate/incorrect response based on the LLM's knowledge, which is the data it has been trained on.

Incorrect responses that the users get without fact-checking are what we refer to as **hallucinations**. It is often seen that if the user asks an ambiguous question or a particularly complex math problem that the model hasn't been trained to answer, it will determine a probabilistic answer that may or may not be factually accurate. This can also occur with large vision models such as text-to-image models, where the model ends up providing an undesirable image as the prompted response.

Hence, how we ask questions to the model and how effectively we can provide a description regarding our question becomes a crucial factor for the model to generate a desirable output.

The method of prompting the model in the right manner while avoiding any ambiguity in your prompts becomes the essence of effective **prompt engineering**. This is not just applicable to the technical community anymore!

Even people with varying technical backgrounds can use LLMs for a range of tasks. Based on the user prompts, the models can offer basic tips on entrepreneurship or provide fundamental insights into website creation through detailed, informative conversations.

Effective prompt engineering techniques pave the way for users to get the desired responses. Furthermore, some companies have been offering high-paying jobs for researchers and personas who can write or adopt effective prompt engineering to get their model to perform responsible actions, thereby enhancing the company's productivity to execute their functions/tasks at an accelerated pace.

This chapter will explain how effective prompt engineering techniques can be applied to LLMs. But first, let's dive into the structure of a prompt and some key ideas that focus on effective prompt techniques.

Components of prompts

How you write a prompt plays a crucial role in guiding the behavior of the model. Prompts contain a few key elements. Let's understand those elements through an example (*Figure 3.1*):

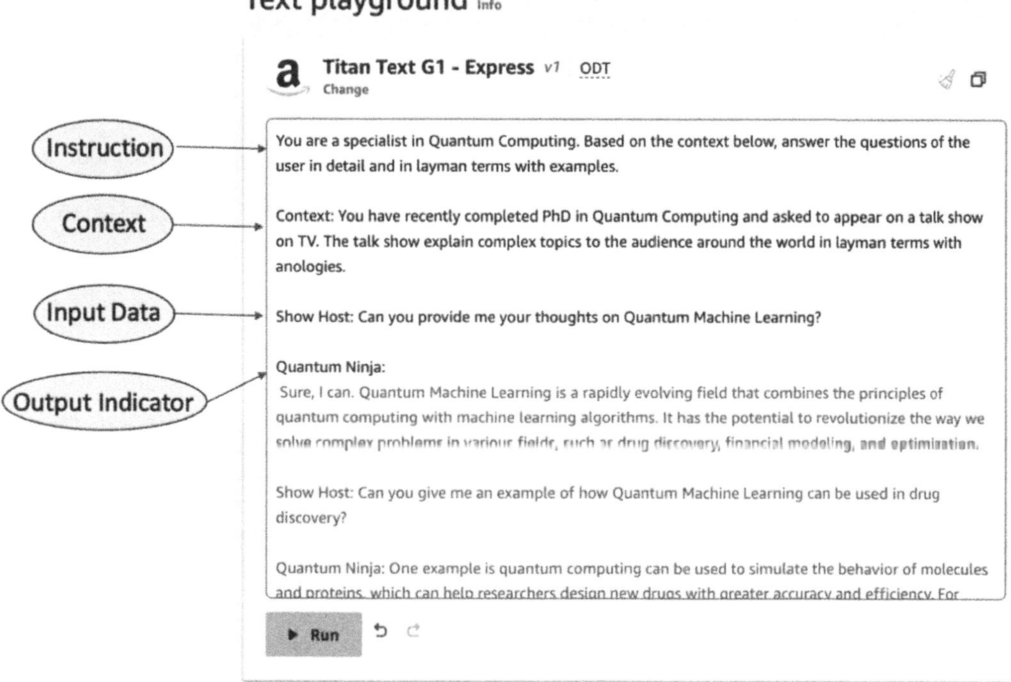

Figure 3.1 – Components of a prompt

Let's take a closer look at the terms highlighted in the preceding figure:

- **Instruction**: With an instruction, you provide a clear and concise description or instruction to the model on how it should perform the task, whether it be summarizing text, translating languages, composing music, or any number of other things. In the preceding figure, you can see that we have asked the model to act as a specialist in quantum computing and answer the user's question in detail and in layman's terms, along with examples.
- **Context**: Context refers to the relevant background information that you provide to the model to enhance its performance. This can include any relevant data, past experiences, or domain-specific knowledge. In the preceding figure, in terms of context, we stated that the model has recently completed a PhD and has been asked to be part of an interview on a talk show that explains complex topics in layman's terms. This primes the model with pertinent knowledge.

- **Input data** (or **user input**): This is the actual question or input that the model needs to process and base its output on. It can be in the form of text, images, audio, and so on, and it can be as simple as a short question, such as `What is Quantum Computing?`. As depicted in the preceding figure, the input question that goes to the model is `Can you provide me your thoughts on Quantum Machine Learning?`.
- **Output indicator**: This is the layout or an indicator that the model should provide its output in. It could be as simple as `Quantum Ninja`, as depicted in the preceding figure, so that the model understands that its output should be in this layout, or it could be in a specific format, such as text, JSON, an audio clip, and so on. Special syntax such as <|*endoftext*|> signals the end of the input and the beginning of the model's output. This special syntax can vary on a per-model basis.

Although prompts need not have all four elements, their form depends on the task. Let's examine a few sample prompts:

Example 1: SQL query

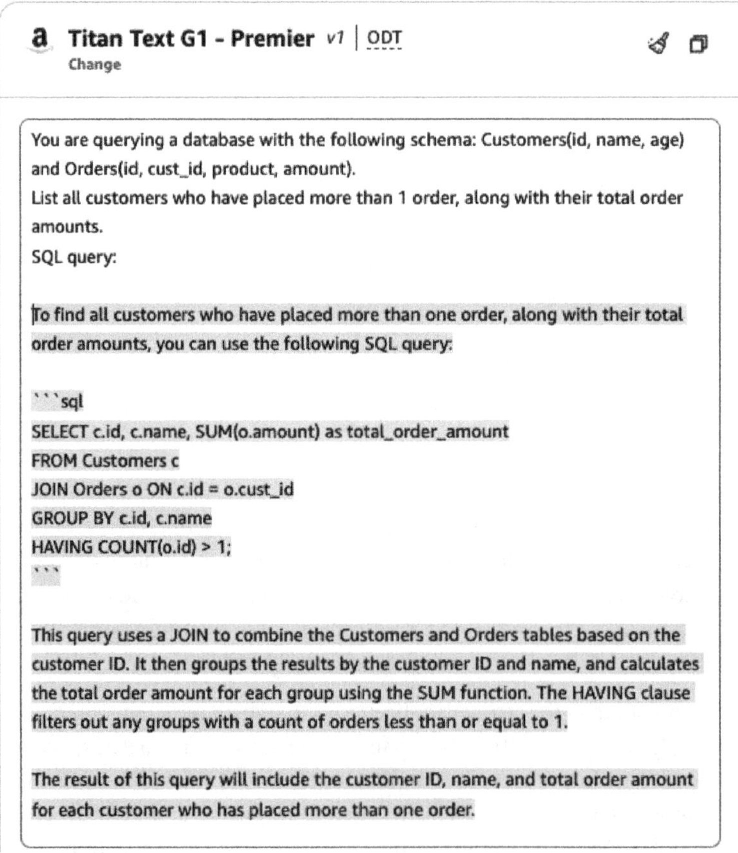

Figure 3.2 – SQL query prompt

As shown in *Figure 3.2*, we are specifying the following prompt elements to the Titan Text G1 – Premier model:

- **Context**: `You are querying a database with the following schema: Customers(id, name, age) and Orders(id, cust_id, product, amount).`
- **Input**: `List all customers who have placed more than 1 order, along with their total order amounts.`
- **Output**: `SQL query:`

This prompt provides clear instructions, relevant schema context, a sample input, and output indicators to produce a suitable SQL query.

Example 2: Recipe generation

Here is another example (*Figure 3.3*):

Text playground Info

Titan Text G1 - Express v1 ODT

[Recipe title: Baked Salmon with Dill]
Baked salmon is a healthy weeknight dinner option perfect with roasted potatoes or rice. The fresh dill adds an aromatic flavor.
[Ingredients:]
Salmon fillet, dill, lemon, salt, pepper, olive oil
[Instructions:] <|endoftext|>

1. Preheat the oven to 400°F.
2. Rinse the salmon fillet and pat it dry with a paper towel.
3. In a bowl, mix together the dill, lemon, salt, pepper, and olive oil.
4. Rub the mixture all over the salmon fillet.
5. Place the salmon fillet on a baking sheet lined with aluminum foil.
6. Bake in the preheated oven for 15-20 minutes, or until the salmon is cooked through.
7. Serve with roasted potatoes or rice.

Figure 3.3 – Recipe prompt

Let's take a closer look:

- **Context**: `Baked salmon is a healthy weeknight dinner option perfect with roasted potatoes or rice. The fresh dill adds an aromatic flavor.`
- **Input data**: `Salmon fillet, dill, lemon, salt, pepper, olive oil.`
- **Output indicator**: < | `endoftext` | >.

The preceding prompt provides the model with the recipe's title, introductory context, ingredients as input data, and <|`endoftext`|> as an output indicator, which signals where the recipe steps should begin.

Prompt engineering applications

Now that we understand how we can communicate with the model, let's learn about some prompt engineering techniques that can aid us in getting better responses from the model.

However, primarily, we need to understand that the optimal prompt engineering approach for any given use case is heavily reliant on the task at hand, as well as the data on which it has been trained.

Some of the tasks that the models on Bedrock excel at are as follows:

- **Classification**: LLMs exhibit prowess in text classification, a supervised learning technique for assigning categories to text. For instance, sentiment analysis involves discerning whether an input passage conveys positive or negative emotion. Some LLMs available via Amazon Bedrock, such as the Amazon Titan models, can also identify toxic, harmless, or fact-based content. Their deep contextual understanding aids the judgment of subtle linguistic cues.
- **Question-answering**: The models can answer questions accurately without external context due to their vast parameters gained from ingesting hundreds of billions of words during pre-training. When provided with relevant documents, their performance further improves by reasoning over the additional context.
- **Summarization**: The models condense lengthy texts into concise summaries that preserve key details, learning to differentiate salient points. Adding such a prompt facilitates rapid analysis of documents.
- **Text generation**: The model can generate original coherent text given a short prompt. Their fluency and semantic consistency allow realistic synthesis of stories, poems, scripts, and more.
- **Code generation**: For a textual description of a programming need, the models can generate executable code in languages such as SQL and Python. For example, a prompt could request text-to-SQL or Python code generation, thereby accomplishing the outlined computational goal.
- **Mathematical reasoning**: The models exhibit an aptitude for mathematical problems provided in text form. This includes numerical calculations, logical deduction, and geometric reasoning. They can further justify solutions with step-by-step explanations.

The breadth of natural language tasks that can be mastered by LLMs on Amazon Bedrock exemplifies their versatility. Their adaptive capacity promises to expand application domains even further.

Now that we've gained insights into applications of prompt engineering in the real world, let's try to unlock some of the most common prompt engineering techniques.

Unlocking prompt engineering techniques

The field of prompt engineering is an active area of research and innovation with new techniques and patterns emerging frequently, driven by the pursuit to improve the performance of the models and generate more natural human-like responses. In this section, we are going to look at some of the most common patterns.

Zero-shot prompting

Zero-shot refers to the ability of LLMs to generate reasonable responses to prompts that it has not been explicitly trained on. It relies solely on a descriptive prompt to specify the desired output, as depicted in *Figure 3.4*:

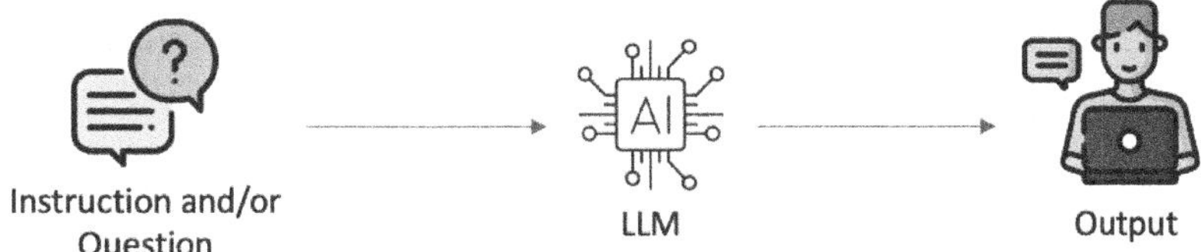

Figure 3.4 – Zero-shot prompting

For instance, a zero-shot prompt to get a poem could be `Write a rhyming poem with 4 stanzas about seasons changing`.

The main advantage of this method is that it's easier; prompt crafting can be done without providing examples in the input. However, output quality can vary without concrete examples to base on.

Few-shot prompting

Few-shot prompting or **few-shot learning** builds on zero-shot's capabilities. As depicted in *Figure 3.5*, on top of instructions/questions, you can provide a few examples that establish a concept or scenario, at which point models can start to generate reasonable continuations:

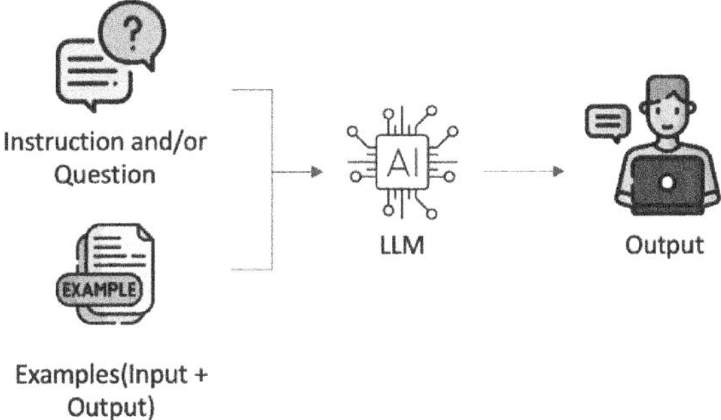

Figure 3.5 – Few-shot prompting

For instance, after showing two or three examples of short conversations about booking a doctor's appointment, LLMs can produce an appointment booking dialog without needing thousands of examples. The key benefit over zero-shot is that few-shot examples help narrow down the context and constrain the generation process, making outputs more precise.

Let's look at some of the examples of few-shot prompting. The following are two inputs that we can use in the poem writing task from the previous sub-section that we can give to the model as examples.

Example 1: `Roses are red, violets are blue, spring brings life anew.`

Example 2: `Summer sun shining bright, long days full of light.`

`Now you write a rhyming poem about autumn changing leaves.`

By analyzing these examples, LLMs can learn the pattern of rhyming four-line stanzas about seasons. It can then follow the template to generate an autumn poem. Balancing creativity and guidance is key in few-shot prompts.

Additional examples of few-shot prompting are available here: `https://www.promptingguide.ai/techniques/fewshot`.

Chain-of-thought prompting

Chain of thought (**CoT**) **prompting** aims to elicit reasoning chains from language models. It involves providing the LLM with a prompt that lays out a reasoning chain or train of thought for the model to follow (*Figure 3.6*).

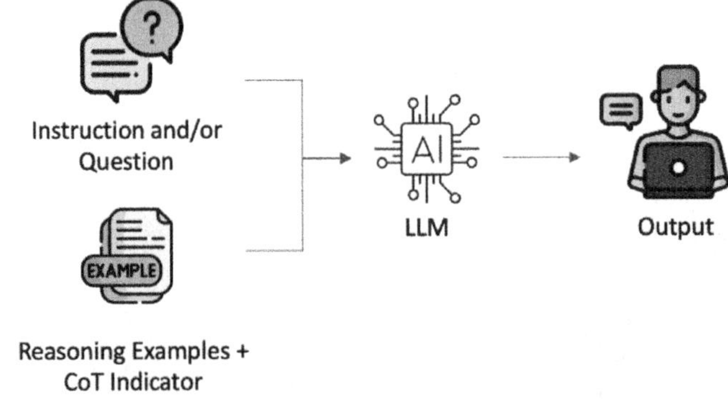

Figure 3.6 – Chain-of-thought prompting

A prompt may start with background context, state a hypothesis or problem, provide reasoning steps, and end with a conclusion to be expanded on. The model then tries to continue the chain of reasoning coherently in its generated text:

Here's an example of a CoT prompt:

```
Recycling is beneficial for the environment because it reduces waste
sent to landfills. Landfills produce methane, a potent greenhouse
gas. They also take up large amounts of space. Recycling reduces
landfill contributions by reusing materials. In conclusion, recycling
helps fight climate change by reducing landfill methane and space
requirements. The main environmental benefits of recycling are...
```

This prompting style guides the LLM to follow the provided reasoning chain and elaborate further on the conclusion statement. The generated text will likely discuss reduced methane emissions and land use from increased recycling in more detail. Hence, chaining further encourages step-by-step logical thinking that focuses on the end goal over open-ended, meandering text.

Let's look at some examples of CoT prompting and the responses:

Example 1:

```
Write a story about a professor exploring a mysterious artifact
```

```
Dr. Jones entered the temple, brushing cobwebs out of her face. In the
center of the room sat a small stone box...
```

```
As she opens the box, a glowing light emerges, illuminating symbols
on the walls
```

```
Squinting in the sudden brightness, Dr. Jones sees the symbols
represent a long-lost ancient language. She reaches towards the box
and feels an energy pulling at her fingertips...
```

Example 2:

```
What are the pros and cons of renewable energy sources?
```

```
Some pros of renewable energies are...
```

```
You missed one major renewable source. Please include geothermal
energy when comparing the pros and cons.
```

```
Some pros of renewable energies like solar, wind, geothermal and
hydroelectric power are low pollution...
```

In this approach, the human can guide and shape the overall narrative or analysis by inserting additional prompts whenever they want to redirect, refine, or expand the model's response. It allows for a more conversational flow based on an initial theme or direction provided by the human.

Additional examples of CoT prompting are available at `https://www.promptingguide.ai/techniques/cot`.

ReAct prompting

Reasoning and Acting (**ReAct**) prompting is derived from the ReAct framework, as introduced in the paper *ReAct: Synergizing Reasoning and Acting in Language Models* (`https://arxiv.org/abs/2210.03629`):

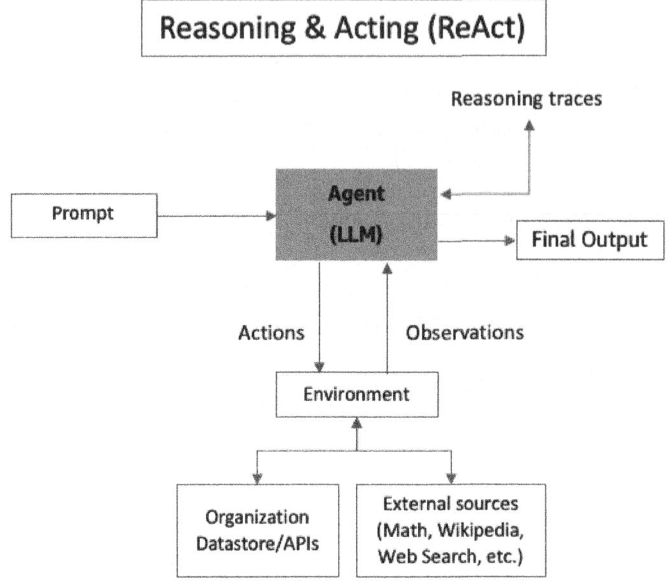

Figure 3.7 – ReAct prompting

This framework generates various reasoning traces. Then, based on those traces, it performs relevant actions. Through this process of reasoning and acting, you can also allow the application to have access to the organization's internal data stores and APIs, or external sources from various tools, websites, web searches, and more, as shown in *Figure 3.7*. This process of generating reasoning traces and performing actions is iterative and occurs until the LLM finds the answer to the user's prompt.

We will discuss ReAct prompting in more detail in *Chapter 10*. For now, let's create a ReAct-SQL tool for deriving a comprehensive response from the model.

Prompt from human: `Provide an updated financial summary report for AnyCompany`

Assistant response:

Thought: The user is asking for financial information about AnyCompany. To answer this, I need to do the following:

- Query the database to find financial records for AnyCompany
- Write a summary of the financial information obtained

So, I will need to use the `sql_db_query` tool.

Action: `sql_db_query`

Action input: `SELECT * FROM financial_db WHERE company = 'AnyCompany';`

`[(260B, 55B, 321B, 2.2T)]`

Answer:

```
AnyCompany has demonstrated strong financial performance with revenue
of $260 billion. With net income of $55 billion, AnyCompany has a 21%
net profit margin, indicating it is highly profitable. AnyCompany also
has a considerable asset base of $321 billion, providing the company
with significant financial resources. With a market capitalization
of $2.2 trillion, AnyCompany is the most valuable public company,
suggesting investors are confident in AnyCompany continued growth and
profitability. Overall, AnyCompany's finances appear very healthy.
```

Similar to the preceding form of prompting patterns, new prompt engineering techniques and patterns are burgeoning these days. More details on prompt engineering can be found in the prompt engineering guide at `https://www.promptingguide.ai/techniques`.

In this section, we uncovered several prompt engineering techniques that are being leveraged in the realm of building Generative AI applications for various use cases. Next, we will work on designing prompts for Amazon Bedrock FMs.

Designing prompts for Amazon Bedrock models

In this section, we're going to cover prompt guidance for some of the models available via Amazon Bedrock. We will kick things off with the Anthropic Claude model and provide details around prompt guidance for this. The majority of the learning for prompt guidance can be inherited from Claude models. Furthermore, for the sake of striking a balance between brevity and detail, we will shine a light on the models from Amazon Titan, AI21 Labs, and Stability AI Stable Diffusion. This will sum up our prompt guidance and associated prompt recommendations for invoking Amazon Bedrock models.

Prompting Anthropic Claude 3

Here are some things to keep in mind while prompting the Anthropic Claude 3 model:

- **Assigning a role/persona via prompts**: Assigning roles or personas to the Claude models aids in improving model performance in several scenarios, which, in turn, improves the model's tonality. For instance, you can assign an expert role for executing a certain task, such as `You are a seasoned Children's Book Author` or `You are a Business Expert`.

  Example: `Imagine you are a kindergarten teacher and have to provide an explanation for rainbows in the sky to the children.:`

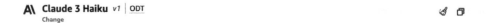

Why do we see rainbows in the sky?

Rainbows are formed when sunlight interacts with water droplets in the atmosphere. Here's a more detailed explanation of how rainbows are produced:

1. Sunlight enters the water droplets: When sunlight hits a raindrop, the light bends (refracts) as it passes from the air into the drop.

2. Reflection inside the drop: The light then reflects off the back of the drop and exits the drop.

3. Dispersion of light: As the light exits the drop, it is dispersed (separated) into its different wavelengths (colors). This is because the different wavelengths of light (red, orange, yellow, green, blue, indigo, violet) bend at slightly different angles.

4. Alignment of colors: The dispersed colors then align in a particular order - red on the outside, violet on the inside - forming the familiar arc of a rainbow.

5. Viewing angle: For an observer to see the rainbow, the sun must be behind them, and the water droplets must be at a specific angle (around 42 degrees) relative to the observer's line of sight.

So in summary, the interaction of sunlight, water droplets, and the physics of refraction and dispersion come together to create the beautiful, multicolored arc we know as a rainbow in the sky.

Figure 3.8 – Anthropic Claude 3 Haiku – simple prompting

Without assigning a role/persona, the answer may be complex to understand, as shown in *Figure 3.8*.

After adding the role/persona, you can see that the output response aligns more with a child's complexity level in *Figure 3.9*:

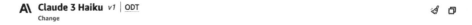

Imagine you are a kindergarten teacher and have to provide an explanation for rainbows in the sky to the children.

clears throat and speaks in a warm, gentle tone

Alright, my little friends, gather round and let's talk about those beautiful rainbows we sometimes see in the sky!

You see, when the sun's light shines through the raindrops in the air, it gets bent and spread out, like how a prism bends and spreads out light. This makes all the different colors in sunlight - red, orange, yellow, green, blue, indigo, and violet - become visible to our eyes. And that's what creates the beautiful rainbow!

The raindrops act like tiny mirrors, reflecting the sunlight and separating it into those lovely, vibrant colors. It's almost like nature's own special light show just for us! Isn't that amazing?

Rainbows are a wonderful reminder that even when it's raining, the sun is still shining up above. They're a special treat that nature gives us, a colorful arc across the sky to brighten our day. So the next time you see a rainbow, remember - it's the sun's light playing peek-a-boo with the raindrops, just for you!

smiles warmly Now, who wants to try and make their own rainbow using a prism or some water? I bet we can make some magic of our own!

Figure 3.9 – Anthropic Claude 3 Haiku – assigning role personas

- **Providing clear and direct instructions to Claude**: It is always advisable to provide simple, clear instructions to the model to generate the desired output. Adding emphasis to skip any additional content/preamble in the output avoids any unnecessary information in the output. For instance, take a look at the input prompts in *Figure 3.10*. One contains an additional sentence on skipping the preamble and the other doesn't provide any further clarification to the input prompt. Since the `Temperature` parameter can be set to a higher value, the output that's generated might be different, as shown here. However, the clear instructions in the latter provide a more direct output without any additional context, as desired by the user:

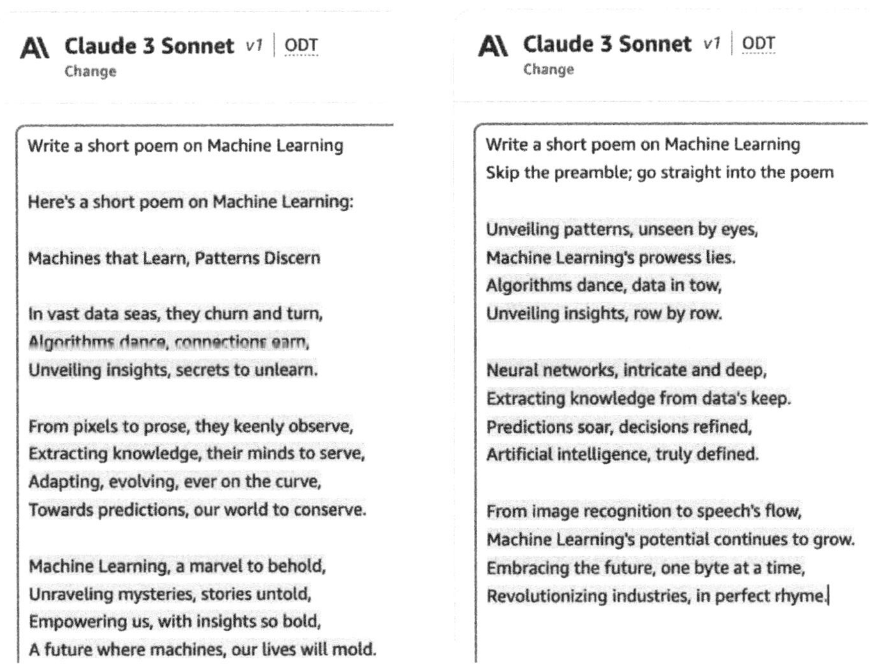

Figure 3.10 – Providing clear and direct instructions

- **Few-shot prompt examples**: Providing examples (as covered in the *Few-shot prompting* section) of some common scenarios aids in the overall performance gain of the model and generating succinct responses with proper formatting.
- **XML tags**: Usage of XML tags, such as `<tag>content</tag>`, can assist in providing a definitive structure in the prompt and the output response. We can provide additional context and clarification to Claude stating a piece of information can be found within the tags to be leveraged for generating the output. In such a way, Claude understands how to frame the output response, by extracting the key relevant information from the tags.

  It's also recommended to separate the input data from the instructions to generate a more structured prompt for easier and more performant processing by the model.

Here's an example of tags:

A\ **Claude 3 Sonnet** *v1* | ODT
Change

Draft a polite email to Bob using the information within the <email> tag below.
<email>
Hope you're doing well. This is to inform you that the task for AnyCompany estimates need to be delivered to the customer by 6 pm EOD.
</email>
Dear Bob,

I hope this email finds you well. I wanted to bring to your attention that the task for AnyCompany estimates needs to be delivered to the customer by 6 pm today, end of day.

Please let me know if you need any assistance or have any questions regarding this matter.

Thank you for your attention to this.

Best regards,
[Your Name]

Figure 3.11 – XML tags

As shown in *Figure 3.11*, we provided a `<email>` tag, which generated a more structured output response from the model.

- **Response limiters and defining the output format**: Anthropic Claude models (especially the 100K and 200K token length models) are capable of providing comprehensive and verbose responses. The user can limit the response length by explicitly stating the word limit, or character count, as part of the prompt to provide a more succinct and relevant output. Let's look at an example:

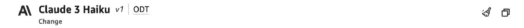

Draft a brief summary on Quantum Computing in 100 words

Quantum computing is a revolutionary field that harnesses the unique properties of quantum mechanics to perform computations beyond the capabilities of classical computers. By leveraging the principles of superposition and entanglement, quantum computers can solve certain problems exponentially faster than traditional computers. This has significant implications for fields such as cryptography, drug discovery, optimization, and simulation. However, the development of practical quantum computers is still a significant challenge, as they require precise control and manipulation of delicate quantum systems. Ongoing research in areas like quantum error correction and hardware design aims to overcome these obstacles and unlock the full potential of quantum computing for transformative applications.

Figure 3.12 – Response limiters

In *Figure 3.12*, we have set the response limiter to 100 words as part of the prompt. Furthermore, specifying the desired output format – be it a list, JSON, paragraph, Markdown, and so on – can lead to more performant and precise output, as desired by the user, which aids in eliminating any irrelevant verbiage from chatty models.

- **Explicit unknown disclaimers**: Providing explicit expressions as disclaimers such as `If you don't know the answer, respond with the following format - My sincere apologies, I'm not aware of the answer` can aid in avoiding any form of hallucination from chatty Claude models. Guardrails for the topics can also be added such that Claude doesn't respond to unwanted inputs. This concept will also be discussed in *Chapter 12*.

Prompting Mistral models

Similar to other models, when working with Mistral models, crafting well-designed prompts is crucial to obtaining high-quality and relevant outputs. Here are some key points to keep in mind while designing the prompts for Mistral models:

- Clearly define the task or objective you want the model to accomplish through the prompt. Are you looking for text classification, summarization, personalization, or something else?
- Provide relevant context, examples, or background information to ground the model's understanding before stating the core prompt. Context helps the model better comprehend the prompt.
- Use clear formatting and delimiters such as #, ###, or <<< >>> to separate different sections of the prompt, such as instructions, examples, and the main query. This enhances the prompt's structure.
- When possible, demonstrate the desired output through examples in a *few-shot* learning style. Showing examples guides the model toward the expected format.
- Specify the role the model should take on, such as a customer service agent or technical writer. Defining a persona makes responses more tailored.
- For an open-ended generation, provide clear instructions on the desired output length and structure through numeric targets such as word counts or the number of sentences/paragraphs.
- Ask the model to include confidence scores or assessments when generating outputs to gauge its certainty levels.
- Consider chaining multiple Mistral models in a sequence, where the output from one model feeds into the next for enhanced capabilities.
- Test and iterate on prompt designs through evaluations to find optimal prompting strategies.

Figure 3.13 shows the Mixtral 8x7B Instruct model being invoked in Amazon Bedrock Playground.

Please note that the <s> and </s> tokens are utilized to denote the **beginning of string** (**BOS**) and **end of string** (**EOS**), respectively, signifying the start and conclusion of the text input. The `[INST]` and `[/INST]` strings tell the model that the content enclosed between them constitutes instructions that the model should adhere to:

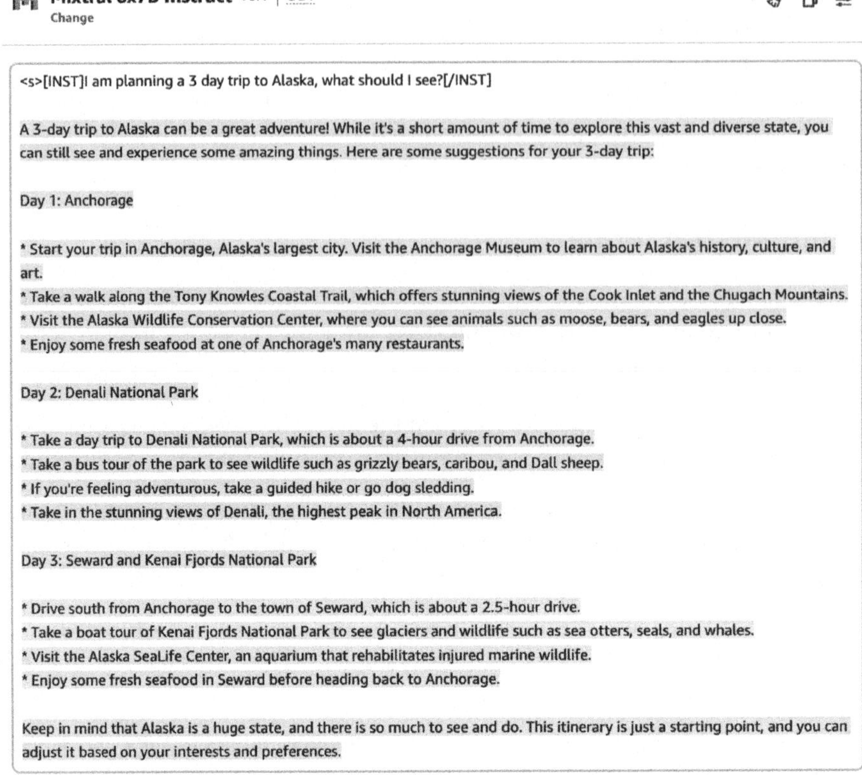

Figure 3.13 – Prompting the Mixtral 8x7B Instruct model

The key is to carefully structure prompts with clear context, examples, instructions, and formatting to steer Mistral models to generate high-quality, tailored outputs matching your needs.

Prompt guidance for Amazon Titan text models

As we learned in *Chapter 1*, Amazon Titan text models are well suited for a plethora of use cases:

- Dialog and roleplay systems
- Text summarization and Q&A
- Machine translation
- Metadata extraction and analysis
- RAG (This will be covered in detail in *Chapter 5*)
- Code generation approaches
- Text and content generation

When generating text outputs with the model, it is often recommended to provide clear instructions on the desired output length and structure to get optimal results. Here are some additional tips for Titan text models:

- Focus prompts on concise, directed questions to get targeted answers by default.
- Systems perform best on single sentences or short paragraphs.
- For longer inputs, place instructions at the end to guide high-quality responses.
- Adding explicit instructions in the prompt produces more tailored results.
- Specify an exact number of words, sentences, bullet points, or paragraphs you want the AI to generate in the prompt. Providing a numerical range (for example, 100-200 words) can also work well. This gives the model a clear target to aim for.
- Avoid vague instructions such as `keep it short` or `summarize briefly`. These are open to interpretation by the AI. Precise numbers remove ambiguity.
- Word count alone may not sufficiently guide output length as sentence lengths can vary. Specifying the number of sentences/paragraphs provides more robust control.
- If the model seems unable to generate a quality response for a prompt, program it to default to a message such as `Unsure about answer` rather than attempt to force a poor response. Here's an example of such a prompt: `Tell me about Quantum Computing. Respond with Unsure about the answer or I don't know in case you are not sure about the question being asked.`
- When relevant, provide context paragraphs for the AI to reference before asking a question. This provides knowledge for an informed response.
- Test different output length instructions to find the right balance between conciseness and adequate detail for your use case. Err on the side of more specificity with numbers.

You can go back to the *Amazon Titan FMs* section in *Chapter 1* if you wish to look at example prompts and responses in Titan models.

AI21 Labs – instruct models

AI21 Labs models work very well with languages other than English, such as Spanish, French, German, Portuguese, Italian, and Dutch. The model is proficient in text summarization, text generation, and Q&A tasks. In this section, we will walk through a few key concepts to be inculcated with AI21 models available via Amazon Bedrock:

- **Output length**: To generate desirable responses from AI12 models, it is advisable to specify the output length – that is, the number of paragraphs, items, and so on or an approximation of the same – instead of using words/characters.

- **Provide short yet detailed task descriptions**: Craft clear, detailed task descriptions to minimize ambiguity. AI21 models excel at following precise instructions for even complex jobs.
- **Avoid negative prompting**: Directly state the target outcome. Avoid negatives such as `no more than x statements`. It is always recommended to state requirements directly and affirmatively.
- **Header usage**: Provide context upfront using an `Instruction:` header to clarify the prompt. Separate prompt sections with newlines to highlight distinct pieces and for readability purposes.
- **Evaluate multiple prompting patterns**: Try both zero-shot and few-shot learning. Pick an ideal approach for your use case. For instance, as depicted in the zero-shot and few-shot examples shown in this chapter, depending on the use case under consideration, you may initiate by providing zero examples and determining the response, and simultaneously compare the response generated from the model after providing certain examples to guide the output. In some cases, there may not be a need to provide a ton of examples if the model can generate a desirable response.

Figure 3.14 depicts a product description summarization example from AI21 Jurassic-2 Ultra within Amazon Bedrock:

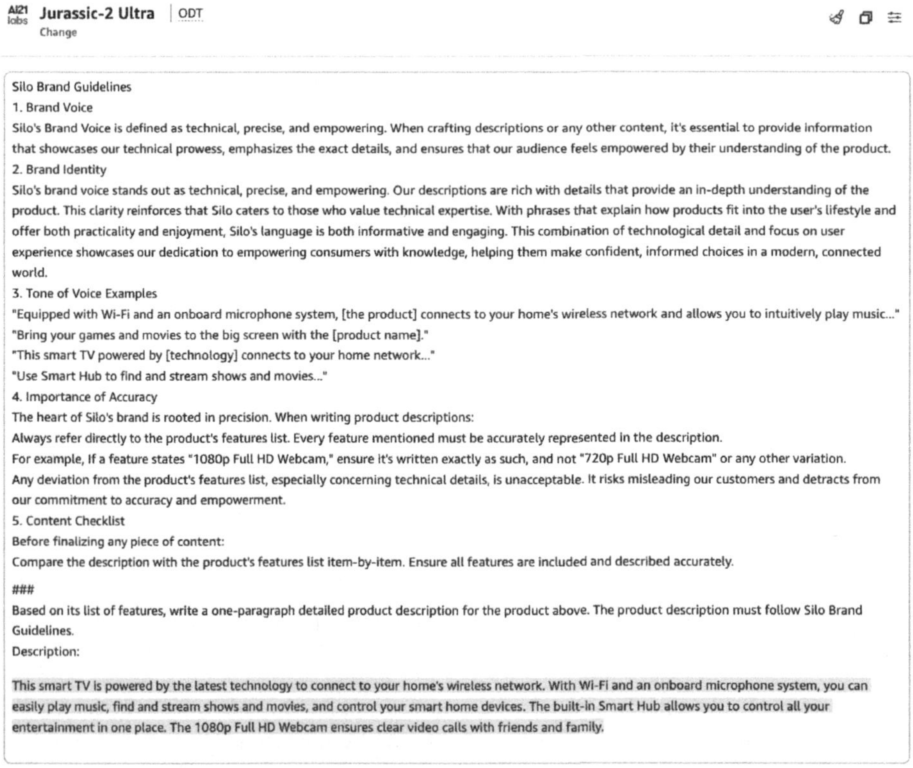

AI21 labs Jurassic-2 Ultra | ODT
Change

Silo Brand Guidelines
1. Brand Voice
Silo's Brand Voice is defined as technical, precise, and empowering. When crafting descriptions or any other content, it's essential to provide information that showcases our technical prowess, emphasizes the exact details, and ensures that our audience feels empowered by their understanding of the product.
2. Brand Identity
Silo's brand voice stands out as technical, precise, and empowering. Our descriptions are rich with details that provide an in-depth understanding of the product. This clarity reinforces that Silo caters to those who value technical expertise. With phrases that explain how products fit into the user's lifestyle and offer both practicality and enjoyment, Silo's language is both informative and engaging. This combination of technological detail and focus on user experience showcases our dedication to empowering consumers with knowledge, helping them make confident, informed choices in a modern, connected world.
3. Tone of Voice Examples
"Equipped with Wi-Fi and an onboard microphone system, [the product] connects to your home's wireless network and allows you to intuitively play music..."
"Bring your games and movies to the big screen with the [product name]."
"This smart TV powered by [technology] connects to your home network..."
"Use Smart Hub to find and stream shows and movies..."
4. Importance of Accuracy
The heart of Silo's brand is rooted in precision. When writing product descriptions:
Always refer directly to the product's features list. Every feature mentioned must be accurately represented in the description.
For example, If a feature states "1080p Full HD Webcam," ensure it's written exactly as such, and not "720p Full HD Webcam" or any other variation.
Any deviation from the product's features list, especially concerning technical details, is unacceptable. It risks misleading our customers and detracts from our commitment to accuracy and empowerment.
5. Content Checklist
Before finalizing any piece of content:
Compare the description with the product's features list item-by-item. Ensure all features are included and described accurately.
###
Based on its list of features, write a one-paragraph detailed product description for the product above. The product description must follow Silo Brand Guidelines.
Description:

This smart TV is powered by the latest technology to connect to your home's wireless network. With Wi-Fi and an onboard microphone system, you can easily play music, find and stream shows and movies, and control your smart home devices. The built-in Smart Hub allows you to control all your entertainment in one place. The 1080p Full HD Webcam ensures clear video calls with friends and family.

Figure 3.14 – Prompting the AI21 Jurassic-2 Ultra model

Further details on prompt engineering and design with AI21 models, along with examples, can be found at `https://docs.ai21.com/docs/prompt-engineering`.

Prompting Meta Llama models

Similar to any other LLM, effective prompting is essential for getting the most out of Llama models. Since the following is standard prompt guidance for any LLM, we will cover some of the best practices here:

- **Clarity and specificity**:
  - Ensure that your prompts are clear, concise, and unambiguous
  - Provide sufficient context and details to guide the model toward the desired output
  - Use precise language and avoid vague or open-ended statements
- **Structure and formatting**:
  - Organize your prompts logically and structure them in a way that aligns with the desired output format
  - Utilize formatting elements such as bullet points, numbered lists, or headings to enhance readability and comprehension
  - Consider providing examples or templates to illustrate the expected format of the output
- **Task framing**:
  - Frame your prompts as specific tasks or instructions for the model to follow
  - Clearly specify the desired action, such as summarizing, generating, or analyzing
  - Provide context about the intended use case or audience for the output
- **Iterative refinement**:
  - Prompting is an iterative process, and you may need to refine your prompts based on the model's responses
  - Analyze the output and identify areas for improvement or clarification
  - Incorporate feedback and adjust the prompt accordingly to steer the model toward better results
- **Fine-tuning and customization**:
  - Explore the possibility of fine-tuning the Llama model on domain-specific data or examples
  - Customize the model's behavior and outputs by incorporating specific instructions or constraints in the prompt
  - Leverage techniques such as prompting with few-shot examples or demonstrations to improve performance

- **Ethical and safety considerations**:
  - Be mindful of potential biases or harmful outputs that the model could generate
  - Incorporate explicit instructions or filters to mitigate risks and ensure the model's responses align with ethical and safety guidelines
  - Monitor and evaluate the model's outputs for any concerning or inappropriate content

Llama models also consider special kinds of tokens. For Llama 3, the following tokens are used:

- The <|`begin_of_text`|> token represents the BOS token.
- The <|`eot_id`|> token indicates the end of the current turn or message.
- The <|`start_header_id`|>`{role}`<|`end_header_id`|> token encloses the role for a particular message, which can be either **system**, **user**, or **assistant**.
- The <|`end_of_text`|> token is equivalent to the EOS token. Upon generating this token, Llama 3 will stop producing any further tokens.

For more details on prompt formats, go to `https://llama.meta.com/docs/model-cards-and-prompt-formats`:

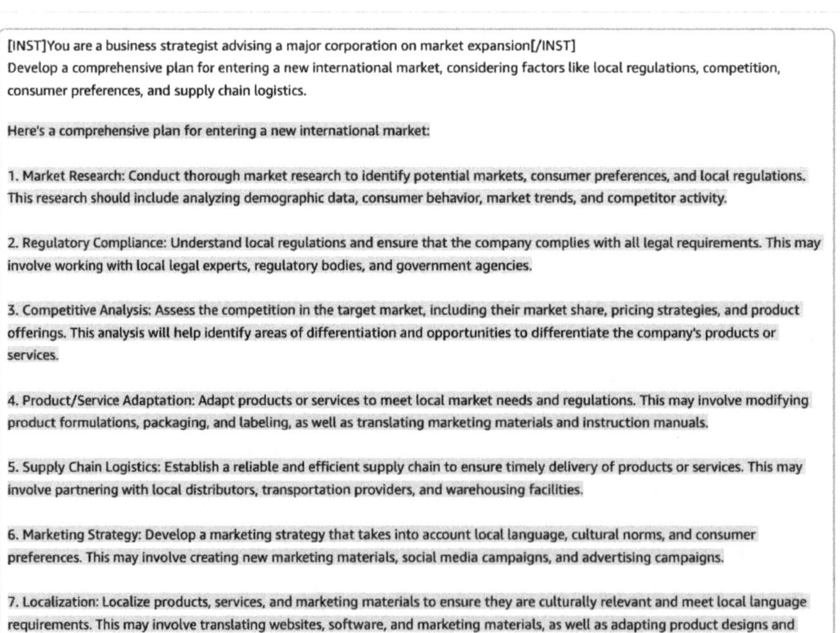

Figure 3.15 – Prompting the Llama2 Chat 70B model

As shown in *Figure 3.15*, the Llama 2 Chat 70B model is being invoked in Amazon Bedrock Playground.

The `[INST]` and `[/INST]` strings tell the model that the content enclosed between them constitutes instructions that the model should adhere to.

If you'd like to learn about the different examples and templates for invoking various models, including any new models being added to Amazon Bedrock, go to `https://docs.aws.amazon.com/bedrock/latest/userguide/prompt-templates-and-examples.html`.

Prompt guidance for Stability AI – Stable Diffusion

Stable Diffusion models (along with Amazon Titan image models) have been gaining popularity in image generation use cases. Here are some key tips for crafting effective prompts when using Stability AI's Stable Diffusion for image generation:

- **Specify the subject clearly**: Start your prompt with a clear description of the desired subject or main element of the image – for example, `A photo of a cat` or `An illustration of a robot`. Being more specific usually produces better results.
- **Indicate the style**: After the subject, specify the desired art style, medium, or aesthetic, such as `in impressionist style` or `a cartoon drawing of`. Styles help steer the output.
- **Use text weights**: Give elements different emphasis by assigning weights, such as `cat:1.5, sitting:1.2, couch:1`. Higher weights make elements more prominent.
- **Add negative prompts**: Adding phrases that should not appear in the image, prefixed by `-`, improves quality by excluding unwanted elements. For example, if you provide `Cars racing on racetrack` as a prompt and give `red car` as a negative prompt, it will exclude red cars from the image's output, as shown in *Figure 3.16*:

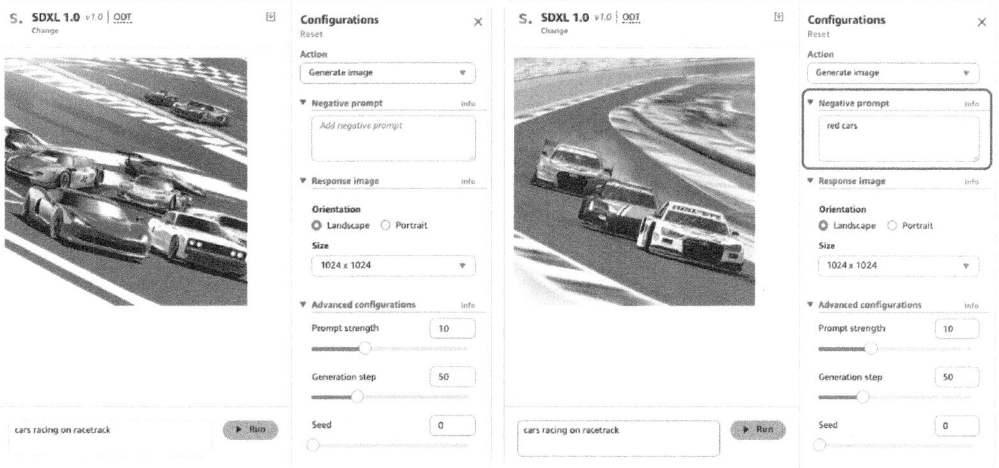

Figure 3.16 – Negative prompt example

- **Be detailed and specific**: Using more descriptive and distinctive words, rather than general terms, produces more tailored results.
- **Adjust parameters**: Parameters such as `--ar`, `--v`, and `--n` control the aspect ratio, vividness, and level of detail, respectively. Tweak them to refine the output.
- Providing additional descriptive details always aids the model in being more performant. The following are examples of such aspects:
  - Specify the medium (painting, drawing, CGI, and so on)
  - Define colors used
  - Describe lighting and shadows
  - Include the artist's name if mimicking a style
  - Mention the website if you're reproducing a specific image
  - Add any other descriptive remarks or adjectives
  - Specify the desired resolution if needed for print or digital use

Let's look at an example.

Prompt: `Portrait photo of an Indian old warrior chief, tribal panther make up, front profile, looking straight into the camera, serious eyes, 50mm portrait photography, hard rim lighting photography-beta -ar 2:3 -beta`

Output response from SDXL 1.0:

Figure 3.17 – Image generation output from SDXL 1.0

When prompted with the same input, the output response from the Titan Image Generator G1 model is as follows:

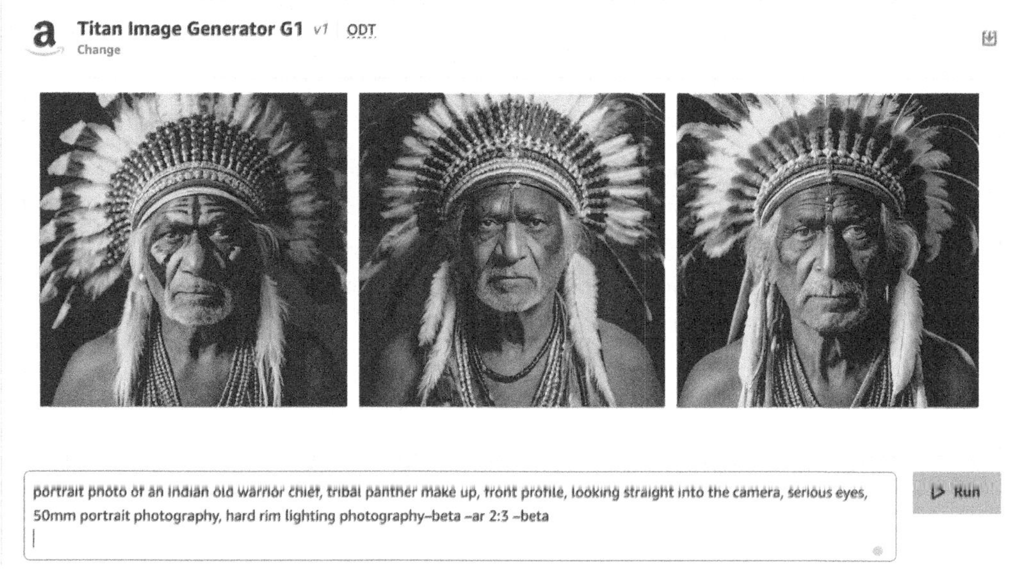

Figure 3.18 – Image generation output from Titan Image Generator

Providing this level of detail and context will help produce a more accurate image that matches your vision. Adjust prompts iteratively to refine results.

You might be wondering why the same prompt generated different outputs from two models. The reason for this is that SDXL is trained on a different set of data than Titan Image Generator, so the output you will see from these models will differ. Think of it this way: SDXL and Titan are two people, who learn from two different books for an exam. During the exam, when they were asked the same question, they would have two different viewpoints, and their answer would be based on the books they read.

If you are trying these prompts in your environment, you might also notice another thing. The output image that you are seeing in your environment might differ from the one shown here, even if you provide the same prompts. The reason for this is to do with the added degree of randomness. These models will generate output based on the inference parameters, such as *Prompt Strength* and *Seed*. We will cover these parameters in detail in *Chapter 9*. However, in short, prompt strength controls how you want the model output to be influenced by the prompt, and the seed is a way to randomize an output image.

Now that you have a good understanding of prompt guidance for FMs provided by Amazon Bedrock, in the next section, we will try to sum up some of the key principles and techniques you must follow when it comes to prompt engineering in various use cases.

Understanding best practices in prompt engineering

To summarize, when crafting prompts, you must adhere to the following key principles:

- **Tailor prompts to your model**: Prompts can contain instructions, context, input, and output indicators. Account for factors such as model size, input data, moderation policies, and more. What works for one model may fail for another:
  - Be clear, concise, and straightforward to avoid any ambiguity.
  - *Output usage in the prompt*: It is often useful to mention the requested output at the end of the prompt – for example, `What are the use cases of renewable resources? List 5 key points.`
  - *Language emphasis*: Using simple flowing language with coherent sentences assists in crafting a better prompt and avoiding isolated phrases.
  - *Get into the model's head*: Craft prompts to nudge it toward helpful behaviors. Think of it as someone who has all the right answers but only for correctly articulated questions.
- **Iteratively refine prompts**: Treat initial prompts as hypotheses and revise them based on model output. The best prompts emerge through an ongoing give-and-take:
  - *Use directives*: If you want the output to be in a particular form, specify it directly within the prompt – for example, `Summarize the chapter in 500 words.`
  - *Provide example responses*: Adding some example responses within the prompt with the expected output can refine the responses more desirably – for example, `Summarize this chapter in one paragraph (1000 characters): [New study shows decreasing activity in region X leads to impairment.]`. Surrounding the example response in brackets indicates the model adheres to the guidelines set by the user while responding in the desired format.
  - *Add constraints*: Constraining prompt responses by format, additional information inclusion, length, and more can lead to more controlled output.
- **Strike the right detail balance**: Too little detail fails to guide the model adequately while excessive verbosity limits creative flourishes. Distill prompts down to concise essence:
  - *Complex task handling*:
    - FMs can hallucinate when dealing with complex tasks. It is advisable to break down the complex task into subtasks or even consider splitting complex tasks into multiple prompts.
    - Provide emphasis by using keywords to ask the model to think step-by-step or provide logical reasoning as it is crafting the output. Provide some key examples in the input for complex tasks.

- *Rinse, lather, repeat*: Iteratively break down and try different prompts to optimize model responses for your goals. Continue adjusting while testing and experimenting to achieve the desired results.
- *Continuous evaluation*: Iteratively reviewing the model's responses to provide the desired quality is a must when it comes to handling different use cases and complex scenarios.

Prompts unlock Generative AI's capabilities but require thoughtfulness to construct properly. Learn your target model's strengths and limitations, iterate carefully on prompt phrasings, and appreciate these systems' ever-evolving nature. Wield prompts judiciously and enjoy the fruits of AI's burgeoning creativity!

Complexity arises in structuring the right prompts to handle intricate goals. But when done well, prompts unlock AI like a skeleton key, opening doors to breathtaking new generative capabilities. The prompt contains the potential; our role is to shape and guide it with thoughtful prompts.

Summary

In this chapter, we learned about several prompt engineering techniques to gain a deeper understanding of prompting patterns and uncovered insights while considering examples of said prompting patterns. Then, we dived into prompt guidance with Amazon Bedrock models for Anthropic Claude, AI21 Labs, Amazon Titan, and Stability AI's Stable Diffusion.

Lastly, we summarized the practical approach to prompt guidance while looking at Amazon Bedrock models that can be applied to various use cases. Through various examples, we learned how to craft the most effective prompts.

At this point, you should have a good understanding of the importance of prompt engineering. Furthermore, you should be able to analyze various prompt techniques and best practices involved in prompt engineering in the context of building Generative AI applications.

In the next chapter, we'll learn how to customize a model using fine-tuning and continued pretraining techniques. We will delve into how fine-tuning works, look at various APIs, analyze the results, and perform inference on our fine-tuned model.

4

Customizing Models for Enhanced Performance

When general-purpose models fall short of delivering satisfactory results for your domain-specific use case, customizing FMs becomes crucial. This chapter delves into the process of customizing FMs while using techniques such as fine-tuning and continued pre-training to enhance their performance. We'll begin by examining the rationale behind customizing the base FM and exploring the mechanics of fine-tuning. Subsequently, we will delve into data preparation techniques to ensure our data is formatted appropriately for creating a custom model using both the AWS console and APIs. We will understand various components within model customization and different customization APIs that you can call from your application.

Furthermore, we will analyze the model's behavior and perform inference. Finally, we will conclude this chapter by discussing guidelines and best practices for customizing Bedrock models.

By the end of this chapter, you will be able to understand the importance and process of customizing a model for your domain-specific use case.

The following key topics will be covered in this chapter:

- Why is customizing FMs important?
- Understanding model customization
- Preparing the data
- Creating a custom model
- Analyzing the results
- Guidelines and best practices

Technical requirements

For this chapter, you need to have access to an *AWS* account. If you don't have one, you can go to `https://aws.amazon.com/getting-started/` and create an AWS account.

Once you have access to an AWS account, you will need to install and configure the AWS CLI (`https://aws.amazon.com/cli/`) so that you can access Amazon Bedrock FMs from your local machine. In addition, you will need to set up the AWS Python SDK (Boto3) since the majority of the code cells we will be executing require it (`https://docs.aws.amazon.com/bedrock/latest/APIReference/welcome.html`). You can set up Python by installing it on your local machine, using AWS Cloud9, utilizing AWS Lambda, or leveraging Amazon SageMaker.

> **Note**
>
> There will be a charge associated with invocating and customizing the FMs of Amazon Bedrock. Please refer to `https://aws.amazon.com/bedrock/pricing/` to learn more.

Why is customizing FMs important?

In the previous chapter, we looked at several prompt engineering techniques to improve the performance of a model. As we also saw in *Chapter 1* (and shown in *Figure 4.1*), these FMs are trained on massive amounts of data (GBs, TBs, or PBs) with millions to billions of parameters, allowing them to understand relationships between words in context to predict subsequent sequences:

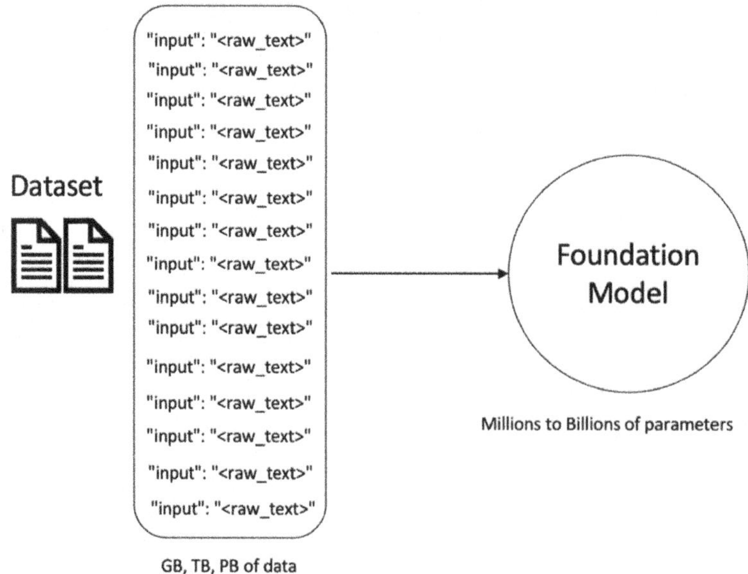

Figure 4.1 – Training an FM

So, why do we need to customize these models?

That's a fair question since a lot of use cases can be directly solved by using prompt engineering and RAG techniques (which we will cover in *Chapter 5*). However, consider a situation where you require the model to adhere to a particular writing style, output format, or domain-specific terminology. For instance, you may need the model to analyze financial earnings reports or medical records accurately. In such cases, the pre-trained models might not have been exposed to the desired writing style or specialized vocabularies, limiting their performance despite effective prompt crafting or RAG implementation.

To bridge this gap and enhance the model's domain-specific language understanding and generation capabilities, customization becomes essential. By fine-tuning the pre-trained models on domain-specific data or adapting them to the desired writing style or output format, you can tailor their performance to meet your unique requirements, ensuring more accurate and relevant responses:

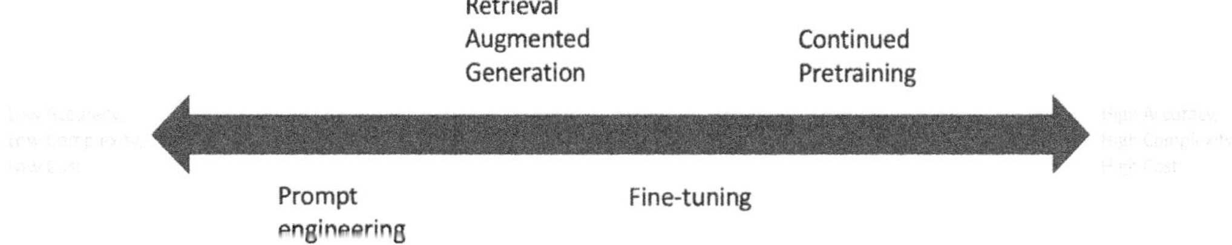

Figure 4.2 – Generative AI performance techniques

If you look at the spectrum of generative AI performance techniques shown in *Figure 4.2* for improving the performance of FMs, it ranges from prompt engineering to training the model from scratch. For domain-specific data, prompt engineering techniques may provide low accuracy, but they involve less effort and are cost-effective. Prompt engineering is a better option if you have a simple task and don't need a new domain-specific dataset. If you would like to understand how prompt engineering works, please go back to *Chapter 3*.

Next on the spectrum with a little bit of increasing complexity, cost, and accuracy is RAG. This technique fetches data from outside the language model, such as from internal knowledge bases or external sources. It is a particularly useful technique when you have large corpora of documents that do not fit the context length of the model. We will discuss RAG in more detail in *Chapter 5*.

Further on the spectrum, customizing the model is essentially more time-consuming and costly. However, it provides greater accuracy to your specialized use case.

There are two customization techniques within Amazon Bedrock: fine-tuning and continued pretraining.

In *fine-tuning*, the model is trained with the labeled dataset – a supervised learning approach. The labeled dataset that you provide will be specific to your use case. Whether you're working in healthcare, finance, or any other field, you can fine-tune your model to become an expert in that particular domain. In healthcare, for example, the model can be fine-tuned for medical specialization, allowing it to understand and interpret medical records with greater accuracy. Similarly, a financial analysis model can be fine-tuned for niche financial analysis, enabling it to identify patterns and trends in financial data that may be missed by traditional algorithms.

To fine-tune a model using your own data, you need to have a sufficient amount of high-quality data that is relevant to the task you want to perform. This data should be labeled and annotated to provide the model with the necessary information for training. As shown in *Figure 4.3*, we can use this labeled dataset to fine-tune the base FM, which then generates a custom model. You can then use the custom model to generate responses that are tailored to your specific domain and use case:

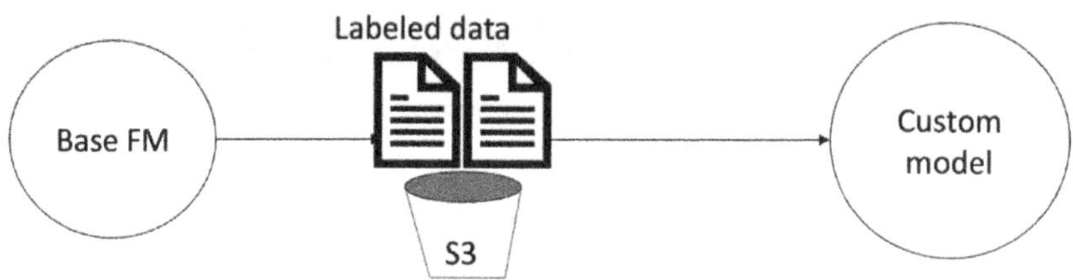

Figure 4.3 – Fine-tuning

For example, let's say you work in the medical industry and would like to summarize a dialog between two doctors discussing the medical report of the patient, extract the information to be put into medical forms, and maybe write it in layman's terms.

In this case, the base FMs might not be trained on the domain-specific dataset. Hence, this is an example scenario where when we perform fine-tuning, we will provide the model with labeled examples of how the prompt and response should look like.

In *continued pre-training*, we adapt to a new domain or train the model to learn the terminologies of an unfamiliar domain. This involves providing additional continuous training to an FM while utilizing large amounts of unlabeled data. When we say unlabeled data, we mean that there is no target label, and the model will learn the patterns from the provided texts. This contrasts with fine-tuning, which involves using smaller quantities of labeled data. *Figure 4.4* highlights the difference between the labeled and unlabeled data that's required for continued pre-training and fine-tuning, respectively:

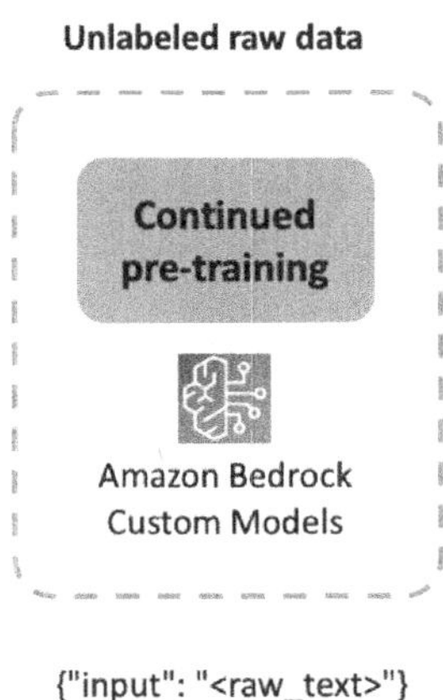

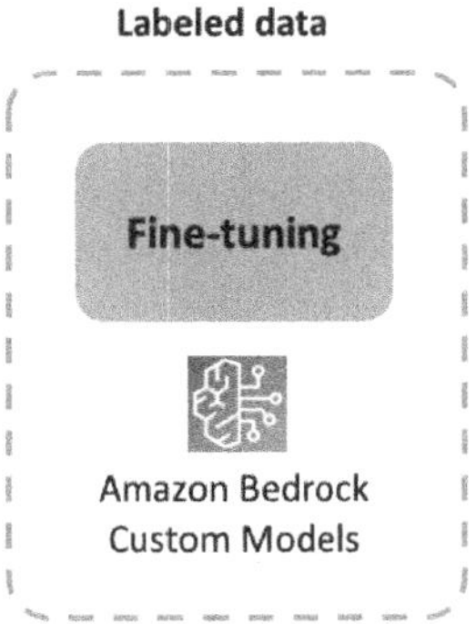

{"input": "<raw_text>"}
{"input": "<raw_text>"}
{"input": "<raw_text>"}

{"prompt": "<prompt text>", "completion": "<expected generated text>"}
{"prompt": "<prompt text>", "completion": "<expected generated text>"}
{"prompt": "<prompt text>", "completion": "<expected generated text>"}

Figure 4.4 – Unlabeled versus labeled data

Examples of continued pre-training can include training the model to learn the terminologies of the financial industry so that it can understand financial reports, or training the model to learn quantum physics by giving it abundant information from books so that it will be able to evaluate/predict the tokens associated with string theory with greater accuracy. Let's say that two physicists are having a dialog around string theory, and we pass that dialog as a context to the base FM (as shown in *Figure 4.5*):

Physicist 1: Hey Maria, how's your dive into string theory going?
Physicist 2: Hey Javier, it's been intense! String theory's mathematical complexity is something else I've been wrapped up in exploring extra dimensions, especially the twisty-turny shapes called Calabi-Yau manifolds.

Physicist 1: Oh yeah, those things are like a puzzle within a puzzle. It's amazing how they represent the hidden structure of our universe. I've been getting lost in their mathematical intricacies too.
Physicist 2: Totally! It feels like we're spelunking in a cave of math and trying to uncovering the rules that govern everything. Lately I've been digging into compactification where those extra dimensions curl up and influence particle physics in subtle ways.

Physicist 1: Compactification's like folding up those dimensions into tiny spaces right? It's wild how it affects the behavior of particles. And speaking of wild have you looked into heterotic string theory lately?
Physicist 2: Oh yeah, heterotic strings are fascinating. They're like this dance between open and closed strings, creating this unified picture of how forces work. And those E8 x E8 symmetry groups? They're like the beat to the song of the universe.

Physicist 1: Exactly! It's like the universe has this underlying harmony we're trying to uncover. But then there's the holographic principle, which adds a whole new layer of complexity
Physicist 2: Yeah, the holographic principle is mind-bending. It's like saying all the information in our universe is encoded on the surface of black holes. It challenges everything we thought we knew about space and information.

Physicist 1: It's a reminder of how much we still have to learn. But that's the beauty of science, right?

What are E8 x E8 symmetry groups ?

E8 x E8 symmetry groups are the beat to the song of the universe in heterotic string theory.

Figure 4.5 – Quantum physicist dialog and question

It could be possible that the base FM we are using here isn't familiar with quantum physics – that is, the base FM hasn't been trained on a dataset related to quantum physics.

So, when we ask the model a question such as `What are E8 x E8 symmetry groups?`, the model hallucinates and doesn't explain this concept since it doesn't know about string theory.

With continued pre-training, we train the model on an unfamiliar domain by providing the base FM with a large amount of unlabeled datasets. For example, we could train the model on textbooks about quantum computing in the desired format, as explained in the *Preparing the data* section, which then creates a custom model (as shown in *Figure 4.6*):

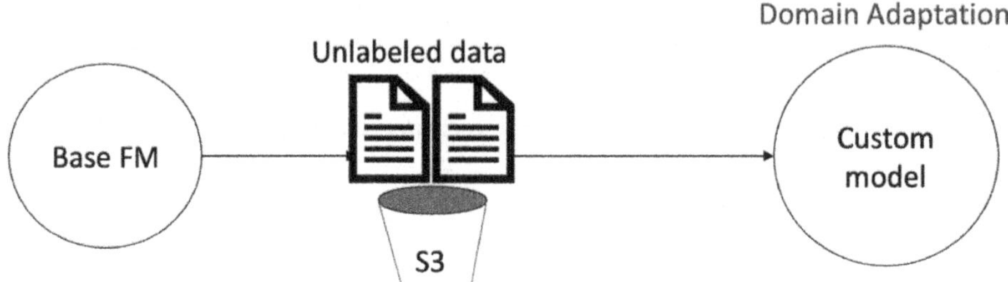

Figure 4.6 – Continued pre-training

Continued pre-training presents certain challenges. As we are training the entire model, the weights and biases are what demand heavy computational resources and diverse unlabeled text data.

When you're deciding whether to use custom models over other methods, such as prompt engineering and RAG, several factors come into play. These include the task that you are working on, the availability of data, computational resources, and cost. Here are some guidelines to help you make an informed decision:

- **Complexity level**: Creating custom models is particularly useful when you have tasks that are complex and require the model to understand intricate details.
- **Specialized data**: Having a sufficient amount of specialized data for creating custom models will provide remarkable results. Make sure your data is clean (free from errors, inconsistencies, and duplicates) and prepared (formatted, transformed, and split into appropriate subsets) before you start the training process.
- **Computational resources and cost**: When you create custom models, you'll need to purchase Provisioned Throughput, which gives you a dedicated capacity to deploy the model. Make sure you review the pricing based on the model type and commitment terms. We will discuss Provisioned Throughput in detail in the *Analyzing the results* section of this chapter.

In addition, creating custom models provides you with greater control over how you want the model to respond. You can customize it precisely to your needs, making it suitable for tasks that require fine-grained customization, such as responding in a specific tone, dialect, or inclusive language.

Let's understand some key concepts of model customization before we start our first model customization job.

Understanding model customization

The principle behind fine-tuning and continued pre-training comes from the broad concept of **transfer learning**, which, as its name suggests, entails transferring knowledge that's been acquired from one problem to other often related but distinct problems. This practice is widely employed in the field of **machine learning** (**ML**) to enhance the performance of models on new tasks or domains.

Model customization is a five-step process:

1. **Identify your use case and data**: Identifying the use case/task and how it solves your organization's business objectives is a critical step. Do you want to summarize legal documents, perform Q&A on medical reports, or do something else? Once you've identified the use case, you must gather enough relevant datasets that you can use for model customization. The dataset should contain examples that the model can learn intricate details from. Remember, how your custom model performs on your task-specific use case depends on the quality of the dataset that you provide for training.
2. **Prepare the dataset**: Once you've gathered the dataset, you have to clean and preprocess it. For fine-tuning, you need to have labeled examples in **JSON lines** (**JSONL**) format. For continued pre-training, you need to have unlabeled examples in JSONL format. We will discuss this in more detail in the *Preparing the data* section.
3. **Select the base pre-trained model**: Once the dataset has been prepared, you have to select an existing base pretrained model that you would like to fine-tune. You can look at the website of the model provider to understand the model attributes. If it is fit for your use case, try prompt engineering techniques to check which model responds closest to what you are looking for, and also evaluate the FMs using **Model evaluation** within Amazon Bedrock or using **Model leaderboards**:

    - *Model evaluation*: Bedrock provides two distinct evaluation methods: automatic evaluation and human evaluation. Automatic evaluation utilizes predefined metrics such as accuracy, robustness, and toxicity screening, whereas with human evaluation, you can define custom metrics such as friendliness, stylistic adherence, or alignment with brand voice. We will have a more detailed discussion on model evaluation in *Chapter 11*.
    - *Model leaderboards*: Several leaderboards are available that rank models based on their performance on various tasks, such as text generation, summarization, sentiment analysis, and more. Some of the most popular leaderboards include **General Language Understanding Evaluation** (**GLUE**), SuperGLUE, HELM, and OpenLLM by HuggingFace.

Please note that although it's good to understand the performance of the FM through leaderboards, for real-world use cases, you have to be cautious and not rely solely on leaderboards as they may lack the robustness required to mirror the complexity of real-world use.

4. **Configure and start the fine-tuning job**: Once you've identified the base FM and the dataset is ready, you can configure the fine-tuning job by specifying hyperparameters, the input and output S3 path for the dataset and store metrics, respectively, and networking and security settings. We will discuss this in more detail in the *Creating a custom model* section.
5. **Evaluate and iterate**: Once the model is ready, you can evaluate and analyze it based on the metrics and logs stored by the model. To do so, you can put aside a validation set that provides the performance metric of the custom model you've created. We will discuss this in more detail in the *Analyzing the results* section.

When we are customizing a model, Amazon Bedrock creates a copy of the base FM, on which we essentially update its model weights. **Weights** are key components in **artificial neural networks** (**ANNs**) and are attached to the inputs (or features). These weights define which features are important in predicting the output and getting better at specific tasks. *Figure 4.7* shows a simplified ANN architecture where these inputs, along with their weights, are processed by **summation** and the **activation function** (both defined in the model algorithm) to get the output (**Y**).

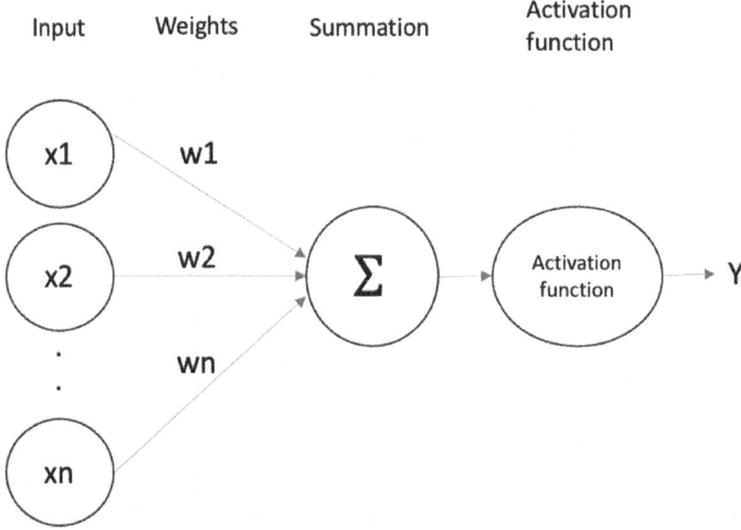

Figure 4.7 – Simplified ANN

For a deeper dive into ANNs, there are numerous online tutorials and courses available that provide in-depth explanations and examples of neural network concepts, architectures, and training techniques. Additionally, textbook classics such as *Neural Networks and Deep Learning, Michael Nielsen, Determination Press* and *Deep Learning, Ian Goodfellow, Yoshua Bengio, and Aaron Courville, MIT Press* offer comprehensive theoretical and mathematical foundations.

When we perform model customization (fine-tuning or continued pre-training), we update the model weights. While updating the model weights, a common problem can occur called **catastrophic forgetting**. This is when the model starts to forget some information it was originally trained on due to weight modifications, which can lead to degraded performance on more generalized tasks. In general, this can happen due to overfitting the training data, which means the model provides an accurate response to the training data but can't generalize well and provides degraded performance on new information. In addition, customizing the model can be costly and resource-intensive, something that requires extensive memory utilization.

To overcome these challenges, a technique called **Parameter-efficient Fine-tuning** (**PEFT**) was introduced in the paper *Parameter-Efficient Transfer Learning for NLP* (`https://arxiv.org/pdf/1902.00751`).

Note that at the time of writing, Bedrock does not support PEFT. However, it's good to have an understanding of the PEFT technique.

PEFT

In PEFT, you don't need to fine-tune all the model parameters, something that can be quite time-consuming, resource-intensive, and costly. Instead, it freezes much of the model weights and you only need to train a small number of them. This makes it memory and compute-efficient, less susceptible to catastrophic forgetting, and cheaper to store the model on the hardware.

When fine-tuning LLMs, various techniques can reduce the number of trainable parameters to improve efficiency. We can categorize these PEFT methods into three main classes:

- **Selective methods**: These update only certain components or layers of the original LLM during fine-tuning. This allows you to focus on the most relevant parts of the model. However, it can result in suboptimal performance compared to full fine-tuning.
- **Reparameterization methods**: These introduce low-rank matrices to compress the original weights. Examples include such as **Low-Rank Adaptation of Large Language Models** (**LoRA**). This reduces parameters while still modifying the whole model. The trade-off is increased memory usage during training.
- **Additive methods**: These keep the original weights of the LLM frozen and add new trainable layers for task-specific adaptation. Additive methods such as **adapters** add the trainable layer inside the encoder or decoder component of the transformer architecture.

The choice of the PEFT approach involves balancing metrics such as parameter and memory efficiency against model quality, training speed, and cost. Selectively updating parts of a model offers one end of this trade-off, while adapters and prompts maximize parameter efficiency at the cost of some architectural changes.

With that, we've covered PEFT and its techniques at a very high level. However, if you are interested in learning more about it, go to `https://github.com/huggingface/peft`. In addition, the *Generative AI with Large Language Models* course provides in-depth information about PEFT methods: `https://www.deeplearning.ai/courses/generative-ai-with-llms/`.

Hyperparameter tuning

In addition to fine-tuning techniques such as PEFT, **hyperparameter tuning** also plays a big role in ensuring a model retains its pretrained knowledge. Hyperparameters are configuration settings that control the model training process, much like knobs that can be tweaked and tuned. Models have various hyperparameters, including the learning rate, number of epochs, batch size, beta, gamma, and more. Each model may require a different set of optimal hyperparameter values, found through experimentation, to achieve the best performance and accuracy.

The **learning rate** hyperparameter controls how quickly the model is adapted to the task. It also controls how much the model's parameters are adjusted during each iteration of the training process. It determines the step size at which the model's parameters are updated based on the calculated gradients (which represent the direction and magnitude of the changes needed to minimize the loss function).

Let's consider an analogy that might help you visualize the learning rate.

Imagine that you're trying to find the lowest point in a hilly landscape, but you're blindfolded. You can only sense the steepness of the slope you're standing on (the gradient) and take steps accordingly. The learning rate determines how big or small those steps should be:

- If the learning rate is too high, you might overshoot the lowest point and end up on the other side of the hill, continually overshooting and never converging to the optimal solution
- If the learning rate is too low, you might take tiny steps and get stuck on a plateau or make painfully slow progress toward the lowest point

The ideal learning rate allows you to take reasonably sized steps that bring you progressively closer to the lowest point (the optimal set of model parameters) without overshooting or getting stuck.

In practice, finding the optimal learning rate is often a matter of experimentation and tuning. Different models and datasets may require different learning rates for the training process to converge effectively.

Now that we understand the concepts behind fine-tuning, let's start the customization process by preparing the data.

Preparing the data

We've already seen why customizing the model is important to improve its accuracy and performance. We've also seen that continued pre-training is an unsupervised learning approach that needs unlabeled data, whereas fine-tuning is a supervised learning approach that needs labeled data.

The type of data we provide to the model can change the way the model responds. If the data is biased or has highly correlated features, you might not get the right responses from the trained custom model. This is true for any ML models you are training, so it is essential to provide high-quality data. While I won't cover data processing and feature engineering concepts in this book, I wanted to highlight their importance. If you wish to learn more about these concepts, you can go through any ML courses and books, such as *Hands-On Machine Learning with Scikit-Learn, Keras, and TensorFlow* by Aurélien Géron, and *Feature Engineering for Machine Learning* by Alice Zheng and Amanda Casari.

The dataset that you need for continued pre-training and fine-tuning should be in JSONL format. The following documentation explains what JSONL format is, its requirements, sample examples, and its validator: https://jsonlines.org/.

Now, let's look at the data preparation techniques we can use for both methods.

Continued pre-training expects the data to be in {"input": "<raw_text>"} format, whereas fine-tuning expects the data to be in {"prompt": "<prompt text>", "completion": "<expected generated text>"} format.

Here are some examples:

- **Continued pre-training**: {"input": "EBITDA stands for Earnings Before Interest, Tax, Depreciation and Amortization"}
- **Fine-tuning**: {"prompt": "What's EBITDA?", "completion": "Earnings Before Interest, Tax, Depreciation and Amortization"}

If your dataset comprises images, then you can fine-tune the text-to-image or image-to-embedding model using Titan Image Generator as the base model. At the time of writing, continued pre-training only supports text-to-text models, not image-generation models.

For image data, fine-tuning expects the data to be in {"image-ref": "s3://path/file1.png", "caption": "caption text"} format.

Once you've prepared the data, you must split it into train and validation datasets and store it in an Amazon S3 bucket. Once you've done this, you can create a custom model.

Creating a custom model

To create a custom model via the AWS console, go to **Custom models** on the Amazon Bedrock console page (https://console.aws.amazon.com/bedrock/home). *Figure 4.8* shows what the **Custom models** page looks like. It provides information on how the customization process works, as well as two tabs called **Models** and **Training jobs**:

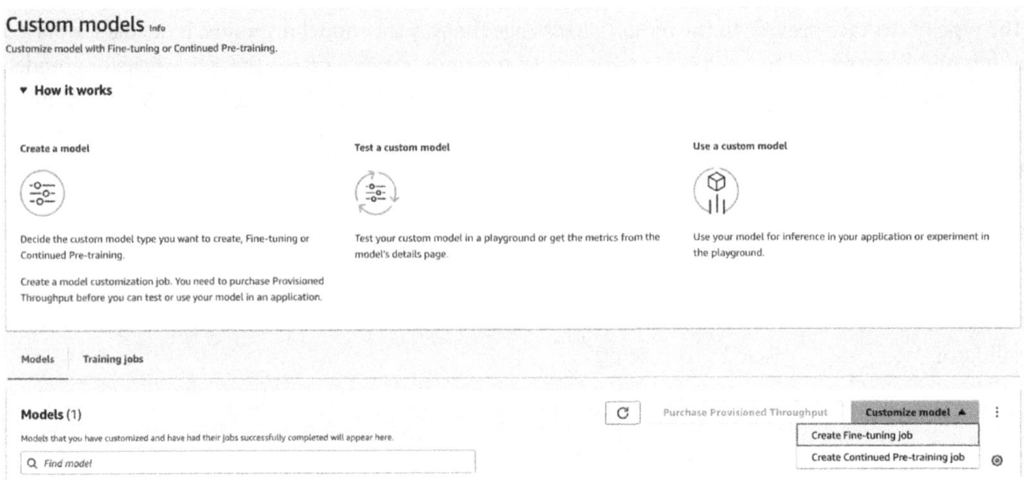

Figure 4.8 – The Bedrock console – Custom models

Under **Customize model** in the **Models** tab, you can select **Create Fine-tuning job** or **Create Continued Pre-training job**. When you select either of these options, you can view details about the job, including its status, under the **Training jobs** tab.

Components of model customization

The main components of model customization (fine-tuning or continued pre-training) include the source model, hyperparameters, and input data, as demonstrated in *Figure 4.9*. These inputs are used to create a training job, which outputs the custom model alongside its metrics and logs:

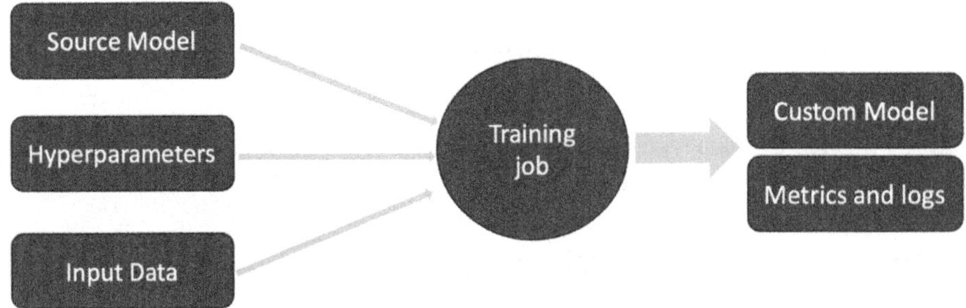

Figure 4.9 – Components of customization job

Let's learn more about these:

- **Source model**: A key component of any customization job is selecting the source model that you wish to customize. You can find a list of all the supported models under the **Model details** section of the **Create Fine-tuning job** and **Create Continued Pre-training job** pages, as shown in *Figure 4.10*:

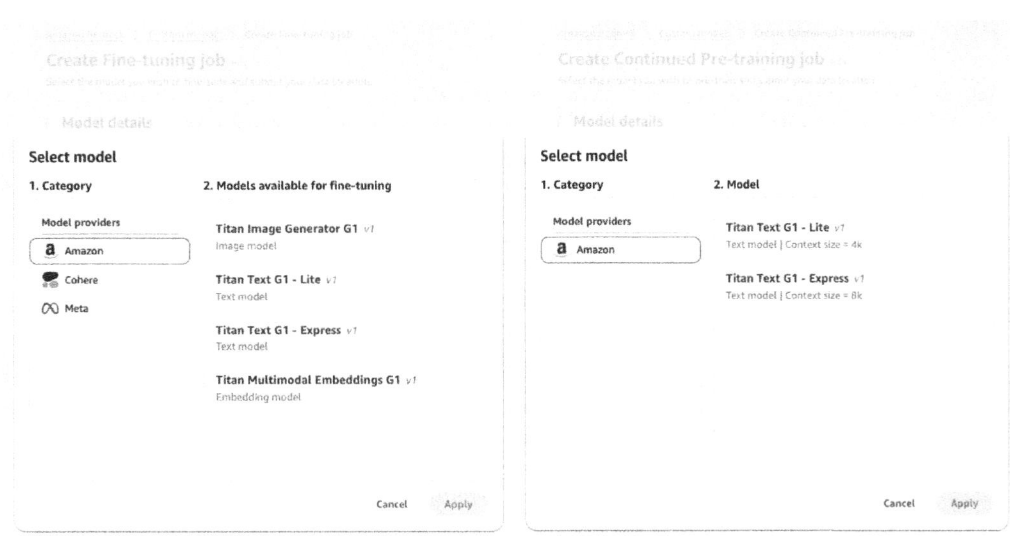

Figure 4.10 – Selecting a model for a customization job

- **Hyperparameters**: Along with the source models, you can specify a set of hyperparameters. These act like external knobs that control how the model is trained. These are different from inference parameters, which are set during the inference process.
- **Input data**: The dataset that is used to train the model is in JSONL format, and it's prepared and stored in an Amazon S3 bucket.
- **Training job**: The inputs (source model, hyperparameters, and input data) are used to create a training job. There are other configuration details, such as VPC settings, which you can use to securely control access to the data in an Amazon S3 bucket, an IAM service role, which provides access to Bedrock to write to an S3 bucket, and model encryption, which you can use encrypt the custom model at rest using a KMS key. We will cover security and privacy in Amazon Bedrock in *Chapter 12*.
- **Custom model**: Once the training process is completed, the custom model is stored in the AWS account owned by the AWS Bedrock Service team.
- **Metrics and logs**: While creating the customization job, you provide the S3 output path where the metrics and logs are stored by the training job. You will see the `step_wise_training_metrics.csv` and `validation_metrics.csv` files inside the S3 output path. We will learn how to evaluate and analyze results in the *Analyzing the results* section.

For now, let's look at the API calls we can use to create a custom model.

APIs

Amazon Bedrock provides several APIs that allow you to create, monitor, and stop customization jobs. This section will examine some of these key APIs: **CreateModelCustomizationJob**, **ListModelCustomizationJob**, **GetModelCustomizationJob**, and **StopModelCustomizationJob**.

Let's dive deeper into each of these API calls:

- **CreateModelCustomizationJob**: This API is used to create a customization job that will start the training process and create a custom model. In this API, you can specify various parameters – for example, you can set `customizationType` to `FINE_TUNING` or `CONTINUED_PRE_TRAINING`, `baseModelIdentifier` as the source model you wish to use, relevant hyperparameters, and the input data (training and validation dataset). Here's an example of the job being used in the Python SDK (Boto3):

```
import boto3
import json
llm = boto3.client(service_name='bedrock')

# Setting customization type
customizationType = "FINE_TUNING"

# Creating customization job
llm.create_model_customization_job(
    jobName="fine-tuning-job",
    customModelName="fine-tuned model",
    roleArn="arn:aws:iam::arn-for-
MyBedrockModelCustomizationRole",
    baseModelIdentifier="arn:aws:bedrock:us-east-1::foundation-
model/foundation-model-id",
    hyperParameters={
        "epochCount": "1",
        "batchSize": "1",
        "learningRate": "0.007",
        "learningRateWarmupSteps": "0"
    },
    trainingDataConfig={"s3Uri": "s3://bucket/path/to/train.
jsonl"},
    validationDataConfig={
        "validators": [{
            "s3Uri": "s3://bucket/folder/validation-file.jsonl"
        }]
    },
    outputDataConfig={"s3Uri": "s3://bucket/folder/
outputdataconfig/"}
)
```

Once you run the preceding code, the training job will start.

- **ListModelCustomizationJob**: You can use this API call to retrieve a list of all the customization jobs that you are running:

```
import boto3
llm = boto3.client(service_name='bedrock')
llm.list_model_customization_jobs()
```

- **GetModelCustomizationJob**: This API call retrieves detailed information about the customization job. Here, you can view the status of the job; it can be `IN_PROGRESS`, `STOPPED`, `FAILED`, or `COMPLETE`. If the model has a status of `FAILED`, you will *not* be charged:

```
import boto3
llm = boto3.client(service_name='bedrock')
fine_tune_job = llm.get_model_customization_job(jobIdentifier='a
rn:aws:bedrock:job-arn-from-create-model-customization')
print(fine_tune_job['status'])
```

  Amazon Bedrock also has integration with Amazon EventBridge, where you can receive a notification whenever there is a status change. We will dive deeper into the EventBridge integration in *Chapter 11*.

- **StopModelCustomizationJob**: If the customization job is `IN_PROGRESS`, and you would like to stop the job for any reason, you can run this API call:

```
import boto3
llm = boto3.client(service_name='bedrock')
llm.stop_model_customization_job(jobIdentifier='arn:aws:bedrock:
job-arn-from-create-model-customization')
```

Once you start the customization job, the time it takes to complete will vary depending on the size of the training dataset you provide. If your dataset contains a few thousand records, the training job can take about an hour, while if the dataset contains millions of records, the training job can take a few days to complete.

Once the customization job has been completed and a custom model has been created, we can analyze the results and perform inference on our model.

Analyzing the results

As mentioned previously, when creating a customization job, we provide an output S3 path, where the metrics and logs are stored by the training job. You will see the `step_wise_training_metrics.csv` and `validation_metrics.csv` files inside the S3 output path. Within these files, you will see information such as the step number, epoch number, loss, and perplexity. You will see these details in both the training and validation sets. Although providing a validation set is optional, doing so allows the performance metrics of the custom model that's been created to be evaluated.

Depending on the size of the dataset, you can decide how much of the validation dataset you would like to hold. If your dataset is small (for example, it contains hundreds or thousands of records), you can use 90% as the training set and 10% as the validation set. If your dataset size is large (for example, it contains hundreds of thousands of records), you can reduce the validation set. So, if you have hundreds of thousands of records, you can use 99% of them as the training set and 1% as the validation set.

Metrics for training and validation

There are two key types of metrics that provide valuable insights into how well the model is learning: loss and perplexity. Let's take a closer look:

- **Loss**: This ranges from 0 to infinity. The loss value that's calculated during training indicates how well the model fits the training data. Meanwhile, the validation loss shows how effectively the model generalizes to new, unseen examples after training is completed. Loss is one of the most commonly used metrics for evaluating the performance of a model during training. In general, lower loss values are preferable and indicate that the model is fitting the data well. Higher loss values suggest that the model's prediction is far off from the actual response and it's making a lot of errors.
- **Perplexity**: This ranges from 1 to infinity. It measures a language model's ability to accurately predict the next token in a sequence. A lower perplexity score corresponds to better predictions and the model's capabilities.

Both loss and perplexity are important metrics for data scientists to analyze when training models with Bedrock. A well-performing training run will show the training and validation loss values converging over time. This convergence indicates that the model is learning from the training data without overfitting.

Inference

Once the job is successful and we've verified the training and validation metrics, we are ready to perform inference on our model. The first thing we need to do is purchase Provisioned Throughput, which gives us a dedicated capacity to deploy the model. At the time of writing, custom Bedrock models can only be deployed through Provisioned Throughput. However, you can also use Provisioned Throughput for base FMs supported by Bedrock.

At the time of writing, three commitment terms are available with Bedrock.

- **No commitment** (priced hourly)
- **1 month**
- **6 months**:

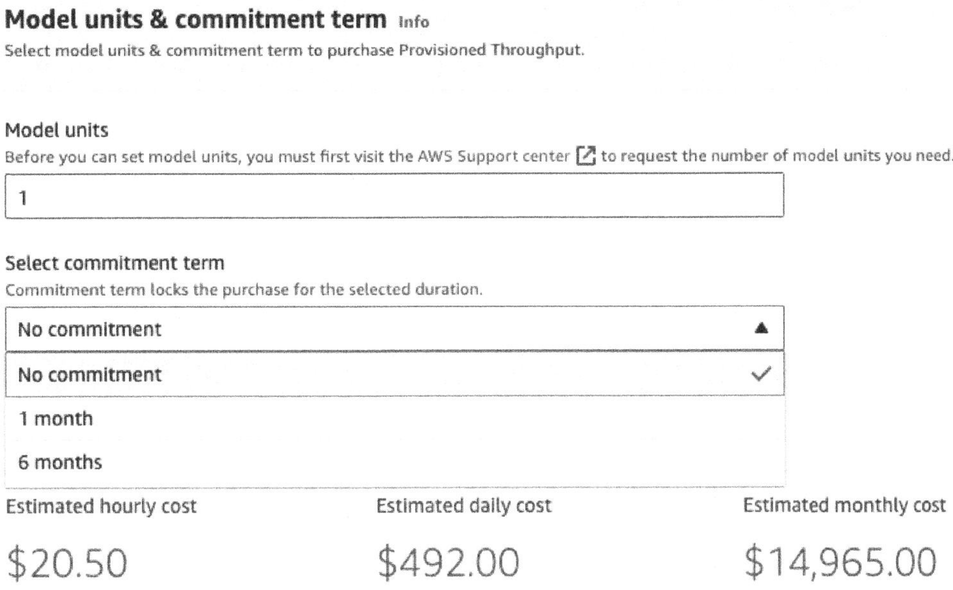

Model units & commitment term Info

Select model units & commitment term to purchase Provisioned Throughput.

Model units

Before you can set model units, you must first visit the AWS Support center to request the number of model units you need.

1

Select commitment term

Commitment term locks the purchase for the selected duration.

No commitment

No commitment

1 month

6 months

Estimated hourly cost $20.50

Estimated daily cost $492.00

Estimated monthly cost $14,965.00

Figure 4.11 – Model units & commitment term

The **No commitment** option is only available for custom models with **Model units** set to `1`. **Model units** are a way to define a throughput that's measured in terms of the maximum number of input and output tokens processed per minute:

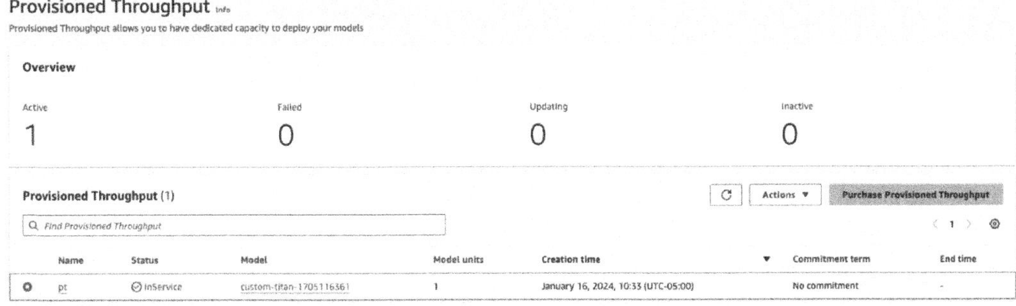

Figure 4.12 – Provisioned Throughput

Once you've purchased Provisioned Throughput, you can see its details in the Bedrock console and via the **ListProvisionedModelThroughputs** and **GetProvisionedModelThroughput** APIs.

Once Provisioned Throughput has an *Active* status, the custom model that you've created will be deployed to an endpoint. At this point, you can perform inference on the model using either the playground experience or through an API. Both options will be discussed next.

Amazon Bedrock playground

Performing inference via the playground experience is pretty straightforward and similar to how you perform inference on base FMs.

Instead of using the base model, you can select the custom model that you've created, at which point you're ready to ask questions or provide a prompt to your model. *Figure 4.13* depicts the process of selecting the **custom-titan-1705116361** model from the Bedrock playground, where it can be fine-tuned on user-provisioned training data:

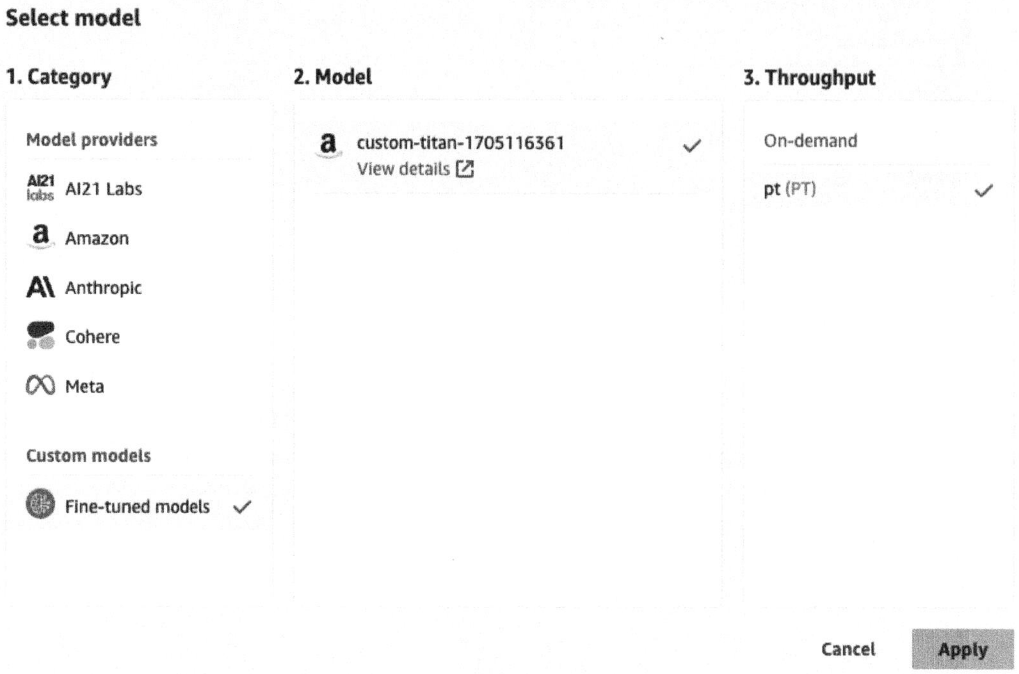

Select model

1. Category	2. Model	3. Throughput
Model providers	custom-titan-1705116361 ✓ View details	On-demand
AI21 Labs		pt (PT) ✓
Amazon		
Anthropic		
Cohere		
Meta		
Custom models		
Fine-tuned models ✓		

Cancel Apply

Figure 4.13 – Select model

Amazon Bedrock API

Bedrock also provides the **InvokeModel** API. This is the same API we used to invoke the base model in *Chapter 2*. The only difference here is that in `modelId`, we should provide the `arn` model of the provisioned endpoint. You can attain this from the **Bedrock Console – Provisioned Throughput** tab or via the **GetProvisionedModelThroughput** API:

```
Bedrock_runtime.invoke_model(
    modelId=arn-provisioned-throughput,
    body="""
{
```

```
  "inputText": "Classify this statement as Positive, Neutral, or
Negative:\\n'I really do not like this!'",
  "textGenerationConfig":{
    "maxTokenCount": 1,
    "stopSequences": [],
    "temperature": 1,
    "topP": 0.9
  }
"""
)
response_body = response["body"].read().decode('utf8')
print(response_body)

print(json.loads(response_body)["results"][0]["outputText"])
```

Now that we understand how to fine-tune models with Amazon Bedrock and leverage Provisioned Throughput, let's learn how to import selective custom models.

Importing custom models in Amazon Bedrock

To leverage the **Import Models** capability within Amazon Bedrock, navigate to the Bedrock console. On the left-hand side panel, under **Foundation models**, click **Imported models**.

Once you land on the **Imported models** page, as shown in *Figure 4.14*, you will be able to create a custom model by importing a model directly from Amazon SageMaker (where you might have customized FMs already) or by importing the model files from an Amazon S3 bucket:

Figure 4.14 – Imported models

At the time of writing, importing a model into Amazon Bedrock creates a custom model that supports the following patterns:

- **Continued pre-training or fine-tuned model**: As explained previously, you can refine the pre-trained model by utilizing proprietary data while the maintaining structural integrity of the original model configuration.
- **Domain adaptation**: You can tailor the custom-imported model to a specific domain. This adaptation process will enhance the model's performance within a target domain by addressing domain-specific variations. For instance, language adaptation can be undertaken so that responses can be generated in regional dialects or languages, such as Tamil or Portuguese.
- **Pre-training from scratch**: As you are aware by now, this approach extends beyond merely customizing weights and vocabulary. This approach provides you with the opportunity to modify fundamental model parameters, including the number of attention heads, hidden layers, or context length. Additionally, techniques such as post-training quantization or integrating base and adapter weights enable further refinement and optimization of the model's architecture.

To initiate the **Import model** job, you can provide the model details, including a relevant model name, import job name, and model import settings.

At the time of writing this book, the imported model can support the Mistral, Flan, Llama2, and Llama3 architectures. As the generative AI landscape evolves, Bedrock may expand the list of supported architectures for model import in the future.

Once a model import job has been completed successfully, the imported model will be listed on the **Models** tab of the **Imported models** page. Here, you can view key details about the imported model, such as its ARN, model ID, and status. From this page, you can also use the imported model for inference by invoking it through the Bedrock API.

Detailed information regarding the different model types and open source architectures that Amazon Bedrock's custom model capability supports can be found at `https://docs.aws.amazon.com/bedrock/latest/userguide/model-customization-import-model.html#model-customization-import-model-architecture`.

> **Note**
>
> Please ensure that your account has sufficient quota limits to execute the **CreateModelImportJob** action. If it doesn't, the following error will be displayed:

Your account does not have the quota limits to perform the CreateModelImportJob action. Please request a quota limit increase through service quotas for the "Imported models per account" to proceed.

Figure 4.15 – Error

You can request for your quota limit to be increased by navigating to `https://us-east-1.console.aws.amazon.com/servicequotas/home/services/bedrock/quotas`.

Throughout this chapter, we've learned how to prepare a dataset, customize an FM, and then check its performance and perform inference. Now, let's look at some of the guidelines and best practices we need to consider while trying to customize a model.

Guidelines and best practices

While customizing a model, it's ideal to consider the following practices for optimal results:

- **Providing the dataset**: The most important thing in ML is the dataset. Most of the time, how your model performs depends on the dataset you provide to train the model. So, providing quality data that's aligned with your use case is important. If you've studied ML in university or worked in this field, you might have learned about various feature engineering and data processing techniques you can use to clean and process the data. For example, you can handle missing values in the dataset, make sure you don't provide biased data, or ensure that the dataset follows the format that the model expects. If you would like to learn more about providing quality data, please read *Feature Engineering for Machine Learning* by Alice Zheng and Amanda Casari. This same principle applies to generative AI since it is essentially a subset of ML.
- **Choosing the right FM**: Next, you need to select the base FM that you are looking to customize. Make sure you look at its attributes, how many tokens it supports, what type of data it's been trained on, and the size of the model. Go through the model cards in the Bedrock console, read through the websites of these models, and look at their performance by using standardized benchmarks such as GLUE, SuperGLUE, HELM, and OpenLLM by HuggingFace. However, keep in mind that you shouldn't completely rely on these benchmark tools as they may not represent the complexity and diversity of real-world applications.
- **Identifying hyperparameters**: Once you have a quality dataset and the right base model has been selected, you need to identify the right hyperparameters for customization. Your goal should be to avoid overfitting; the model should be able to generalize well to the new unseen information. There are several hyperparameters that you can adjust, such as the number of epochs, batch size, learning rate, early stopping, and others. You can find a list of hyperparameters that all the Bedrock models support at `https://docs.aws.amazon.com/bedrock/latest/userguide/custom-models-hp.html`.
- **Evaluating performance**: Once you've fine-tuned the model, evaluate its performance using the validation dataset. The **validation dataset** is the dataset that's held back from training the model and is used for evaluating it instead. To learn more about data splitting, go to `https://mlu-explain.github.io/train-test-validation/`. Here, you can look at different metrics, such as loss and perplexity, or use techniques such as accuracy, **Bilingual Evaluation Understudy** (**BLEU**), and **Recall-Oriented Understudy for Gisting Evaluation** (**ROUGE**) scores. For context, BLEU scores indicate the quality assessment of machine-

generated translations compared to reference translations set provided by human translators. The ROUGE score is useful for text summarization tasks, wherein evaluation is conducted based on the quality of machine-generated summaries compared to the respective reference summaries created by humans. If the model doesn't provide the desired performance results, you have to readjust the hyperparameters or bring in more datasets. Once the model is ready to be used and provides the desired evaluation results, you can perform inference on the model.

- **Adapting the model for specific domains**: Customizing the model to a business domain is a promising approach for improving productivity and efficiency. By tailoring the model to the specific needs of a particular industry, we can enable it to perform tasks that were previously impossible or inefficient and create a more competitive and successful business.

Adopting these practices can help you make the most of customizing an FM and harnessing the true power of generative AI.

Summary

In this chapter, we explored two model customization techniques, fine-tuning and continued pre-training, the need to customize a model, and understood the concepts behind fine-tuning and continued pre-training. Further, we prepared our dataset, created a custom model, evaluated the model, and performed inference.

Lastly, we discussed some of the guidelines and best practices you need to consider when customizing your FM.

In the next chapter, we're going to uncover the power of RAG in solving real-world business problems by using an external data source. We will delve into the various use cases and sample architectures and implement RAG with Amazon Bedrock.

5
Harnessing the Power of RAG

By now, we know the FMs are trained using large datasets. However, the data used to train FMs might not be recent, and this can cause the models to hallucinate. In this chapter, we will harness the power of RAG by augmenting the model with external data sources to overcome the challenge of hallucination.

We will explore the importance of RAG in generative AI scenarios, how RAG works, and its components. We will then delve into the integration of RAG with Amazon Bedrock, including a fully managed RAG experience by Amazon Bedrock called Knowledge Bases. The chapter will then take a hands-on approach to the implementation of Knowledge Bases and using APIs.

We will explore some real-world scenarios of RAG and discuss a few solution architectures for implementing RAG. You will also be introduced to implementing a RAG framework using Amazon Bedrock, LangChain orchestration, and other generative AI systems. We will end by examining current limitations and future research directions with Amazon Bedrock in the context of RAG.

By the end of this chapter, you will be able to understand the importance of RAG and will be able to implement it with Amazon Bedrock. Learning these methods will empower you to apply the concept of RAG in your own enterprise use cases and build production-level applications, such as conversational interfaces, question answering systems, or module summarization workflows.

Here are the key topics that will be covered in this chapter:

- Decoding RAG
- Implementing RAG with Amazon Bedrock
- Implementing RAG with other methods
- Advanced RAG techniques
- Limitations and future directions

Technical requirements

This chapter requires you to have access to an AWS account. If you don't have one already, you can go to `https://aws.amazon.com/getting-started/` and create an AWS account.

Secondly, you will need to install and configure AWS CLI (`https://aws.amazon.com/cli/`) after you create an account, which will be needed to access Amazon Bedrock FMs from your local machine. Since the majority chunk of code cells we will be executing is based in Python, setting up an AWS Python SDK (Boto3) (`https://docs.aws.amazon.com/bedrock/latest/APIReference/welcome.html`) would be beneficial at this point. You can carry out the Python setup in these ways: install it on your local machine, or use AWS Cloud9, or AWS Lambda, or leverage Amazon SageMaker.

> **Note**
>
> There will be a charge associated with the invocation and customization of FMs of Amazon Bedrock. Please refer to `https://aws.amazon.com/bedrock/pricing/` to learn more.

Decoding RAG

RAG is an approach in NLP that combines large-scale retrieval with neural generative models. The key idea is to retrieve relevant knowledge from large corpora and incorporate that knowledge into the text-generation process. This allows generative models such as Amazon Titan Text, Anthropic Claude, and **Generative Pre-trained Transformer 3** (**GPT-3**) to produce more factual, specific, and coherent text by grounding generations in external knowledge.

RAG has emerged as a promising technique to make neural generative models more knowledgeable and controllable. In this section, we will provide an overview of RAG, explain how it works, and discuss key applications.

What is RAG?

Traditional generative models, such as BART, T5 or GPT-4 are trained on vast amounts of text data in a self-supervised fashion. While this allows them to generate fluent and human-like text, a major limitation is that they lack world knowledge beyond what is contained in their training data. This can lead to factual inconsistencies, repetitions, and hallucinations in the generated text.

RAG aims to ground generations in knowledge by retrieving relevant context from large external corpora. For example, if the model is generating text about Paris, it could retrieve *Wikipedia* passages about Paris to inform the generation. This retrieved context is encoded and integrated into the model to guide the text generation.

Augmenting generative models with retrieved knowledge has been shown to produce more factual, specific, and coherent text across a variety of domains.

The key components of RAG systems are the following:

- A GenAI model – specifically, an FM or LLM – that can generate fluent text (or multi-modal) outputs.
- A corpus of data to retrieve relevant information from (for example, *Wikipedia*, web pages, documents).
- Retriever module, which encodes the input query and retrieves relevant passages from the knowledge corpus based on relevance to the query.
- Re-ranker to select the optimal contextual information by re-scoring and ranking the retrieved passages based on relevance to the query. (This step is optional in building basic RAG systems but becomes crucial when building enterprise-scale systems with advanced RAG techniques).
- Fusion module to integrate retrieval into the language model. This can involve techniques such as concatenation or allowing the language model to condition on relevant external knowledge.
- Other components may also include query reformulation, hybrid search techniques, and multi-stage retrieval, which will be covered later in this chapter.

In order to gain a better understanding of RAG approaches, let us walk through a simple example:

- **Input query**: `What are the key events in the life of Marie Curie?`
- **Retriever module**: The retriever module encodes the query `What are the key events in the life of Marie Curie?` into a dense vector representation. It then searches through the knowledge corpus (for example, *Wikipedia*, web pages) to find relevant passages. For example, it may retrieve the following:

    I. `Marie Curie was a Polish physicist and chemist who conducted pioneering research on radioactivity...`

    II. `In 1903, Curie became the first woman to win a Nobel Prize for her study of spontaneous radiation...`

    III. `Curie won a second Nobel Prize in 1911, this time in chemistry, for her discovery of the elements radium and polonium...`

- **Re-ranker**: The re-ranker scores and re-ranks the retrieved passages based on their relevance to the original query using cross-attention. It may determine that passages *II* and *III* are more relevant than *I*.

- **Fusion module**: The top re-ranked passages (for example, *II* and *III*) are then integrated into the generative language model, either by concatenating them, summarizing them, or allowing the model to attend over them; that is, focus on different parts of the retrieved passages as needed while generating the output.

  Note that the goal of the fusion step is to provide the generative language model with the most pertinent external knowledge in a manner that allows effective conditioning of the generated output on that knowledge, leading to more accurate, informative, and grounded responses.

- **Output**: The language model can then generate a fluent answer by conditioning on the relevant retrieved knowledge:

  ```
  The key events in the life of Marie Curie include:
  ```

  - `In 1903, she became the first woman to win a Nobel Prize for her study of spontaneous radiation (radioactivity).`
  - `In 1911, she won a second Nobel Prize in chemistry for her discovery of the elements radium and polonium.`

- By retrieving relevant knowledge from an external corpus and integrating it into the language model, the RAG system can generate a more informative and accurate response, overcoming the limitations of relying solely on the model's training data.

> **Note**
>
> Dense vector representations, also known as dense embeddings or dense vectors, are a way of encoding meaning and semantic relationships in a numerical format that can be effectively processed by machines. This allows techniques such as cosine similarity to identify semantically related words/texts even without exact keyword matches. Dense vectors power many modern NLP applications, such as semantic search, text generation, translation, and so on, by providing effective semantic representations as inputs to **deep learning** models.

We will further dive deep into these components in the *Components of RAG* section. Since you now have a brief understanding of RAG, it's time to realize the importance of RAG in the context of the GenAI universe.

Importance of RAG

Before we dive into how RAG works and its components, it's important to understand why RAG is needed. As LLMs become more capable of generating fluent and coherent text, it also becomes more important to ground them in factual knowledge and guard against potential hallucinations. If you ask an LLM questions pertaining to recent events, you might notice the model to be hallucinating. With RAG, you can augment the latest knowledge as context to the model to improve content quality by reducing the chance of factual errors.

Another major advantage of RAG is overcoming the limited context length (input token limit) of the model. When providing pieces of text as a context that fits within the token limit of the model, you may not need to use RAG and leverage in-context prompting. However, if you want to provide a large corpus of documents as a context to the model, using RAG would be a better approach. However, RAG is beneficial even when the corpus can fit in the context due to needle-in-a-haystack problems, which can affect retrieval accuracy. To summarize, RAG becomes specifically useful in two primary use cases:

- When the corpus size exceeds that of the context length
- When we want to dynamically provide context to the model instead of feeding it the entire corpus in context

RAG has many potential applications for improving GenAI. It can help build contextual chatbots that rely on real enterprise data. It can enable personalized search and recommendations based on user history and preferences. A RAG approach can also aid real-time summarization of large documents by retrieving and condensing key facts. For example, applying RAG to summarize extensive legal texts or academic papers allows for the extraction and condensation of important information, providing succinct summaries that capture the core points. Overall, RAG is an important technique for overcoming some limitations of current generative models and grounding them in factual knowledge. This helps make the generated content more useful, reliable, and personalized.

Key applications

Compared to other LLM customization techniques, such as prompt engineering or fine-tuning, RAG offers several advantages:

- **Flexibility of knowledge source**: The knowledge base can be customized for each use case without changing the underlying LLM. Knowledge can be easily added, removed, or updated without costly model retraining. This is especially useful for organizations whose knowledge is rapidly evolving.
- **Cost-effective**: RAG allows a single-hosted LLM to be shared across many use cases through swappable knowledge sources. There is no need to train bespoke models for each use case, which means greater cost efficiency.
- **Natural language queries**: RAG relies on natural language for context retrieval from the knowledge source, unlike prompt engineering, which uses rigid prompt templates. This enables users to be more flexible when working with the models.

For most organizations with a custom knowledge pool of information, RAG strikes a balance between cost, flexibility, and usability. Prompt engineering is sufficient for small amounts of context, while full model fine-tuning entails high training costs and rigid knowledge. RAG allows easy knowledge base updates and sharing of LLMs across use cases.

For example, RAG is well suited for **business-to-business Software-as-a-Service (B2B SaaS)** companies that manage evolving document bases across many customers. A single-hosted LLM can handle queries across clients by swapping their context documents, eliminating the need for per-client models.

Now that we understand the importance and potential applications of RAG in different scenarios, let us jump into exploring the working of RAG.

How does RAG work?

Figure 5.1 provides a high-level overview of how RAG works:

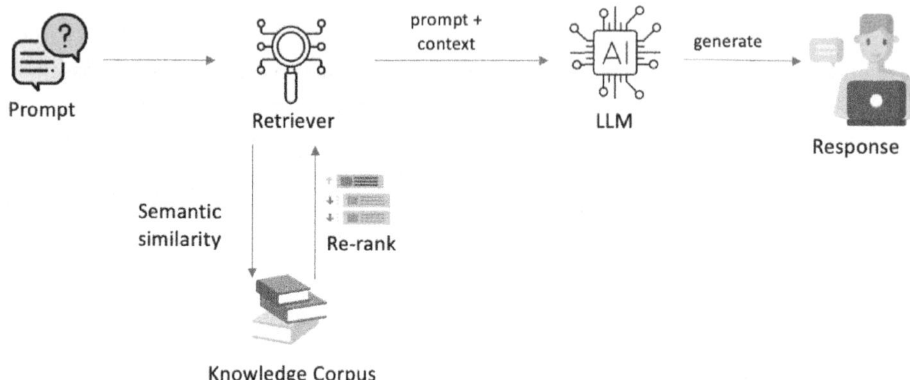

Figure 5.1 – Simplified RAG

Let us now understand these steps in detail:

1. Given a prompt from the user, the retriever module is invoked to encode the input query in a dense vector representation.
2. The retriever module then finds relevant context (passages or documents) from the knowledge corpus, based on maximum inner product similarity (semantic similarity) between the query vector and pre-computed dense vector representations of the corpus contents.
3. An optional re-ranker module can then re-score and re-rank the initially retrieved results and select the best context passages to augment the generation. The re-ranker helps surface the most relevant passages.
4. The top-ranked retrieved contexts are fused with the input query to form an augmented prompt (query and context).
5. The generative model, i.e. the FM or LLM then produces the output text conditioned on both the original query prompt and the retrieved relevant knowledge contexts.
6. In some RAG systems, the retrieval and re-ranking process can be repeated during the generation step to dynamically retrieve more relevant knowledge as the output is being generated.

The key benefits of RAG are ensuring that the generated outputs are grounded in accurate and up-to-date information from trusted external sources, providing source citations for transparency, and reducing hallucinations or inaccuracies from the language model's training data alone.

RAG systems meet enterprise requirements for GenAI, such as being comprehensive, trustworthy, transparent, and credible by properly sourcing, vetting, and customizing the underlying data sources and models for specific use cases.

Components of RAG

As explained earlier, once a query is received, relevant context is retrieved from the knowledge source and condensed into a context document. This context is then concatenated with the original query and fed into the LLM to generate a final response. The knowledge source acts as a dynamic long-term memory, in a way that can be frequently updated, while the LLM contributes its strong language generation capabilities.

The knowledge base

A key component of RAG models is the knowledge base, which contains the external knowledge used for retrieval. The knowledge base stores information in a format optimized for fast retrieval, such as dense vectors or indexes.

Popular knowledge sources used in RAG include *Wikipedia*, news archives, books, scientific papers, and proprietary knowledge bases created specifically for RAG models. The knowledge can consist of both structured (for example, tables and lists) and unstructured (for example, free text) data.

In a typical RAG scenario, the textual contents of the documents (or web pages) that make up the knowledge corpus and need to be converted into dense vector representations or embeddings are encoded data into smaller chunks. To preserve this structure of tables or lists while encoding, more advanced encoding techniques are used that can embed entire tables/lists as a single vector while retaining their row/column relationships.

Long unstructured text passages are typically chunked or split into smaller text segments or passages of a maximum length (for example, 200 tokens). Each of these chunks or passages is then encoded independently into a dense vector representation.

This embedding process typically happens asynchronously or as a batch process, separate from and ahead of time before any user queries are received by the RAG system.

The embeddings for the entire document corpus are pre-computed and stored before the system is deployed or used for any query answering. This pre-computation step is necessary for the following reasons:

- The document corpus can typically be very large (for example, *Wikipedia* has millions of articles)
- Embedding the full corpus at query time would be extremely slow and inefficient
- Pre-computed embeddings allow fast maximum inner product search at query time

By embedding the sources asynchronously ahead of time, the RAG system can quickly retrieve relevant documents by comparing the query embedding against the pre-computed document embeddings using efficient vector similarity search methods such as cosine similarity, Euclidean distance, **Microprocessor without Interlocked Pipelined Stages** (**MIPS**), or **Facebook AI Similarity Search** (**FAISS**). Readers are encouraged to review the paper *A Survey on Efficient Processing of Similarity Queries over Neural Embeddings* (`https://arxiv.org/abs/2204.07922`), which debriefs methods on efficient processing of similarity queries.

Note that the sizes and scope of the knowledge base has a major influence on the capabilities of the RAG system. Larger knowledge bases with more diverse, high-quality knowledge provide more contextual information for the model to draw from, based on the user's questions.

Retriever module

The retriever module is responsible for finding and retrieving the most relevant knowledge from the knowledge base for each specific context. The input to the retrieval model is typically the prompt or context from the user.

The embedding model encodes the prompt into a vector representation and matches it against encoded representations of the knowledge base to find the closest matching entries.

Common retrieval methods include sparse methods such as **Term Frequency-Inverse Document Frequency** (**TF-IDF**) or **Best Match 25** (**BM25**), as well as dense methods such as semantic search over embedded representations from a dual-encoder model. The retrieval model ranks the knowledge and returns the top *k* most relevant pieces back to the generative model.

The tighter the integration between the retrieval model and the generative model, the better the retrieval results.

Conditioning the generative model

The key aspect that makes the RAG process generative is the conditional generative model. This model takes the retrieved knowledge along with the original prompt and generates the output text.

The knowledge can be provided in different ways to condition the generation:

- Concatenating the retrieved text to the prompt
- Encoding the retrieved text into dense vectors
- Inserting the retrieved text into the input at particular positions

For example, in a typical scenario, the retrieved knowledge is augmented with the input prompt and fed to the LLM to provide a succinct response to the end user. This allows the LLM to directly condition the text generation on the relevant facts and context. Users are encouraged to check out the paper *Leveraging Passage Retrieval with Generative Models for Open Domain Question Answering* (`https://arxiv.org/pdf/2007.01282.pdf`) in order to gain a deeper understanding of the complexity of RAG in the realm of question answering frameworks.

The generative model is usually a large pre-trained language model such as GPT-4, Anthropic Claude 3, Amazon Titan Text G1, and so on. The model can be further fine-tuned end to end on downstream RAG tasks, if needed, in order to optimize the integration of the retrieved knowledge for domain-specific use cases. Now, let us dive into exploring RAG with Amazon Bedrock.

Implementing RAG with Amazon Bedrock

Prior to responding to user queries, the system must ingest and index the provided documents. This process can be considered as *step 0*, and consists of these sub-steps:

- Ingest the raw text documents into the knowledge base.
- Preprocess the documents by splitting them into smaller chunks to enable more granular retrieval.
- Generate dense vector representations for each passage using an embedding model such as Amazon Bedrock's Titan Text Embeddings model. This encodes the semantic meaning of each passage into a high-dimensional vector space.
- Index the passages and their corresponding vector embeddings into a specialized search index optimized for efficient **nearest neighbor** (**NN**) search. These are also referred to as **vector databases**, which store numerical representations of text in the form of vectors. This index powers fast retrieval of the most relevant passages in response to user queries.

By completing this workflow, the system constructs an indexed corpus ready to serve relevant results for natural language queries over the ingested document collection. The passage splitting, embedding, and indexing steps enable robust ranking and retrieval capabilities.

The flow diagram depicted in *Figure 5.2* exemplifies the overall flow of the RAG process as described previously:

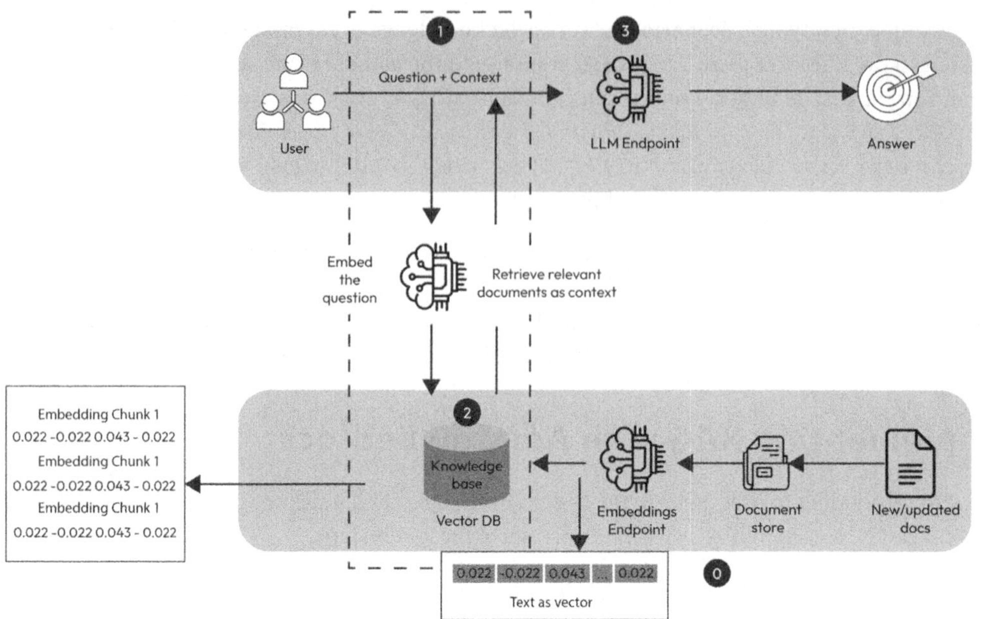

Figure 5.2 – RAG with Amazon Bedrock

When documents have been properly indexed, the system can provide contextual answers to natural language questions through the following pipeline:

- **Step 1**: Encode the input question into a dense vector representation (embedding) using an embedding model, such as the Amazon Titan Text Embeddings model or Cohere's embedding model, both of which can be accessed via Amazon Bedrock. This captures the semantic meaning of the question.
- **Step 2**: Compare the question embedding to indexed document embeddings using cosine similarity or other distance metrics. This retrieves the most relevant document chunks. Append the top-ranking document chunks to the prompt as contextual information. This provides relevant background knowledge for the model.
- **Step 3**: Pass the prompt with context to an LLM available on Amazon Bedrock such as Anthropic Claude 3, Meta Llama 3, or Amazon Titan Text G1 - Express. This leverages the model's capabilities to generate an answer conditioned on the retrieved documentation.

Finally, return the model-generated answer, which should show an understanding of the question in relation to the contextual documents.

The system thus leverages Amazon Bedrock FMs to provide natural language question answering grounded in relevant documentation and context. Careful indexing and encoding of documents enable seamless integration of retrieval with generative models for more informed and accurate answers.

Here is an example of RAG implementation with Amazon Bedrock and Amazon OpenSearch Serverless as a vector engine: `https://aws.amazon.com/blogs/big-data/build-scalable-and-serverless-rag-workflows-with-a-vector-engine-for-amazon-opensearch-serverless-and-amazon-bedrock-claude-models/`.

Now that we have discussed some details around implementing RAG with Amazon Bedrock, let us dive deep into tackling use cases using RAG through Knowledge Bases on Amazon Bedrock.

Amazon Bedrock Knowledge Bases

Amazon Bedrock provides a fully managed RAG experience with Knowledge Bases, handling the complexity behind the scenes while giving you control over your data. Bedrock's Knowledge Base capability enables the aggregation of diverse data sources into a centralized repository of machine-readable information. Knowledge Bases automate the creation of vector embeddings from your data, store them in a managed vector index, and handle embedding, querying, source attribution, and short-term memory for production RAG.

The key benefits of Knowledge Bases in Amazon Bedrock include the following:

- **Seamless RAG workflow**: There's no need to set up and manage the components yourself. You can just provide your data and let Amazon Bedrock handle ingestion, embedding, storage, and querying.
- **Custom vector embeddings**: Your data is ingested and converted into vector representations tailored to your use case with a choice of embedding models.
- **Attribution and memory**: The `RetrieveAndGenerate` API within Amazon Bedrock provides attribution back to source documents and manages conversation history for contextual responses.
- **Flexible integration**: Incorporate RAG into your workflows with API access and integration support for other GenAI tools.

Amazon Bedrock Knowledge Base setup

Objectively speaking, the following steps facilitate Knowledge Base creation and integration:

1. Identify and prepare data sources for ingestion
2. Upload data to **Amazon Simple Storage Service** (**Amazon S3**) for centralized access
3. Generate embeddings for data via FMs and persist in a vector store
4. Connect applications and agents to query and incorporate Knowledge Base into workflows

To create ingestion jobs, follow the next steps:

1. **Set up your Knowledge Base**: Before you can ingest data, you need to create a knowledge base. This involves defining the structure and schema of the knowledge base to ensure it can store and manage the data effectively.
2. **Prepare your data source**:
   - Ensure your data is stored in Amazon S3. The data can be in various formats, including structured (for example, CSV, JSON) and unstructured (for example, text files, PDFs).
   - Organize your data in a way that makes it easy to manage and retrieve.
3. **Create an ingestion job**:
   - Navigate to the AWS Bedrock console and go to the **Knowledge base** section.
   - Select the option to create a new ingestion job.
   - Provide the necessary details, such as the name of the job, the S3 bucket location, and the data format.
   - Configure the job to specify how the data should be processed and ingested into the knowledge base.
4. **Configure sync settings**:
   - Set up the sync settings to ensure the knowledge base is updated with the most recent data from your S3 location.
   - You can configure the sync to run at regular intervals (for example, daily or weekly) or trigger it manually as needed.
   - Ensure that the sync settings are optimized to handle large volumes of data efficiently.
5. **Run the ingestion job**:
   - Once the job is configured, you can start the ingestion process.
   - Monitor the job's progress through the AWS Bedrock console. You can view logs and status updates to ensure the job is running smoothly.

Now that we have a basic understanding of the ingestion process, let us walk through these details thoroughly.

In order to initiate this pipeline within the AWS console, one can navigate to the **Orchestration** section within the Amazon Bedrock page, as shown in *Figure 5.3*:

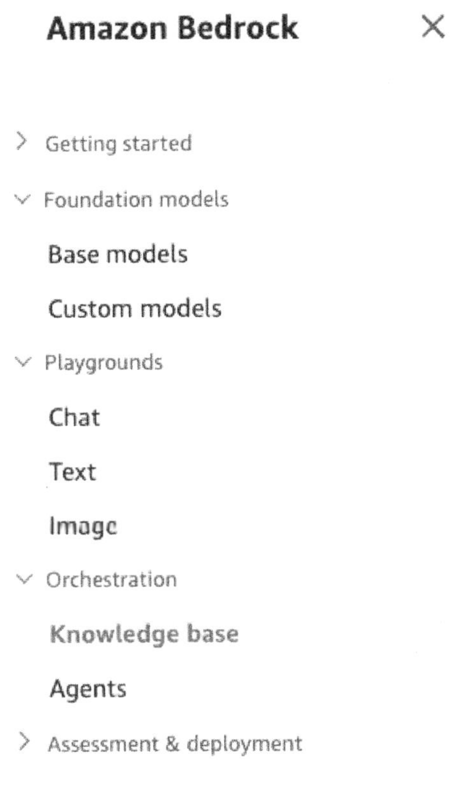

Figure 5.3 – Knowledge base

Now, let's look at these steps in greater depth:

1. Click on **Knowledge base** and enter the details pertaining to the knowledge base you intend to create. You can provide a custom knowledge base name, description, and the respective **Identity and Access Management** (**IAM**) permissions for creating either a new service role or leveraging an existing service role for the knowledge base. You can also provide tags to this resource for easy searching and filtering of your resource or tracking AWS costs associated with the service in the knowledge base details section.

2. In the next step, you will set up the data source by specifying the S3 location where the data to be indexed resides. You can specify a particular data source name (or leverage the default pre-filled name) and provide the S3 URI (Uniform Resource Identifier) of the bucket containing the source data, as depicted in *Figure 5.4*:

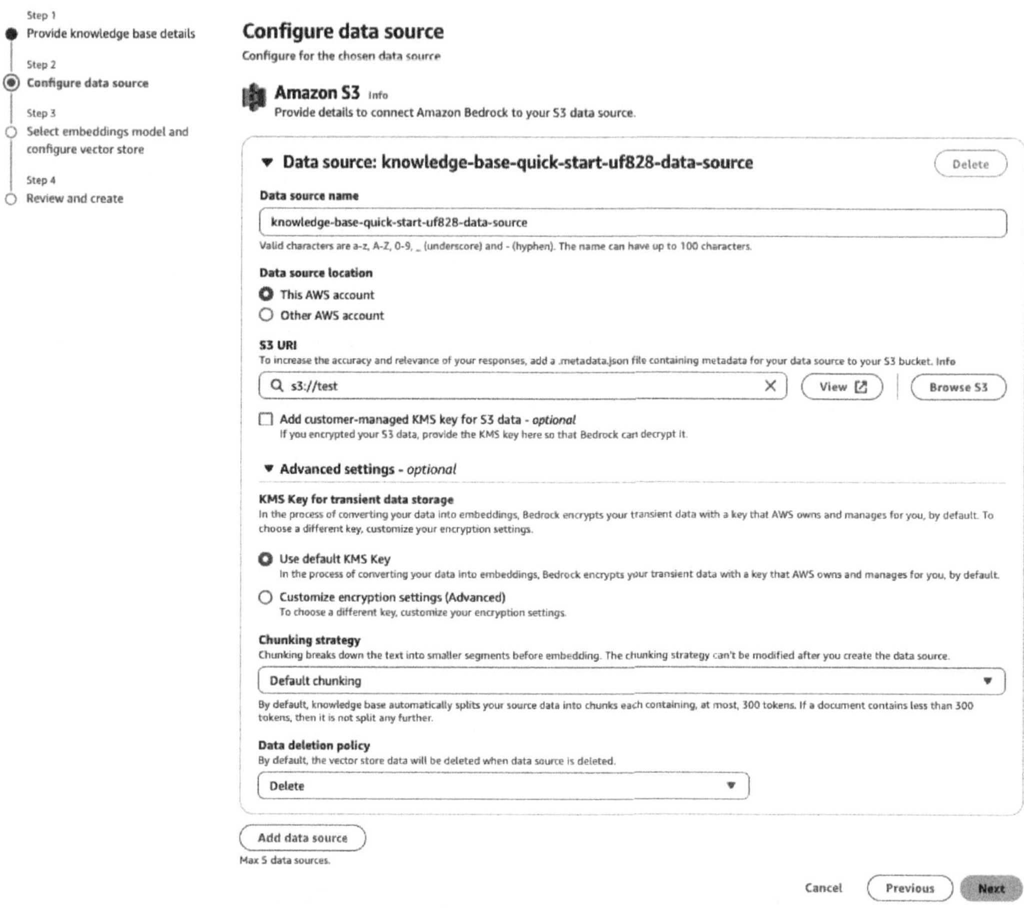

Figure 5.4 – Knowledge base: Set up data source

3. You can also provide a customer-managed **Key Management Service** (**KMS**) key you used for encrypting your S3 data, in order to allow the Bedrock service to decrypt it when ingesting the given data into the vector database. Under **Advanced settings** (as shown in *Figure 5.5*), users have the option to choose the default KMS key or customize encryption settings by choosing a different key of their choice by entering the **Amazon Resource Name** (**ARN**) or searching for their stored customized key (or creating a new AWS KMS key on the fly). Providing a customer-managed KMS key for encrypting S3 data sources ingested by Amazon Bedrock is desired for enhanced data security, compliance, and control. It allows data sovereignty, key

rotation/revocation, **separation of duties** (**SoD**), auditing/logging capabilities, and integration with existing key management infrastructure. By managing your own encryption keys, you gain greater control over data protection, meeting regulatory requirements and aligning with organizational security policies for sensitive or regulated data:

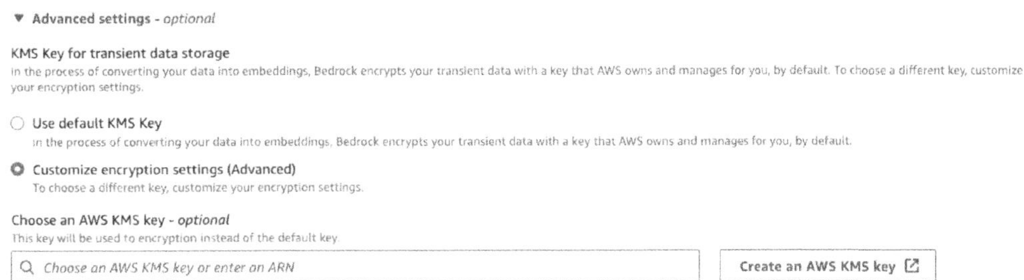

Figure 5.5 – Knowledge base: Advanced settings

Under **Chunking strategy** (as shown in *Figure 5.6*), users have the option to select how to break down text in the source location into smaller segments before creating the embedding. By default, the knowledge base will automatically split your data into tiny chunks each containing, at most, 300 tokens. If a document or, in other words, source data contains fewer than 300 tokens, it is not split any further in that case:

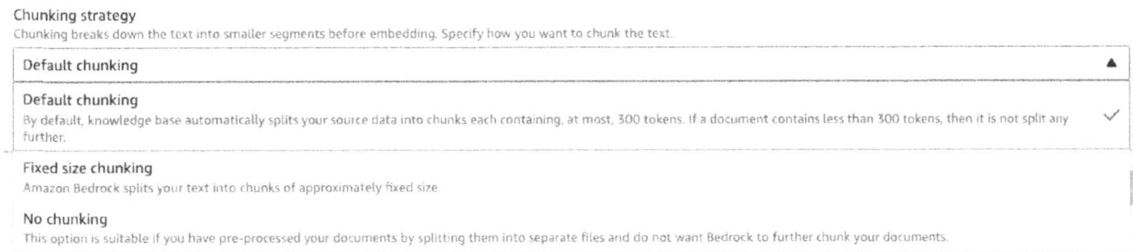

Figure 5.6 – Knowledge base: Chunking strategy

Alternatively, you have the option to customize the chunk size using **Fixed size chunking** or simply opt for **No chunking** in case you have already preprocessed your source documents into separate files of smaller chunks and don't intend to chunk your documents any further using Bedrock.

In the next stage, users will select an embedding model to convert their selected data into an embedding. Currently, there are four embeddings models that are supported, as shown in *Figure 5.7*. Further, under **Vector database**, users have the option to go with the recommended route – that is, select the quick create option, which will create an Amazon OpenSearch Serverless vector store in the background automatically in the respective account of their choice:

Note

Vector embeddings are numeric representations of text data that encode semantic or contextual meaning. In NLP pipelines, text documents are passed through an embedding model to convert the chunks, including discrete tokens such as words into dense vectors in a continuous vector space. Good vector representations allow **machine learning** (**ML**) models to understand similarities, analogies, and other patterns between words and concepts. In other words, if the vector representations (embeddings) are trained well on a large dataset, they will capture meaningful relationships in the data. This allows ML models that use those embeddings to recognize things such as the following:

- Which words are similar in meaning (for example, *king* and *queen*)

- Which concepts follow an analogical pattern (for example, *man* is to *king* as *woman* is to *queen*)

- Other patterns in how the concepts are represented in the embedding space

The well-trained embeddings essentially provide the ML models with a numeric map of the relationships and patterns inherent in the data. This makes it easier for the models to then learn and make inferences about those patterns during training on downstream tasks.

Hence, simply put, good embeddings help ML models understand similarities and relationships between words and concepts rather than just treating them as isolated data points.

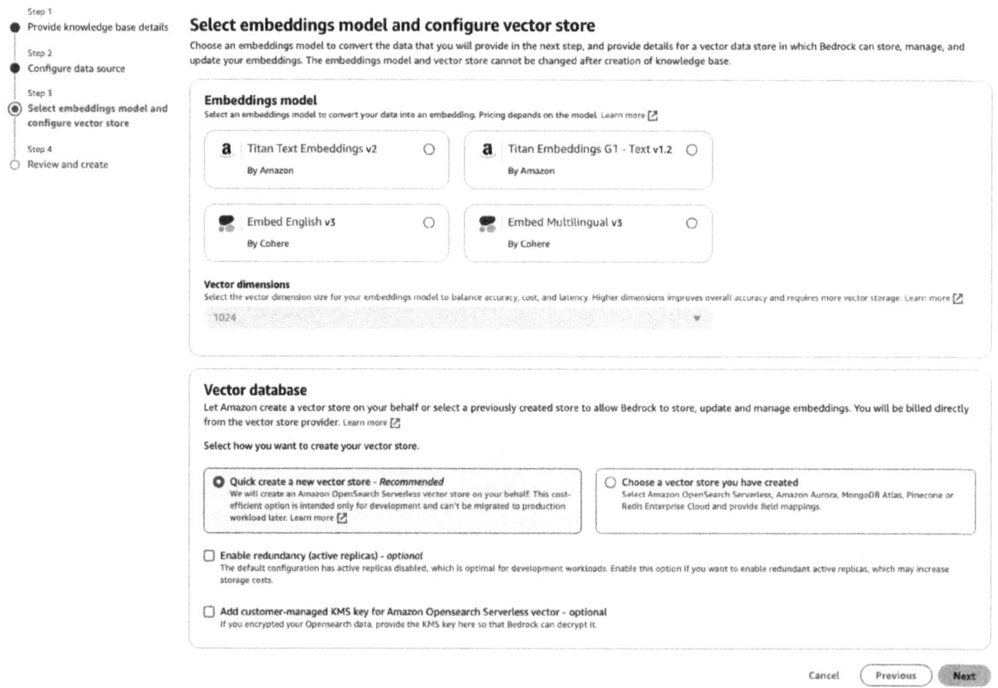

Figure 5.7 – Knowledge base: Configure vector store

Alternatively, you have the option to choose your own vector store (as shown in *Figure 5.8*). At the time of writing this book, you have the option to select **Vector engine for Amazon OpenSearch Serverless**, **Amazon Aurora**, **MongoDB Atlas**, **Pinecone**, or **Redis Enterprise Cloud**. Once selected, you can provide the field mapping to proceed with the knowledge base creation final setup. Depending on the use case, developers or teams may opt for one vector database over another. You can read more about the role of vector datastores in GenAI applications at `https://aws.amazon.com/blogs/database/the-role-of-vector-datastores-in-generative-ai-applications/`:

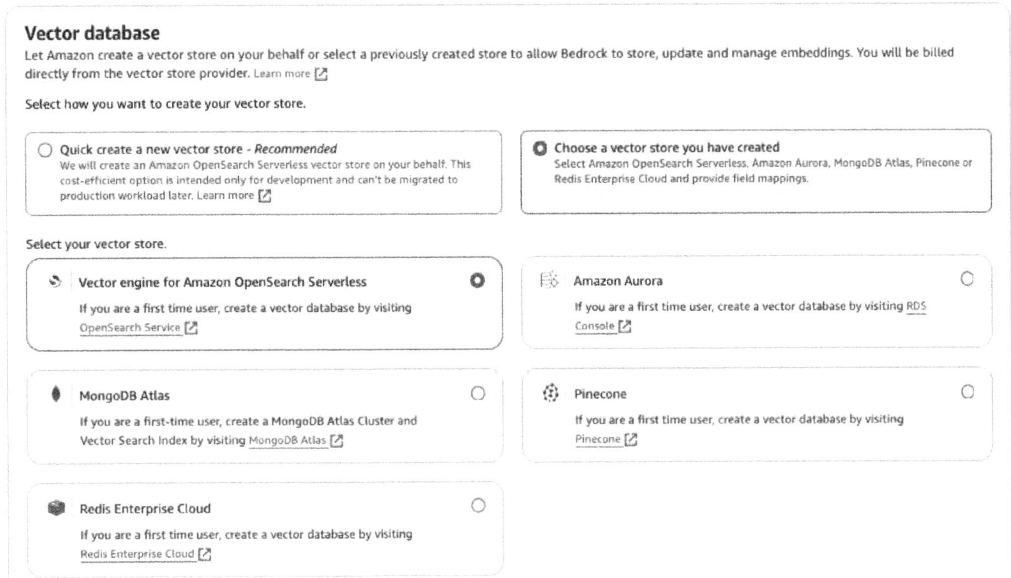

Figure 5.8 – Knowledge base: Vector database

You can check out `https://aws.amazon.com/blogs/aws/preview-connect-foundation-models-to-your-company-data-sources-with-agents-for-amazon-bedrock/` to learn more about how you can set up your own vector store with Pinecone, OpenSearch Serverless, or Redis.

Assuming that you opt for the default route, involving the creation of a new Amazon OpenSearch Serverless vector store, you can proceed and click on **Create knowledge base** post reviewing all the provided details as depicted in *Figure 5.9*:

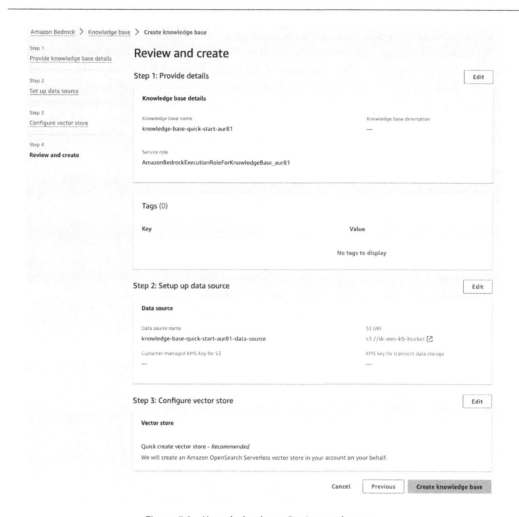

Figure 5.9 – Knowledge base: Review and create

Once created, you can sync the information to ensure the knowledge base is ingesting and operating on the most recent data stored in your Amazon S3 location. After syncing is completed for the knowledge base, users can test said knowledge base by selecting the appropriate model suitable for their use case by clicking on **Select Model**, as shown in *Figure 5.10*:

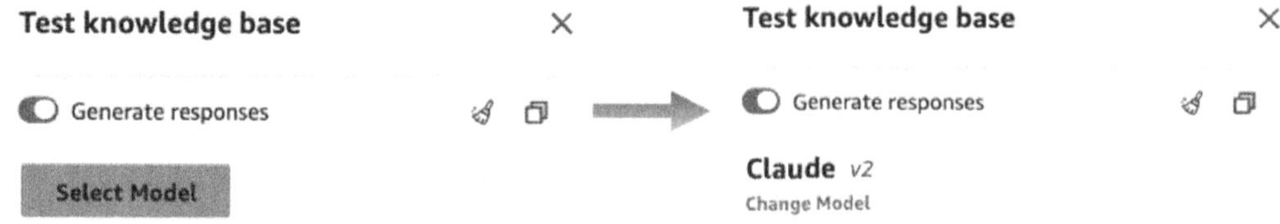

Figure 5.10 – Test knowledge base: Select Model

Once the appropriate model has been selected, you can test it by entering a particular query in the textbox and receiving a particular response generated by the model, depicted in *Figure 5.11*:

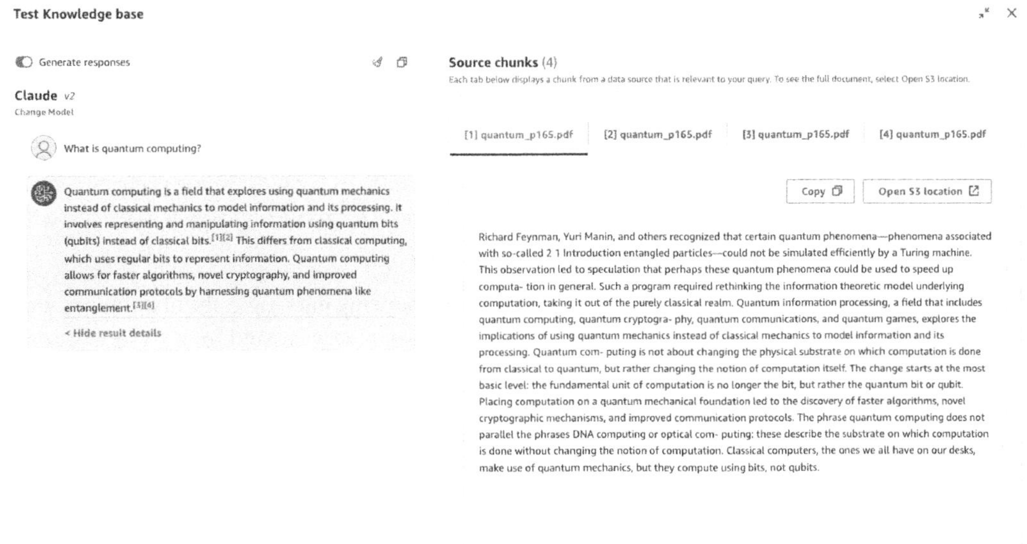

Figure 5.11 – Test Knowledge base

At its core, Amazon Bedrock transforms the user's query into vector representations of meaning; that is, embeddings. It then searches the knowledge base for relevant information using these embeddings as the search criteria. Any knowledge retrieved is combined with the prompt engineered for the FM, providing essential context. The FM integrates this contextual knowledge into its response generation to answer the user's question. For conversations spanning multiple turns, Amazon Bedrock leverages its knowledge base to maintain conversation context and history, delivering increasingly relevant results.

Additional information for testing the knowledge base and inspecting source chunks can be found at `https://docs.aws.amazon.com/bedrock/latest/userguide/knowledge-base-test.html`.

To ensure your knowledge base is always up to date, it is essential to automate the syncing process. This can be achieved by using AWS Lambda functions or AWS Step Functions to trigger ingestion jobs based on specific events or schedules.

AWS Lambda is a serverless compute service that allows you to run code without provisioning or managing servers. You can create Lambda functions to automate tasks such as triggering data ingestion jobs, processing data, or sending notifications. Lambda functions can be triggered by various events, including file uploads to Amazon S3, changes to DynamoDB tables, or scheduled events using Amazon CloudWatch Events.

AWS Step Functions is a serverless function orchestrator that allows you to coordinate multiple AWS services into business workflows. You can create state machines that define a series of steps, including Lambda functions, data processing tasks, and error-handling logic. Step Functions can be particularly useful for orchestrating complex data ingestion pipelines or ML workflows.

Regularly monitoring and managing data sources is crucial to maintain their relevance and accuracy. **Amazon CloudWatch** is a monitoring and observability service that provides data and actionable insights across your AWS resources. You can utilize CloudWatch to set up alarms and notifications for any issues or anomalies in the data syncing process. CloudWatch can monitor metrics such as Lambda function invocations, Step Functions executions, and Amazon S3 bucket activity, allowing you to proactively identify and address potential issues.

Adhering to best practices for data management, such as organizing data logically, maintaining data quality, and ensuring data security, is vital. AWS provides various services and tools to support data management best practices:

- You can organize your data in Amazon S3 buckets and leverage features such as versioning, lifecycle policies, and access controls to maintain data quality and security.
- **AWS Glue** is a fully managed **extract, transform, and load** (**ETL**) service that can help you prepare and move data reliably between different data stores. Glue can be used to clean, transform, and enrich your data before ingesting it into your knowledge base.
- **AWS Lake Formation** is a service that helps you build, secure, and manage data lakes on Amazon S3. It provides features such as data cataloging, access control, and auditing, which can help ensure data security and governance.

Regular reviews and updates of the knowledge base should be conducted to remove outdated information and incorporate new, relevant data. AWS provides services such as **Amazon Kendra** and **Amazon Comprehend** that can help you analyze and understand your knowledge base content, identify outdated or irrelevant information, and suggest updates or improvements.

Tracking actionable metrics, such as search success rate, user engagement, and data freshness, is also important. These metrics can help continuously improve the knowledge base, ensuring it meets the needs of its users effectively.

Amazon CloudWatch can be used to collect and analyze metrics from various AWS services, including your knowledge base application. You can create custom metrics, dashboards, and alarms to monitor the performance and usage of your knowledge base.

By leveraging AWS services such as Lambda, Step Functions, CloudWatch, S3, Glue, Lake Formation, Kendra, and Comprehend, you can automate the syncing process, monitor and manage data sources, adhere to data management best practices, and track actionable metrics to ensure your knowledge base remains up to date, relevant, and effective in meeting the needs of your users.

Readers are encouraged to visit the Amazon Bedrock RAG GitHub repository (`https://github.com/aws-samples/amazon-bedrock-rag`) to explore and implement a fully managed RAG solution using Knowledge Bases for Amazon Bedrock.

API calls

For users who wish to invoke Bedrock outside of the console, the `RetrieveAndGenerate` API provides programmatic access to execute this same workflow. This allows Bedrock's capabilities to be tightly integrated into custom applications via API calls rather than console interaction. The `RetrieveAndGenerate` API gives developers the flexibility to build Amazon Bedrock-powered solutions tailored to their specific needs. *Figure 5.12* illustrates the RAG workflow using Amazon Bedrock's `RetrieveAndGenerate` API:

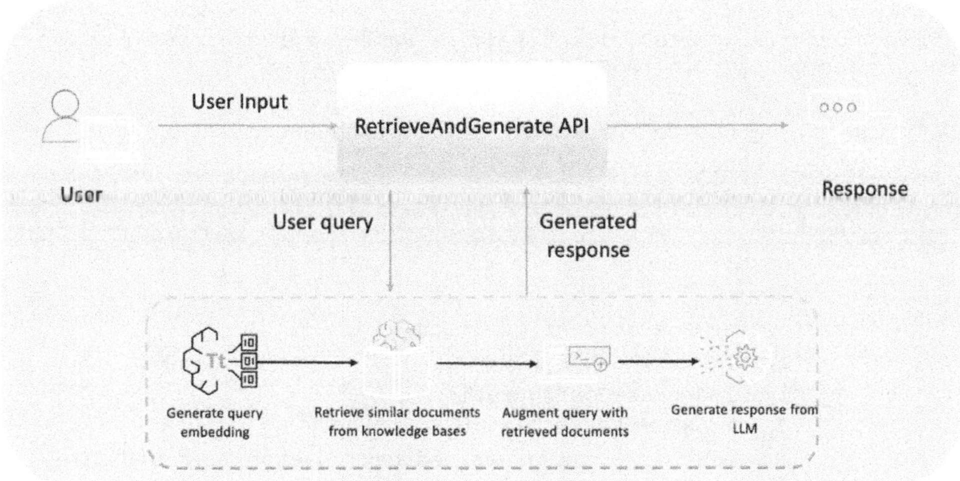

Figure 5.12 – RetrieveAndGenerate API

In the `RetrieveAndGenerate` API, the generated response output contains three components: the text of the model-generated response itself, source attribution indicating where the FM retrieved information from, and the specific text excerpts that were retrieved from those sources as part of generating the response. The API provides full transparency by returning not just the final output text but also the underlying source materials and attributions that informed the FM's response generation process. This allows users to inspect both the final output as well as the intermediate retrieved texts that were used by the system during response generation.

The following is a code sample for running the same operation as showcased in the console using the API.

> **Note**
>
> Ensure you have the latest version of the `boto3` and `botocore` packages prior to running the code shown next. In case the packages are not installed, run the following command in your Jupyter notebook. Note that `!` will not be needed if you're running Python code from a Python terminal:
>
> ```
> !pip install boto3 botocore
> ```

```
#import the main packages and libraries
import os
import boto3
import botocore
import json

bedrock_agent_rn = boto3.client(service_name='bedrock-agent-runtime',
region_name=os.environ['AWS_REGION'])

#Defining the method to invoke the RetrieveAndGenerate API
def retrieveAndGenerate(input, kb_Id):
    return bedrock_agent_rn.retrieve_and_generate(
        input={
            'text': input
        },
        retrieveAndGenerateConfiguration={
            'type': 'KNOWLEDGE_BASE',
            'knowledgeBaseConfiguration': {
                'knowledgeBaseId': kb_Id,
                'modelArn': 'arn:aws:bedrock:us-east-1::foundation-
model/anthropic.claude-instant-v1'
                }
            }
        )

#Invoking the API to generate the desired response
response = retrieveAndGenerate("What is Quantum Computing?",
"PGOWBGYODD")["output"]["text"]
print(response)
```

> **Note**
>
> This script assumes that readers have already created a knowledge base and ingested the relevant documents, following the procedures outlined in the preceding section. With this prerequisite fulfilled, invoking the `RetrieveAndGenerate` API will enable the system to fetch the associated documents using the provided code sample.

The code provided will print the extracted text output to display the relevant information from the data source in context to the input query, formatted as desired. The response is generated by contextualizing pertinent details from the data source with respect to the specifics of the input query. The output is then formatted and presented in the requested structure. This allows customized extraction and formatting of relevant data from the source to provide responses tailored to the input query in a suitable structure.

> **Note**
>
> Please ensure you have the right permissions to invoke Amazon Bedrock APIs by navigating to IAM roles and permissions, searching for the respective role (if you are running the notebook in Amazon SageMaker, search for the execution role that was assigned when you created the Amazon SageMaker domain), and attaching Amazon Bedrock policies for invoking Bedrock models and Bedrock agent runtime APIs.

Yet another resourceful Amazon Bedrock API, the `Retrieve` API, enables more advanced processing and utilization of the retrieved text segments. This API transforms user queries into vector representations, performs similarity searches against the knowledge base, and returns the most relevant results along with relevance scores. The `Retrieve` API provides users with more fine-grained control to build custom pipelines leveraging semantic search capabilities. Through the `Retrieve` API, developers can orchestrate subsequent stages of text generation based on the search results, implement additional relevance filtering, or derive other workflow optimizations. *Figure 5.13* exemplifies the usage of the `Retrieve` API in Amazon Bedrock in a RAG pipeline:

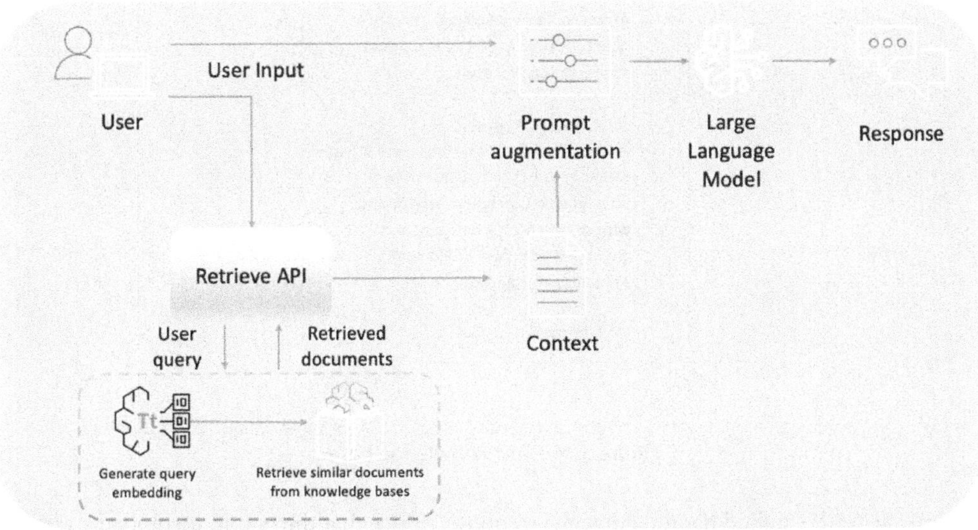

Figure 5.13 – Retrieve API

Within the Amazon Bedrock console, you can toggle the switch to disable the **Generate responses** feature and rely solely on retrieval. This configuration setting allows us to view the raw retrieval results without any generative text being produced. We can pose the same question `What is Quantum Computing?` again. *Figure 5.14* showcases the generated responses retrieved from the knowledge base pertaining to the question on quantum computing. Note that Amazon Bedrock cites the references along with the generated responses:

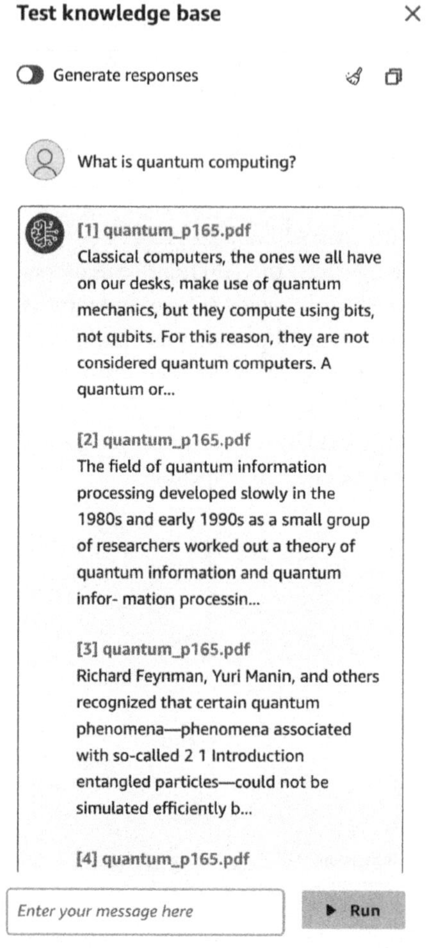

Figure 5.14 – Test knowledge base

This time, instead of a fluid natural language response, notice that the output displays the retrieved text chunks alongside links to the original source documents from which they were extracted. This approach provides transparency by explicitly showing the relevant information retrieved from the knowledge base and its provenance.

Note

Ensure you have the latest version of the `boto3` and `botocore` packages prior to running the code shown next. In case the packages are not installed, run the following command in your Jupyter notebook. Note that `!` will not be needed if you're running Python code from a Python terminal:

```
!pip install boto3 botocore
```

Leveraging the `Retrieve` API using `boto3` looks like this:

```
#import the main packages and libraries
import os
import boto3
import botocore

bedrock_agent_rn = boto3.client(service_name='bedrock-agent-runtime',
region_name = os.environ['AWS_REGION'])

#Defining the method to invoke the RetrieveAndGenerate API
def retrieve(query, kb_Id, number_Of_Results=3):
    return bedrock_agent_rn.retrieve(
        retrievalQuery= {
            'text': query
        },
        knowledgeBaseId=kb_Id,
        retrievalConfiguration= {
            'vectorSearchConfiguration': {
                'numberOfResults': number_Of_Results
            }
        }
    )

#Invoking the API
output_response = retrieve("What is Quantum Computing?", "PG0WBGY0DD")
["retrievalResults"]

print(output_response)
```

The `Retrieve` API returns a response containing the retrieved text excerpts, as well as metadata about the source of each excerpt. Specifically, the response includes the location type and URI of the source data from which each text chunk was retrieved. Additionally, each retrieved text chunk is accompanied by a relevancy score. This score provides an indication of how closely the semantic content of the retrieved chunk matches the user's input query. Text chunks with higher scores are more relevant matches to the query compared to chunks with lower scores. By examining the scores of the retrieved chunks, the user can focus on the most relevant excerpts returned by the `Retrieve` API. Therefore, the `Retrieve` API provides not only the retrieved text but also insightful metadata to enable productive utilization of the API response.

By tapping into the custom chunking and vector store capabilities within the RAG framework, you gain more fine-grained control over how your NLP workflows operate under the hood. Expertly applying these customizations helps ensure RAG is tailored to your specific needs and use cases. Note that at the time of writing this book, when creating a data source for your knowledge base, you can specify the chunking strategy in the `ChunkingConfiguration` object:

```
chunking_config = {
    "chunkingStrategy": "FIXED_SIZE", # or "NONE"
    "fixedSizeChunkingConfiguration": {
        "chunkSize": 200 # Chunk size in tokens
    }
}
```

Let's look at this in a bit more detail:

- `FIXED_SIZE` allows you to set a fixed chunk size in tokens for splitting your data sources
- `NONE` treats each file as a single chunk, giving you full control over pre-chunking your data

Further information on using the API with the AWS Python SDK can be found at `https://aws.amazon.com/blogs/aws/knowledge-bases-now-delivers-fully-managed-rag-experience-in-amazon-bedrock/`.

Knowledge Bases for Amazon Bedrock reduces the complexity of RAG, allowing you to enhance language generation with your own grounded knowledge. The capabilities open new possibilities for building contextual chatbots, question answering applications, and other AI systems that need to generate informed specific responses.

Let us further explore how the RAG approach can be implemented using the LangChain orchestrator and other GenAI systems.

Implementing RAG with other methods

Amazon Bedrock is not the only way to implement RAG, and in this section, we will learn about the other ways. Starting with LangChain, we will also look at some other GenAI systems.

Using LangChain

LangChain provides an excellent framework for building RAG models by integrating retrieval tools and LLMs. In this section, we will look at how to implement RAG with LangChain using the following components:

- **LLMs**: LangChain integrates with Amazon Bedrock's powerful LLMs using Bedrock's available FM invocation APIs. Amazon Bedrock can be used to generate fluent NL responses after reviewing the retrieved documents.
- **Embedding model**: Text embedding models available via Amazon Bedrock, such as Amazon Titan Text Embeddings, generate vector representations of text passages. This allows comparing textual similarity in order to retrieve relevant contextual information to augment the input prompt for composing a final response.
- **Document loader**: LangChain provides a PDF loader to ingest documents from local storage. This can be replaced by a loader to retrieve enterprise documents.
- **Vector store**: An in-memory store such as FAISS index embeddings can be used for fast retrieval. A persistent store such as AWS OpenSearch could also be used from an enterprise perspective. Alternatively, other vector stores, such as Chroma DB, Weaviate, Pinecone, and **Relational Database Service** (**RDS**) and PostgreSQL with `pgvector`, can be leveraged based on the use case.
- **Index**: The vector index matches input embeddings with stored document embeddings to find the most relevant contexts.
- **Wrapper**: LangChain provides a wrapper class that abstracts away the underlying logic, handling retrieval, embeddings, indexing, and generation.

The RAG workflow via LangChain orchestration is as follows:

- Ingest a collection of documents into the document loader
- Generate embeddings for all documents using the embedding model
- Index all document embeddings in the vector store
- For an input question, generate its embedding using the embedding model
- Use the index to retrieve the most similar document embeddings
- Pass the relevant documents to the LLM to generate a natural language answer

By orchestrating retrieval and generation in this way, LangChain provides an easy yet powerful framework for developing RAG models. The modular architecture allows flexibility, extensibility, and scalability. For more details on RAG implementation with LangChain, follow the steps in the Amazon Bedrock workshop at `https://github.com/aws-samples/amazon-bedrock-workshop/blob/main/06_OpenSource_examples/01_Langchain_KnowledgeBases_and_RAG_examples/01_qa_w_rag_claude.ipynb`.

Other GenAI systems

RAG models can be integrated with other GenAI tools and applications to create more powerful and versatile AI systems. For instance, RAG's knowledge retrieval capabilities can be combined with conversational agents built on Amazon Bedrock. This allows the agents to perform multi-step tasks and leverage external knowledge bases to generate responses that are more contextually relevant.

Additionally, the RAG knowledge base retrieval enables seamless integration of RAG into custom GenAI pipelines. Developers can retrieve knowledge from RAG indexes and fuse it with LangChain's generative capabilities. This unlocks new use cases such as building AI assistants that can provide expert domain knowledge alongside general conversational abilities.

Further information on LangChain retrievers can be found at `https://python.langchain.com/docs/integrations/retrievers`.

We will cover more details about agents for Amazon Bedrock in *Chapter 10* where we will uncover more RAG-based integration with Amazon Bedrock agents.

With Amazon Bedrock's managed approach, incorporating real-world knowledge into FMs has become more accessible than ever. Now, let us uncover some advanced RAG techniques that are rapidly growing as a mechanism to improve upon current RAG approaches.

Advanced RAG techniques

While basic RAG pipelines involve retrieving relevant documents and directly providing them as context to the LLM, advanced RAG techniques employ various methods to enhance the quality, relevance, and factual accuracy of generated responses. These advanced techniques go beyond the naive approach of simple document retrieval and context augmentation, aiming to optimize various stages of the RAG pipeline for improved performance.

Let's now look at some key areas where advanced RAG techniques focus.

Query handler – query reformulation and expansion

One key area of advancement is query reformulation and expansion. Instead of relying solely on the user's initial query, advanced RAG systems employ NLP techniques to generate additional related queries. This increases the chances of retrieving a more comprehensive set of relevant information from the knowledge base. Query reformulation can involve techniques such as the following:

- **Synonym expansion**: Adding synonyms or related terms to the original query to increase the chances of retrieving relevant information. Here are some examples:
  - *Original query*: `"Hurricane formation"`
  - *Expanded query*: `"Hurricane formation" OR "Tropical cyclone genesis" OR "Tropical storm development"`
- **Query rewriting**: Using an LLM to rewrite or rephrase the original user query to improve retrieval quality. Here are some examples:
  - *Original query*: `What causes hurricanes?`
  - *Rewritten query*: `Explain the meteorological conditions and processes that lead to the formation of hurricanes or tropical cyclones.`
- **Entity extraction**: Identifying key entities in the query and expanding with related concepts can assist in optimal results. Here are some examples:
  - *Original query*: `When was the first iPhone released?`
  - *Extracted entities*: `iPhone`
  - *Expanded query*: `iPhone AND ("product launch" OR "release date" OR "history")`
- **Multi-query retrieval**: Using the LLM to generate multiple related queries and retrieve results for each before combining them. Here are some examples:
  - *Original query*: "`Causes of the American Civil War`"
  - *Generated queries*:
    - `What were the key political and economic factors that led to the American Civil War?`
    - `How did the issue of slavery contribute to starting the American Civil War?`
    - `What were the major events and incidents that precipitated the outbreak of the Civil War in America?`

Figure 5.15 illustrates an overview of a query handler with rewriting and re-ranking mechanisms:

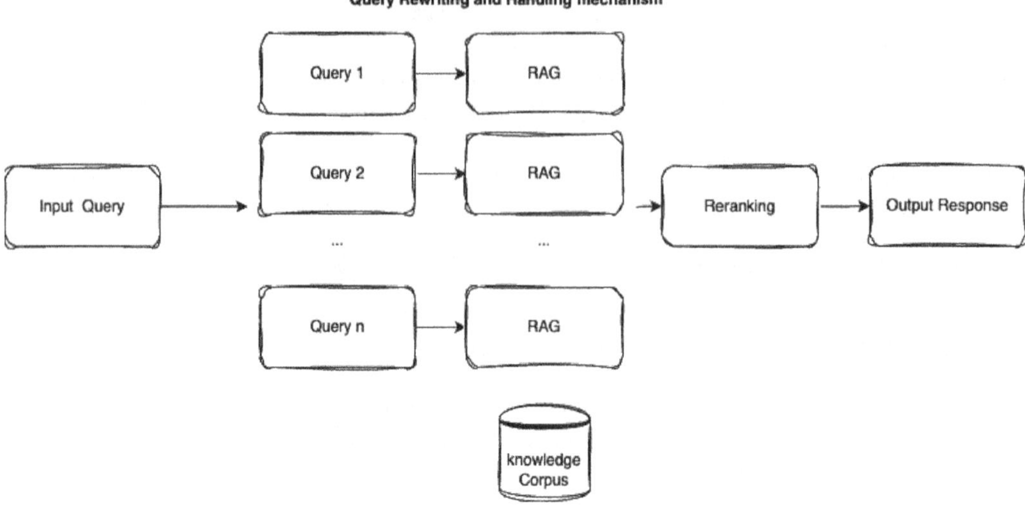

Figure 5.15 – Query handler with rewriting and re-ranking mechanisms

By retrieving information for multiple reformulated queries, the system can gather a richer context to better understand the user's intent and provide more complete and accurate responses.

Hybrid search and retrieval

Advanced RAG systems often employ hybrid retrieval strategies that combine different retrieval methods to leverage their respective strengths. For example, a system might use sparse vector search for initial filtering, followed by dense vector search for re-ranking and surfacing the most relevant documents. Other hybrid approaches include the following:

- Combining keyword matching with vector similarity search
- Using different retrieval methods for different types of data (for example, structured versus unstructured)
- Hierarchical retrieval, where coarse-grained retrieval is followed by fine-grained re-ranking

Here's a simple example to illustrate hybrid search and retrieval:

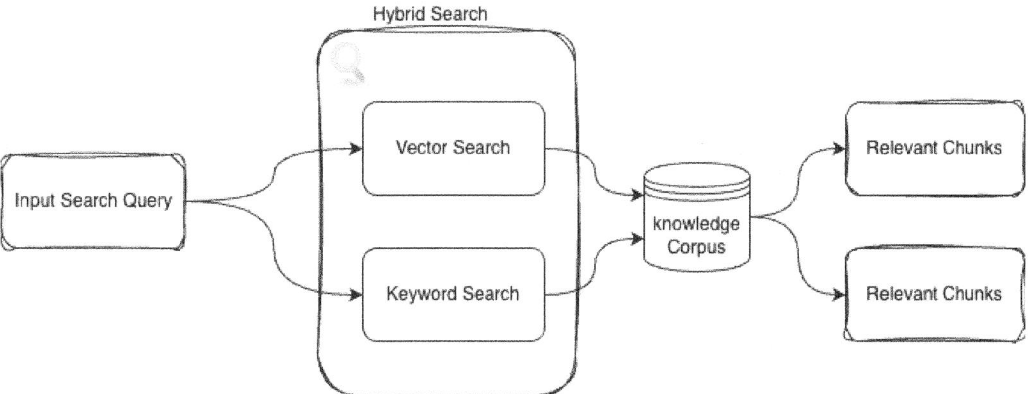

Figure 5.16 – Hybrid search and retrieval approach

Let's say you are searching for information about `apple products` on a website that sells electronics and grocery items.

The hybrid search approach combines two retrieval methods:

- **Keyword search (sparse vector)**: This method looks for exact keyword matches in the text data. For the query `apple products`, it will retrieve documents/pages that contain the words `apple` and `products`, such as the following:
  - `Buy the latest Apple iPhone models here`
  - `Apple MacBook Pro laptops on sale`
  - `Apple cider and apple juice in the grocery section`
- **Semantic/vector search (dense vector)**: This method maps the query and documents into vector representations in a high-dimensional space. It then finds documents whose vectors are closest/most similar to the query vector, capturing semantic relatedness beyond just keyword matching.

  For `apple products`, it may retrieve documents such as the following:
  - `Top tech gadgets and accessories for students` (semantically related to electronics/products)
  - `Healthy fruits and snacks for kids' lunchboxes` (semantically related to apple as a fruit)

The hybrid search can then combine and re-rank the results from both retrieval methods:

1. `Buy the latest Apple iPhone models here`
2. `Apple MacBook Pro laptops on sale`
3. `Top tech gadgets and accessories for students`

4. `Apple cider and apple juice in the grocery section`
5. `Healthy fruits and snacks for kids' lunchboxes`

By combining keyword matching (for brand/product names) and semantic understanding (for broader context), the hybrid approach can provide more comprehensive and relevant search results compared to using just one method.

The key benefit is retrieving documents that are relevant both lexically (containing the exact query keywords) and semantically (related conceptually to the query intent), improving overall search quality.

Embedding and index optimization

The quality of the vector embeddings and indexes used for retrieval can significantly impact the performance of RAG systems. Advanced techniques in this area include the following:

- **Embedding fine-tuning**: Instead of using a general pre-trained embedding model, the embedding model can be fine-tuned on domain-specific data to better capture the semantics and nuances of that domain.

  For example, if building a RAG system for a medical question answering task, the embedding model can be further fine-tuned on a large corpus of medical literature, such as research papers, clinical notes, and so on. This allows the model to better understand domain-specific terminology, abbreviations, and contextual relationships.

- **Index structuring and partitioning**: Instead of storing all document embeddings in a single flat index, the index can be structured or partitioned in ways that improve retrieval efficiency; for example, clustering, hierarchical indexing, and metadata filtering:

  - **Clustering**: Documents can be clustered based on their embeddings, and separate indices created for each cluster. At query time, the query embedding is compared against cluster centroids to identify the relevant cluster(s) to search within.
  - **Hierarchical indexing**: A coarse-level index can first retrieve relevant high-level topics/categories, and then finer-grained indices are searched within those topics.
  - **Metadata filtering**: If document metadata such as type, source, date, and so on is available, the index can be partitioned based on that metadata to allow filtering before vector search.

  Figure 5.17 depicts an advanced retrieval mechanism enriched with metadata:

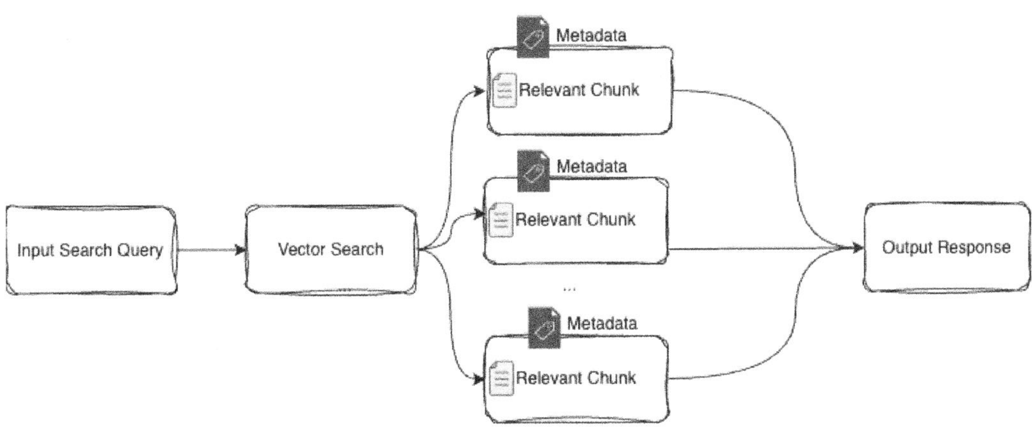

Figure 5.17 – Retrieval mechanism enriched with metadata

- **Approximate NN (ANN) indexing**: For very large vector indices, techniques such as **Hierarchical Navigable Small World** (**HNSW**), FAISS, or **Approximate Nearest Neighbors Oh Yeah** (**Annoy**) can be used to create ANN indices. This allows trading off some accuracy for massive computational speedups in retrieval time over brute-force search. Interested readers can read more details about indexing for NN search in the paper *Learning to Index for Nearest Neighbor Search* (`https://arxiv.org/pdf/1807.02962`).
- **Index compression and quantization**: The size of vector indices can be reduced through compression and quantization techniques without significantly impacting retrieval accuracy. This includes methods such as product quantization, scalar quantization, residual quantization, and so on.

The paper *Vector Quantization for Recommender Systems: A Review and Outlook* (`https://arxiv.org/html/2405.03110v1`) provides a detailed overview of vector quantization for recommender systems. By optimizing the embeddings and indexes, advanced RAG systems can improve the relevance and comprehensiveness of the retrieved information, leading to better overall performance.

Retrieval re-ranking and filtering

Even after initial retrieval, advanced RAG systems often employ additional re-ranking and filtering techniques to surface the most relevant information. These techniques include the following:

- **Cross-attention re-ranking**: Using more expensive cross-attention models can be leveraged in order to re-score and re-rank initially retrieved documents based on their relevance to the query. The paper *Multi-Vector Attention Models for Deep Re-ranking* (`https://aclanthology.org/2021.emnlp-main.443.pdf`) provides a mechanism for deep re-ranking using multi-vector attention models.

- **Learned re-rankers**: Training neural networks or other ML models specifically for the task of re-ranking retrieved documents can assist in improving the search results augmented with the input query.
- **Filtering and pruning**: Removing less relevant or redundant documents from the initial retrieval set based on various heuristics or models can provide contextual optimization.

For example, the user may ask a query: `What were the causes of the American Civil War?`

Here are some examples of initial retrieval via vector search:

- `The issue of slavery was a primary cause of the Civil War...`
- `Economic differences between North and South led to tensions...`
- `The election of Abraham Lincoln in 1860 triggered secession...`
- `The Missouri Compromise failed to resolve slavery expansion...`
- `The Underground Railroad helped enslaved people escape...`

Here are some examples of re-ranking:

- `The election of Abraham Lincoln in 1860 triggered secession...`
- `The issue of slavery was a primary cause of the Civil War...`
- `The Missouri Compromise failed to resolve slavery expansion...`
- `Economic differences between North and South led to tensions...`
- `The Underground Railroad helped enslaved people escape...`

Here are the top 3 re-ranked and filtered results:

- `The election of Abraham Lincoln in 1860 triggered secession...`
- `The issue of slavery was a primary cause of the Civil War...`
- `The Missouri Compromise failed to resolve slavery expansion...`

The top 3 re-ranked and filtered results are then provided as context to the language model for generating a final response about the causes of the Civil War, focused on the most relevant information.

By re-ranking and filtering the retrieved information, advanced RAG systems can provide the LLM with a more focused and relevant context, improving the quality and factual accuracy of the generated responses.

Figure 5.18 demonstrates a complete architectural flow using Amazon Bedrock and some of the advanced RAG techniques (re-ranking with hybrid search mechanism) in order to further enhance the output response:

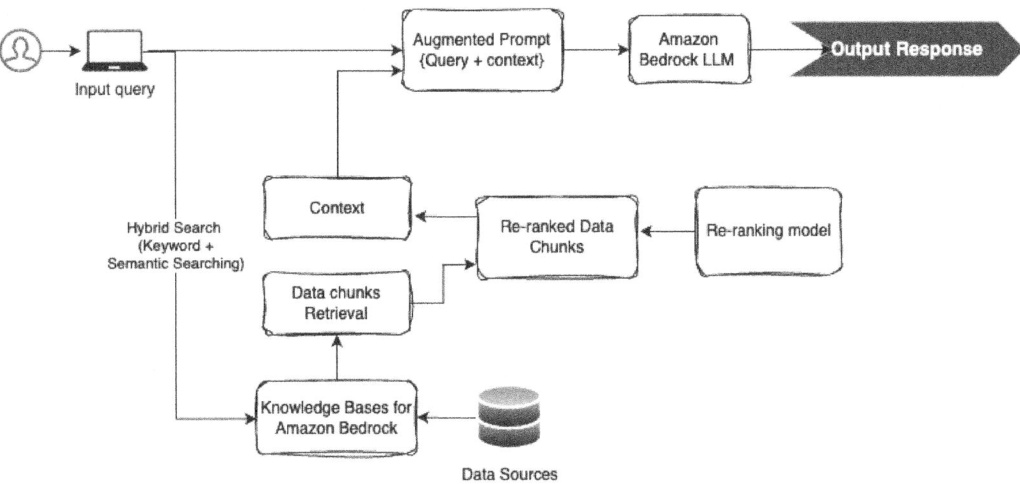

Figure 5.18 – Advanced RAG approach with Amazon Bedrock

As depicted in *Figure 5.18*, employing hybrid search (natively available) within Knowledge Bases for Amazon Bedrock can greatly enhance contextual search quality. Additionally, instead of parsing the data chunks directly to the LLM, feeding the retrieved data chunks to a re-ranker model in order to rank the contextual results can further improve the quality of the output. Cohere Rerank, Meta's Dense Passage Retrieval, BERT for re-ranking, or open source models in Hugging Face (`cross-encoder/ms-marco-MiniLM-L6-v2`) are a few examples of re-ranking models that can be utilized for such ranking optimization tasks. Finally, once the augmented prompt is created with an enhanced query and optimized context, wherein the prompt is parsed to the Amazon Bedrock LLM for outputting a desirable response.

In such a manner, advanced RAG techniques can aim to enhance the quality, relevance, and factual accuracy of language model outputs by improving various stages of the RAG pipeline by incorporating these techniques. Readers are encouraged to visit `https://aws.amazon.com/blogs/machine-learning/create-a-multimodal-assistant-with-advanced-rag-and-amazon-bedrock/` to learn how to implement **multimodal RAG (mmRAG)** with Amazon Bedrock using advanced RAG techniques. This solution also uncovers comprehensive solutioning by leveraging advanced LangChain capabilities.

The paper *RQ-RAG: Learning to Refine Queries for Retrieval Augmented Generation* (`https://arxiv.org/html/2404.00610v1`) walks through yet another advanced RAG approach – **Refine Query for RAG (RQ-RAG)**, which can aid in further optimization of queries by equipping it with capabilities for explicit rewriting, decomposition, and disambiguation.

Since we have uncovered deeper details into RAG functionality, training, and its implementation with Bedrock and other GenAI systems, one should also keep in mind some limitations and research problems. This provides an opportunity for us to evolve with further enhancements with RAG and lead GenAI pathways with more insightful thought processes. Some of the limitations and future directions are discussed in the next section.

Limitations and future directions

While promising, RAG models also come with challenges and open research problems, including the following:

- **Knowledge selection**:One of the critical challenges in RAG is determining the most relevant and salient knowledge to retrieve from the knowledge base. With vast amounts of information available, it becomes crucial to identify and prioritize the most pertinent knowledge for the given context. Existing retrieval methods may struggle to capture the nuances and subtleties of the query, leading to the retrieval of irrelevant or tangential information. Developing more sophisticated query understanding and knowledge selection mechanisms is a key area of research.
- **Knowledge grounding**: Seamlessly integrating retrieved knowledge into the generation process is a non-trivial task. RAG models need to understand the retrieved knowledge, reason over it, and coherently weave it into the generated text. This process requires advanced **NL understanding** (**NLU**) and **NL generation** (**NLG**) capabilities, as well as a deep understanding of the context and discourse structure. Failure to ground the retrieved knowledge properly can lead to inconsistencies, incoherence, or factual errors in the generated output.
- **Training objectives**: One of the major limitations of RAG is the lack of large-scale supervised datasets for end-to-end training. Creating such datasets requires extensive human annotation, which is time-consuming and costly. Additionally, defining suitable training objectives that balance the retrieval and generation components is challenging. Existing training objectives may not adequately capture the complexity of the task, leading to sub-optimal performance.
- **Knowledge base construction**: The quality and coverage of the knowledge base play a crucial role in the effectiveness of RAG models. Creating broad-coverage knowledge bases that span diverse domains and topics is a daunting task. Existing knowledge bases may be incomplete, biased, or outdated, limiting the model's ability to retrieve relevant information. Furthermore, ensuring the accuracy and factual correctness of the knowledge base is essential but challenging, especially for rapidly evolving or controversial topics.
- **Multi-step reasoning**: RAG systems often struggle with combining retrieved knowledge across multiple steps to perform complex reasoning or inference tasks. Technical domains frequently require multi-step reasoning, such as deriving conclusions from multiple premises, following intricate logical chains, or synthesizing information from diverse sources. Current RAG systems may lack the capability to effectively integrate and reason over retrieved knowledge in a coherent and logical manner, limiting their applicability in scenarios involving intricate reasoning processes.

- **Evaluation**: Evaluating the performance of RAG models is challenging due to the complexity of the task. Traditional metrics for text generation, such as perplexity or **BiLingual Evaluation Understudy** (**BLEU**) scores, may not adequately capture the factual correctness, coherence, and consistency of the generated output. Developing robust evaluation methodologies that consider these aspects, as well as the quality of the retrieved knowledge, is an open research problem. Readers are encouraged to check out Ragas (`https://docs.ragas.io/en/v0.1.6/index.html`), which is essentially a framework to assist you evaluate your RAG pipelines at scale.

Despite these limitations, RAG holds significant promise for enhancing the capabilities of GenAI models by leveraging external knowledge sources. Addressing these challenges will be crucial for the widespread adoption and success of RAG in various applications, such as question answering, dialogue systems, and content generation.

Key research priorities going forward include improving retrieval precision, developing more sophisticated fusion methods, exploring efficient large-scale training techniques, and creating better evaluation benchmarks.

Future directions

Researchers are exploring advanced techniques such as dense passage retrieval, learned sparse representations, and hybrid approaches that combine symbolic and neural methods. Additionally, incorporating external knowledge sources beyond traditional corpora, such as structured databases or knowledge graphs, could significantly improve retrieval precision and context understanding.

Developing more sophisticated fusion methods is another critical area of research. While current approaches such as retrieval-augmented language models have shown promising results, they often rely on simple concatenation or attention mechanisms to fuse retrieved information with the language model's generation. Researchers are investigating more advanced fusion techniques that can better capture the complex relationships between retrieved knowledge and the generation context, potentially leveraging techniques from areas such as multi-modal learning, **graph neural networks** (**GNNs**), and neuro-symbolic reasoning.

Exploring efficient large-scale training techniques is essential for scaling RAG to massive knowledge sources and complex domains. Current systems are often trained on relatively small datasets due to computational constraints, limiting their ability to effectively leverage vast knowledge repositories. Researchers are investigating techniques such as distributed training, knowledge distillation, and efficient retrieval indexing to enable training on large-scale knowledge sources while maintaining computational feasibility.

Finally, creating better evaluation benchmarks is crucial for accurately assessing the performance of RAG systems and driving progress in the field. Existing benchmarks often focus on specific tasks or domains, making it challenging to evaluate the generalization capabilities of these systems. Researchers are working on developing more comprehensive and challenging benchmarks that cover a wider range of knowledge sources, domains, and generation tasks, as well as incorporating more sophisticated evaluation metrics that go beyond traditional measures such as perplexity or BLEU scores.

By addressing these key research priorities, the field of RAG can continue to advance, enabling the development of more powerful and versatile language generation systems that can effectively leverage vast knowledge repositories to produce high-quality, informative, and context-relevant text.

Summary

RAG is a rapidly evolving technique that overcomes knowledge limitations in neural generative models by conditioning them on relevant external contexts. We uncovered how training LLMs with a RAG approach works and how to implement RAG with Amazon Bedrock, the LangChain orchestrator, and other GenAI systems. We further explored the importance and limitations of RAG approaches in the GenAI realm. As indicated, early results across a variety of domains are promising and demonstrate the potential of grounding text generation in real-world knowledge. As research addresses current limitations, retrieval augmentation could enable GenAI systems that are factual, informative, and safe.

In the next chapter, we will delve into practical applications by employing various approaches on Amazon Bedrock. We will commence with a text summarization use case, and then explore insights into the methodologies and techniques in depth.

Part 2: Amazon Bedrock Architecture Patterns

In this part, we will explore various architectural patterns and use cases for leveraging the powerful capabilities of Amazon Bedrock. These include text generation, building question answering systems, entity extraction, code generation, image creation, and developing intelligent agents. In addition, we will dive deep into the real-world applications, equipping you with the knowledge and skills to maximize Amazon Bedrock's capabilities in your own projects.

This part contains the following chapters:

- *Chapter 6, Generating and Summarizing Text with Amazon Bedrock*
- *Chapter 7, Building Question Answering Systems and Conversational Interfaces*
- *Chapter 8, Extracting Entities and Generating Code with Amazon Bedrock*
- *Chapter 9, Generating and Transforming Images Using Amazon Bedrock*
- *Chapter 10, Developing Intelligent Agents with Amazon Bedrock*

6

Generating and Summarizing Text with Amazon Bedrock

In this chapter, we will explore architecture patterns for generating and summarizing text with Amazon Bedrock. You will learn about applications of text generation and how text generation works with Amazon Bedrock. Then, we will use some prompt engineering techniques, including contextual prompting, and orchestration using LangChain. After, we will explore text summarization using small texts/files, summarizing large articles and books, and discover use cases and patterns for text summarization.

By the end of this chapter, you will be able to understand and implement text generation and summarization with Amazon Bedrock in real-world use cases.

Here are the key topics that will be covered in this chapter:

- Generating text
- Summarizing text
- Creating a secure serverless solution

Technical requirements

This chapter requires you to have access to an AWS account. If you don't have one already, you can go to `https://aws.amazon.com/getting-started/` and create one.

Secondly, you will need to install and configure the AWS CLI (`https://aws.amazon.com/cli/`). You will use this to access Amazon Bedrock FMs from your local machine. Since the majority of the code cells we will be executing are based in Python, setting up an AWS Python SDK (Boto3) (`https://docs.aws.amazon.com/bedrock/latest/APIReference/welcome.html`) would be beneficial at this point. You can carry out the Python setup in any way: install it on your local machine, or use AWS Cloud9, or utilize AWS Lambda, or leverage Amazon SageMaker. If you're using Jupyter Notebook with the AWS Python SDK to interact with Amazon Bedrock, make sure you run the following code cell in the notebook to import the essential libraries and create a Bedrock runtime client:

```
#Ensure you have the latest version of boto3 & langchain
!pip install -U boto3 langchain-community

#import the main packages and libraries
import boto3
import json

#Create bedrock runtime client
bedrock_client = boto3.client('bedrock-runtime') #Select the desired
region
```

> **Note**
>
> There will be a charge associated with invoking and customizing the FMs of Amazon Bedrock. Please refer to `https://aws.amazon.com/bedrock/pricing/` to learn more.

Generating text

Text generation plays a crucial role in various sectors, from marketing and advertising to journalism and creative writing. The significance of this technique lies in its capacity to streamline content creation processes, boost productivity, and unlock new realms of creativity.

One of the key advantages of text generation is its potential to save valuable time and resources. Traditional content creation methods can be time-consuming and labor-intensive, often requiring extensive research, writing, and editing efforts. But by using generative AI models, businesses and individuals can quickly produce initial drafts, outlines, or complete pieces of content, freeing up valuable time for other tasks.

Furthermore, text generation empowers content creators to explore new narrative avenues and push the boundaries of their creativity. By providing a starting point or a framework, these tools can spark fresh ideas and facilitate the exploration of unconventional storytelling techniques or unique writing styles. This capability is particularly valuable in industries where originality and distinctiveness are highly prized, such as fiction writing, advertising campaigns, or brand storytelling initiatives.

In addition to creative applications, text generation also holds immense potential in fields that demand high volumes of informative and factual content. For instance, news reporting, scientific publications, technical documentation, and text generation can aid in the rapid dissemination of accurate and up-to-date information. By leveraging vast data repositories and subject matter expertise, these tools can generate comprehensive reports, summaries, or articles, ensuring that relevant information is readily available to the intended audience.

Moreover, text generation offers exciting opportunities for personalization and customization. By analyzing user preferences, demographics, and contextual data, these tools can tailor content so that it resonates with specific target audiences, enhancing engagement and fostering stronger connections with readers or customers.

Let's look at some real-world applications of text generation in detail.

Text generation applications

While the applications of text generation are endless, here are a few examples to get you started:

- **Generating product descriptions**: Amazon Bedrock's text generation capabilities can be leveraged to automate the creation of product descriptions for marketing teams. By inputting the product's features, specifications, and key benefits, the FM can generate compelling and SEO-optimized descriptions that highlight the unique selling points of the product. This can significantly streamline the process of creating product descriptions, saving time and resources for marketing teams.

  The generated descriptions can be tailored to different target audiences, tone, and style preferences, ensuring a consistent and engaging brand voice across various channels. Additionally, the FM can be customized on existing product descriptions, allowing it to learn and mimic the desired writing style and formatting.

- **Media articles and marketing campaigns generation**: Amazon Bedrock's text generation capabilities can be utilized for creating high-quality content for media articles, blog posts, and marketing campaigns. By providing relevant information, data, and guidelines, the FM can generate well-structured and coherent articles that can be used for content marketing, thought leadership, or news dissemination.

  The FM can be trained on existing content, enabling it to understand and mimic the tone, style, and formatting preferences of specific publications or brands. It can also generate attention-grabbing headlines, engaging introductions, and compelling **calls to action** (**CTAs**) for marketing campaigns.

- **Personalized email and message composition**: Amazon Bedrock can be utilized to compose personalized emails, messages, and other written communications for customer outreach, marketing campaigns, or even internal communications. By leveraging customer data and preferences, the FM can generate highly tailored and engaging content, enhancing customer experience and increasing brand loyalty.

- **Healthcare**: Clinical documentation is a critical aspect of healthcare, but it can be time-consuming and prone to errors. Bedrock can assist healthcare professionals in streamlining the note-taking and documentation process by generating accurate and comprehensive clinical notes based on conversations or dictations during patient encounters. Amazon offers another service called *AWS HealthScribe* that's powered by Amazon Bedrock and is specifically designed to do that. To learn more about AWS HealthScribe, go to `https://aws.amazon.com/healthscribe/`.

Bedrock can be employed to generate personalized health and wellness recommendations tailored to an individual's unique health profile, lifestyle, and preferences. By analyzing data from various sources, such as **electronic health records** (**EHRs**), wearable devices, and self-reported information, Bedrock can provide tailored recommendations for diet, exercise, stress management, and preventive care.

Text generation systems with Amazon Bedrock

If you have been following the previous chapters, you may have already tried generating text on Amazon Bedrock. But just as a reminder, a simple text generation system looks like this:

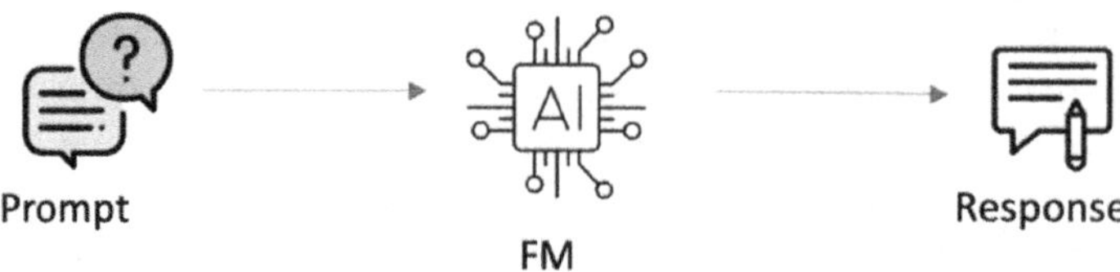
Prompt
AI
FM
Response

Figure 6.1 – Simple text generation system

You provide a prompt to the model and say something like `Compose an email to a customer support team`. Even if you don't provide any context, the model will generate a sample email for you (as shown in *Figure 6.2*):

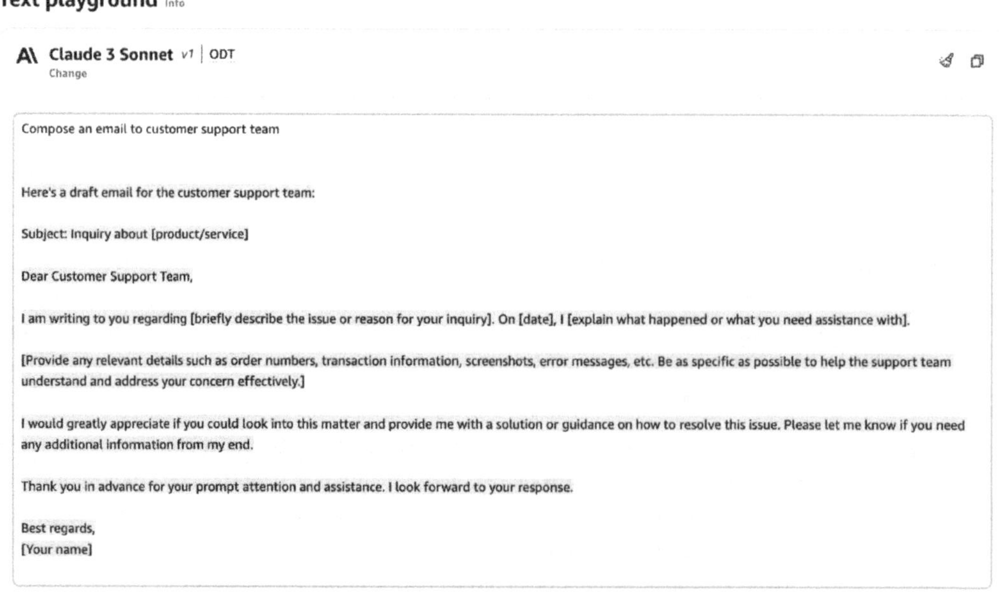
Amazon Bedrock > Text playground
Text playground Info
Claude 3 Sonnet v1 | ODT
Change
Compose an email to customer support team
Here's a draft email for the customer support team:
Subject: Inquiry about [product/service]
Dear Customer Support Team,
I am writing to you regarding [briefly describe the issue or reason for your inquiry]. On [date], I [explain what happened or what you need assistance with].
[Provide any relevant details such as order numbers, transaction information, screenshots, error messages, etc. Be as specific as possible to help the support team understand and address your concern effectively.]
I would greatly appreciate if you could look into this matter and provide me with a solution or guidance on how to resolve this issue. Please let me know if you need any additional information from my end.
Thank you in advance for your prompt attention and assistance. I look forward to your response.
Best regards,
[Your name]

Figure 6.2 – Generating an email

In your Jupyter Notebook environment with the AWS Python SDK, run the following sample script to invoke the AI21 Jurassic model. Make sure you import the essential libraries and create the Bedrock runtime client first, as mentioned in the *Technical requirements* section:

```
prompt_data = """Human: Compose an email to a customer support team.
Assistant:
"""

body = json.dumps({"prompt": prompt_data, "maxTokens": 200})
modelId = "ai21.j2-mid-v1"  # change this to use a different version
from the model provider
accept = «application/json»
contentType = «application/json»

response = bedrock_client.invoke_model(body=body, modelId=modelId,
accept=accept, contentType=contentType)
response_body = json.loads(response.get("body").read())
print(response_body.get("completions")[0].get("data").get("text"))
```

Now, based on the model that you select, the response's structure and output may vary. *Figure 6.3* shows the response from the AI21 Jurassic model:

```
Dear Customer Support Team,

I am writing this email because I have a question. I hope you can answer my question.

My question is about the return policy. I would like to return a product I bought from your website, but I can't find any information about how to do it o
n your website.

I hope you can help me.

Sincerely,
```

Figure 6.3 – AI21 Jurassic output

Here, we provided a simple prompt without providing any context or information. Now, let's move on to the advanced architecture patterns of text generation and understand contextual prompting.

Generating text using prompt engineering

In the previous section, we looked at a pattern of text generation where we did not provide any context or information to the model. Let's use some of the prompt engineering techniques we learned about in *Chapter 3*:

- **Zero-shot contextual prompting**: Here, we will provide detailed context in the prompt in a zero-shot fashion:

  ```
  prompt = """
  Human: Write a descriptive and engaging travel guide section
  about a lesser-known but beautiful destination, capturing the
  local culture, cuisine, and must-see attractions in a way that
  ```

```
inspires wanderlust.
Assistant:"""
body = json.dumps({"prompt": prompt,"max_tokens_to_sample":
500})
modelId = "anthropic.claude-v2"  # change this to use a
different version from the model provider
accept = «application/json»
contentType = «application/json»
response = bedrock_runtime.invoke_model(body=body,
modelId=modelId, accept=accept, contentType=contentType)
response_body = json.loads(response.get("body").read())
print(response_body.get("completion"))
```

Running the preceding code will generate a response similar to the one shown in *Figure 6.4*:

```
Here is a draft travel guide section about a lesser-known but beautiful destination:

Uncover the Hidden Gem of Cesky Krumlov, Czech Republic

Nestled in the hills of Southern Bohemia lies a fairy-tale medieval town that feels frozen in time. Cesky Krumlov
is a hidden gem that remains largely off the typical tourist trails, but offers a transported journey into the pas
t with its beautifully preserved old town center.

As you wander the cobblestone streets, you'll be immersed in architecture spanning Gothic, Renaissance, and Baroqu
e styles. The crown jewel is the 13th century Cesky Krumlov Castle, towering over the Vltava River with its sprawl
ing complex of 40 buildings. Inside, marvel at the ornate staterooms and immerse yourself in the stories of noble
families from eras past.

The delight is in the details - peak into quiet courtyard gardens, stroll the charming arcades, and admire the col
orful facades of centuries-old burgher houses. As the sun sets, grab a local Pilsner beer in one of the riverside
restaurants and watch the fading light reflect off the river and castle above.

Czech cuisine shines in Cesky Krumlov, so sample local specialties like roasted duck, dumplings, hearty stews, and
the world-famous Budvar beer. For delicious dining with unbeatable atmosphere, head to riverside eateries like Krc
ma V Satlavske and Hospoda 99.

Cesky Krumlov charms with its small town pace, thriving arts scene, and stunning natural surroundings. Just steps
away from the old town you can hike forest trails or meander through the castle gardens and grounds. Come in June
to experience the Five-Petalled Rose Festival, where medieval lore springs to life with costumes, banners, and the
ater.

This destinations feels like a fairy tale brought to life, offering an utterly captivating glimpse into Bohemia's
past. Let the wonder of Cesky Krumlov capture your imagination and take you back in time during your travels throu
gh Czech Republic.
```

Figure 6.4 – Zero-shot contextual prompt response

In the preceding scenario, we used the Amazon Bedrock API – `invoke_model` – and passed the prompt, configuration parameters, and model ID. If you want to learn more about the various Bedrock APIs that are available, you are encouraged to revisit *Chapter 2*.

- **Few-shot contextual prompting**: Here, we will provide some examples in our prompt so that the model can start to generate reasonable continuations:

```
prompt = """
Human: Here are some examples of product descriptions:

Example 1:
```

```
Product: Apple iPhone 13 Pro
Description: The iPhone 13 Pro is a smartphone designed and
manufactured by Apple Inc. It features a 6.1-inch Super Retina
XDR display, a powerful A15 Bionic chip, and an advanced triple-
camera system with improved low-light performance and 3x optical
zoom. The phone also boasts 5G connectivity, longer battery
life, and a durable Ceramic Shield front cover.

Example 2:
Product: Sony WH-1000XM4 Noise Cancelling Headphones
Description: Experience exceptional audio quality with the
Sony WH-1000XM4 Noise Cancelling Headphones. These over-
ear headphones feature industry-leading noise cancellation
technology, allowing you to immerse yourself in your music
without distractions. The responsive touch controls and long-
lasting battery life make them ideal for everyday use, while the
comfortable design ensures hours of listening pleasure.

Example 3:
Product: Instant Pot Duo Crisp + Air Fryer
Description: The Instant Pot Duo Crisp + Air Fryer is a
versatile kitchen appliance that combines the functions of
an electric pressure cooker, air fryer, and more. With its
EvenCrisp technology, you can achieve crispy, golden results
using little to no oil. The easy-to-use control panel and 11
built-in smart programs allow you to cook a wide variety of
dishes with ease, making it a must-have for any modern kitchen.

Your task: Generate a product description for the following
product:
Product: Sony A7 III Mirrorless Camera
Assistant:"""
body = json.dumps({"prompt": prompt, "max_tokens_to_sample":
500})
modelId = "anthropic.claude-v2"
accept = "application/json"
contentType = "application/json"
response = bedrock_runtime.invoke_model(body=body,
modelId=modelId, accept=accept, contentType=contentType)
response_body = json.loads(response.get("body").read())
print(response_body.get("completion"))
```

Here, we provided three examples in our prompt to tell the model how our response should look. Then, we invoked the model to generate a product description for `Sony A7 III Mirrorless Camera`. We received the response shown in *Figure 6.5*:

```
Here is a product description for the Sony A7 III Mirrorless Camera:

Capture stunning images with the Sony A7 III Mirrorless Camera. This full frame camera delivers excellent image qu
ality with its 24.2MP back-illuminated Exmor R CMOS sensor and advanced BIONZ X image processor. The 693-point hyb
rid AF system provides incredibly fast, precise focusing in any lighting condition. With an impressive ISO range e
xpandable to 204,800, 4K video capabilities, and a durable magnesium alloy body, the A7 III empowers you to shoot
professionally in any situation. Whether you're shooting portraits, landscapes, sports or video, the A7 III's outs
tanding quality and reliable performance will enable you to consistently produce impressive results.
```

Figure 6.5 – Few-shot contextual prompting response

- **Zero-shot prompting with LangChain**: Here, we will use LangChain's integration of Bedrock API. LangChain acts as an abstraction layer, simplifying the interaction with the Bedrock API before routing your request to the appropriate API endpoint (the Amazon Bedrock `invoke_model` API in this case):

> **Note**
>
> At the time of writing, we used `langchain_community.llms` library to import *Bedrock*. However, based on the updates from the LangChain community, it may be susceptible to change. For updated information on importing the LangChain package, please visit `https://python.langchain.com/v0.2/docs/integrations/platforms/`.

```
from langchain_community.llms import Bedrock

inference_modifier = {"max_tokens_to_sample": 4096,
"temperature": 0.5, "top_k": 250, "top_p": 1, "stop_sequences":
["\n\nHuman"],}
llm = Bedrock(model_id="anthropic.claude-v2",  client=bedrock_
client, model_kwargs=inference_modifier,)

response = llm("""
Human: Write a descriptive and engaging travel guide section
about a lesser-known but beautiful destination, capturing the
local culture, cuisine, and must-see attractions in a way that
inspires wanderlust.
Assistant:""")

print(response)
```

Upon running the preceding code snippet, we can see that the model can generate a descriptive response, as requested (as shown in *Figure 6.6*):

```
Here is a draft travel guide section about a lesser-known but beautiful destination:

Discover the Hidden Gem of Cesky Krumlov, Czech Republic

Nestled in the hills of Bohemia along the Vltava River, the medieval town of Cesky Krumlov is a
fairytale village that feels frozen in time. With its winding cobblestone streets, pastel-hued
architecture, and dramatic castle towering over the river, this charming town looks like something
straight out of a storybook. Though not as famous as Prague, Cesky Krumlov deserves a spot on any
Central Europe itinerary for its breathtaking scenery, rich history, and delightful old-world
ambiance.

The heart of Cesky Krumlov is its UNESCO-recognized historic center, where 13th-century shops and
taverns rub shoulders with Baroque and Renaissance buildings. Wander through the lively squares and
get lost down the quaint backstreets while soaking up the relaxed, small-town vibes. Don't miss the
main square, with its impressive Town Hall, or the castle complex, which dates back to 1240 when it
was built by the noble Rosenberg family.

Beyond the main town, serene countryside awaits. Follow the river downstream through the forested
valley to discover secluded swimming holes and riverside beaches. Hike up to grand mountaintop
vistas, go white water rafting over rapids, or enjoy a hot air balloon ride for a bird's eye view
over the rolling landscape. Savor a fresh pint at one of the local microbreweries back in town while
listening to live folk music in a cozy cellar bar.

Cesky Krumlov also boasts excellent regional cuisine. Be sure to try the local specialty, a thick
sourdough dumpling dish called knedliky, along with hearty Czech beers like Pilsner Urquell. Sample
sweet and savory crepes from the medieval Latran Street market, or indulge in chocolate cake and hot
chocolate at one of the vintage cafés on the main square. For a unique dining experience, book a
medieval feast in the castle complete with costumed servers, candlelight, and a multi-course menu of
roasted meats and stew.

With its timeless beauty and wealth of cultural charms, Cesky Krumlov deserves a spot on every
traveler's bucket list. Come savor the history, scenery, and hospitality of this hidden gem in the
hills of Bohemia.
```

Figure 6.6 – Zero-shot prompting with LangChain

- **Contextual generation with LangChain**: Here, we will provide instructions and context in our prompts before sending them to the model:

```
from langchain_community.llms import Bedrock

inference_modifier = {'max_tokens_to_sample':4096,
"temperature":0.5, "top_k":250, "top_p":1, "stop_sequences":
["\n\nHuman"]}

llm = Bedrock(model_id = "anthropic.claude-v2", client = boto3_
bedrock, model_kwargs = inference_modifier)
from langchain.prompts import PromptTemplate
product_description_prompt = PromptTemplate(   input_
variables=["product_name", "product_category", "key_features"],
    template="""
You are a professional copywriter tasked with creating an
engaging and informative product description for a new Amazon
product.

Product Name: {product_name}
Product Category: {product_category}
Key Features: {key_features}
```

```
Write a compelling product description that highlights the key
features and benefits of the product, while keeping the tone
engaging and persuasive for potential customers.

Product Description:
«»»
)

prompt = product_description_prompt.format(
    product_name="Smart Home Security Camera",
    product_category="Home Security",
    key_features="- 1080p HD video recording\n- Motion
detection alerts\n- Two-way audio communication\n- Night vision
capabilities\n- Cloud storage for recorded footage")
response = llm(prompt)
product = response[response.index('\n')+1:]
print(product)
```

In this scenario, we used the LangChain implementation of Bedrock. We defined a prompt template for creating a product description and invoked the Anthropic Claude model to generate a product description of a smart home security camera. The prompt template is essentially a reusable template for constructing prompts. Within the prompt template, you can provide the context, input variables, task, and some few-shot examples for the model to reference. To learn more about prompt templates, go to `https://python.langchain.com/v0.2/docs/concepts/#prompt-templates`.

The following figure shows the response from providing the preceding code snippet:

```
Keep your home safe and secure with the new Smart Home Security Camera. With crisp 1080p HD video,
this advanced camera captures every detail day or night thanks to night vision technology. Get
motion detection alerts instantly sent to your phone whenever the camera detects movement - you'll
always know what's happening at home even when you're away.

See, hear, and speak to visitors with clear two-way audio communication. Not only can you monitor
your home closely, you can also deter intruders by talking through the camera's built-in microphone
and speaker. Video footage is securely stored in the cloud, allowing you to review events any time
through the easy-to-use app.

Feel at ease knowing your home is protected by this smart security camera. With customizable motion
detection, real-time notifications, and excellent low-light capabilities, you'll have 24/7 peace of
mind. Set up is a breeze with simple wireless connectivity.

Bring smart home technology to your home security with the Smart Home Camera. Order today to start
monitoring your home from anywhere, any time!
```

Figure 6.7 – Contextual generation with LangChain

Now that we've looked at various text generation patterns, let's look at how we can perform summarization using Amazon Bedrock.

Summarizing text

Text summarization is a highly sought-after capability that holds immense value across diverse domains. It involves the intricate task of condensing lengthy text documents into concise and coherent summaries that capture the essence of the original content. These summaries aim to preserve the most salient information while omitting redundant or irrelevant details, thereby enabling efficient consumption and comprehension of extensive textual data.

Text summarization finds applications in a wide range of sectors, from research and academia to journalism, business intelligence, and legal documentation. With the exponential growth of textual data generated daily, the need for effective summarization techniques has become increasingly paramount. Imagine sifting through voluminous reports, news articles, or legal documents – text summarization emerges as a powerful tool to distill the core information, saving time and cognitive effort for professionals and researchers alike.

Let's look at some of the real-world applications of text summarization:

- **Content curation**: In today's information-rich world, text summarization plays a pivotal role in curating and condensing vast amounts of data. This allows users to quickly grasp the essence of lengthy articles, reports, or online content without having to read every word.
- **News aggregation**: News aggregators and media platforms can leverage text summarization to provide concise summaries of breaking news stories, enabling users to stay informed about the latest developments without getting bogged down by extensive details.
- **Research assistance**: Researchers and academics can benefit from text summarization techniques to quickly identify the most pertinent information from a vast corpus of literature, saving them valuable time and effort.
- **Customer service**: Text summarization can enhance customer service by automatically generating concise summaries of lengthy customer inquiries or feedback, allowing support agents to quickly comprehend the crux of the issue and provide timely responses.
- **Legal and financial domains**: In industries where accurate representation of original text is critical, such as legal or financial sectors, text summarization techniques can be employed to generate summaries of contracts, agreements, or reports, ensuring that key information is not overlooked.
- **Email management**: Email clients or productivity tools can leverage text summarization to provide concise overviews of long email threads or conversations, helping users quickly grasp the key points without having to read through every message.
- **Meeting recap**: Text summarization can be applied to meeting transcripts or notes, generating succinct summaries that capture the most important discussions, decisions, and action items, enabling participants to quickly review and follow up on critical points.

- **Social media monitoring**: Businesses and organizations can utilize text summarization to analyze and summarize vast amounts of social media data, such as customer feedback, product reviews, or brand mentions, enabling them to stay informed about public sentiment and respond promptly.
- **Knowledge extraction**: Text summarization techniques can be used to extract and summarize relevant knowledge from large datasets or knowledge bases, making it easier to access and leverage valuable information for various applications, such as decision-making or knowledge management systems.
- **Educational resources**: Text summarization can be applied to educational materials, such as textbooks or online courses, to generate concise summaries or study aids, helping students grasp key concepts and prepare for exams more efficiently.

While the list of applications is endless and spans across every industry, let's look at how summarization systems work with Amazon Bedrock. We will learn about two approaches:

- Summarization of small files
- Summarization of large files

By small files, we mean pieces of text that fit into the context length of the model. This could range from a couple of sentences to a few paragraphs. On the other hand, by large files, we mean large documents or book(s) worth of information that does not fit into the context length of the model. It is important to note that there is no one-size-fits-all that works across all models. Every model, including their different versions, might have a different context length. For example, Cohere Command R+ has a context length of 128K tokens, while Cohere Command Light has a context length of 4,000 tokens.

Summarization of small files

Small files can include meeting notes, blog posts, news articles, email messages, and call transcripts. These files are then used as a context for the prompt and sent to the model. The prompt here could be as simple as `Summarize the content`. The model then processes the file and provides you with the summarized response. *Figure 6.8* shows the process of small file summarization:

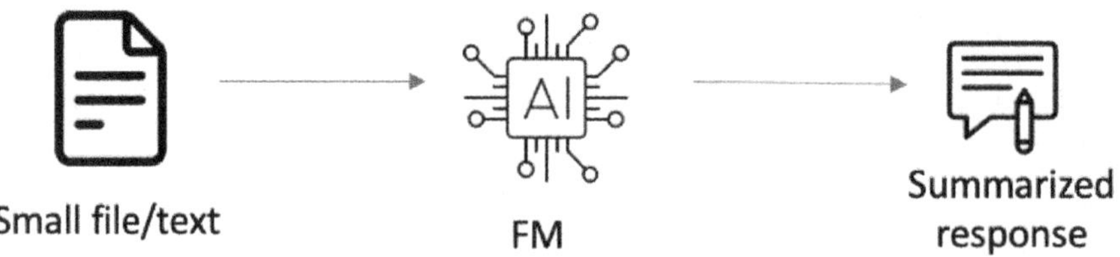

Figure 6.8 – Small file summarization

Let's consider an example of a news article from Yahoo! Finance. Since the news article fits into the context length of the model, we will use that as a context in the prompt, `Summarize the following news article`, and send it to the model. The model will then process the request and provide the summarized response, as shown in *Figure 6.9*:

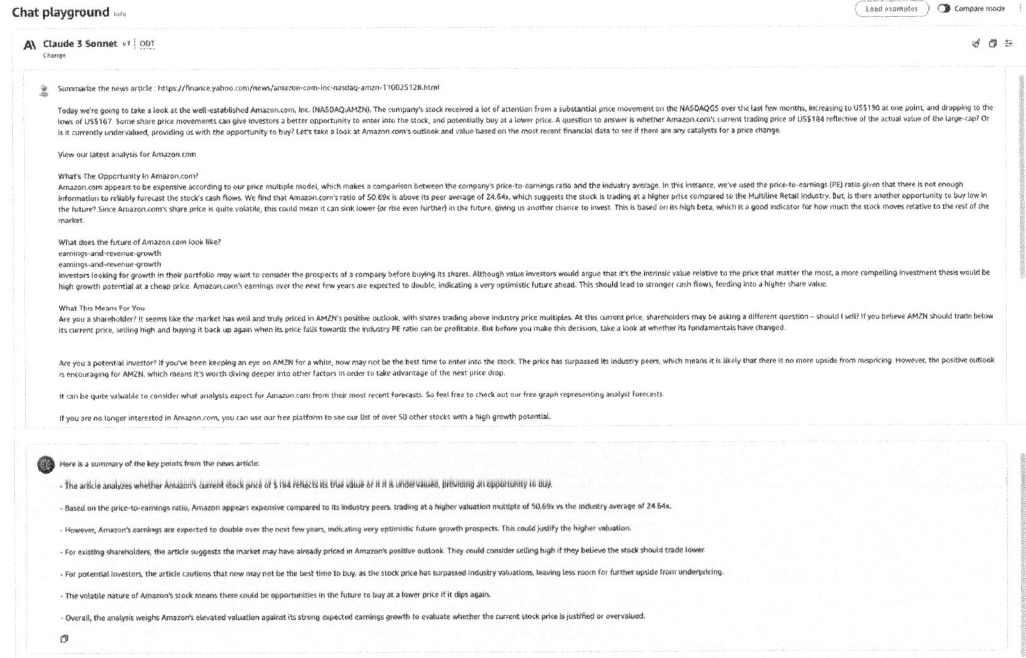

Figure 6.9 – Summarization of a news article

There are a couple of ways to summarize small files in Bedrock. If you're using the AWS Python SDK, you can pass the small file text into the prompt directly, as shown in the following code. However, if you would like to summarize a couple of paragraphs, you can utilize *prompt templates* to place the text dynamically within the prompts and use LangChain to invoke the model:

```
prompt = """
Today we're going to take a look at the well-established Amazon.com,
Inc. (NASDAQ:AMZN). The company's stock led the NASDAQGS gainers with
a relatively large price hike in the past couple of weeks. The recent
jump in the share price has meant that the company is trading at
close to its 52-week high. With many analysts covering the large-cap
stock, we may expect any price-sensitive announcements have already
been factored into the stock's share price. But what if there is
still an opportunity to buy? Let's take a look at Amazon.com's outlook
and value based on the most recent financial data to see if the
opportunity still exists.


Check out our latest analysis for Amazon.com
```

```
What's The Opportunity In Amazon.com?
Great news for investors - Amazon.com is still trading at a fairly
cheap price. According to our valuation, the intrinsic value for the
stock is $238.66, but it is currently trading at US$174 on the share
market, meaning that there is still an opportunity to buy now. What's
more interesting is that, Amazon.com's share price is quite volatile,
which gives us more chances to buy since the share price could sink
lower (or rise higher) in the future. This is based on its high beta,
which is a good indicator for how much the stock moves relative to the
rest of the market.

Can we expect growth from Amazon.com?
earnings-and-revenue-growth
earnings-and-revenue-growth
Future outlook is an important aspect when you're looking at buying
a stock, especially if you are an investor looking for growth in your
portfolio. Buying a great company with a robust outlook at a cheap
price is always a good investment, so let's also take a look at the
company's future expectations. With profit expected to more than
double over the next couple of years, the future seems bright for
Amazon.com. It looks like higher cash flow is on the cards for the
stock, which should feed into a higher share valuation.

What This Means For You
Are you a shareholder? Since AMZN is currently undervalued, it may
be a great time to accumulate more of your holdings in the stock.
With a positive outlook on the horizon, it seems like this growth has
not yet been fully factored into the share price. However, there are
also other factors such as financial health to consider, which could
explain the current undervaluation.


Are you a potential investor? If you've been keeping an eye on AMZN
for a while, now might be the time to enter the stock. Its buoyant
future outlook isn't fully reflected in the current share price yet,
which means it's not too late to buy AMZN. But before you make any
investment decisions, consider other factors such as the strength
of its balance sheet, in order to make a well-informed investment
decision.

Diving deeper into the forecasts for Amazon.com mentioned earlier
will help you understand how analysts view the stock going forward.
Luckily, you can check out what analysts are forecasting by clicking
here.

If you are no longer interested in Amazon.com, you can use our free
platform to see our list of over 50 other stocks with a high growth
potential.
"""
```

```
body = json.dumps({"inputText": prompt,
                   "textGenerationConfig":{
                       "maxTokenCount":4096,
                       "stopSequences":[],
                       "temperature":0,
                       "topP":1
                   },
                  })
modelId = 'amazon.titan-tg1-large' # change this to use a different
version from the model provider
accept = 'application/json'
contentType = 'application/json'
response = bedrock_client.invoke_model(body=body, modelId=modelId,
accept=accept, contentType=contentType)
response_body = json.loads(response.get('body').read())
print(response_body.get('results')[0].get('outputText'))
```

The response is shown in *Figure 6.10*:

```
Amazon.com, Inc. (NASDAQ:AMZN) is trading at close to its 52-week high, with many analysts covering
the large-cap stock. The intrinsic value for the stock is $238.66, but it is currently trading at
US$174 on the share market, meaning that there is still an opportunity to buy now. The company's
share price is volatile, giving us more chances to buy since the share price could sink lower (or
rise higher) in the future. With profit expected to more than double over the next couple of years,
the future seems bright for Amazon.com. However, there are also other factors such as financial
health to consider, which could explain the current undervaluation.
```

Figure 6.10 – Small file summarization response

We have parsed a news article (`https://finance.yahoo.com/news/us-174-time-put-amazon-110026932.html`) from Yahoo! Finance as a sample context to the prompt and invoked the Titan text model to generate the summarized response, as shown in the preceding figure.

Now, let's look at the techniques for summarizing large files.

Summarization of large files

Large files can include large documents or book(s) worth of information that do not fit into the context length of the model. When we say large documents, this includes 10-K reports, **Federal Open Market Committee** (**FOMC**) reports, public health reports, clinical study reports, e-magazines, service documentation, and more. The 10-K report for Amazon is an example of a large file: `https://www.sec.gov/Archives/edgar/data/1018724/000101872424000008/amzn-20231231.htm`.

When working with large files for summarizing text, several challenges are involved:

- **Context length limitations**: All FMs, such as the ones used in Amazon Bedrock, have a maximum context length or input size that they can process at once. This limit varies from model to model, but it is typically in the range of a few thousand tokens (words or word pieces). For example, you can find FMs such as the Anthropic Claude 3 family with 200k tokens. When working with large documents that exceed this context length, it becomes impossible to summarize the entire document accurately and coherently. The model may miss important information or fail to capture the overall context and nuances present in the original text.
- **Hallucinations**: Hallucination is a phenomenon where models generate output that is not grounded in the input data or contains factual inconsistencies. This issue can become more prevalent when dealing with large documents as the model might struggle to maintain coherence and faithfulness to the original text. As the input size increases, the model may start generating plausible-sounding but factually incorrect information, potentially leading to inaccurate summaries.
- **Memory and computational constraints**: Summarizing large documents can be computationally intensive and may require significant memory resources. Generative AI models need to process and store the entire input text, as well as intermediate representations and generated outputs. When working with very large documents, you might experience performance degradation due to the high computational demands if they're not handled with dedicated compute capacity (see the *Provisioned throughput architecture* section in *Chapter 12*).
- **Context understanding**: Large documents often contain complex structures, such as sections, subsections, and cross-references. Generative AI models may struggle to accurately capture and understand the relationships and dependencies between different parts of the document. This can lead to summaries that lack coherence or fail to accurately represent the overall structure and flow of the original content.
- **Topic drift and coherence**: As the length of the input text increases, it becomes more challenging for the models to maintain focus and coherence throughout the summarization process. The model may drift away from the main topic or fail to properly connect and transition between different aspects of the document, resulting in summaries that lack cohesion or clarity.

To address these challenges, let's look at summarizing large files using LangChain.

Text summarization using LangChain's summarization chain

Using LangChain, we are going to break down large files into smaller, more manageable chunks and process them sequentially. *Figure 6.11* shows the architecture of large text summarization using LangChain:

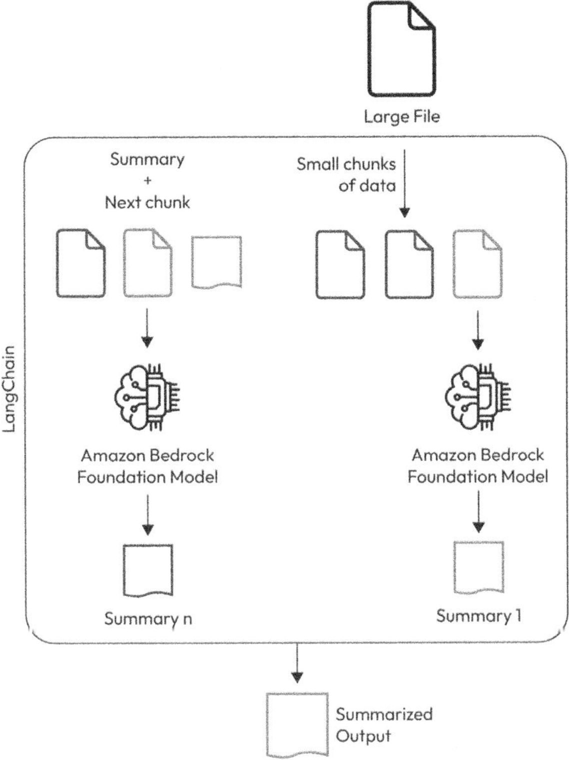

Figure 6.11 – Large file summarization in LangChain

Here's how the process works:

1. **Data ingestion**: The first step in the process is to load a large document or file into the system. This involves loading the file from an Amazon S3 bucket or downloading it directly from the internet. The files you can provide can be in the form of text, PDF, Word documents, and more.
2. **Chunking**: Once the document has been loaded, the LangChain utility is employed to split the content into multiple smaller chunks. The chunking process can be based on various criteria, such as character or word count, sentence boundaries, or even semantic segmentation techniques. The size of the chunks is typically determined by the limitations of the model being used for summarization. Even though there are a variety of chunking techniques, `RecursiveCharacterTextSplitter` is recommended for general text, as per the LangChain documentation: `https://python.langchain.com/v0.2/docs/how_to/recursive_text_splitter/`.

   It recursively splits the text into smaller chunks until each chunk's size falls below a specified threshold. The splitting process leverages separators (`"\n\n"`, `"\n"`), which ensures that individual paragraphs remain intact within a single chunk, rather than being fragmented across multiple chunks.

3. **Summarization chain**: The next step is to use the chunks and perform summarization. LangChain provides three summarization chains – *stuff*, *map_reduce*, and *refine*. Let's take a closer look:

    - `stuff`: As the name suggests, this chain stuffs all the chunks into a single prompt.
    - `map_reduce`: The map-reduce chain is a powerful pattern that allows you to split a large task into smaller subtasks, process them independently, and then combine the results. In the context of text summarization, this chain type is used to break down a long text document into smaller chunks, summarize each chunk independently using an LLM, and then combine the summaries into a final summarized output.
    - `refine`: This chain starts by summarizing the first chunk. Then, `refine` takes this summary and combines it with the second chunk to generate a new summary that encompasses both pieces of information. This process continues, where the latest summary is combined with the next chunk, and a new summary is generated. This iterative approach repeats until all the chunks have been incorporated into the final summary.

    To load any of these summarization chains, you can call `load_summarize_chain` and provide the chain type:

    ```
    from langchain.chains.summarize import load_summarize_chain
    summary_chain = load_summarize_chain(llm=llm, chain_type="map_
    reduce", verbose=False)
    ```

4. **Final summary**: Based on the summarization chain you select and once all the chunks have been processed, the final summary represents a condensed version of the entire original document.

The notebook at `https://github.com/aws-samples/amazon-bedrock-workshop/blob/main/06_OpenSource_examples/00_Langchain_TextGeneration_examples/05_long-text-summarization-titan%20Langchain.ipynb` showcases the use of long text summarization using LangChain. In this example, it uses `map_reduce` as the chain type. We recommend that you try out different chain types and provide any blog posts, files, or news articles as a prompt.

Now that we've summarized large files using the LangChain chain type, let's say we want to summarize a whole book or multiple books' worth of information. In such scenarios, where large manuscripts or books need to be summarized, the RAG approach can be potentially beneficial. However, please note that the summarized response might not contain some essential elements from the book – in other words, there could be information loss. Various advanced RAG techniques, such as query refinement, can be utilized to retrieve the summarized response and essential elements from the text. To learn more about query refinement for RAG, please take a look at the paper *RQ-RAG: Learning to Refine Queries for Retrieval Augmented Generation* (`https://arxiv.org/html/2404.00610v1`).

To learn more about how RAG works and some advanced RAG techniques, please refer to *Chapter 5*.

Next, we'll look at text summarization via Amazon Bedrock Knowledge Base.

Amazon Bedrock Knowledge Base

In *Chapter 5*, we looked at how Amazon Bedrock Knowledge Base works and how to set it up. Let's see an example of summarization using Knowledge Base.

We have put the *Attention is All You Need* research paper in our data store Amazon S3 bucket and synced it with our Bedrock Knowledge base, as shown in *Figure 6.12*:

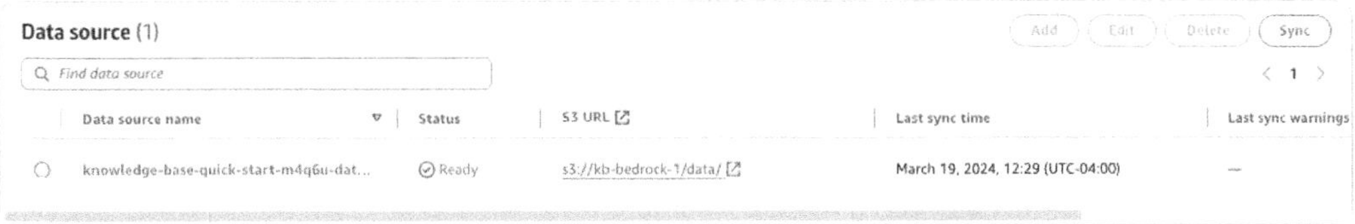

Figure 6.12 – Knowledge Base data source

Select the model and provide a prompt to summarize the content. You will see the response from the LLM, as shown in *Figure 6.13*:

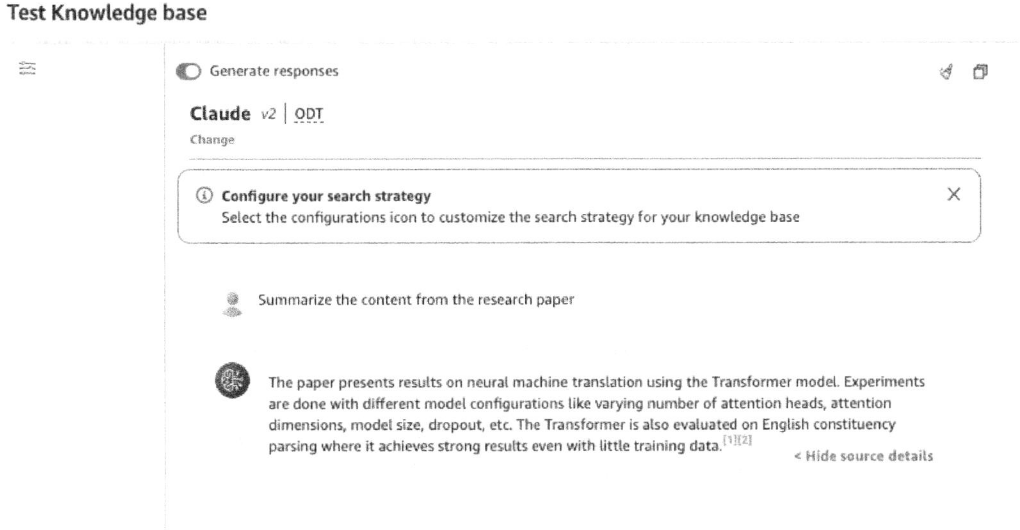

Figure 6.13 – Test Knowledge base

If you would like to try this via APIs, you can call the **Retrieve** API or the **RetrieveAndGenerate** API. The Retrieve API accesses and retrieves the relevant data from Knowledge Base, whereas the RetrieveAndGenerate API, in addition to retrieving the data, generates the response based on the retrieved results. For more details on Amazon Bedrock Knowledge Base, please refer to *Chapter 5*.

In this section, we discussed how to utilize text summarization systems with Amazon Bedrock. Summarizing small files is straightforward and involves utilizing the model's context length. However, summarizing large files requires chunking and specialized techniques such as LangChain's summarization chains, RAG, or Amazon Bedrock Knowledge Base to handle context length limitations, hallucination, computational constraints, and coherence issues.

Now that we have looked at generating and summarizing text using Amazon Bedrock, let's look at how organizations can use these techniques and create a secure serverless solution involving other AWS services.

Creating a secure serverless solution

When working with Generative AI models from Amazon Bedrock, organizations can develop an application that is secure and serverless. Instead of interacting directly with Amazon Bedrock using SDKs, they can have an interactive chatbot that abstracts away any complexity, provides a rich customer experience, and boosts overall productivity.

Figure 6.14 shows an architecture diagram of how the user can interact with the web-based chatbot developed via AWS Amplify and have conversations, generate text in various forms, and perform language translation, text summarization, and more:

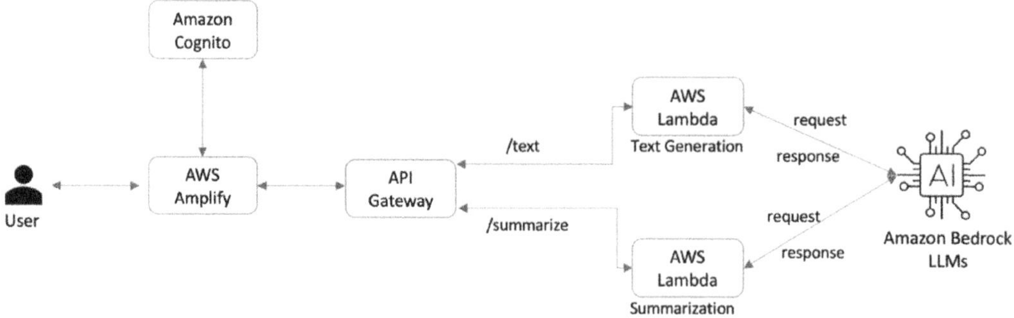

Figure 6.14 – Serverless enterprise application with Amazon Bedrock

Let's take a closer look at this process:

1. **User interaction with the chatbot on AWS Amplify**: AWS Amplify is a comprehensive set of tools and services that simplify the development and deployment of full-stack cloud-powered web and mobile applications. The user initiates the workflow by interacting with a chatbot integrated into a web application developed using AWS Amplify.
2. **User authentication and authorization with Amazon Cognito**: Amazon Cognito is a robust user identity management service provided by AWS. When the user interacts with the chatbot, AWS communicates with Amazon Cognito to perform user authentication and authorization. Amazon Cognito supports various authentication methods, including traditional username/

password combinations, social identity providers (for example, Google or Facebook), and multi-factor authentication. It also provides features for user registration, account recovery, and secure storage of user data.

3. **API Gateway as a centralized entry point**: Once the user has been authenticated and authorized, their request is routed through an API gateway, which acts as a centralized entry point for APIs. API Gateway is a fully managed service that simplifies the process of creating, publishing, maintaining, monitoring, and securing APIs.
4. **Text generation with AWS Lambda and Amazon Bedrock LLMs**: For text generation, API Gateway sends the request (`/text`) to an AWS Lambda function that performs invocation calls to Amazon Bedrock LLMs:

    I. This Lambda function will take the user's input or prompt and pass it to Amazon Bedrock LLMs to generate relevant and coherent text. For example, the user can ask to generate an email or prepare a travel itinerary for a particular destination.

    II. Once the Amazon Bedrock LLMs have generated the requested text, the Lambda function receives the response and sends it back to the user through API Gateway. Here, API Gateway acts as an intermediary, facilitating the communication between the client (that is, the chatbot) and the backend services (Lambda functions and Amazon Bedrock LLMs).

5. **Text summarization with AWS Lambda and Amazon Bedrock LLMs**: For text summarization, API Gateway sends a separate request (`/summarize`) to another AWS Lambda function specifically designed to perform invocation calls to Amazon Bedrock LLMs for summarization tasks:

    I. This Lambda function performs invocation calls to Amazon Bedrock LLMs to summarize text based on the user's input or prompt and the provided context (small or large files).

    II. After the Amazon Bedrock LLM has generated the summarized text, the Lambda function receives the response and sends it back to the user via API Gateway.

By separating the text generation and summarization tasks into different Lambda functions and API Gateway routes, the application can efficiently handle different types of requests and leverage the specialized capabilities of Amazon Bedrock LLMs for each task.

This workflow highlights the flexibility and modular nature of AWS services, allowing multiple components to be integrated to build complex applications. AWS Lambda functions act as computational engines that make invocation calls to Amazon Bedrock LLMs to perform text generation and summarization.

By breaking down the application into smaller, independent components, developers can easily maintain, update, and scale individual parts of the system without affecting the entire application.

If you're curious about trying out the serverless chatbot with Amazon Bedrock, check out `https://github.com/aws-samples/amazon-serverless-chatbot-using-bedrock`.

At this point, you should understand and be able to implement text generation and summarization with Amazon Bedrock in real-world use cases.

Summary

In this chapter, we dived into the architecture patterns for generating and summarizing text using Amazon Bedrock. The first part of this chapter covered text generation. We looked at the fundamentals of text generation through prompt engineering techniques, in-line context training, and orchestration with LangChain. Then, we explored various use cases and patterns for text generation that you can apply to real-world scenarios.

The second part of this chapter covered text summarization. We discussed both extractive and abstractive summarization approaches and their respective applications. Furthermore, we examined the systems and techniques that can be employed for text summarization using Amazon Bedrock.

In the next chapter, we will explore building question-answering and conversational interfaces.

7

Building Question Answering Systems and Conversational Interfaces

In this chapter, we will delve into the realm of **question answering** (**QA**) and conversational interfaces, harnessing the power of Amazon Bedrock. The chapter begins with unveiling real-world use cases of QA with Amazon Bedrock, demonstrating the practical applications and benefits of this technology. Moving forward, the chapter will cover architectural patterns for QA on both small and large documents, providing a solid foundation to understand the underlying mechanics. Additionally, the concept of conversation memory will be explained, allowing for the storage and utilization of chat history, thereby enabling more contextually aware and coherent conversations.

The chapter will also dive into the concept of embeddings and their significance within the architectural flow of QA systems. Furthermore, we will learn about prompt engineering techniques for chatbots, equipping you with the skills to craft effective prompts and enhance the performance of their conversational interfaces. Contextual awareness will also be addressed, explaining how to develop chatbots that can seamlessly integrate and leverage external files and data sources.

Finally, we will conclude by exploring real-world use cases of conversational interfaces, showcasing the diverse applications and potential impact of this technology across various domains.

The key topics that will be covered in this chapter include the following:

- QA overview
- Document ingestion with Amazon Bedrock
- Conversational interfaces

Technical requirements

This chapter requires you to have access to an AWS account. If you don't have it already, you can go to `https://aws.amazon.com/getting-started/` and create an AWS account.

Secondly, you will need to install and configure the AWS CLI (`https://aws.amazon.com/cli/`) after you create an account, which will be needed to access Amazon Bedrock FMs from your local machine. Since a major chunk of the code cells we will execute is based in Python, setting up the AWS SDK for Python (Boto3) (`https://docs.aws.amazon.com/bedrock/latest/APIReference/welcome.html`) will be beneficial at this point. You can carry out the Python setup in the following ways – install it on your local machine, use AWS Cloud9, utilize AWS Lambda, or leverage Amazon SageMaker.

> **Note**
> There is a charge associated with the invocation and customization of the FMs of Amazon Bedrock. Refer to `https://aws.amazon.com/bedrock/pricing/` to learn more.

QA overview

QA systems are designed to understand natural language queries and provide relevant answers based on a given context or knowledge source. These systems leverage advanced NLP techniques and machine learning models to comprehend the intent behind a user's question, extracting the most appropriate response from the available information.

Let's consider an example scenario of a typical QA system: suppose you are a content writer for a technology company and you need to explain the concept of **optical character recognition** (**OCR**) to your audience. A QA system could assist you in this task by providing relevant information from its knowledge base, or by analyzing a given text corpus related to OCR.

Here's how a QA system might handle a query such as `What is optical character recognition used for?`:

- **Query understanding**: The system first analyzes the query to understand the user's intent and extract key entities and concepts. In this case, it recognizes that the query asks about the use cases or applications of optical character recognition.
- **Context retrieval**: The system then searches its knowledge base or the provided text corpus to find relevant information related to OCR and its applications. It may identify passages or paragraphs that discuss OCR's purpose and practical uses.

- **Answer extraction**: After retrieving the relevant context, the system employs advanced NLP techniques, such as named entity recognition, relation extraction, and semantic analysis, to identify the most relevant information that directly answers the query. It may extract specific use cases or applications of OCR from the text.
- **Answer generation**: Finally, the system composes a concise and natural-sounding answer based on the extracted information. For example, it might respond with something like the following:

```
"Optical character recognition (OCR) is used to convert text in
images, scanned documents, or handwritten text into machine-readable
and editable text format. It has several applications, including:
Digitizing printed documents, books, and archives for easier storage
and search.
Extracting text from images or photographs for indexing or further
processing.
Automating data entry tasks by extracting information from forms,
invoices, or receipts.
Enabling text-to-speech capabilities for visually impaired users.
Facilitating translation of text between languages by first converting
it to editable format."
```

The system may also provide additional context, examples, or relevant information to enhance the user's understanding of the topic.

Theoretically speaking, all of this looks perfect and straightforward. However, let's ponder over some challenges in this situation.

Since these QA systems are designed to automatically generate responses to inquiries by analyzing and extracting relevant information from a provided set of data or text sources, they may or may not explicitly contain the complete answer to the given query. In order words, a system's ability to infer and combine disparate pieces of information from various contexts is crucial, as the complete answer may not be readily available in a single, self-contained statement within the provided data.

QA poses a significant challenge, as it necessitates models to develop a deep comprehension of the semantic meaning and intent behind a query, rather than merely relying on superficial keyword matching or pattern recognition. This elevated level of language understanding is crucial for accurately identifying the relevant information required to formulate a suitable response, even when the exact phrasing or terminology differs between the query and the available context.

Overcoming these hurdles is essential for developing intelligent systems that can engage in fluid dialogue, provide accurate information, and enhance user experiences across a wide range of domains and applications.

At the time of writing, tons of generative AI use cases have spawned in a short period. Enterprises are scaling their conversational interfaces – chatbots and QA systems – with the goal of reducing manual labor and replacing existing frameworks with automated generative AI systems.

One of the most promising applications of LLMs and generative AI technology is, in fact, QA. Being able to ask natural language questions and receive accurate, relevant answers could transform how we interact with information and computers.

Potential QA applications

The applications for a robust QA system are far-reaching across many industries and domains:

- **Customer service**: Allow customers to ask questions and receive tailored help and troubleshooting in a natural language rather than search documentation
- **Research and analytics**: Allow analysts and researchers to ask open-ended exploratory questions to discover insights across large datasets
- **Education**: Create intelligent tutoring systems where students can ask follow-up questions and receive explanations at their level
- **Knowledge management**: Make an organization's data, documentation, and processes more accessible by allowing natural language queries

Of course, as with any generative AI system, there are concerns around factual accuracy, safety, and potential misuse that must be carefully addressed as QA systems are developed and deployed.

Nonetheless, the ability to break down barriers between humans and information through natural language queries represents a key frontier in AI's advancement. With FMs available on Amazon Bedrock, such QA systems powered by LLMs provide an exciting glimpse at that future.

QA systems with Amazon Bedrock

Enterprise-grade QA systems are usually built on the foundation of cutting-edge NLP techniques, including transformer architectures and transfer learning. They should be designed to understand the nuances of human language, enabling it to comprehend complex queries and extract relevant information from various data sources.

One of the key advantages of Amazon Bedrock is its ability to handle open-ended questions that require reasoning and inference. Unlike traditional QA systems that rely on predefined rules or patterns, Bedrock can understand the underlying context and provide thoughtful responses based on the information it has learned.

With a plethora of FMs available on Amazon Bedrock, developers, data scientists or generative AI enthusiasts can build applications or services that can potentially excel at dealing with ambiguity and uncertainty. If the available information is incomplete or contradictory, these engaging applications can provide responses that reflect their level of certainty, or they can request additional information, making the interaction more natural and human-like.

Moreover, Amazon Bedrock is highly scalable and can be easily integrated into various applications and platforms, such as chatbots, virtual assistants, and knowledge management systems. Its cloud-based architecture and high availability nature ensure that it can handle high volumes of queries and adapt to changing data and user requirements.

QA without context

In scenarios where no additional context or supporting documents are provided, QA systems must rely solely on their pre-trained knowledge to generate responses. This type of open-domain **QA without context** presents several key challenges compared to scenarios where context is given. Some of these challenges are as follows:

- **Knowledge scope and completeness**: When no context is provided, the QA system's knowledge comes entirely from what was present in its training data. This makes the scope and completeness of the training data extremely important. Ideally, the training data should cover a wide range of topics with factual accuracy. However, training datasets can have gaps, biases, or errors, which then get encoded into the model's knowledge.
- **Querying the right knowledge**: Without context to ground the question, the QA system must accurately map the question to the relevant areas of knowledge in its parameters. This requires strong natural language understanding capabilities to correctly interpret the query, identify key entities/relations, and retrieve the appropriate factual knowledge to formulate a response.
- **Hallucination**: A critical challenge is hallucination – when the model generates incorrect information that contradicts its training data. Without grounding context, there are fewer constraints on what a model may generate. Hallucinations can range from subtle mistakes to completely fabricated outputs presented with high confidence.

Prompt examples and templates for QA without context

When an LLM is asked a question without any additional context, it can be difficult for the LLM to understand the question and generate an accurate answer. It can be like providing them with a puzzle with missing pieces. Prompt engineering helps us provide the missing pieces, making it easier for LLMs to understand our questions and deliver accurate answers.

Thus, careful prompt engineering is required to steer generation in the right direction and encourage well-calibrated, truthful responses. There are three main techniques for prompt engineering in QA without context:

- **Query reformulation**: This involves rephrasing the initial question to better match the model's knowledge. For example, instead of asking `What is the capital of France?`, you could ask `What city is the capital of France?`. Let's take another example. Instead of asking `What caused the extinction of dinosaurs?` (a broad question), the reformulated prompt would look like `What is the most widely accepted theory for the extinction of dinosaurs?` (which focuses on a specific aspect).

- **Model priming**: This involves providing instructions in the prompt to better communicate the desired output format. For example, you could prompt the LLM to provide a short answer, a list of possible answers, or a paragraph of text. For example, instead of asking `What are the Great Lakes?`, you could ask `Provide a list of the five Great Lakes of North America` (which specifies a desired answer format).
- **Attribution calibration**: This involves encouraging models to estimate and communicate their confidence level in their answers. This can help users to better understand the reliability of the information that the LLM provides. Say that you simply ask `Who wrote Hamlet?` This seems like a straightforward question, but the LLM might be unsure whether it's referring to the authorship of the original play or a modern adaptation. Instead, you could ask the model with attribution calibration in a certain manner, such as `Can you tell me definitively who wrote the original play Hamlet? Based on my understanding of literature, I am very likely (or less certainly) correct in my answer`. This version of the prompt offers a range of confidence levels (`very likely` or `less certain`) instead of just `confident` or `unsure`. This allows the LLM to express a more nuanced level of certainty based on the information it has processed.
- In addition to the preceding techniques, you should leverage system prompts in order to shape the interpretation and response of LLMs when queried by the end users. Think of system prompts as carefully crafted instructions that are meant to guide the model's behavior, directing it toward the desired outcome.
- For instance, when crafting prompts for role-playing scenarios, system prompts can define the personality traits, communication style, and domain knowledge the AI should exhibit. Imagine you're creating a virtual assistant. Through system prompts, you can specify a helpful, informative persona, ensuring that the FM uses language and knowledge appropriate for the role.
- Additionally, system prompts can help maintain consistency in the model's responses, especially during prolonged interactions. By outlining the persona and desired tone throughout the prompts, you ensure that the model stays true to its character, fostering trust and a more natural user experience.
- For an example of system prompts with the Anthropic Claude model, we encourage you to peruse through `https://promptengineering.org/claudes-system-prompt-a-prompt-engineering-case-study/`. You should always keep in mind that the best prompts will depend on the specific question and the capabilities of the LLM you use. Experiment with different phrasing and templates to find what works best for your needs.
- By using prompt engineering, it is always possible to improve the accuracy and reliability of LLMs on QA tasks without context.

Simple question prompts

One of the most straightforward ways to prompt a generative model is to pose a direct question, formatted within triple quotes in the case of a multiline comprehensive prompt within the code. Let's experiment with an example in the Amazon Bedrock chat playground.

In order to execute run simple QA prompts in Amazon Bedrock playground, let's head back to the AWS console and navigate to the Amazon Bedrock landing page. Once you reach the landing page, scroll through the left pane and click on the **Chat** option under **Playgrounds**.

Select a particular model in the chat playground by navigating to **Select Model**. In our example, let's select the **Jurassic-2 Ultra** FM and initiate the conversation with the following example in *Figure 7.1*.

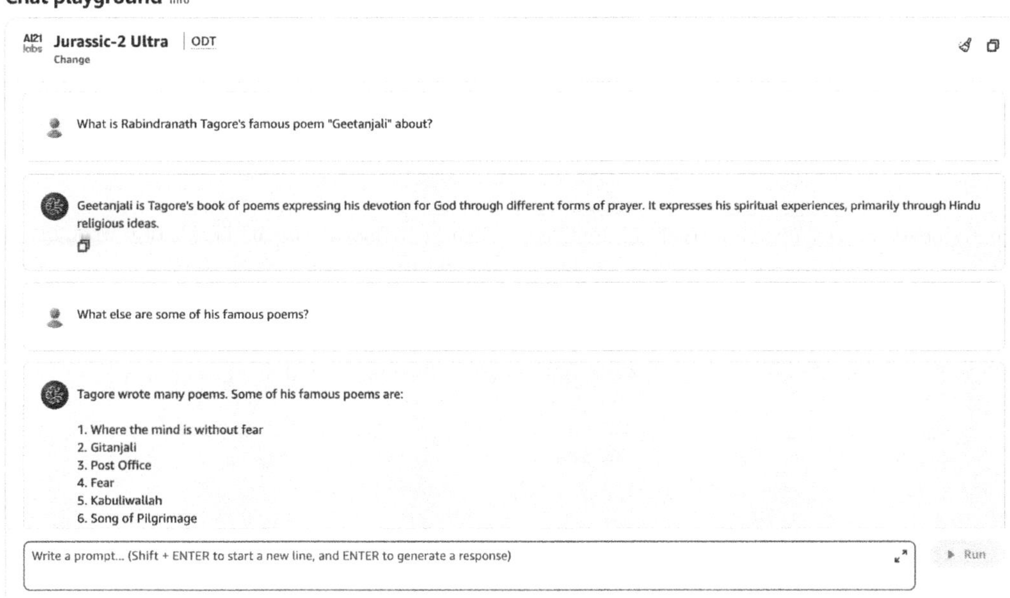

Figure 7.1 – A simple prompt with Amazon Bedrock models in the chat playground

As depicted in the preceding example, a simple prompt such as `What is Rabindranath Tagore's famous poem "Geetanjali" about?` was used without any context provided to the model. In order to further the chat with the model, a follow-up question was also asked, `What else are some of his famous poems?`, to which the model provided a decent response. (You can run this sample prompt in your Bedrock playground with other models and continue the conversation chain to witness any differences in the responses.)

You can also leverage **Compare mode** in **Chat Playground** by toggling the slider at the right side of the **Chat Playground** window, as shown in *Figure 7.2*, and execute a similar prompt against multiple FMs available on Amazon Bedrock. As visible in the following figure, three models are compared on a particular question. Note the third model was added by clicking on the + option on the right side.

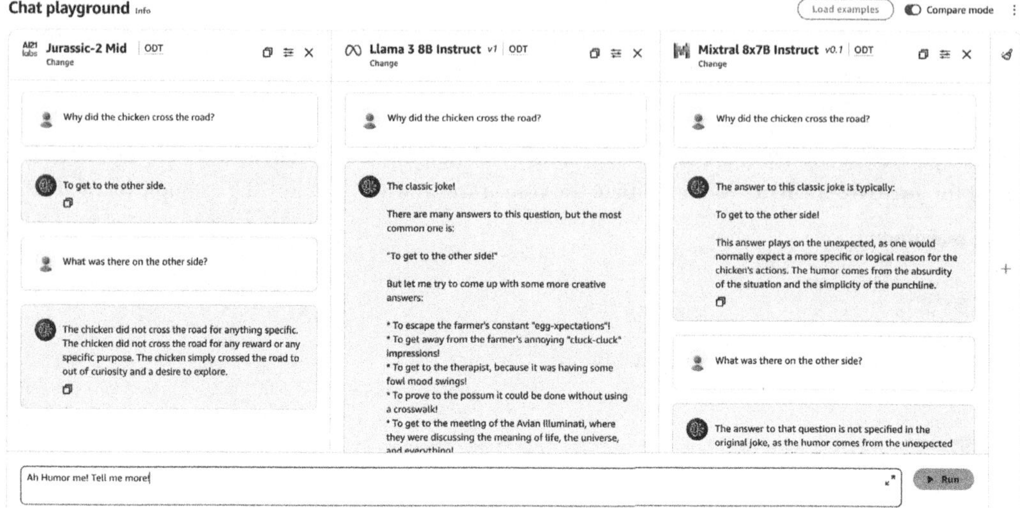

Figure 7.2 – Simple QA prompting with Compare Mode in Amazon Bedrock

Similarly, by using Amazon Bedrock APIs, the models can be prompted in a QA context:

```
prompt = """You are an expert AI assistant. You will answer questions
in a succinct manner. If you are unsure about the
answer, say 'I am not sure about this answer'

Question: How can I connect my old Samsung TV with my Mac laptop?
Answer:"""
parameters = {
    "maxTokenCount":1024,
    "temperature":0.1,
    "topP":0.8,
    "stopSequences":[]
    }
```

Using the preceding prompt, the FM available in Amazon Bedrock can be invoked; the model can then provide a particular response. You are encouraged to run this prompt with the Amazon Titan model and capture the response as an exercise.

Model encouragement and constraints

Optionally, you can encourage the model by framing the prompt in a motivational way. By combining model encouragement and constraints, you can create more effective prompts that guide the LLMs to generate high-quality responses.

Here are some examples:

- Providing context and specific keywords can encourage the model to generate more accurate responses
- Setting length and format constraints can help the model generate responses that are concise and structured
- Restricting the model to a specific domain or topic can help it generate responses that are more accurate and relevant

A prompt example can be formatted in the following order:

```
You are an expert in explaining complex scientific concepts in a
clear and engaging manner. Your ability to break down intricate
topics into understandable terms makes you an invaluable resource
for educational purposes.
```

```
Constraints: Assume your audience consists of college students or
professionals with a basic understanding of computer science and
physics. Your explanation should be accessible yet informative,
covering both theoretical and practical aspects of quantum computing.
```

This is followed by the question:

```
Could you please provide a comprehensive overview of quantum computing,
including its principles, potential applications, and the challenges
it faces?
```

Figure 7.3 illustrates the sample usage of model encouragement, along with constraints to invoke the Meta Llama model on Amazon Bedrock's chat playground.

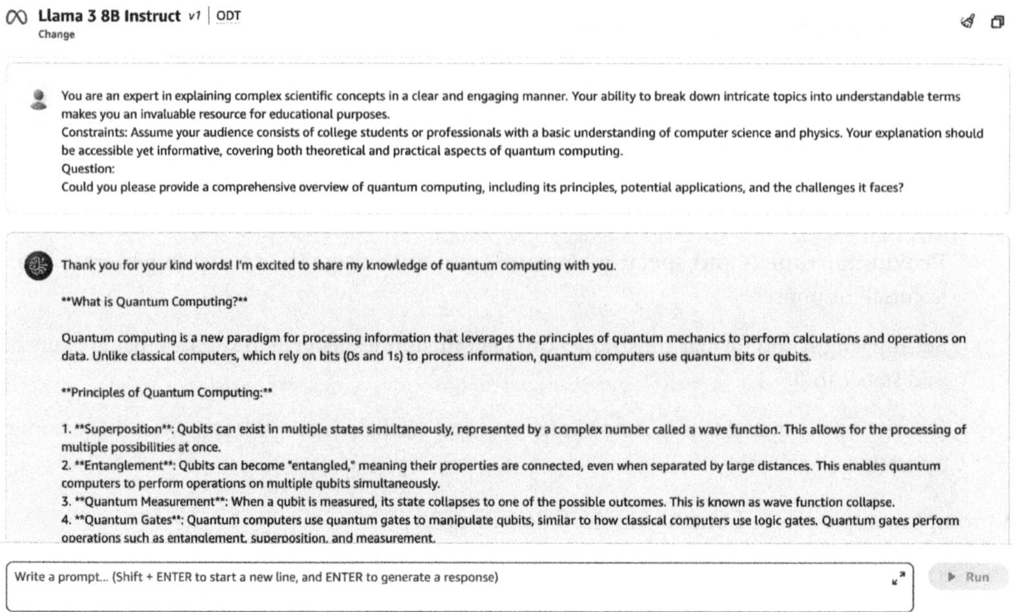

Figure 7.3 – A simple prompt example of using model encouragement and constraints on the Meta Llama 3 model in Amazon Bedrock's chat playground

You are encouraged to execute the prompt at your end and note the difference in responses with/without the constraints and model encouragement. You will notice that this type of prompt can help prime the model to provide a thoughtful, thorough response.

Here is another example for you to execute, either in Amazon Bedrock's chat playground or by using Amazon Bedrock APIs to invoke the model:

```
You have an excellent grasp of complex machine learning concepts and can explain them in a clear and understandable way.

Could you please explain the concept of gradient descent in machine learning?

Please keep your explanation concise and suitable for readers with a basic understanding of machine learning.
```

Let's say you invoke an FM with a hypothetical question without any relevant context. In some cases, it may end up hallucinating. *Figure 7.4* illustrates a fascinating scenario where the model ends up hallucinating when queried about an imaginary BMX Subaru bike, which doesn't really exist in real life!

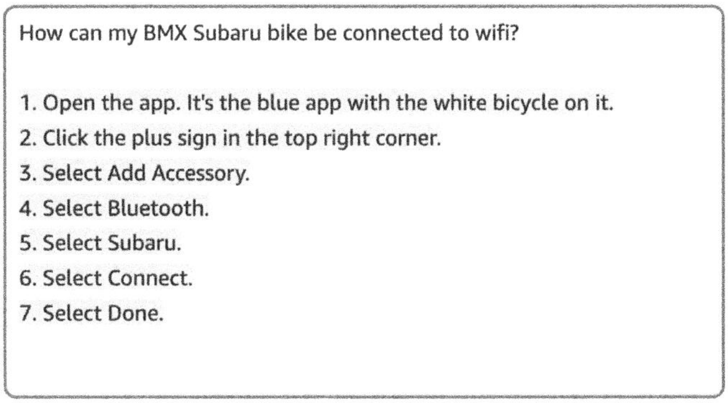

How can my BMX Subaru bike be connected to wifi?

1. Open the app. It's the blue app with the white bicycle on it.
2. Click the plus sign in the top right corner.
3. Select Add Accessory.
4. Select Bluetooth.
5. Select Subaru.
6. Select Connect.
7. Select Done.

Figure 7.4 – A QA prompt sample without context in Amazon Bedrock's chat playground

If proper prompt instructions are provided with context, the model will strive to find the relevant content within the context and then provide a reasonable desirable response.

Keep in mind that while QA without context is extremely challenging, strategies such as constitutional AI and iterative refinement techniques that leverage and re-combine the model's internal knowledge in novel ways can help improve performance on open-domain QA.

> Note
>
> **Constitutional AI** is an area of AI research concerned with developing AI systems that adhere to ethical principles and legal frameworks. It can involve designing AI systems that are fair, transparent, and accountable and respect human rights and privacy.

QA with context

QA with context involves providing an input text and a question, and the language model must generate an answer based solely on the information contained within the given text. This task requires the model to comprehend the context, identify relevant details, and synthesize a coherent response that directly addresses the query while avoiding introducing external information.

For this use case, it is beneficial to structure the prompt by presenting the input text first, followed by the question. This ordering allows the model to fully process the context before attempting to formulate an answer, potentially improving response quality and accuracy. As indicated in the previous section, incorporating techniques such as model encouragement can further enhance performance on QA tasks.

The ideal prompt will have the following structure:

```
input_text: {{text}}

question: {{question}}

answer:
```

Now, let's see what the content of the prompt would be like:

Input_text:

`"""The Arctic fox (Vulpes lagopus) is a small fox native to the Arctic regions of the Northern Hemisphere and common throughout the Arctic tundra biome. It is well adapted to living in cold environments, with dense fur insulation and a compact body shape that limits exposure to the cold. Adults weigh 3-5 kg (6.6-11 lb) and have a body length of 46-68 cm (18-27 in). Their thick fur is an insulating blanket that keeps them warm even in the depths of an Arctic winter. The Arctic fox has a deep, thick underfur that insulates it from the cold and a dense, insulating guard hair coat on top."""`

Question: `What are some key adaptations that allow the Arctic fox to survive in cold Arctic environments?`

Example output:

```
"The Arctic fox has several key adaptations that allow it to survive
in the cold Arctic environments:
1. Dense fur insulation to keep it warm.
2. A compact body shape that limits exposure to the cold.
3. A thick underfur that insulates it from the cold.
4. A dense, insulating guard hair coat on top.
These physical adaptations, such as thick fur coats and compact
body shape, enable the Arctic fox to withstand the extreme cold
temperatures of the Arctic tundra region."
```

The preceding example prompt showcases a scenario where an answer about the Arctic fox's physical adaptations to cold environments is provided, and the question prompts the model to identify and summarize the relevant details from the text.

Next, let's walk through an example prompt of QA with context using Amazon Bedrock APIs:

```
# Import the respective libraries
import boto3
import botocore
import os
import json
import sys

#create bedrock runtime client
bedrock_runtime = boto3.client('bedrock-runtime')

#Provide the model paramters
```

```
model_parameters = {
      "maxTokenCount":1024,
      "temperature":0,
      "stopSequences":[],
      "topP":0.9
      }

#Provide relevant context to the model
context= """Using your Apple Watch to locate a misplaced iPhone is a
handy feature that can save you a lot of time and frustration. The
process typically begins by opening the Control Center on your watch
by swiping up from the bottom of the watch face. From there, you'll
see an icon that looks like a ringing iPhone - tapping this will
remotely activate a loud pinging sound on your iPhone, even if it's
on silent mode. If you're within earshot, simply follow the sound to
track down your missing device. Alternatively, you can use the FindMy
app on your Apple Watch, which provides a map showing the last known
location of your iPhone. Tap the "Devices" tab, select your iPhone,
and it will display its location, as well as give you the option to
force it to emit a sound to aid in your search. For an even quicker
option, you can simply raise your wrist and ask Siri "Hey Siri, find
my iPhone," and the virtual assistant will attempt to pinpoint the
location of your iPhone and provide directions. However, for any of
these methods to work, your iPhone must be powered on, connected to
a cellular or WiFi network, and have the Find My feature enabled in
Settings under your Apple ID. As long as those criteria are met,
your Apple Watch can be a powerful tool for tracking down a wandering
iPhone."""

#Take the entire context/excerpt provided above and augment to the
model along with the input question

question = "How can I find my iPhone from my Apple watch in case I
lose my phone?"
prompt_data = f""" Answer the user's question solely only on the
information provided between <></> XML tags. Think step by step and
provide detailed instructions.
<context>
{context}
</context>

Question: {question}
Answer:"""
#Now, you can Invoke the foundation model using boto3 to generate the
output response.

body = json.dumps({"inputText": prompt_data, "textGenerationConfig":
model_parameters})
accept = "application/json"
```

```
contentType = "application/json"

# You can change this modelID to use an alternate version from the
model provider
modelId = "amazon.titan-tg1-large"

response = bedrock_runtime.invoke_model(
    body=body, modelId=modelId, accept=accept,
contentType=contentType)

generated_response_body = json.loads(response.get("body").read())
print(generated_response_body.get("results")[0].get("outputText").
strip())
```

Run the preceding code, and try to invoke the Amazon Bedrock FM on your own to test the results. The generated output may look akin to *Figure 7.5*:

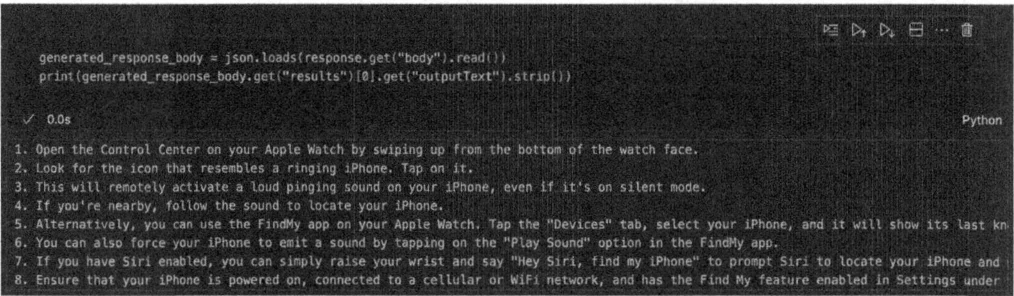

Figure 7.5 – Example output generated from an Amazon Bedrock FM

After executing the code to invoke the model, you will observe that the model can generate an appropriate response in most cases by leveraging the information provided as context.

Now that we have covered prompt engineering with QA use cases on Bedrock, let's walk through document ingestion frameworks with Amazon Bedrock.

Document ingestion with Amazon Bedrock

The architectural pattern for QA systems with context can be broadly divided into two categories – *QA on small documents* and *QA on large documents on knowledge bases*. While the core components remain similar, the approach and techniques employed may vary, depending on the size and complexity of the input data.

QA on small documents

For QA systems designed to handle small documents, such as paragraphs or short articles, the architectural pattern typically follows a pipeline approach consisting of the following stages:

1. **Query processing**: The natural language query is preprocessed by converting it to a vector representation.
2. **Document retrieval**: Relevant documents or passages are retrieved from the corpus based on the query keywords or semantic similarity measures. For smaller documents, retrieval can be straightforward; you can directly embed and index the entire document or passage within your vector store. In another scenario, since the input documents are smaller in nature, there might not be a need to split them into smaller chunks as long as they can fit within the token size limit of the model. Once inspected, the document can be directly parsed in context within the model prompt template.
3. **Passage ranking**: Once retrieved, the passages are ranked by their relevance to the query. This ranking can be done using techniques such as **term frequency-inverse document frequency (TF-IDF)** semantic similarity, or specialized neural ranking models. Automation of passage ranking can be made possible using an orchestrator or type or vector database. For instance, Amazon Kendra has a SOTA semantic searching mechanism built in to perform relevance ranking.
4. **Answer extraction**: The top-ranked passages are analyzed to identify the most relevant spans or phrases that potentially answer the query. This stage often involves techniques such as named entity recognition, coreference resolution, and QA models. Hence, in the case of generative AI frameworks, relevant context extraction can be performed by these LLMs without the need to explicitly invoke complicated techniques.
5. **Answer scoring and ranking**: The extracted answer candidates are scored and ranked based on their confidence or relevance to the query, using techniques such as answer verification models or scoring functions. There are some re-ranking models, such as Cohere Rerank, that can also be leveraged to improve recall performance.
6. **Answer generation**: The top-ranked answer is generated, potentially involving post-processing steps such as formatting, rephrasing, or generating natural language responses.

This pipeline approach is well-suited for QA on small documents, as it allows for efficient retrieval and ranking of relevant passages, followed by targeted answer extraction and scoring, without the need to split the document into chunks or process it in a different way.

Let's walk through an example of small document ingestion with Amazon Bedrock.

For small document ingestion with Amazon Bedrock and LangChain, you can use the **TextLoader** or **PDFLoader** to load the documents directly into memory. In LangChain, `TextLoader` and `PDFLoader` are actually *Python* classes, not software components. Here's a brief explanation:

- `TextLoader` and `PDFLoader` are used to load and parse text and PDF documents, respectively.
- These classes are part of LangChain's document loader functionality, which helps in preparing documents for further processing in AI applications.

Here's an example with TextLoader.

> **Note**
>
> As shown in the previous chapters, ensure that the necessary libraries for LangChain are installed along with Chroma DB. We are using Chroma DB only for example purposes. You can leverage other vector databases, such as Chroma, Weaviate, Pinecone, and Faiss, based on their use case. If Chroma DB is not installed, execute `!pip install chromadb` before running the following code.

```
from langchain.document_loaders import TextLoader
from langchain.text_splitter import CharacterTextSplitter
from langchain.vectorstores import Chroma

# Load the document
loader = TextLoader('path/to/document.txt')
documents = loader.load()

# Split the documents into chunks
text_splitter = CharacterTextSplitter(chunk_size=1000, chunk_
overlap=200)
texts = text_splitter.split_documents(documents)

# Create embeddings and store in Chroma vector store
from langchain_community.embeddings import BedrockEmbeddings
embeddings = BedrockEmbeddings()
db = Chroma.from_documents(texts, embeddings)
```

QA for large documents on knowledge bases

When dealing with large documents on knowledge bases, the architectural pattern may need to be adapted to handle the scale and complexity of the data. A common approach is to incorporate techniques from information retrieval and open-domain QA systems. The following steps highlight the process of ingesting large documents, creating a vector index, and creating an end-to-end QA pipeline:

1. **Knowledge base construction**: The large corpus or knowledge base is preprocessed, indexed, and structured in a way that facilitates efficient retrieval and querying.

2. **Query processing**: Similar to the small document case, the natural language query is preprocessed by converting it to a vector representation.
3. **Document or passage retrieval**:
   - **Chunking**: For larger documents, directly embedding the entire document might not be ideal. You should consider chunking the document into smaller, more manageable segments such as paragraphs or sentences.
   - **Small-to-big retrieval**: In this case, the following process is followed:
     i. Embed and search using smaller chunks during retrieval.
     ii. Identify relevant chunks based on their retrieved scores.
     iii. Use the retrieved chunk IDs to access and provide the corresponding larger document segment to the LLM for answer generation. This way, the LLM has access to the broader context, while retrieval leverages smaller, more focused units.
   - **Efficiency**: Chunking and *small-to-big* retrieval can help improve efficiency by reducing the computational load of embedding and searching massive documents.
4. **Passage re-ranking**: The retrieved passages or knowledge base entries may undergo further reranking or filtering based on their relevance to the query, using techniques such as neural re-rankers or semantic similarity measures.
5. **Answer extraction and generation**: Depending on the nature of the query and the knowledge base, answer extraction and generation may involve techniques such as multi-hop reasoning, knowledge graph traversal, or generating natural language responses from structured data.
6. **Answer scoring and ranking**: Similar to the small document case, the extracted answer candidates are scored and ranked based on their confidence factor or relevance to the query.
7. **Answer presentation**: The final answer or set of answers is presented to the user, potentially involving formatting, summarization, or generating natural language explanations.
8. **Additional points worth considering**:
   - **Adaptive retrieval limits**: Depending on the complexity of the query and document collection, setting an adaptive limit on the number of retrieved documents can optimize performance.
   - **Compression**: Techniques such as summarization or information extraction can pre-process large documents to condense information without losing context, further aiding the LLM during answer generation.

This approach is particularly useful for QA systems operating on large, diverse, and potentially unstructured knowledge bases, as it leverages information retrieval techniques to efficiently retrieve and rank relevant information before answer extraction and generation.

For large document ingestion, it is recommended to use Amazon Bedrock's knowledge bases to handle the ingestion workflow and store the embeddings in a vector database, as detailed in *Chapter 5*.

Regardless of the document size, modern QA systems tend to incorporate advanced techniques, such as transformer-based language models, graph neural networks, and multi-task learning. Additionally, techniques such as transfer learning, few-shot learning, and domain adaptation are commonly employed to adapt QA models to different domains or knowledge bases.

It's important to note that the specific implementation details and techniques employed may vary depending on the requirements, constraints, and resources available for a particular QA system. The architectural pattern serves as a general framework, providing a solid foundation to understand the underlying mechanics and guide the design and development of QA systems tailored to different use cases and domains.

QA implementation patterns with Amazon Bedrock

In this section, we will explore different patterns pertaining to QA. First, we will look at how to ask queries to a model directly. Thereafter, another approach using RAG will be covered wherein we will add contextual information. Let us begin!

The baseline approach: unbound exploration in the realm of knowledge

In this initial pattern, we embark on a journey where questions are posed directly to the model, unencumbered by external constraints. The responses we receive are rooted in the model's foundational knowledge. However, as you clearly understand by now, this approach presents a formidable challenge – the outputs are broad and generic, devoid of the nuances and specifics that define a customer's unique business landscape. *Figure 7.6* depicts the journey of said user when interacting with Amazon Bedrock and using direct prompts, with small documents within the prompt to invoke the model.

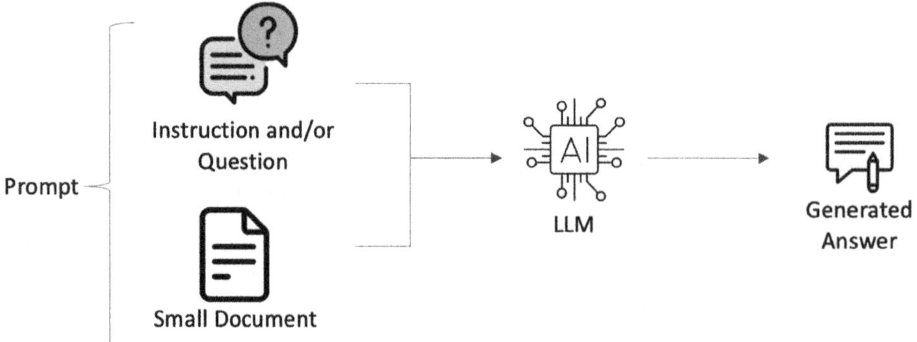

Figure 7.6 – Prompting the Bedrock LLM for QA generation with direct input prompts

Note that we covered this approach in detail when we illustrated how to leverage the Amazon Bedrock Titan model to provide informative responses to user queries, as showcased in the *QA with context* section

As shown previously, the example demonstrated how the Bedrock Titan model can generate responses without any contextual information provided. Subsequently, we manually incorporated context into the model's input to enhance the quality of its responses. It's important to note that this approach does not involve any RAG to incorporate external knowledge into the model's output.

While this straightforward approach can work well for short documents or singleton applications, it may not scale effectively for enterprise-level QA scenarios. In such cases, where large volumes of enterprise documents need to be considered, the entire context may not fit within the prompt sent to the model, necessitating more advanced techniques.

The RAG approach: contextual illumination

In this second pattern, we will embark on a more refined journey, one that harnesses the power of RAG. Here, we artfully weave our questions with relevant contextual information, creating a tapestry that is more likely to contain the answers or insights that we seek. This approach is analogous to entering the library with a well-curated reading list, guiding us toward the shelves that hold the knowledge we desire.

However, even in this enhanced approach, a limitation persists – the amount of contextual information we can incorporate is bound by the context window imposed by the model. It's akin to carrying a finite number of books in our metaphorical backpack, forcing us to carefully curate the contextual information we bring along, lest we exceed the weight limit and leave behind potentially crucial insights.

As you learned in *Chapter 5*, RAG combines the use of embeddings to index the corpus of documents, building a knowledge base, and the use of an LLM to perform the embeddings, with the goal of eventually extracting relevant information from a subset of documents within this knowledge base. In preparation for RAG, the documents comprising the knowledge base are split into chunks of a fixed or variable size. These chunks are then passed through the model to obtain their respective embedding vectors. Each embedding vector, along with its corresponding document chunk and additional metadata, is stored in a vector database, optimized for efficient similarity searches between vectors.

Figure 7.7 illustrates a RAG-based workflow using Amazon Bedrock in the context of a QA generation framework.

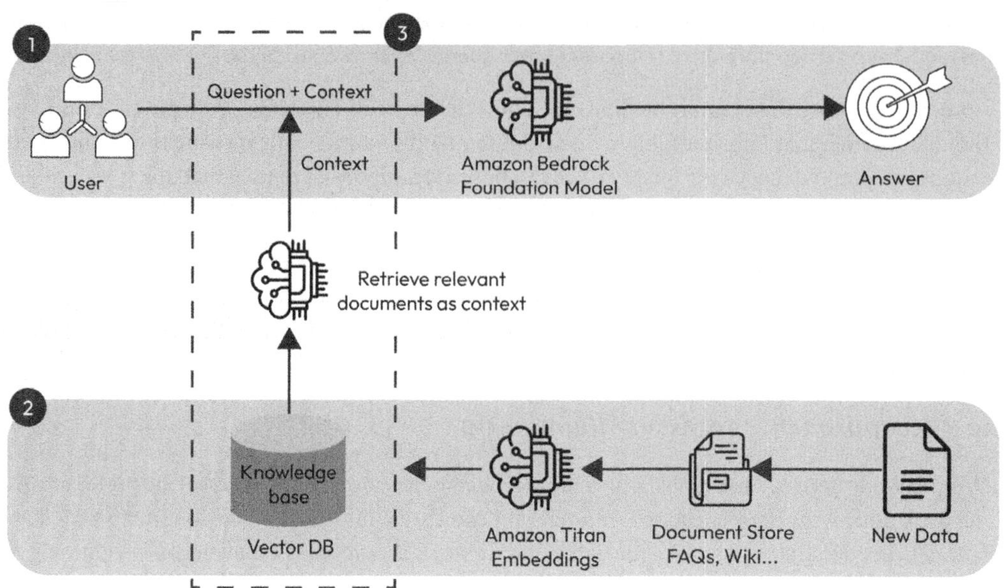

Figure 7.7 – QA with Amazon Bedrock using the RAG approach

By leveraging this RAG approach, we can tap into a vast repository of contextual information, allowing our generative AI models to produce more informed and accurate outputs. However, we must remain mindful of the token limitations and carefully curate the contextual information we incorporate. Doing so would ensure that we strike a balance between the breadth and depth of the domain knowledge (being parsed to the model to provide a response instead of the model hallucinating), while staying within the model's constraints.

In this approach, we will build upon the code discussed in the previous section on small document ingestion. However, you will find differentiating snippets in the code – specifically around identifying a similarity with the query from the source data and leveraging the pertinent information, augmented for the prompt in order to invoke the LLM:

```
#importing the respective libraries
from langchain.document_loaders import TextLoader
from langchain.text_splitter import CharacterTextSplitter
from langchain.vectorstores import Chroma
!pip install chromadb
Import boto3
Import botocore

#Create client side Amazon Bedrock connection with Boto3 library
region = os.environ.get("AWS_REGION")
bedrock_runtime = boto3.client(
```

```
    service_name='bedrock-runtime',
    region_name=region,
)

# Load the document
loader = TextLoader('path/to/document.txt')
documents = loader.load()

# Split the documents into chunks
text_splitter = CharacterTextSplitter(chunk_size=1000, chunk_
overlap=200)
texts = text_splitter.split_documents(documents)

# Create embeddings and store in Chroma vector store
from langchain_community.embeddings import BedrockEmbeddings
embeddings = BedrockEmbeddings(client=boto3_bedrock, model_id="amazon.
titan-embed-text-v1")

db = Chroma.from_documents(texts, embeddings)

# Enter a user query
query = "Enter your query here"

#Perform Similarity search by finding relevant information from the
embedded data

retriever = db.similarity_search(query, k=3)
full_context = '\n'.join([f'Document {indexing+1}: ' + i.page_content
for indexing, i in enumerate(retriever)])

print(full_context)

#Since we have the relevant documents identified within "full_
context", we can use the LLM to generate an optimal answer based on
the retreived documents. Prior to that, let us format our prompt
template before feeding to the LLM.

prompt_template = f"""Answer the user's question solely only on the
information provided between <></> XML tags. Think step by step and
provide detailed instructions.
<context>
{full_context}
</context>

Question: {query}
Answer:"""
```

```
PROMPT = PromptTemplate.from_template(prompt_template)

#Prompt data input creation to feed to the LLM
prompt_data_input = PROMPT.format(human_input=query, context=context_
string)
#Now, you can Invoke the foundation model using boto3 to generate the
output response.

body = json.dumps({"inputText": prompt_data_input,
"textGenerationConfig": model_parameters})
accept = "application/json"
contentType = "application/json"

# You can change this modelID to use an alternate version from the
model provider
modelId = "amazon.titan-tg1-large"

response = bedrock_runtime.invoke_model(
    body=body, modelId=modelId, accept=accept,
contentType=contentType)

generated_response_body = json.loads(response.get("body").read())
print(generated_response_body.get("results")[0].get("outputText").
strip())
```

Executing this code will give you an understanding of aptly structuring the prompt template and invoking the model to generate a desirable response.

You are further encouraged to execute the code on different documents and experiment with different vector DBs and FMs to gain a deeper understanding of this approach.

Users should target finding relevant documents to provide accurate answers to their queries. Two of the key challenges that users experience when working on their generative AI use cases may include the following:

- Managing large documents that exceed the token limit
- Identifying the most relevant documents for a given question

To tackle these challenges, the RAG approach proposes the following strategy:

- **Document preparation and embeddings**: Before answering questions, the documents must be processed and stored in a document store index, as shown in the *Document ingestion with Amazon Bedrock* section. The steps involved include the following:

    I. Load the documents.

    II. Process and split them into smaller, manageable chunks.

III. Create numerical vector representations (embeddings) of each chunk using the Amazon Bedrock Titan Embeddings model or alternate embeddings models.

IV. Create an index using the chunks and their corresponding embeddings.

- **Question handling**: Once the document index is prepared, users can ask questions, and relevant document chunks will be fetched based on the query. The following steps will be executed:

I. Create an embedding of the input question.

II. Compare the question embedding with the embeddings in the index.

III. Fetch the *Top K* relevant document chunks.

IV. Add those chunks as part of the context in the prompt.

V. Send the prompt to the Amazon Bedrock FM.

VI. Receive a contextual answer based on the retrieved documents.

By following this approach within the code, we can leverage the power of generative AI, embeddings, and vector datastores to provide accurate and context-aware responses to user queries, even when dealing with large document sets.

Now that we have uncovered QA answering systems in detail, it's time to uncover the realm of its derivative – aka conversational interfaces.

Conversational interfaces

Conversational interfaces, such as virtual assistants or chatbots, have found widespread application across various domains, including customer service, sales, and e-commerce, offering swift and efficient responses to users. They can be accessed through diverse channels, such as websites, messaging applications, and social media platforms, thereby ensuring a seamless user experience.

Chatbot using Amazon Bedrock

In the realm of generative AI, Amazon Bedrock provides a robust platform for developing and deploying chatbots. *Figure 7.8* highlights the overall conversational flow inculcated with Amazon Bedrock with chat history integration. The flow involves the following steps:

1. A given user asks a particular question via the interface to the appropriate Bedrock LLM.
2. The model stores the conversational history to a particular database, say DynamoDB. The chat history and the question are appended to form an augmented prompt. The conversational history is stored in a database, such as DynamoDB. This history, along with the current user query, is used to create an augmented prompt. This augmented prompt is then used to inform the generative AI model, which improves the chatbot's responses in future interactions. By incorporating the conversational history, the chatbot can avoid prompting the user with questions they have already been asked. This fosters a more natural and engaging conversation.

3. The augmented prompt is retrieved to get the relevant response from the LLM.
4. The conversation continues in the form of feedback, wherein the output generated is then fed back in the form of a conversation chain to continue the ongoing interaction with the user.

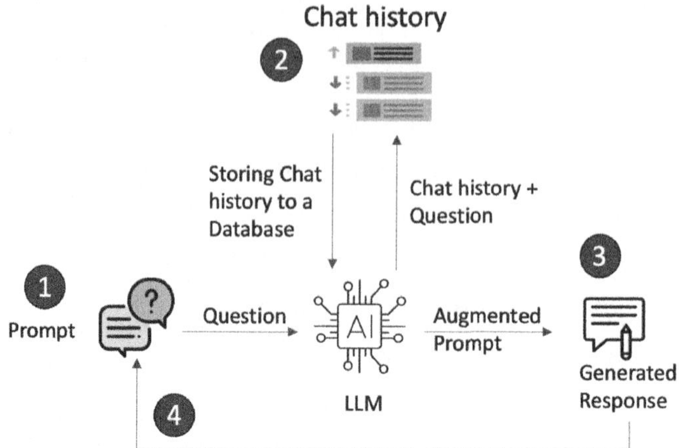

Figure 7.8 – A conversational flow with Amazon Bedrock

The use cases for chatbots built on Amazon Bedrock are diverse and versatile, catering to a wide range of scenarios:

- **Basic chatbot – zero shot**: This use case involves the development of a basic chatbot that leverages a pre-trained FM to engage in conversational interactions without any additional context or prompting. For instance, the following prompt can be provided:

```
You are a friendly and helpful conversational AI assistant. You should
engage in natural language conversations on a wide range of topics,
answering questions to the best of your knowledge and abilities. If
you are unsure about something, you can respond politely that you don't
have enough information about that particular topic. Your main goal is
to provide useful information to users in a conversational manner. You
do not need any additional context or examples to start conversing.
```

- **Prompt-based chatbot (LangChain)**: In this scenario, the chatbot is designed to operate within a specific context defined by a prompt template. Leveraging the LangChain library, developers can create chatbots that can engage in contextualized conversations, providing relevant and tailored responses. For instance, the following code snippet showcases how Langchain can be used with a prompt template and engage with the user in a conversational chain:

```
from langchain import PromptTemplate, LLMChain
from langchain_community.llms import Bedrock
```

```
# Define the prompt template
template = """You are a helpful travel assistant. You will be
provided with information about a user's travel plans, and your
task is to provide relevant suggestions and recommendations
based on their preferences and requirements.
Travel Details: {travel_details}
Using the information provided, suggest some activities,
attractions, restaurants, or any other recommendations that
would enhance the user's travel experience. Provide your
response in a conversational and friendly tone."""

# Create the prompt template object
prompt = PromptTemplate(template=template, input_
variables=["travel_details"])
```

Now, users can create the LLM chain and provide a sample prompt, such as the following one, and invoke the model accordingly:

```
# Sample user input
user_travel_details = """I'm planning a 5-day trip to Paris with
my family (two adults and two children, ages 8 and 12). We're
interested in exploring the city's history, architecture, and
cultural attractions. We also enjoy trying local cuisine and
engaging in family-friendly activities."""
```

- **A persona-driven chatbot**: This use case involves the creation of chatbots with well-defined personas or roles. For instance, a career coach chatbot can be developed to engage in dialogues with users, offering guidance and advice on career-related matters, while maintaining a consistent persona throughout the interaction. For example, a chatbot can be used as a teaching assistant, providing students with information and answering their questions. The chatbot can be designed to match the personality of a teacher, or it can take on a more playful persona to make learning more engaging. Yet another scenario can involve a persona-driven chatbot in a customer service or healthcare sector. Specifically, a chatbot in healthcare can be used to provide patients with information about their health conditions or to answer questions about medications. The chatbot can be designed to be empathetic and understanding, and it can use language that is easy for patients to understand.
- **Context-aware chatbot**: In this advanced use case, the chatbot is designed to understand and respond based on contextual information provided through external files. By generating embeddings from these files, the chatbot can comprehend and incorporate the provided context into its responses, delivering highly relevant and context-specific interactions. For instance, the examples provided in *Chapter 5* on RAG highlight a context-aware Chatbot use case, where a prompt is provided with the context extracted from ingested documents/external files to augment the prompt with the matched context.

These use cases demonstrate the versatility and power of chatbots built on Amazon Bedrock, enabling developers to create conversational interfaces tailored to diverse user needs and scenarios.

Empowering chatbot development with Amazon Bedrock and the LangChain framework

In the realm of conversational interfaces, such as chatbots, maintaining context and retaining memory across interactions is paramount. This is true not only for short-term exchanges but also for long-term conversations, where the ability to recall and build upon previous interactions is crucial.

As discussed in the previous section on QA systems in greater detail (in addition to *Chapter 5*), LangChain provides memory components in two distinct forms to address this need. First, it offers a suite of helper utilities designed to manage and manipulate previous chat messages. These utilities are modular and highly versatile, enabling their integration into various workflows and applications.

Secondly, LangChain streamlines the process of incorporating these memory utilities into chains, which are fundamental building blocks to create complex conversational systems. By leveraging LangChain's abstractions and easy-to-use interfaces, developers can effortlessly define and interact with different types of memory components, enabling the creation of sophisticated and context-aware chatbots.

Whether you're building a simple QA bot or a complex, multi-turn conversational agent, LangChain's memory management capabilities, combined with its integration with Amazon Bedrock, empower you to craft intelligent and engaging chatbot experiences.

Crafting context-aware conversational interfaces – the fundamental pillars

As detailed in the *QA systems with Amazon Bedrock* section, the cornerstone of developing a context-aware chatbot lies in the generation of contextual embeddings. As you are aware by now, this initial phase entails an ingestion process that feeds your data through an embedding model, wherein these embeddings are then meticulously stored in a specialized data structure, often referred to as a vector store, facilitating efficient retrieval and manipulation.

Figure 7.9 depicts a process where documents or files are taken as input, processed, or transformed, and then converted into embeddings that are stored in a vector store.

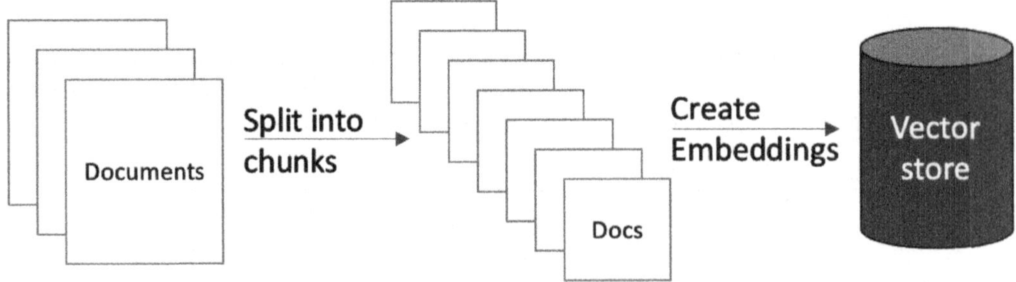

Figure 7.9 – Chunking large documents and storing embeddings in a vector store

Identical to QA system implementation patterns with Bedrock, the second critical component in the orchestration of user interactions can be defined as the **request handling mechanism**. This intricate process involves receiving user input, interpreting the intent and context, invoking the appropriate models or services, and synthesizing the relevant responses. It acts as the central hub, choreographing the various components to deliver a seamless and contextually relevant conversational experience. In our scenario, this form or orchestrator or request handling hub can be executed with Langchain or Amazon Bedrock agents. *Figure 7.10* illustrates the QA conversational interface workflow to retrieve a relevant response from the chunked documents, by extracting the desired information from the vector store.

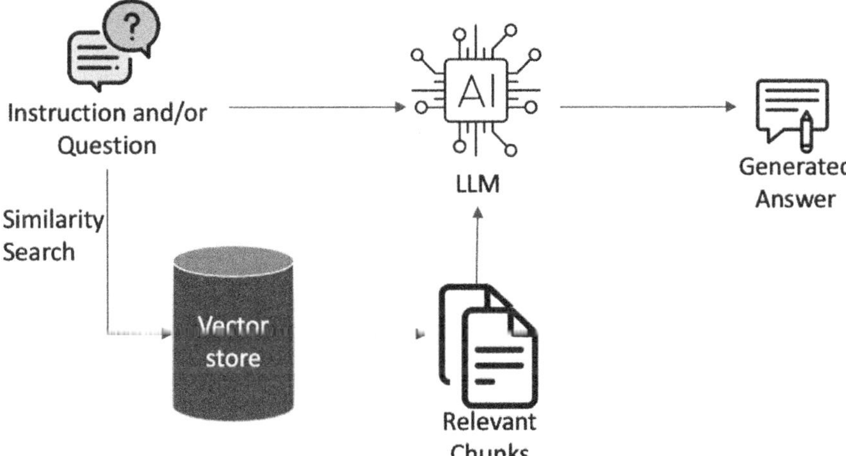

Figure 7.10 – A QA conversational workflow with a similarity search and chunking the relevant information

Within this request handling phase, the system leverages the previously generated embeddings, employing sophisticated algorithms to identify the most pertinent information from the vector store. This contextual retrieval enables the chatbot to provide responses that are tailored to the specific conversational thread, accounting for the user's intents, previous utterances, and the overarching conversational context.

Now, let's dive into a context-aware architectural workflow in the case of conversational interfaces.

A context-aware chatbot architectural flow

The process flow for this architecture (also depicted in *Figure 7.11*) is as follows:

1. Initially, the contextual documents are transformed into numerical embeddings using a powerful embeddings model, such as Amazon's Titan Embeddings model. These embeddings are stored in a specialized vector database for efficient retrieval.
2. The user's query is encoded into a numerical representation using an embeddings model, enabling the system to understand its semantic meaning.

3. The user's query embeddings and the chat history are fed into an FM, specifically the text embeddings model, which searches the vector database for the most relevant contextual information.
4. The vector database returns the contextual embeddings that best match the query, allowing the LLM to generate a response that incorporates the relevant context.

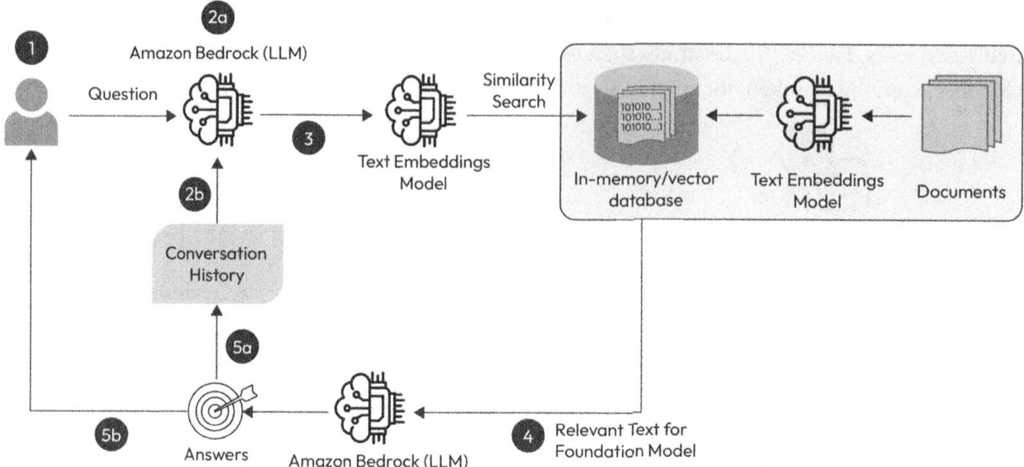

Figure 7.11 – A conversational architectural flow for context-aware chatbots

The code for this architectural flow using Amazon Titan is available at `https://github.com/aws-samples/amazon-bedrock-workshop/blob/main/06_OpenSource_examples/02_Langchain_Chatbot_examples/00_Chatbot_Titan.ipynb`.

Additional examples with different FMs from Anthropic, AI21 Labs, and Meta are also available on the Amazon Bedrock samples page at the same link. More examples will continue to be added to Amazon Bedrock GitHub Samples over time for users to experiment and leverage for their enterprise use cases.

Furthermore, information on building a contextual chatbot application using Knowledge Bases with Amazon bedrock can be found here: `https://aws.amazon.com/blogs/machine-learning/build-a-contextual-chatbot-application-using-knowledge-bases-for-amazon-bedrock/`.

We also encourage you to read about a well-defined QA bot built on an AWS solution, expanding your horizon of possibilities to build an enterprise-level conversational chatbot: `https://aws.amazon.com/blogs/machine-learning/deploy-generative-ai-self-service-question-answering-using-the-qnabot-on-aws-solution-powered-by-amazon-lex-with-amazon-kendra-and-amazon-bedrock/`.

In the realm of generative AI, QA patterns and conversational interfaces represent the ever-evolving journey of knowledge acquisition and dissemination. As we navigate these paths, we continually seek innovative ways to refine our queries, augment our context, and push the boundaries of what is possible, all in the pursuit of unlocking the treasure trove of knowledge that lies within these remarkable models.

As enterprises continue to embrace generative AI and seek more intelligent and automated solutions, Amazon Bedrock stands out as a powerful tool to build advanced QA systems that can enhance customer experiences, streamline operations, and unlock new possibilities in human-computer interactions.

Summary

In this chapter, we explored architectural intricacies and key components that power modern QA interfaces and chatbots. We gained insights into prompt engineering techniques that facilitate natural and engaging conversations. We further illustrated how QA systems and conversational systems can be designed seamlessly with Amazon Bedrock, highlighting the architectural workflow for these patterns.

In the next chapter, we will uncover more potential use cases and applications of generative AI with Amazon Bedrock. We will gain a deeper understanding of entity extraction and code generation using Amazon Bedrock and its potential real-world use cases.

8

Extracting Entities and Generating Code with Amazon Bedrock

This chapter uncovers the realm of entity extraction, a crucial technique in NLP. We will explore the intricacies of entity extraction applications, providing a comprehensive understanding of implementing entity extraction using Amazon Bedrock. Through real-world use cases, you will gain insights into the practical applications of entity extraction across various domains.

Furthermore, the chapter will guide you through the exciting world of generative AI for code generation. We will investigate the underlying principles and methodologies that enable AI systems to generate code snippets, functions, and even entire applications. You will learn how to leverage Amazon Bedrock to streamline your development workflows and enhance productivity.

By mastering these techniques, you will be equipped with the knowledge and skills to tackle complex NLP tasks and harness the power of generative AI in your coding endeavors.

The following topics will be covered in detail:

- Entity extraction – a comprehensive exploration
- Industrial use cases of entity extraction – unleashing the power of unstructured data
- Entity extraction with Amazon Bedrock
- Code generation with LLMs – unleashing the power of AI-driven development

Technical requirements

This chapter requires you to have access to an AWS account. If you don't have one already, you can go to `https://aws.amazon.com/getting-started/` and create an AWS account.

Secondly, you will need to install and configure the AWS CLI from `https://aws.amazon.com/cli/` after you create an account, which will be needed to access Amazon Bedrock FMs from your local machine. Since the majority of the code cells we will be executing are based on Python, setting up an AWS Python SDK (Boto3) at `https://docs.aws.amazon.com/bedrock/latest/APIReference/welcome.html` would be beneficial at this point. You can carry out the Python setup in the following manner: install it on your local machine, use AWS Cloud9 or AWS Lambda, or leverage Amazon SageMaker.

> **Note**
>
> There will be a charge associated with the invocation and customization of Amazon Bedrock FMs. Please refer to `https://aws.amazon.com/bedrock/pricing/` to learn more.

Entity extraction – a comprehensive exploration

In the era of big data and information overload, the ability to extract meaningful insights from unstructured text data has become increasingly valuable. **Entity extraction**, a subfield of NLP, plays a pivotal role in this endeavor by identifying and classifying named entities within text, such as people, organizations, locations, and more. This process not only facilitates information retrieval and knowledge management but also enables a wide range of applications, including **question-answering**, sentiment analysis, and **decision support systems** (**DSSs**).

The journey of entity extraction began with simple pattern-matching and rule-based systems, which relied heavily on manually crafted rules and lexicons. These methods, while useful, lacked scalability and robustness when dealing with diverse and complex datasets.

Hence, traditionally, entity extraction has been a challenging task, requiring extensive manual effort and domain-specific knowledge. However, the advent of generative AI, particularly LLMs, has revolutionized this field, offering more accurate, scalable, and efficient solutions. In this chapter, we will explore the various techniques employed by LLMs on Amazon Bedrock for entity extraction, diving into their underlying architectures, strengths, and limitations.

Deep learning approaches

The advent of machine learning introduced statistical models that leveraged feature engineering. These models, including **hidden Markov models** (**HMMs**) and **conditional random fields** (**CRFs**), represented a significant step forward. They utilized hand-crafted features and probabilistic frameworks to improve extraction accuracy. However, their performance was still limited by the quality and comprehensiveness of the features engineered by experts.

Neural networks marked a paradigm shift in entity extraction by automating feature learning and capturing intricate patterns within the data. Early applications of neural networks, such as **recurrent NNs** (**RNNs**) and **long short-term memory networks** (**LSTMs**), demonstrated the potential of deep learning in handling sequential data and extracting entities with greater accuracy.

While models such as BERT and its successors represent a significant leap in NLP, our focus will remain on models and techniques that align with the practical applications and tools used in Bedrock. We will explore some deep learning approaches and models that have proven effective in various scenarios and are relevant to our framework.

Transformer-based models

Transformer architectures, introduced by the seminal paper *Attention is All You Need* (*Vaswani et al., 2017*: `https://arxiv.org/abs/1706.03762`), have become the backbone of many SOTA LLMs for entity extraction. These models employ self-attention mechanisms to capture long-range dependencies within the input text, enabling them to better understand the context and relationships between entities.

BERT, developed by Google AI, is a prominent example of a transformer-based model that has achieved exceptional results in various NLP tasks, including entity extraction. It is a bidirectional model, meaning it can process text in both directions simultaneously, allowing it to capture contextual information more effectively than its predecessors.

Sequence labeling and CRFs

Entity extraction can be framed as a sequence labeling problem, where each token in the input text is assigned a label indicating its entity type (for example, person, organization, location) or a non-entity label. LLMs can be trained to perform this task by leveraging techniques such as CRFs or the more recent **bidirectional LSTM with CRF** (**BiLSTM-CRF**) architecture.

CRFs are probabilistic graphical models that can effectively capture the dependencies between labels in a sequence, making them well suited for entity extraction tasks. They model the conditional probability of label sequences given the input text, allowing for the incorporation of rich features and contextual information.

BiLSTM-CRF models combine the strengths of BiLSTMs for capturing long-range dependencies and CRFs for sequence labeling. This hybrid approach has shown impressive performance in entity extraction, particularly in scenarios where entities may span multiple tokens or have complex structures.

Rule-based systems

While deep learning approaches have gained significant traction in recent years, rule-based systems remain valuable tools in the entity extraction domain. These systems rely on manually crafted rules and patterns to identify and classify entities within text, leveraging domain-specific knowledge and expert insights. These rules can be augmented to the prompt template when invoking Amazon Bedrock in order to generate a desirable response from the FMs. For example, in a medical application, the rule-based component might identify drug names, dosages, and patient information using predefined patterns.

Regular expressions and pattern matching

Regular expressions and **pattern-matching** techniques are fundamental building blocks of rule-based entity extraction systems. These methods allow for the definition of patterns that can match and extract specific entity types, such as phone numbers, email addresses, or specific named entities (for example, company names and product names).

While regular expressions can be effective for well-defined and structured entity types, they may struggle with more complex or ambiguous entities that require contextual understanding. Nevertheless, they remain valuable tools, particularly in combination with other techniques or as a preprocessing step for more advanced methods. Here are some examples:

- **Ruleset**: Define rules using regular expressions and pattern matching to identify specific entities such as drug names, dosages, and patient information
- **Example rules**:
  - Drug names can be identified using a dictionary of known drug names
  - Dosages can be extracted using patterns such as `\d+mg` (for example, `500mg`)
  - Patient information can be identified through patterns such as `Patient: [A-Za-z]+`

Gazetteer lists and dictionaries

Gazetteer lists and **dictionaries** are curated collections of known entities, often organized by entity type or domain. These resources can be used to match and extract entities within text by performing lookups against predefined lists.

For example, a gazetteer of geographic locations can be employed to identify and extract mentions of cities, countries, or other places in a given text. Similarly, dictionaries of person names or organization names can ease the extraction of these entity types.

While gazetteer lists and dictionaries can be highly accurate for the entities they cover, they may struggle with ambiguity, variations, or newly emerging entities not present in the predefined lists. Additionally, maintaining and updating these resources can be a labor-intensive process, especially in rapidly evolving domains.

Hybrid approaches

In practice, many entity extraction systems employ a combination of deep learning and rule-based techniques, leveraging the strengths of both approaches to achieve optimal performance. These hybrid approaches aim to strike a balance between the flexibility and generalization capabilities of deep learning models and the precision and interpretability of rule-based systems.

Ensemble methods

Ensemble methods involve combining the outputs of multiple entity extraction models, potentially using different architectures or techniques, to improve overall performance. This approach can leverage the strengths of individual models while mitigating their weaknesses, resulting in more robust and accurate entity extraction.

For example, an ensemble system might combine the predictions of a transformer-based model such as BERT with those of a rule-based system or a gazetteer lookup. The outputs of these models can be combined using various strategies, such as majority voting, weighted averaging, or more sophisticated ensemble learning techniques.

Hybrid architectures

Hybrid architectures integrate deep learning and rule-based components within a single model, allowing for the seamless integration of both approaches. These architectures often involve a deep learning component for learning representations and capturing contextual information, combined with rule-based components for incorporating domain-specific knowledge or handling well-defined entity types.

One example of a hybrid architecture is the use of LLMs for entity representation learning, followed by a rule-based component for entity classification or extraction. The LLM component can learn rich representations of the input text, capturing contextual information and long-range dependencies, while the rule-based component can leverage expert knowledge and precise patterns for entity identification and classification. For instance, consider an application designed to extract financial information from corporate earnings reports. Here's a detailed example of how a hybrid architecture can be implemented:

- **LLM for initial text processing**: FMs available on Amazon Bedrock can process the entire earnings report, generating detailed representations of text segments. They capture the context and nuances of financial terminology, ensuring a deep understanding of phrases such as `revenue`, `net income`, and `operating expenses`.
- **Ruleset**: Develop a set of rules tailored to financial documents. For instance, rules might include the following:
    - Identifying dollar amounts following keywords such as `revenue`, `net income`, or `expenses`.
    - Extracting dates and fiscal periods using regular expressions.
    - Recognizing company-specific terminology and abbreviations.

The rule-based system analyzes the LLM-generated representations, applying these rules to accurately extract specific financial entities.

Let's now look at how the representations are integrated and optimized:

- **Pipeline**: The system processes the earnings report through the LLM, which outputs rich text representations. These representations are then fed into the rule-based component.
- **Output**: The final output includes precisely extracted financial entities, such as revenue figures, net income amounts, and fiscal periods, all verified and categorized according to the predefined rules.

By employing such a hybrid approach on Amazon Bedrock, the application leverages the comprehensive text understanding provided by LLMs and the precision and reliability of rule-based extraction methods. This approach ensures that entity extraction is more accurate and contextually aware, making it useful for complex domains such as financial analysis.

In order to gain a deeper understanding of hybrid LLM frameworks, readers are encouraged to read these papers: *Hybrid LLM-Rule-based Approaches to Business Insights Generation from Structured Data* (`https://arxiv.org/pdf/2404.15604`) and *An innovative hybrid approach for extracting named entities from unstructured text data* (`https://www.researchgate.net/publication/332676137_An_innovative_hybrid_approach_for_extracting_named_entities_from_unstructured_text_data`).

In this section, we covered different approaches (deep learning, rule-based, and hybrid approaches) associated with entity extraction. Now that we have a basic understanding of these approaches, let us dive into some industrial use cases of entity extraction.

Industrial use cases of entity extraction – unleashing the power of unstructured data

Entity extraction has numerous applications across various domains, ranging from information retrieval and knowledge management to DSSs and **business intelligence** (**BI**). In this section, we will explore some practical use cases and applications of entity extraction with GenAI:

- **Knowledge graph construction**: Knowledge graphs are structured representations of entities and their relationships, enabling efficient storage, retrieval, and reasoning over vast amounts of information. Entity extraction plays a crucial role in the construction of knowledge graphs by identifying and classifying entities from unstructured text data, which can then be used to populate the graph's nodes and edges. For instance, let us use the following :
    - **Text**: `Google was founded by Larry Page and Sergey Brin while they were Ph.D. students at Stanford University.`

With entity extraction, the following information can be extracted:

- **Entities identified**:
    - `Google (Organization)`
    - `Larry Page (Person)`
    - `Sergey Brin (Person)`
    - `Stanford University (Organization)`

- **Role in knowledge graph construction**: These identified entities are classified and used to populate nodes within the knowledge graph. The relationships between the entities, such as `founded by` (`Google` -> `Larry Page and Sergey Brin`) and `studied at` (`Larry Page and Sergey Brin` -> `Stanford University`), are established as edges connecting the nodes. This structured representation allows for efficient querying and reasoning over the information.
- **Resulting knowledge graph snippet**:
    - **Nodes**:
        - `Google (Organization)`
        - `Larry Page (Person)`
        - `Sergey Brin (Person)`
        - `Stanford University (Organization)`
    - **Edges**:
        - `Google -> Founded by -> Larry Page`
        - `Google -> Founded by -> Sergey Brin`
        - `Larry Page -> Studied at -> Stanford University`
        - `Sergey Brin -> Studied at -> Stanford University`

LLMs on Amazon Bedrock can be employed for accurate and scalable entity extraction, facilitating the creation of comprehensive knowledge graphs from diverse data sources, such as news articles, scientific publications, or social media posts. These knowledge graphs can power various applications, including question answering systems, recommendation engines, and decision support tools. Here are some examples:

- **Biomedical and scientific literature analysis**: Entity extraction is particularly valuable in the biomedical and scientific domains, where vast amounts of unstructured text data are generated through research publications, clinical notes, and other sources. Identifying and classifying entities such as genes, proteins, diseases, and chemical compounds can enable researchers and healthcare professionals to quickly navigate and extract insights from this wealth of information.

LLMs in Amazon Bedrock can be fine-tuned on domain-specific datasets to achieve high accuracy in extracting biomedical and scientific entities. These models can assist in literature review processes, drug discovery pipelines, and the development of knowledge bases for precision medicine and personalized healthcare.

- **BI and competitive analysis**: In the business world, entity extraction can be leveraged for competitive analysis, market research, and BI applications. By extracting entities such as company names, product names, and industry-specific terms from news articles, social media posts, and other online sources, businesses can gain valuable insights into their competitors, market trends, and customer sentiment.

  Amazon Bedrock APIs can be coupled with **BI platforms** (**BIPs**) and analytics tools, enabling real-time entity extraction and analysis of vast amounts of unstructured data. This can empower data-driven decision-making, strategic planning, and the identification of new business opportunities.

- **Social media monitoring and sentiment analysis**: Social media platforms generate a constant stream of user-generated content, containing valuable information about public opinion, trends, and sentiment toward various entities, such as brands, products, or public figures. Entity extraction plays a crucial role in social media monitoring and sentiment analysis by identifying the relevant entities within this unstructured data.

LLMs in Amazon Bedrock can be employed to accurately extract entities from social media posts, enabling sentiment analysis and opinion mining around these entities. This can provide businesses with valuable insights into customer feedback, brand perception, and potential issues or opportunities, allowing them to respond proactively and shape their marketing and communication strategies accordingly.

In this section, we covered industrial applications applicable in the context of entity extraction. Keep in mind that the number of these use cases can increase exponentially as we uncover more diverse scenarios across different industries. Now, let us learn how to leverage Amazon Bedrock for entity extraction use cases.

Entity extraction with Amazon Bedrock

At its core, entity extraction with GenAI involves providing a prompt that instructs the model to identify and classify relevant entities within a given text input. The key is constructing prompts that are clear, consistent, and provide enough examples for the model to understand the desired behavior.

The Amazon Bedrock service, with the ability to invoke LLMs in a serverless manner, provides a scalable and cost-effective solution for entity extraction. This service allows developers to leverage pre-trained models or fine-tune them on custom datasets, enabling tailored entity extraction for specific domains or use cases.

Structuring prompts for entity extraction

When designing prompts for entity extraction tasks, it's essential to provide clear instructions and examples to the model. A well-structured prompt typically includes the following components:

- **Task description**: Begin by explicitly stating the task at hand, such as `Identify and classify the following entities in the given text.`
- **Entity types**: Provide a list of entity types the model should recognize, such as `Person`, `Organization`, `Location`, and so on.
- **Example inputs and outputs**: Include one or more examples of input text with the corresponding entities annotated. This helps the model understand the desired output format and learn from real-world instances.

The following is an example prompt:

```
'''
Task: Identify and classify the following entities in the given text:

Entity Types: Person, Organization, Location

Input Text: "Michael Jordan, the legendary basketball player for
the Chicago Bulls, announced his retirement from the NBA after an
illustrious career."

The output looks like this:

  [Person: Michael Jordan], [Organization: Chicago Bulls], [Location:
  NBA]

Let's look at another example:

Input Text: "Apple Inc., the tech giant based in Cupertino, California,
unveiled its latest iPhone model at a press event."

The output looks like this:

  [Organization: Apple Inc.], [Location: Cupertino], [Location:
  California]

'''
```

Let's explore these use cases through a code example and generate an output by invoking an Anthropic Claude 3 Sonnet FM on Amazon Bedrock.

> **Note**
>
> Please ensure that you have the required libraries, such as `boto3`, installed to run the code. If not, please install the library using the `pip install boto3` command in your editor.
>
> Additionally, ensure that you have enabled access to the models available on Amazon Bedrock. For further documentation on model access on Bedrock, please visit `https://docs.aws.amazon.com/bedrock/latest/userguide/model-access.html`.

```
# Import the respective libraries
import boto3
import botocore
import os
import json
import sys

#Create client-side Amazon Bedrock connection with Boto3 library
region = os.environ.get("AWS_REGION")
bedrock_runtime = boto3.client(service_name='bedrock-runtime',region_
name=region)

prompt_data = """
Human: You are a helpful AI assistant. If you are unsure about the
answer, say I do not know. Skip the preamble.
Task: Identify and classify the following entities in the given text:
Entity Types: Person, Organization, Location

Input Text: "Michael Jordan, the legendary basketball player for
the Chicago Bulls, announced his retirement from the NBA after an
illustrious career."

Assistant:
"""
messages=[{ "role":'user', "content":[{'type':'text','text': prompt_
data}] }]

body=json.dumps(
        {
            "anthropic_version": "bedrock-2023-05-31",
            «max_tokens»: 512,
            «messages»: messages,
            «temperature»: 0.1,
            "top_p": 1
        }
    )
```

```
response = bedrock_runtime.invoke_model(body=body, modelId="anthropic.
claude-3-sonnet-20240229-v1:0")
response_body = json.loads(response.get('body').read())

print(response_body['content'][0].get("text"))
```

Here's a sample output from the FM:

```
print(response_body['content'][0].get("text"))

Person: Michael Jordan
Organization: Chicago Bulls, NBA
Location: -
```

Figure 8.1 – Sample output

While this basic structure works for simple cases, more advanced prompting techniques are needed for robust, production-level entity extraction.

Incorporating context and domain knowledge

Entity extraction scenarios often benefit from contextual information and domain-specific knowledge. By providing relevant background or domain-specific details within the prompt, you can enhance the model's understanding and improve its ability to accurately identify entities.

Here's an example prompt with context:

```
Task: Identify and classify entities related to sports in the given
text.

Entity Types: Athlete, Team, Tournament, Sport

Context: This text discusses sports events, teams, and athletes
involved in various sports competitions.

Input Text: "Serena Williams, a well renowned Tennis player, defeated
Venus Williams to win 23rd Grand Slam title at the 2017 Australian
Open."

The output looks like this:

  [Athlete: Serena Williams], [Athlete: Venus Williams], [Tournament:
  Grand Slam], [Tournament: Australian Open], [Sport: tennis]
```

In *Figure 8.2*, the code sample for the preceding use case is depicted. It's important to note that the code does not explicitly mention the installed libraries. It is assumed that users have already pre-installed the required Python packages and libraries, as detailed in the previous code sample:

```
#Create client side Amazon Bedrock connection with Boto3 library
region = os.environ.get("AWS_REGION")
bedrock_runtime = boto3.client(service_name='bedrock-runtime',region_name=region)

#Provide the model paramters
model_parameters = {
    "anthropic_version": "bedrock-2023-05-31",
    "max_tokens_to_sample":1024,
    "temperature":0}


prompt_data = """
Human: You are a helpful AI assistant. If you are unsure about the answer, say I do not know. Skip the preamble.
Task: Identify and classify entities related to sports in the given text.
Entity Types: Athlete, Team, Tournament, Sport

Context: This text discusses sports events, teams, and athletes involved in various sports competitions.

Input Text: "Serena Williams, a well renowned Tennis player, defeated Venus Williams to win 23rd Grand Slam title at the 2017 Australian Open."

Assistant:
"""

messages=[{ "role":'user', "content":[{'type':'text','text': prompt_data}]}]

body=json.dumps(
        {
            "anthropic_version": "bedrock-2023-05-31",
            "max_tokens": 512,
            "messages": messages,
            "temperature": 0.1,
            "top_p": 1
        }
    )

response = bedrock_runtime.invoke_model(body=body, modelId="anthropic.claude-3-sonnet-20240229-v1:0")
response_body = json.loads(response.get('body').read())

print(response_body['content'][0].get("text"))

Athlete: Serena Williams, Venus Williams
Tournament: Australian Open
Sport: Tennis
```

Figure 8.2 – Prompting Amazon Bedrock FM for entity extraction with contextual information

It might produce favorable output for certain FMs based on the input instructions. However, in other scenarios, it has the potential to generate hallucinated or irrelevant additional information, as demonstrated in *Figure 8.3*. Therefore, employing few-shot prompting can be advantageous for entity extraction in such cases:

```
[105]: modelId = "ai21.j2-jumbo-instruct"  # change this to use a different version from the model provider
       accept = "application/json"
       contentType = "application/json"

       response = invoke_model(body, modelId, accept, contentType)
       response_body = json.loads(response.get("body").read())

       print(response_body.get("completions")[0].get("data").get("text"))


       Serena Williams: Athlete,
       : Tournament,
       tennis: Sport
```

Figure 8.3 – AI21 Labs J2 Jumbo Instruct FM output

Leveraging few-shot learning

As you are aware, few-shot learning involves providing the model with a small number of labeled examples during training or inference. This approach can be particularly effective for entity extraction tasks, as it allows the model to learn from a limited set of high-quality examples and generalize to new, unseen data.

Here's an example prompt with few-shot learning:

```
Task: Identify and classify entities related to technology companies
in the given text.

Entity Types: Company, Product, Location

Few-Shot Examples:

Input Text: "Microsoft, based in Redmond, Washington, unveiled its
latest operating system, Windows 11, at a virtual event."

The output looks like this:

  [Company: Microsoft], [Product: Windows 11], [Location: Redmond],
  [Location: Washington]

Here's another example:

Input Text: "Google's parent company, Alphabet Inc., announced plans
to expand its data center operations in Iowa and Nevada."

The output looks like this:

  [Company: Alphabet Inc.], [Company: Google], [Location: Iowa],
  [Location: Nevada]

Let's look at another example:

Input Text: "Samsung Electronics, the South Korean tech giant, launched
its new flagship smartphone, the Galaxy S22, featuring a powerful
camera and improved battery life."

The output looks like this:

  [Company: Samsung Electronics], [Product: Galaxy S22], [Location:
  South Korea]
```

```
Now, look at the following use case:

Your Input Text: "Amazon, the e-commerce behemoth based in Seattle, Washington, unveiled its latest line of Echo smart speakers and Alexa-powered devices at a hardware event."

```
```

Let's craft a code sample for the preceding use case and invoke the Amazon Titan model on Amazon Bedrock:

```
# Import the respective libraries
import boto3
import botocore
import os
import json
import sys

#Create client-side Amazon Bedrock connection with Boto3 library
region = os.environ.get("AWS_REGION")
bedrock_runtime = boto3.client(service_name='bedrock-runtime',region_
name=region)

prompt_data = """Task: Identify and classify entities related to
technology companies in the given text.
Entity Types: Company, Product, Location

Few-Shot Examples:
Input Text: "Microsoft, based in Redmond, Washington, unveiled its
latest operating system, Windows 11, at a virtual event."
Output: [Company: Microsoft], [Product: Windows 11], [Location:
Redmond], [Location: Washington]

Input Text: "Google's parent company, Alphabet Inc., announced plans
to expand its data center operations in Iowa and Nevada."
Output: [Company: Alphabet Inc.], [Company: Google], [Location: Iowa],
[Location: Nevada]

Input Text: "Samsung Electronics, the South Korean tech giant,
launched its new flagship smartphone, the Galaxy S22, featuring a
powerful camera and improved battery life."
Output: [Company: Samsung Electronics], [Product: Galaxy S22],
[Location: South Korea]

Your Input Text: "Amazon, the e-commerce behemoth based in Seattle,
Washington, unveiled its latest line of Echo smart speakers and Alexa-
powered devices at a hardware event."
```
```

```
Output:
"""

body = {
    "inputText": prompt_data
}
modelId = "amazon.titan-tg1-large"
accept = «application/json»
contentType = «application/json»

response = invoke_model(body, modelId, accept, contentType)
response_body = json.loads(response.get("body").read())

print(response_body.get("results")[0].get("outputText"))
```

Executing the preceding code generates the following output, as shown in *Figure 8.4*:

```
[Company: Amazon], [Product: Echo smart speakers, Alexa-powered
devices], [Location: Seattle], [Location: Washington]
```

```
body = {
    "inputText": prompt_data
}
modelId = "amazon.titan-tg1-large"
accept = "application/json"
contentType = "application/json"

response = invoke_model(body, modelId, accept, contentType)
response_body = json.loads(response.get("body").read())

print(response_body.get("results")[0].get("outputText"))
[Company: Amazon], [Product: Echo smart speakers, Alexa-powered devices], [Location: Seattle], [Location: Washington]
```

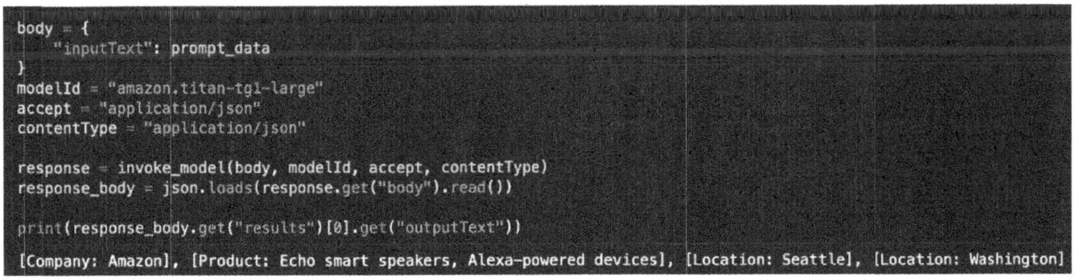

Figure 8.4 – Generated output from Amazon Titan FM

Therefore, in this example, the prompt offers a set of labeled instances to assist the model in understanding the entity extraction task within the technology domain. Through the utilization of few-shot learning, the model can proficiently generalize to unfamiliar input text, all while upholding a high level of accuracy.

Iterative refinement and evaluation

Prompt engineering constitutes an iterative process that frequently necessitates refinement and evaluation. As you explore various prompts and techniques, it's vital to assess the model's performance through automatic model evaluation or human evaluation methods, as elaborated upon in *Chapter 11*. Through careful analysis of the model's outputs and identifying areas for enhancement, you can iteratively refine your prompts, thereby augmenting the overall accuracy of your entity extraction system.

Take a look at the following example of model analysis and refinement:

'''

Initial Prompt:

Task: Identify and classify entities in the given text.

Entity Types: Person, Organization, Location

Input Text: "Elon Musk, the CEO of Tesla Inc., announced plans to build a new Gigafactory in Austin, Texas."

The output looks like this:

```
[Person: Elon Musk], [Organization: Tesla Inc.], [Location: Austin]
```

Output Analysis: The model correctly identified the person and organization entities but missed the location "Texas."

Refined Prompt:

Task: Identify and classify entities in the given text, including nested or multi-word entities.

Entity Types: Person, Organization, Location

Input Text: "Elon Musk, the CEO of Tesla Inc., announced plans to build a new Gigafactory in Austin, Texas."

The output looks like this:

```
[Person: Elon Musk], [Organization: Tesla Inc.], [Location: Austin,
Texas]
```

'''

By refining the prompt to include instructions for handling nested or multi-word entities, the model's performance improved, correctly identifying the location as Austin, Texas.

We encourage users to run the provided code on Amazon Bedrock to extract pertinent entities using the Claude 3 model and the `Messages` API. As mentioned earlier, please ensure that access to these models on Amazon Bedrock is enabled. For further documentation on accessing models on Bedrock, please visit `https://docs.aws.amazon.com/bedrock/latest/userguide/model-access.html`.

> **Note**
>
> Make sure you have the `boto3` library installed, as explained in the previous chapters. If not, please install the latest version using the following command: `pip install boto3`.

```
#importing the relevant libraries
import boto3
import json

#Creating Bedrock client and region
bedrock_client = boto3.client('bedrock-runtime',region_name='us-
east-1')

prompt = """
Task: Identify and classify entities in the given text.
Entity Types: Person, Organization, Location
Input Text: "Elon Musk, the CEO of Tesla Inc., announced plans to
build a new Gigafactory in Austin, Texas.
Output:
"""

messages = [{ "role":'user', "content":[{'type':'text','text':
prompt}]}]
max_tokens=512
top_p=1
temp=0.5
system = "You are an AI Assistant"


body=json.dumps(
        {
            "anthropic_version": "bedrock-2023-05-31",
            «max_tokens»: max_tokens,
            «messages»: messages,
            "temperature": temp,
            "top_p": top_p,
            "system": system
        }
    )

response = bedrock_client.invoke_model(body= body, modelId =
"anthropic.claude-3-sonnet-20240229-v1:0")

response_body = json.loads(response.get('body').read())
print(response_body)
```

Printing `response_body` as shown in the preceding snippet might yield the following output, as expected:

```
{'id': 'msg_01RqxLfg6hEEu1K8jY3g8gzq',
  'type': 'message',
  'role': 'assistant',
  'content': [{'type': 'text',
    'text': 'Person: Elon Musk\nOrganization: Tesla Inc.\nLocation: Austin, Texas'}],
  'model': 'claude-3-sonnet-28k-20240229',
  'stop_reason': 'end_turn',
  'stop_sequence': None,
  'usage': {'input_tokens': 71, 'output_tokens': 23}}
```

Hence, by leveraging effective prompt engineering techniques with Amazon Bedrock, such as providing clear instructions, relevant examples, and handling ambiguity, GenAI models can be guided to perform high-quality entity extraction across several use cases and different domains. As with any AI application, it requires careful design, testing, and refinement to build a truly production-ready system.

As LLMs continue to grow in size and complexity, their capabilities in entity extraction are expected to further improve, enabling more accurate and robust solutions.

Ongoing research also focuses on integrating external knowledge sources such as knowledge graphs or ontologies into LLMs for entity extraction. By embedding structured knowledge into the model's architecture or training regimen, these methods have the potential to enrich the model's comprehension of entities and their interconnections, thereby potentially enhancing both performance and interpretability.

Check the following AWS blog showcasing the integration of **intelligent document processing** (**IDP**) in the context of entity extraction automation using AWS AI/ML services such as Amazon Textract with Amazon Bedrock and LangChain: `https://aws.amazon.com/blogs/machine-learning/intelligent-document-processing-with-amazon-textract-amazon-bedrock-and-langchain/`.

This solution proves particularly beneficial for handling handwritten or scanned documents, encompassing the extraction of pertinent data from various file formats such as PDF, PNG, TIFF, and JPEG, regardless of the document layout. The Amazon Textract service facilitates the automatic extraction of text, handwriting, and data from such scanned documents.

Consequently, this solution capitalizes on the strengths of each component: Amazon Textract for precise data extraction, Amazon Bedrock for streamlined data processing pipelines, and LangChain for seamlessly integrating LLMs into the workflow. Overall, the blog post offers a pragmatic solution for automating document processing tasks, underscoring the advantages of leveraging AWS services and open source frameworks such as LangChain to develop intelligent applications. Therefore, it holds substantial potential for diverse document processing scenarios, providing dynamic adaptability to evolving data patterns.

Additional examples of entity extraction with Bedrock have been added here: `https://github.com/aws-samples/amazon-bedrock-workshop/blob/main/01_Text_generation/04_entity_extraction.ipynb`. Users are encouraged to run and execute the code cells to gain a much better understanding of entity extraction using Amazon Bedrock for GenAI use cases.

Now that you have grasped the concepts of entity extraction in more detail, we will dive into more code generation scenarios in the universe of Amazon Bedrock.

Code generation with LLMs – unleashing the power of AI-driven development

As the field of AI continues to evolve, one of the most exciting and promising areas is the use of LLMs for code generation, especially in the case of developer productivity gains. Customers can leverage state-of-the-art LLMs available on Amazon Bedrock to generate high-quality code, revolutionizing the way developers approach software development.

The code generation process

The code generation process with Amazon Bedrock is straightforward and user-friendly. Developers can interact with the platform through a web-based interface or via an API, as discussed in the previous chapters. The process typically involves the following steps:

1. **Problem description**: The developer provides a natural language description of the desired functionality or task that they want the code to perform.
2. **Context and constraints**: The developer can optionally provide additional context, such as programming language preferences, coding styles, or specific libraries or frameworks to be used.
3. **LLM code generation**: Amazon Bedrock's LLMs analyze the problem description and any provided context and generate the corresponding code.
4. **Code refinement**: The generated code can be iteratively refined through additional prompts or feedback from the developer, allowing for a collaborative and interactive process.
5. **Code integration**: The final generated code can be seamlessly integrated into the developer's project or code base.

Benefits of code generation with Amazon Bedrock

Leveraging LLMs for code generation offers numerous benefits to developers, including the following:

- **Increased productivity**: With Amazon Bedrock, developers can quickly generate code for various tasks and functionalities, reducing the time and effort required for manual coding
- **Improved code quality**: The code generated by Amazon Bedrock's LLMs can provide high-quality outputs, adhering to best practices and coding standards based on the iterative refinement of the prompts

- **Reduced errors**: LLMs can help reduce the likelihood of common coding errors, such as syntax errors or logical flaws, by generating correct and coherent code with prompt engineering
- **Exploration and prototyping**: Bedrock enables developers to rapidly explore and prototype different ideas and approaches, facilitating more efficient and creative problem-solving
- **Accessibility**: By leveraging natural language descriptions and FMs for code generation purposes (Llama, Claude, Titan, Mistral, and so on), Amazon Bedrock makes code generation more accessible to developers with varying levels of expertise or backgrounds

Limitations and considerations

While LLM-based code generation offers numerous advantages, it is important to be aware of their limitations and considerations:

- **Specialized domain knowledge**: LLMs may not always generate code that requires highly specialized domain knowledge or complex algorithms. Human expertise and review may still be necessary in certain cases.
- **Security and compliance**: Generated code should be thoroughly reviewed and tested to ensure it adheres to security best practices and any relevant compliance requirements.
- **Integration and maintenance**: Generated code may need to be adapted and maintained over time as requirements or dependencies change.
- **Ethical considerations**: As with any AI system, it is crucial to ensure LLMs are used responsibly and ethically, considering potential biases or unintended consequences.

Use cases and examples

Amazon Bedrock's code generation capabilities can be applied to a wide range of use cases across various domains and programming languages. Some examples include the following:

- **Web development**: Developers can generate code using Bedrock for web applications, APIs, or user interfaces using languages such as JavaScript, Python, or Ruby.
- **Data processing and analysis**: Developers can leverage Bedrock to write code for data manipulation, analysis, and visualization tasks using languages such as Python or R.
- **Mobile app development**: Bedrock can be utilized to generate code for mobile applications using languages such as Swift, Kotlin, or React Native.
- **Embedded systems and Internet of Things (IoT) devices**: Developers can create code for embedded systems, microcontrollers, or IoT devices using languages such as C, C++, or Rust with the assistance of Bedrock models.
- **Scientific computing**: Bedrock can aid in writing code for scientific simulations, numerical calculations, or data processing tasks using languages such as MATLAB, Julia, or Fortran through its code generation features.

Now, let's look at a few examples of code generation, debugging, or code transformation use cases with Amazon Bedrock.

Prompt engineering examples with Amazon Bedrock

Here is a sample prompt given to a Claude 3 Sonnet model within Amazon Bedrock to adopt the role of a Python developer and perform a code generation task:

```
Human: You are an expert Python developer tasked with coding a web
scraper for an experienced developer. The scraper should extract data
from multiple web pages and store the results in a SQLite database.
Write clean, high-quality Python code for this task, including
necessary imports. Do not write anything before the ```python block.
After writing the code, carefully check for errors. If errors exist,
list them within <error> tags and provide a new corrected version.
If no errors, write "CHECKED: NO ERRORS" within <error> tags.

Assistant:
```

Let us execute this prompt in code using Anthropic Claude 3 model on Amazon Bedrock. As covered in the previous sections, please ensure you have the necessary libraries installed and have the required permissions to invoke the model on Amazon Bedrock:

```
# Import the respective libraries
import boto3
import botocore
import os
import json
import sys

#Create client side Amazon Bedrock connection with Boto3 library
region = os.environ.get("AWS_REGION")
bedrock_runtime = boto3.client(service_name='bedrock-runtime',region_
name=region)

# Adding prompt example here:
prompt_data = """Human: You are an expert Python developer tasked
with coding a web scraper for an experienced developer. The scraper
should extract data from multiple web pages and store the results
in a SQLite database. Write clean, high-quality Python code for this
task, including necessary imports. Do not write anything before the
```python block. After writing the code, carefully check for errors.
If errors exist, list them within <error> tags and provide a new
corrected version. If no errors, write "CHECKED: NO ERRORS" within
<error> tags.
Assistant:
"""
```
```

```
# Using Messages API with Anthropic Claude
messages=[{ "role":'user', "content":[{'type':'text','text': prompt_
data}]}]

body=json.dumps(
        {
            "anthropic_version": "bedrock-2023-05-31",
            «max_tokens»: 512,
            «messages»: messages,
            «temperature»: 0.1,
            "top_p": 1
        }
    )

response = bedrock_runtime.invoke_model(body=body, modelId="anthropic.
claude-3-sonnet-20240229-v1:0")
response_body = json.loads(response.get('body').read())
```

We won't dive into the entirety of the output generated, but provided in *Figure 8.5* is a code snippet generated as a result of invoking a Claude 3 Sonnet model via Amazon Bedrock API with the preceding prompt:

```
print(response_body['content'][0].get("text"))
```python
import requests
from bs4 import BeautifulSoup
import sqlite3

# Connect to SQLite database
conn = sqlite3.connect('scraped_data.db')
c = conn.cursor()

# Create table if it doesn't exist
c.execute('''CREATE TABLE IF NOT EXISTS scraped_data
             (url TEXT, title TEXT, content TEXT)''')

# List of URLs to scrape
urls = ['https://www.example.com/page1', 'https://www.example.com/page2', 'https://www.example.com/page3']

# Loop through URLs and scrape data
for url in urls:
    response = requests.get(url)
    soup = BeautifulSoup(response.content, 'html.parser')

    # Extract title and content
    title = soup.find('h1').text
    content = soup.find('div', {'class': 'content'}).text

    # Insert data into database
    c.execute("INSERT INTO scraped_data VALUES (?, ?, ?)", (url, title, content))
    conn.commit()

# Close database connection
conn.close()
```
```

Figure 8.5 – Output code snippet generated by invoking Claude 3 Sonnet model via Amazon Bedrock

Figure 8.6 shows yet another example of a code debugging use case, leveraging a Llama 2 Chat 13B model available on Amazon Bedrock within the chat playground:

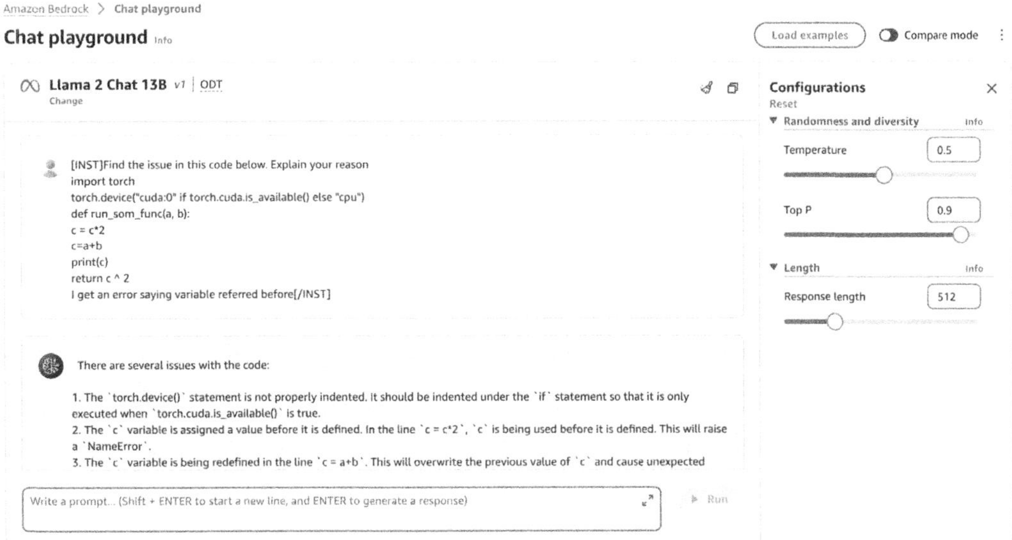

Figure 8.6 – Code debugging using Llama 2 Chat 13B model on Amazon Bedrock

Now, let's take a look at a code translation scenario. Here's an example prompt for a code translation use case with a Mixtral 8X7B instruct model on Amazon Bedrock, followed by a generated output:

```
# Import the respective libraries
import boto3
import botocore
import os
import json
import sys

#Create client-side Amazon Bedrock connection with Boto3 library
region = os.environ.get("AWS_REGION")
bedrock_runtime = boto3.client(service_name='bedrock-runtime',region_
name=region)

prompt="""
[INST] You are an AI code translator specialized in converting
code between different programming languages while preserving
functionality, readability, and style. Your task is to translate the
provided Python code to JavaScript.
Here is a brief description of the code's purpose:

This code defines a class called 'BankAccount' that represents a basic
```

```
bank account. It has methods to deposit and withdraw money, as well as
to check the account balance.

Python code is in the following code block:
```python
class BankAccount:
    def __init__(self, initial_balance=0):
        self.balance = initial_balance

    def deposit(self, amount):
        self.balance += amount

    def withdraw(self, amount):
        if self.balance >= amount:
            self.balance -= amount
        else:
            print("Insufficient funds")

    def check_balance(self):
        return self.balance
```
Translate the above Python code to JavaScript, maintaining clear
variable naming, proper indentation, and adding comments to explain
any non-trivial logic or language-specific constructs used in the
translation.
After translating the code, carefully review your work for any errors
or inconsistencies. If errors are found, list them within `<error>`
tags and provide a corrected version. If no errors are present, write
"CHECKED: NO ERRORS" within `<error>` tags.
[/INST]"""

#Model ID and parameter details
modelId = 'mistral.mixtral-8x7b-instruct-v0:1'
accept = 'application/json'
contentType = 'application/json'

body = json.dumps({
    'prompt': prompt,
    'max_tokens': 1000,
    'top_p': 0.9,
    'temperature': 0.2,
})

#Output response
response = bedrock_runtime.invoke_model(body=body.encode('utf-8'), #
```

```
Encode to bytes
      modelId=modelId,
      accept=accept,
      contentType=contentType)
response_body = json.loads(response.get('body').read().
decode('utf-8'))
print(response_body.get('outputs')[0].get('text'))
```

The translated JavaScript code output looks like this:

````
Here's the Python code translated into JavaScript with clear variable
naming, proper indentation, and comments explaining non-trivial logic
or language-specific constructs used in the translation:

```javascript
// Define the BankAccount class
class BankAccount {
  // Initialize the balance property with an initial_balance of 0
  constructor(initial_balance = 0) {
    this.balance = initial_balance;
  }

  // Deposit method to add amount to the balance
  deposit(amount) {
    this.balance += amount;
  }

  // Withdraw method to subtract amount from the balance if there are
sufficient funds
  withdraw(amount) {
    if (this.balance >= amount) {
      this.balance -= amount;
    } else {
      console.log("Insufficient funds");
    }
  }

  // Check_balance method to return the current balance
  check_balance() {
    return this.balance;
  }
}
```
````

```
After reviewing the translated code, no errors or inconsistencies were
found.

<error>NO ERRORS</error>
```

In this example, the prompt provides context about the code's purpose and the original Python code and instructs Code Llama to translate it to JavaScript. The model is asked to maintain clear variable naming and proper indentation and add comments to explain non-trivial logic or language-specific constructs.

The generated output shows the translated JavaScript code, with the class structure and methods translated correctly while preserving the original functionality. After translating the code, the model has carefully reviewed its work and indicated `CHECKED: NO ERRORS` within `<error>` tags, signifying that the translation is correct and error-free.

This example demonstrates how a prompt can be crafted to guide Code Llama (or similar AI code models) to perform code translation tasks while ensuring the translated code is verified and correct. Note that it is always a best practice to perform a human evaluation of the generated output to verify the accuracy of these models and rectify any issues.

Users are encouraged to try these examples within the Amazon Bedrock playground or leveraging Amazon Bedrock APIs with several other models such as Amazon Titan, Cohere Command, Meta Llama, and alternate variations of Anthropic Claude or Mistral models to test the generated output and refine it further.

Users are further invited to explore this code sample where Amazon Bedrock LLMs are being invoked with zero-shot prompting to generate SQL and Python programs: `https://github.com/aws-samples/amazon-bedrock-workshop/blob/main/01_Text_generation/01_code_generation_w_bedrock.ipynb`.

Entity extraction with GenAI represents a significant step forward in our ability to extract valuable insights from unstructured text data. By leveraging the power of LLMs and combining them with rule-based techniques, hybrid approaches offer accurate, scalable, and domain-adaptable solutions for a wide range of applications. As we continue to push the boundaries of these areas, we can expect to unlock new opportunities for knowledge discovery, decision support, and data-driven innovation across various industries and domains.

The field of LLM-based code generation is also rapidly evolving, and Amazon Bedrock is at the forefront of this exciting development. As LLMs become more advanced and the available training data continues to grow, the capabilities and applications of code generation will expand further. Amazon Bedrock represents a significant step forward in the realm of code generation, empowering developers to leverage the power of LLMs to increase productivity, improve code quality, and explore new ideas more efficiently. As this technology continues to mature, it has the potential to revolutionize the way software is developed and open up new possibilities for innovation across various industries and domains.

Summary

This chapter commenced with an in-depth exploration of entity extraction, uncovering its fundamentals, techniques, and best practices. It then transitioned to showcasing potential industrial applications of entity extraction, highlighting real-world use cases that demonstrate the power of unlocking valuable insights from unstructured data across various sectors.

Recognizing the pivotal role of prompt engineering, the chapter further provided a comprehensive guide to crafting effective prompts, equipping readers with strategies and guidelines to optimize entity extraction performance. Shifting gears, the discussion then centered on the transformative potential of code generation with LLMs on Amazon Bedrock. We gained insights into the capabilities and limitations of LLMs in driving AI-based development, as well as methodologies for leveraging these cutting-edge models.

Finally, the chapter culminated with a compelling exploration of practical use cases for code generation, demonstrating how this technology can accelerate innovation and boost productivity across various domains. Through real-world examples and case studies, readers witnessed firsthand the profound impact of code generation on streamlining development processes and unleashing new possibilities. In the following chapter, we are going to explore image generation use cases with Amazon Bedrock, along with its potential applications. Stay tuned!

9

Generating and Transforming Images Using Amazon Bedrock

By now, we have explored several LLMs capable of generating textual responses. This chapter explores generating images using select FMs that are available on Amazon Bedrock. We will start with an overview of image generation, wherein we will examine model architectures such as GANs and **variational autoencoders** (**VAEs**) Then, we will cover some real-world applications of image generation and multimodal models available within Amazon Bedrock. Furthermore, we will dive deeper into several multimodal design patterns, as well as some ethical considerations and safeguards that are available with Amazon Bedrock.

By the end of this chapter, you will have gained an understanding of implementing image generation and its design patterns with Amazon Bedrock for real-world use cases.

Here are the key topics that will be covered in this chapter:

- Image generation overview
- Multimodal models
- Multimodal design patterns
- Ethical considerations and safeguards

Technical requirements

This chapter requires you to have access to an AWS account. If you don't have one already, you can go to `https://aws.amazon.com/getting-started/` and create one.

Secondly, you will need to install and configure AWS CLI at `https://aws.amazon.com/cli/` after you create an account, which will be needed to access Amazon Bedrock FMs from your local machine. Since the majority of the code cells that we will be executing are based in Python, setting up an AWS Python SDK (Boto3) at `https://docs.aws.amazon.com/bedrock/latest/APIReference/welcome.html` would be beneficial at this point. You can carry out the Python setup in any way. Install it on your local machine, or use AWS Cloud9, or utilize AWS Lambda, or leverage Amazon SageMaker.

> **Note**
>
> There will be a charge associated with the invocation and customization of the FMs of Amazon Bedrock. Please refer to `https://aws.amazon.com/bedrock/pricing/` to learn more.

Image generation overview

Image generation has been a fascinating and rapidly evolving field. Since the dawn of advanced deep learning techniques and increasing computational power, machines have gained the remarkable ability to create highly realistic and sophisticated images from scratch or based on textual prompts. This ability has opened up a vast array of applications across various domains, including the creative industries, media and entertainment, advertising, product packaging, and many others.

The history of image generation can be traced back to early developments in computer vision and pattern recognition. Researchers and scientists have long sought to understand and replicate the human visual perception system, paving the way for the initial techniques in image synthesis and manipulation. However, the true breakthrough in image generation came with the emergence of deep learning, specifically the introduction of GANs and VAEs.

Please note that we are highlighting these techniques for historical reference. Current image generation FMs do not use these techniques.

What are GANs and VAEs?

GANs, introduced by Ian Goodfellow and his colleagues in 2014, revolutionized the field of image generation. You can read more about it on `https://arxiv.org/pdf/1406.2661`. GANs employ a unique training approach whereby two neural networks are pitted against each other in competition. The first network is known as the **generator**, which is tasked with generating synthetic samples that mimic real data. For example, the generator could produce new images, texts, or audio clips. The second network is called the **discriminator**. Its role is to analyze examples, both real and synthetic, to classify which ones are genuine and which have been artificially generated.

Through this adversarial process, the generator learns to produce increasingly convincing fakes that can fool the discriminator. Meanwhile, the discriminator evolves in its ability to detect subtle anomalies that reveal synthetic samples. Their competing goals drive both networks to continuously improve. A demonstration of GANs can be seen at `https://thispersondoesnotexist.com/`. By refreshing the page endlessly, users are presented with an endless stream of novel human faces. However, none of those faces are real – all are synthetic portraits created solely by a GAN trained on vast databases of images of real human faces. The site offers a glimpse into how GANs can synthesize highly realistic outputs across many domains.

Since the inception of GANs, numerous advancements and variations have been implemented, leading to remarkable achievements in image generation. Techniques such as StyleGAN, BigGAN, and diffusion models have pushed the boundaries of image quality, resolution, and diversity. These models can generate photorealistic images of human faces, landscapes, objects, and even artistic creations, blurring the line between artificial and real.

VAEs, on the other hand, are a simpler means to train generative AI algorithms. They also utilize two neural networks: **encoders** and **decoders**. Encoders learn the patterns in the data by mapping it into lower-dimensional latent space; decoders use these patterns from the latent space and generate realistic samples.

One of the most exciting developments in image generation has been the integration of NLP capabilities. Models such as DALL-E, Stable Diffusion, and Midjourney have empowered users to generate images simply by providing textual descriptions or prompts. This fusion of language and vision has opened up new avenues for creative expression, rapid prototyping, and data augmentation for various ML tasks.

While the advancements in image generation are remarkable, it is crucial to address the ethical considerations and potential risks associated with this technology. Issues such as deepfakes, biases, and misuse for malicious purposes must be carefully addressed to ensure the responsible and ethical deployment of these powerful tools. We will look at this topic in detail in the *Ethical considerations and safeguards* section of this chapter.

Let us look at some real-world applications for image generation models.

Real-world applications

The applications of image generation are endless. Here are some of the real-world applications of image generation:

- **Advertising and marketing**: In the world of advertising and marketing, visuals play a crucial role in capturing attention and conveying messages effectively. With image generation, you can revolutionize marketing campaigns by producing unique, visually striking images tailored to specific target audiences. Marketers can leverage Bedrock models to generate personalized product advertisements, social media visuals, and eye-catching graphics that resonate with their desired demographics. Furthermore, marketers can create variations of images based on customer preferences, ensuring that marketing materials are highly relevant and engaging.
- **Graphic design and content creation**: Graphic designers and content creators often face the challenge of conceptualizing and visualizing ideas before executing them. With Bedrock's image generation models, you can streamline this process by relying on this powerful tool for generating initial concepts, illustrations, and visual assets. Designers can use image generation models to explore different styles, compositions, and color schemes, facilitating quick iterations and experimentation. Additionally, content creators can leverage Bedrock models to generate unique and captivating images for blog posts, articles, or other marketing materials, enhancing their visual appeal and potential for engagement.

- **Product visualization and prototyping**: Effective product visualization is essential for iterating designs, gathering feedback, and showcasing offerings. With Bedrock image generation models, businesses can generate realistic visualizations of product designs, allowing for rapid prototyping and evaluation before investing in physical prototypes. Bedrock models can create images of products in various environments or from different angles, providing stakeholders with a comprehensive understanding of the product's appearance and functionality. This capability can significantly accelerate the product development cycle and aid in marketing and sales efforts.
- **Gaming and virtual environments**: The gaming and **Virtual Reality** (**VR**) industries heavily rely on visually immersive experiences. Bedrock's image generation models can empower developers to create unique textures, environments, and assets for video games, VR, or **Augmented Reality** (**AR**) applications. Bedrock image models can generate custom avatars, character designs, and intricate visual elements based on user specifications or game narratives. In addition, developers can enhance the realism and diversity of their virtual worlds, offering players a more engaging and personalized experience.
- **Architecture and interior design**: Visualizing architectural designs and interior spaces is crucial for architects and interior designers, as well as their clients. Bedrock image models can generate realistic renderings of proposed designs, allowing stakeholders to immerse themselves in the envisioned spaces before construction or renovation. Bedrock's capabilities can aid in visualizing different materials, furniture arrangements, and lighting conditions, enabling architects and designers to refine their concepts and present compelling proposals to clients or decision-makers.
- **Fashion and apparel**: In the fashion and apparel industry, Amazon Bedrock image models can generate unique textile designs, patterns, and clothing styles, enabling fashion designers to explore new concepts and stay ahead of trends. Additionally, Bedrock can create visualizations of clothing items on different body types or in various environments, allowing customers to preview how garments would look in real life before making a purchase. This capability can enhance the shopping experience and reduce return rates.
- **Scientific visualization**: Effective communication of scientific data, phenomena, and simulations is crucial in research and education. Amazon Bedrock's image generation models can assist scientists and researchers in creating visual representations of complex concepts, making them more accessible and understandable. Bedrock models can generate illustrations, diagrams, or 3D models for scientific publications, presentations, or educational materials, facilitating knowledge transfer and fostering a deeper understanding of intricate topics.
- **Art and creative expression**: Artists can leverage Bedrock image models to explore new styles, techniques, and concepts by generating unique and imaginative images based on textual prompts or conceptual frameworks.
- **E-commerce and product catalogs**: In the e-commerce landscape, high-quality product images are essential for attracting customers and driving sales. Amazon Bedrock image models can generate visually appealing and accurate product images for online catalogs or e-commerce

platforms, reducing the need for extensive photoshoots and the associated costs. These models can also create visualizations of customized products or configurations based on customer preferences, enhancing the shopping experience and enabling personalization at scale.

Now that we have looked at some real-world applications, let us explore various multimodal models and their inner workings.

Multimodal models

So far in this book, we have looked at single-modal model architecture patterns, such as text-to-text generation, that includes QA, summarization, code generation, and so on. Let us now expand our understanding to another type of generative AI model: multimodal models.

Multimodal models are a type of model that can understand and interpret more than one modality, such as image, audio, and video, as shown in *Figure 9.1*.

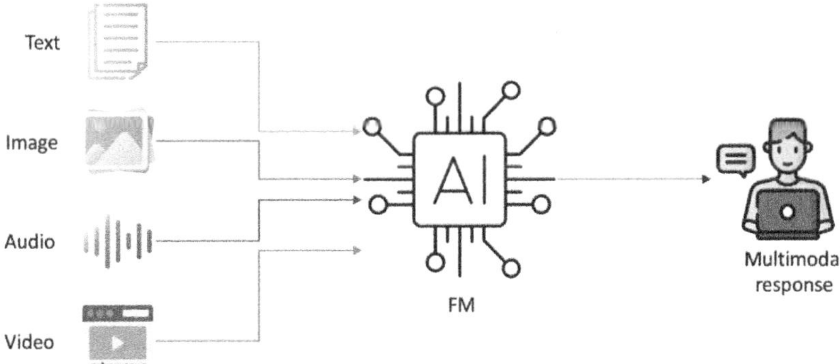

Figure 9.1 – Multimodality

The response received from these models can also be multimodal. Behind the scenes, these FMs comprise multiple single-modal neural networks that process text, image, audio, and video separately.

Now let us look at the multimodality models that are available within Amazon Bedrock.

Stable Diffusion

Stable Diffusion is a state-of-the-art image generation model that has gained significant attention in the field of generative AI. Unlike many other image generation models, Stable Diffusion employs a unique diffusion-based approach, which sets it apart from other methods or techniques.

At the heart of Stable Diffusion is the concept of **diffusion**, which involves a forward and a reverse diffusion process. In **forward diffusion**, Gaussian noise is progressively added to an image until it becomes entirely random. The model then learns to reverse this process, gradually removing the noise to reconstruct the original image. This reversal is called **reverse diffusion** and is the key to Stable Diffusion's impressive performance.

This diffusion process has several key components:

- **Contrastive Language-Image Pre-Training** (**CLIP**): CLIP is a neural network trained on a vast dataset of image-text pairs, enabling it to understand the semantic relationships between visual and textual representations. This component plays a crucial role in bridging the gap between natural language prompts and their corresponding visual manifestations.
- **U-Net**: This serves as a backbone for the image generation process. U-Net is a convolutional neural network designed for image-to-image translation tasks such as segmentation and denoising. Segmentation is the process whereby the images are partitioned into multiple segments or sets of pixels to locate objects and boundaries. Denoising removes the noise from an image to improve its quality. In the context of Stable Diffusion, U-Net is responsible for generating and refining the output image based on the input prompt and guidance from CLIP.
- **VAE**: This is another critical component that helps ensure that the generated images are coherent and realistic. In Stable Diffusion, VAE encodes the generated image into a compressed representation, which is then decoded to produce the final output image.

As shown in *Figure 9.2*, here is a high-level overview of how the whole process works:

1. The user provides a natural language prompt describing the desired image.
2. The CLIP model analyzes the prompt and generates a corresponding embedding, representing the semantic meaning of the text.
3. The U-Net architecture takes this embedding as input, along with an initial random noise image.
4. Through a series of convolutional and deconvolutional operations, U-Net iteratively refines the noise image, guided by the CLIP embedding, to produce an image that matches the input prompt.
5. The generated image is then passed through the VAE, which encodes and decodes it, ensuring coherence and realism.
6. The final output image is produced, reflecting the user's prompt.

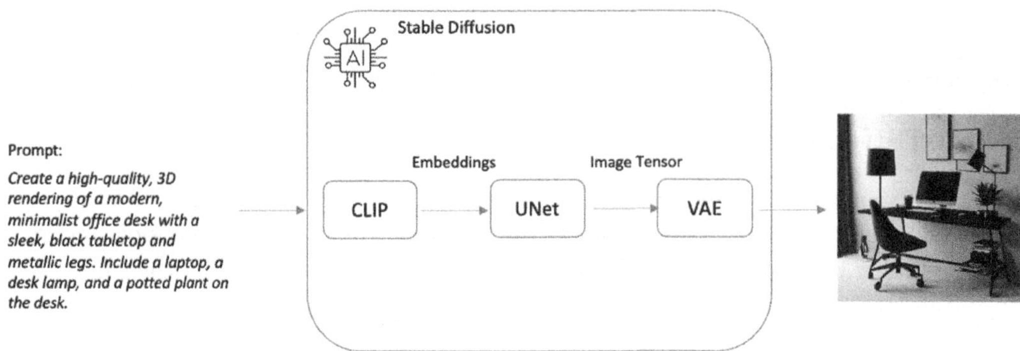

Figure 9.2 – The Stable Diffusion process

By combining these architectural elements, Stable Diffusion is able to generate high-quality, diverse images that are both visually appealing and semantically coherent with the input prompts. In order to understand the detailed workings of the diffusion process, readers are encouraged to read the research paper *On the Design Fundamentals of Diffusion Models: A Survey*. It can be found on: `https://arxiv.org/pdf/2306.04542.pdf`.

This paper explains how diffusion models work by gradually adding noise to training data and then learning to reverse that process to generate new samples. The paper highlights the wide range of applications for diffusion models, including image editing, text-to-image generation, and 3D object creation.

Additionally, readers are recommended to explore the *How Diffusion Models Work* course from DeepLearning.AI at `https://learn.deeplearning.ai/courses/diffusion-models/`.

Titan Image Generator G1

Titan Image Generator G1 is a proprietary image generation model by Amazon that allows users to generate images from text, edit existing images, and create variations of images. The model is designed to make it easy for users to iterate on image concepts by generating multiple image options based on text descriptions. The model is trained on diverse high-quality datasets, so it can understand complex prompts with multiple objects and generate realistic images.

This model supports image editing capabilities such as editing with text prompts using a built-in segmentation model, generating variations of the image, inpainting with an image mask, and outpainting to extend or change the background of an image. You can upload an existing image and provide instructions or prompts to modify specific aspects of the image. The model can intelligently alter the composition, add or remove elements, change colors, or apply various artistic styles, all while preserving the overall coherence and realism of the original image.

We will dive deeper into these capabilities in the *Multimodal design patterns* section.

Titan Multimodal Embeddings

The **Titan Multimodal Embeddings** model is part of the Amazon Titan family of models designed for use cases such as image search and similarity-based recommendation with high accuracy and fast response.

The Titan Multimodal Embeddings model's core strength lies in its ability to generate high-dimensional vector representations for both textual and visual data. These embeddings encapsulate the semantic relationships between different modalities, allowing for efficient and effective search and retrieval operations.

The model supports up to 128 tokens as input text in English, as well as image sizes of up to 25 MB, and converts those to vector embeddings. The default embedding size is 1024 dimensions, providing a rich representation that captures nuanced details and complex relationships. However, you can also configure smaller vector dimensions to optimize for speed and cost, depending on your specific use case and performance requirements.

Anthropic Claude 3 – Sonnet, Haiku, and Opus

Anthropic Claude 3 Model variants – *Claude 3 Sonnet*, *Claude 3 Haiku*, and *Claude 3 Opus* – are the most recent and advanced family of Anthropic Claude models available on Amazon Bedrock. All these models have multimodal capabilities, meaning that they are able to perceive and analyze images as well as text input, with a 200K context window. We encourage you to refer to the *Anthropic Claude* section in *Chapter 1* if you would like to go over their details again.

Now that we have looked at the multimodal models available within Amazon Bedrock, let us explore some of the design patterns.

Multimodal design patterns

With multimodal design patterns, we integrate different modalities, such as text, images, audio, and so on. With the multimodal models available, the ability to generate, manipulate, and understand images from text or other input modalities has become increasingly important in a wide range of applications, from creative design to scientific visualization and beyond.

Numerous patterns can be created with multimodal models. In this section, we are going to cover some of the common patterns.

Text-to-image

With a text-to-image pattern, you provide the text as a prompt to the model. The model will then generate an image based on that prompt, as shown in *Figure 9.3*.

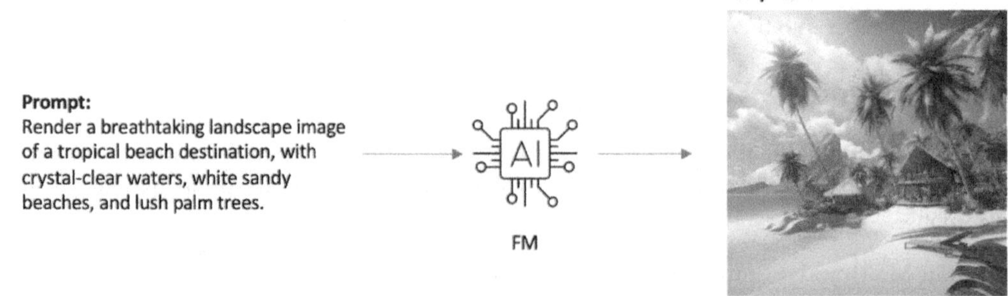

Figure 9.3 – A text-to-image pattern

Parameters

At the core of image generation models are a set of customizable inference parameters and controls that allow users to get the desired image from the model. Let us look at these parameters:

- **Negative prompt**: Specify elements, content, or details you want to exclude from the generated image. For example, we can add negative prompts such as `Cloud` and `seating bench` to exclude them from the image, as shown in *Figure 9.4*.

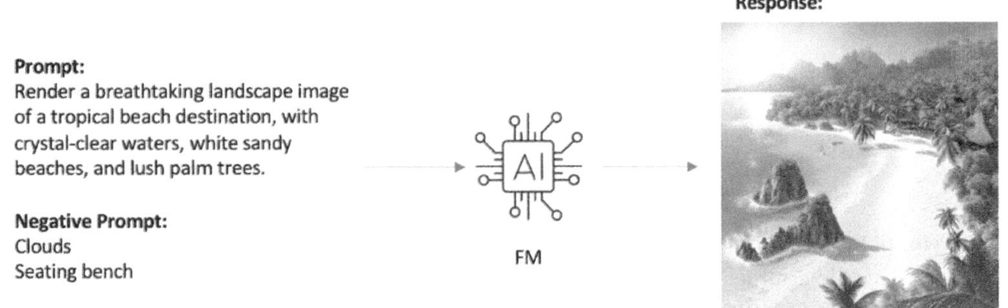

Figure 9.4 – A text-to-image pattern with negative prompts

- **Reference image**: This provides users the ability to input a reference image to the model, which can be leveraged by the model as a baseline to generate its response (generated image). For instance, if we use the image generated from the preceding figure and pass it as a reference along with the prompt, the prompt would be something like this:

```
A futuristic cityscape at night, with towering skyscrapers made
of glass and metal. The buildings are illuminated by neon lights
in shades of blue, purple, and pink. The streets are lined with
holographic billboards and advertisements.
```

The model will use the reference image and the prompt to generate a new image, as shown in *Figure 9.5*.

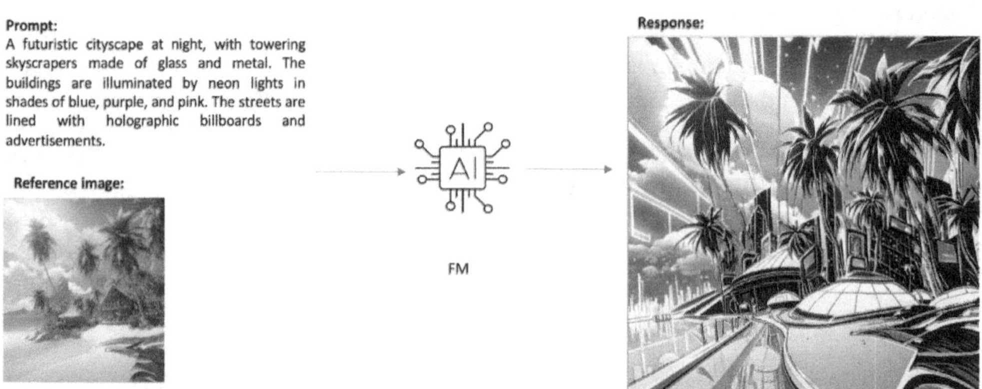

Figure 9.5 – A text-to-image pattern using a reference Image

- **Prompt Strength (cfg_scale)**: Prompt strength, also known as **Classifier-Free Guidance scale** (*cfg_scale*) determines the degree to which the generated image adheres to the provided text prompt. A higher value indicates that the image generation process will adhere more closely to the text prompt, while a lower value allows for more creative interpretation and diversity in the generated images. Using a cfg_scale value somewhere in the middle (*10-15*) is generally recommended, as it strikes a balance between faithfully representing the text prompt and allowing for artistic expression. However, the optimal value may vary depending on your use case or what you are looking for, complexity of the prompt, and the desired level of detail in the generated image.
- **Generation Step (steps)**: The *steps* parameter in Stable Diffusion refers to the number of iterations or cycles the algorithm goes through to generate an image from the input text. It's an important setting that affects the quality and detail of the final image. Here is how it works:
    - The process starts with random noise, and with each step, some of that noise is removed, gradually revealing the intended image.
    - More steps generally lead to higher-quality images with more detail, but there's a point of diminishing returns.
    - The ideal number of steps can vary depending on the complexity of the image you're trying to generate and your personal preferences. However, going much higher may not significantly improve the image but will increase generation time.
    - For simple subjects or scenes, fewer steps (around *10-15*) may be sufficient. But for more complex or detailed images, you may want to increase the steps to *40-50* or even more, depending on how much detailed you are looking for.

What we discussed are just some of the parameters. The following figure highlights additional parameters for Stable Diffusion.

Parameters	Description
text_prompt	This is the textual description or instructions you provide to the model which it uses to generate the corresponding image.
weight	This is the strength that is applied to the model. If the value of weight is less than zero, it is identifies as negative prompt
height and width	These parameters determine the dimensions (size) of the generated image, specifying the number of pixels along the vertical and horizontal axes, respectively.
cfg_scale	This value controls the balance between the model's adherence to the text prompt and its ability to generate diverse and creative outputs.
clip_guidance _preset	This setting influences how closely the generated image follows the semantic content of the text prompt, ranging from a literal interpretation to a more abstract or creative representation.
sampler	This parameter determines the algorithm used by the model to generate the image, affecting the quality, diversity, and computational requirements of the output.
samples	This value specifies the number of independent images the model should generate based on the provided prompt and other parameters.
seed	This parameter allows you to set a specific starting point for the random number generator used by the model, enabling reproducibility of results.
steps	This value determines the number of iterations or steps the model takes during the image generation process, potentially affecting the quality and detail of the output.
style_preset	This parameter allows you to apply pre-defined artistic styles or visual aesthetics to the generated image. It's like using a filter or preset in a photo editing app, where you can choose from options like "line-art," "3d-model" or "cinematic" to give your image a distinct look and feel. These presets can significantly alter the color palette, texture, and overall vibe of the output.
extras	Additional parameters for Experimental or in-development feature. Use with Caution

Figure 9.6 – Stable Diffusion text-to-image parameters

For a more detailed description of these parameters, you can go through the Stable Diffusion documentation at `https://platform.stability.ai/docs/api-reference#tag/Image-to-Image`.

If you are using Amazon Titan Image Generator, here is the list of parameters that you can use: `https://docs.aws.amazon.com/bedrock/latest/userguide/model-parameters-titan-image.html`.

Image search

Image search has emerged as a powerful tool that enables users to explore and leverage vast collections of visual data. With FMs from Amazon Bedrock, you can perform image searches to understand and interpret visual content. You can identify and understand various elements within an image, such as objects, scenes, colors, textures, and even abstract concepts. To illustrate the power of image search, let's consider a practical example.

Imagine you're a fashion retailer with an extensive catalog of clothing items. With Bedrock, you can upload your product images and leverage the image search capabilities to enable customers to find visually similar items. For instance, a customer could upload a picture of a dress that they like and Bedrock would return a set of visually similar dresses from your catalog, facilitating a more engaging and personalized shopping experience.

One powerful approach to image search is based on multimodal embeddings, which allow for the representation of both text and images in a vector space. These vectors capture the visual features and semantic information of the images. The vectors, along with metadata such as image paths, are then stored in a searchable index vector database such as OpenSearch Serverless, FAISS, or Pinecone. This technique enables searching for images using text queries or finding similar images based on a given image (or a combination of text and image).

When a user initiates a search, their input (text, image, or both) is also converted into a vector representation using the same multimodal embedding model. The search vector is then compared against the vectors in the index and the most similar vectors are retrieved based on the vector similarity scores. This approach allows for flexible and intuitive image search, as users can search using natural language descriptions, upload example images, or combine text and images for more precise results. For example, you could search for `a red sports car on a city street` and the model would return relevant images from its data store that match both the visual and textual criteria.

As you might have recognized by now, this process is similar to the RAG process that we discussed in *Chapter 5*. The difference here is that the model is retrieving the images from its data store and is not generating new images. Here is a great example to try out multimodal embedding and searching: `https://github.com/aws-samples/amazon-bedrock-workshop/blob/main/04_Image_and_Multimodal/bedrock-titan-multimodal-embeddings.ipynb`.

Image search with multimodal embeddings has numerous real-world applications across various domains. In e-commerce platforms, it can be used to enhance product search and recommendation systems, allowing customers to find visually similar products or to search for items using natural language descriptions or example images. In the media and entertainment industry, it can assist in content organization, tag suggestion, and copyright infringement detection by identifying similar or duplicate images.

Image understanding

The Anthropic Claude 3 models – Sonnet, Haiku, and Opus – introduce the image understanding capability, through which the model can analyze the image and provide you with a response based on what you are looking to know. For example, you can provide an image of a kitchen or a living room and ask the model to provide a detailed description of the image or write a fictional story based on the image.

Example 1

Use the following prompt: `Provide a detailed description of this image.`

This image depicts a luxurious and well-designed kitchen interior. The room features dark wood cabinetry, contrasted by light marble countertops and backsplash. The kitchen has an expansive layout with a large central island that serves as both a prep area and dining space, with several wooden stools surrounding it.

The room is illuminated by several pendant lights, creating a warm and inviting atmosphere. The stainless steel appliances, including a refrigerator and range, are integrated seamlessly into the design. The kitchen also includes a built-in oven and microwave, as well as a range hood with a bronze finish that complements the overall color scheme.

The room has a mix of open shelving and closed cabinets, providing both display and storage space. The large windows allow natural light to flood the space, highlighting the attention to detail in the design and the high-quality materials used throughout the kitchen.

Overall, this image showcases a beautifully designed, functional, and luxurious kitchen space that would be well-suited for a modern, high-end home.

Figure 9.7 – Image understanding and a detailed description in the output

In *Figure 9.7*, we have provided the image of a kitchen to the Anthropic Claude 3 model and asked it to provide a detailed description of the image. The model is able to provide minute details such as **`the room features dark wood cabinetry, contrasted by light marble countertops`**, and so on.

Example 2

Use the following prompt: `Write a fictional story based on the image attached.`

The grand library exuded an air of timeless elegance. The ornate chandelier cast a warm glow over the room, illuminating the rows of leather-bound volumes that lined the towering shelves. A plush, tufted leather sofa beckoned visitors to sink into its comfortable embrace and lose themselves in the pages of a captivating book.

As the light from the setting sun filtered through the large windows, it danced across the intricate Persian rug, casting dancing shadows on the polished wooden floors. The crackling fire in the ornate fireplace added a cozy ambiance, hinting at the countless stories that had been shared and cherished within these hallowed walls.

This room was a sanctuary, a place where the mind could wander freely, unencumbered by the demands of the outside world. The richly appointed furnishings and the carefully curated collection of books suggested a world of mystery, adventure, and intellectual pursuit. One could almost hear the whispers of scholars, philosophers, and dreamers who had come before, their legacies etched into the very fabric of the room.

In this enchanting space, the boundaries between reality and imagination blurred, inviting the visitor to embark on their own journey of discovery, whether it be through the pages of a beloved tome or the expansive reaches of their own imagination. The library stood as a testament to the power of knowledge, the allure of the written word, and the timeless appeal of a space dedicated to the pursuit of wisdom and understanding.

Figure 9.8 – Image understanding with a fictional story

In *Figure 9.8*, you can see that the model has generated a fictional story based on the image of a library provided to it.

Example 3

Use the following prompt: `Provide the list of items/objects present in the image and explain each item.`

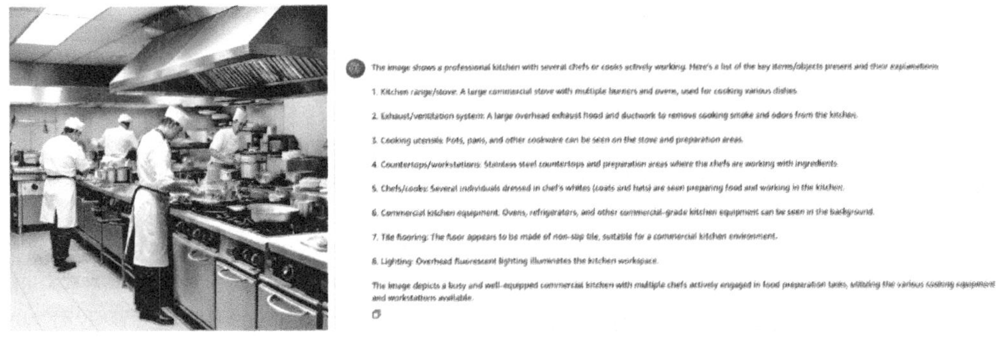

Figure 9.9 – Image understanding with object identification

In *Figure 9.9*, the model is able to identify the items and objects in the image along with their details, showcasing the image classification/object recognition capability.

The Claude models' image understanding capabilities are not limited to those discussed in the preceding examples. They can also be utilized for tasks such as image captioning, creating detailed image descriptions, identifying subjects, and answering questions about the contents of an image. You can look at various use cases of image understanding at `https://docs.anthropic.com/claude/docs/use-cases-and-capabilities#vision-capabilities`.

To use this capability within the Amazon Bedrock console, you can follow the ensuing steps:

1. Go to Amazon Bedrock Console at `https://console.aws.amazon.com/bedrock`.
2. Navigate to **Chat Playground**.
3. Click on **Select model**. Choose the **Anthropic Claude 3 Sonnet**, **Anthropic Claude 3 Haiku**, or **Anthropic Claude 3 Opus** model.
4. Attach the image you want to analyze and provide the prompt based on what you are looking for, as shown in *Figure 9.10*.

Figure 9.10 – How to analyze an image using the Anthropic Claude 3 models

If you are using AWS SDK, you can use Anthropic's `Messages` API to create a chat application and provide an image for understanding. Here is some example AWS Python SDK code for a multimodal message to the Claude 3 Sonnet model: `https://docs.aws.amazon.com/bedrock/latest/userguide/model-parameters-anthropic-claude-messages.html#api-inference-examples-claude-multimodal-code-example`.

Image-to-image patterns

When it comes to image-to-image generation, the model takes an existing image as input and modifies it based on the prompt or instructions you provide. This is different from text-to-image generation, whereby the model creates an entirely new image from scratch based solely on a textual description or prompt. In image-to-image generation, on the other hand, the model uses the existing image as a starting point and then applies the necessary changes or transformations to produce the desired output image. This can involve adjusting various aspects such as colors, textures, objects, or even the overall composition of the image, all guided by the prompt. It's like having a clay model and reshaping it to your desired outcome rather than starting from a lump of raw clay. The ability to modify and manipulate existing images opens up a range of creative possibilities and use cases, from enhancing and editing photographs to creating artistic interpretations or visualizations.

A simple example of image-to-image generation is shown in *Figure 9.11*.

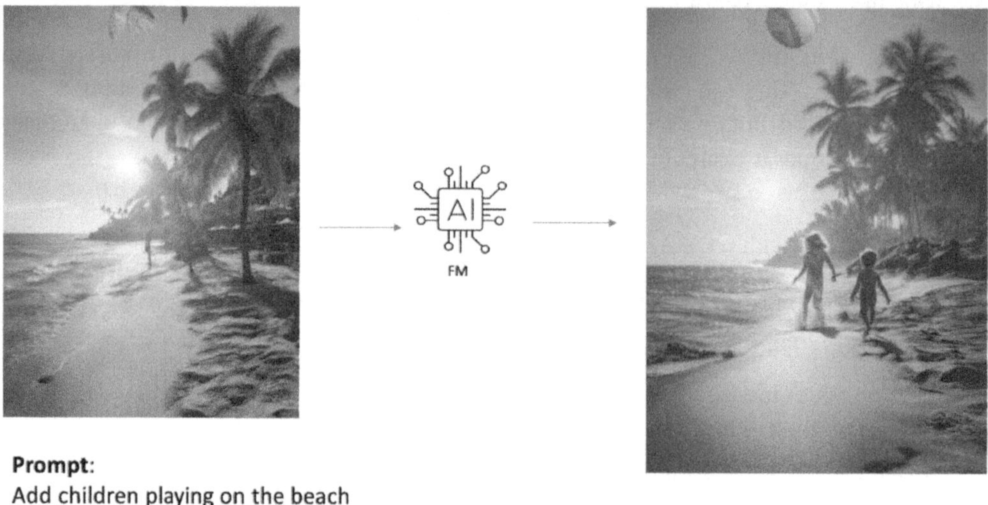

Figure 9.11 – Simple image-to-image generation

When using the Stable Diffusion model for image-to-image generation, there are a few additional parameters to consider along with the text-to-text parameters mentioned in *Figure 9.6*. These additional parameters are highlighted in *Figure 9.12*.

Parameters	Description
init_image	This is where the image is passed in base64 format
init_image_mode	Controls the influence of init_image. Possible values: IMAGE_STRENGTH or STEP_SCHEDULE
image_strength	When init_image_mode is set to IMAGE_STRENGTH, this parameter comes into play. It dictates the degree to which the initial image affects the diffusion process. Values closer to 1 result in generated images that strongly resemble the initial image, whereas values approaching 0 yield images that diverge significantly from the source
step_schedule_start	This optional parameter, ranging from 0 to 1, skips a proportion of the initial diffusion steps, allowing the init_image to influence the early stages of the generation process. Lower values give more weight to the init_image, while higher values give more weight to the diffusion steps during the early stages.
step_schedule_stop	This optional parameter, ranging from 0 to 1, skips a proportion of the final diffusion steps, allowing the init_image to influence the later stages of the generation process. Lower values give more weight to the init_image, while higher values give more weight to the diffusion steps during the later stages.

Figure 9.12 – Stable Diffusion image-to-image parameters

You can learn more about them here: `https://platform.stability.ai/docs/api-reference#tag/Image-to-Image/operation/imageToImage`.

Next, let us look at some image-to-image patterns.

Image variation

Image variation, also known as **image-to-image translation** or **style transfer**, is a powerful technique in generative AI that allows for the creation of new and unique images by modifying existing ones. This process involves taking an input image and applying a desired style or transformation to it, resulting in an output image that combines the content of the original with the desired aesthetic or visual characteristics.

One real-world example of image variation is in the field of fashion design. Designers can take an existing garment or accessory and apply various styles, patterns, or textures to create new and innovative designs without starting from scratch. This not only saves time and resources but also allows for rapid experimentation and iteration, enabling designers to explore a vast range of possibilities.

Another example can be found in the art world, where image variation techniques can be used to create unique and expressive artworks. Artists can take a simple photograph or painting and apply various artistic styles, such as impressionism, cubism, or abstract expressionism, to create entirely new pieces that blend the original content with the desired artistic style. This opens up new avenues for creative expression and allows artists to explore unconventional and thought-provoking visual interpretations.

Image variation also has applications in the fields of interior design and architectural visualization. Designers and architects can take existing spaces or structures and apply different materials, textures, or lighting conditions to visualize how a space might look with different design choices. This can be invaluable in helping clients understand and appreciate proposed designs, as well as in enabling designers to quickly iterate and refine their concepts.

With Bedrock, you can utilize Titan Image Generator to create image variations. Let us try the following prompt and run it through Titan Image Generator:

```
A delicate, nature-inspired pattern with intricate illustrations of
birds, butterflies, and foliage, perfect for a romantic, bohemian
dress or scarf.
```

Figure 9.13 – Image variation

As shown in *Figure 9.13*, Titan Image Generator will create an image (**Original Image**). You can generate image variations that leverage the **Original Image** as a reference, along with an optional prompt that can be provided to the model.

Masking

Amazon Bedrock models – Amazon Titan Generator and Stable Diffusion – offer two powerful image editing techniques: *masking* and *painting*.

With masking, we define specific areas within an image and mask them, either to be preserved or redrawn. This masking can be done either via an image file or a prompt.

Image masking

The approach of **image masking** utilizes a separate image file, known as the **mask image**, to specify the pixels to be masked or preserved in the original image. The mask image must adhere to the following requirements:

- **Identical dimensions and resolution as the original image**: When using image masking, it's crucial that the mask image has the exact same dimensions and resolution as the original image that you want to mask. This ensures that each pixel in the mask image corresponds to a pixel in the original image, allowing for precise masking. If the dimensions or resolutions differ, the masking process may produce distorted or undesired results.

  For example, if your original image has a resolution of 1920 x 1080 pixels, the mask image must also have a resolution of 1920 x 1080 pixels. Any discrepancy in the dimensions or resolution will cause the mask to misalign with the original image, leading to undesirable masking effects.

- **No alpha channel**: The mask image should not have an alpha channel, which is a separate component in some image formats that represents transparency. While the PNG format supports transparency through an alpha channel, for image masking purposes, the mask image should rely solely on color values (**Red, Green, Blue** (**RGB**) or grayscale) to represent masked and unmasked regions.

  The absence of an alpha channel simplifies the masking process and ensures that the masking is based solely on the pixel colors, without any additional transparency information. This approach is often preferred for its simplicity and compatibility with a wide range of image processing tools and libraries.

- **RGB or grayscale color mode**: The mask image can be either in RGB or grayscale color mode. In the context of image masking, the color mode determines how the masking is interpreted:

  - **RGB color mode**: In this mode, each pixel in the mask image is represented by a combination of red, green, and blue values. The masking process typically interprets black pixels (ones with RGB values of `0, 0, 0`) as masked areas, while any non-black pixels are considered unmasked regions.

  - **Grayscale color mode**: In grayscale mode, each pixel is represented by a single value ranging from `0` (black) to `255` (white). The masking process interprets pixels with a value of `0` as masked areas, while pixels with non-zero values are considered unmasked regions.

The choice between RGB and grayscale color modes depends on your specific use case and on the tools or libraries you're using for image masking. Some tools may have a preference for one color mode over the other.

For example, let's assume that you work in the Food and Beverages industry and you want to mask out certain food items from an image to create a transparent layer for a menu design. Suppose that you want to mask the bowl of chips in the image that follows and maybe remove it from your menu. *Figure 9.14* shows the original image and the masked image, where the masking is done on the bowl of chips.

Original Image

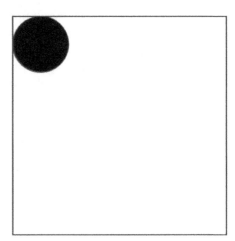

Image Mask

Figure 9.14 – Image masking

If you want to experiment with image masking, you can use online photo editing tools or apps. There is also the **Python Image Library** (**PIL**), a very popular Python library that is worth checking out at: `https://pillow.readthedocs.io/en/stable/reference/Image.html`.

In addition, we recommend that you experiment with the following GitHub examples from the Amazon Bedrock workshop that showcase image masking and painting: `https://github.com/aws-samples/amazon-bedrock-workshop/tree/main/04_Image_and_Multimodal`.

Mask prompting

Mask prompting involves masking images through the use of textual prompts. These textual prompts serve as a guide to the model to comprehend the desired masking area within an image.

The benefit of using mask prompting as opposed to image masking lies in the dynamic nature of mask prompting. You can effortlessly modify the masking by simply altering the textual prompt, allowing for rapid iteration and experimentation. This flexibility allows artists, designers, and content creators to explore a vast array of visual concepts and narratives without being constrained by traditional image editing tools.

In addition, mask prompting can be seamlessly integrated into various workflows and applications, enabling seamless collaboration and enhancing productivity. For instance, in the field of visual storytelling, writers and directors can leverage this feature to conceptualize and refine their vision, while designers can quickly prototype and iterate on visual concepts before committing to a final design.

To ensure the integrity and originality of the content generated, Amazon Bedrock has implemented robust measures to safeguard against plagiarism and unethical practices. We will discuss ethical considerations and safeguards in the upcoming section.

Let's take the same example from the preceding figure. Instead of image masking, we want to apply a mask prompt. We'll say that you want to remove the bowl of chips from the original image. With mask prompting, you can provide the `only bowl of chips` prompt and then further perform painting.

Original Image

Generated Image - Inpainting

Figure 9.15 – Mask prompting

In *Figure 9.15*, we performed inpainting and changed the bowl of chips to a bowl of apple slices. Let us discuss painting in more detail.

Painting

Painting is a technique whereby you can fill in the masked regions within an image or extend it using an image generation model. There are two methods of painting: inpainting and outpainting.

Inpainting

With **inpainting**, you are essentially reconstructing or filling in missing, masked, or corrupted portions of the image. This technique is particularly useful in scenarios where an image has been damaged or obscured, or where it contains unwanted elements that need to be removed or replaced. By providing the image generation model with the surrounding context and effective prompts, it can intelligently generate and blend new content in the designated areas, seamlessly reconstructing the masked regions.

Let us look at some examples:

- **Inpainting removal**: Suppose that you want to remove the masked object within an image. In that case, you can perform inpainting removal. Let's take an example of a beautiful scenic landscape as shown in *Figure 9.16* and say that you want to remove the telephone line from the original image. You can specify the mask prompt as `telephone line` and provide an empty prompt text (`""`).

Original Image

Mask prompt: telephone pole

Prompt text: ""

In-painted Image

Figure 9.16 – Inpainting removal

- **Inpainting replacement**: Suppose that you want to replace any object or scene within the image. In that case, you can perform inpainting replacement. As shown in *Figure 9.17*, you can specify within the prompt text what you want to replace.

Original Image

Prompt text:
replace telephone line with the tree

In-painted Image

Figure 9.17 – Inpainting replacement

Outpainting

Outpainting is the process of extending the image beyond its original boundaries, or in other words painting outside the masked regions. Outpainting is useful in scenarios where the original image or artwork needs to be extended or augmented with additional elements, environments, or perspectives.

Let us look at an example.

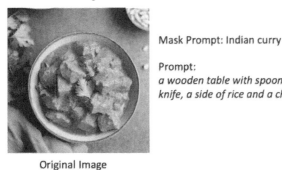

Figure 9.18 – Outpainting

In *Figure 9.18*, you can see that we are painting outside the masked image or prompt (in this case, `Indian curry`) to add some details. These include the background of a wooden table, as well as adding a spoon, a knife, a side of rice, and a chai.

If you want to understand the prompt engineering best practices for the Titan Image Generator model, please check out `https://tinyurl.com/titan-image-generator-prompt`

Now that we have looked at different patterns of multimodal and image patterns, let us look at the ethical considerations and available safeguards within Amazon Bedrock to ensure the responsible use of Generative AI.

Ethical considerations and safeguards

Generative AI models, particularly those capable of generating highly realistic images, raise significant ethical concerns regarding the potential spread of misinformation and deepfakes. As these models are becoming increasingly powerful and accessible, it is crucial to address these ethical challenges proactively to promote the responsible development and deployment of this technology.

One of the primary ethical concerns surrounding image generation models is the risk of creating and disseminating misleading or manipulated content. With the ability to generate photorealistic images from text prompts comes the potential for malicious actors to create and spread false or fabricated visual information. This can have far-reaching consequences, such as undermining trust in media, spreading disinformation, and even influencing political or social narratives.

To address this major ethical challenge, it is crucial for organizations and researchers to prioritize responsible development and deployment of a generative AI life cycle. When using Amazon Bedrock, users can utilize its **watermark detection** feature for images generated by Amazon Titan Image Generator.

The watermark detection capability in Amazon Bedrock is designed to promote transparency and accountability in the use of AI-generated images. By embedding an invisible watermark in every image created by the model, content creators, news organizations, risk analysts, and others can quickly verify whether an image has been generated using Amazon Titan Image Generator.

This approach serves two primary ethical purposes:

- It helps combat the spread of misinformation and deepfakes by providing a mechanism to verify the authenticity of images. This can help build trust and credibility in visual content, particularly in domains where the integrity of information is critical, such as journalism, law enforcement, and scientific research.
- The watermark detection feature promotes transparency and accountability in the use of image generation models. By making it easier to identify AI-generated content, it encourages responsible and ethical practices among content creators and stakeholders, fostering a more open dialogue around the use of this technology.

To try out watermark detection, you can simply navigate to **Watermark detection** in the Amazon Bedrock console and upload an image. Amazon Bedrock then analyzes the image to detect watermarks embedded by Amazon Titan.

In addition to detecting the watermark, you will also receive a confidence score, which determines the level of confidence (or certainty) with which the model is able to identify that the image was generated by Amazon Titan. Usually, you will see a high confidence score when there has been little to no modification in the image. However, if you make some modifications to the generated image, you might see a lower confidence score.

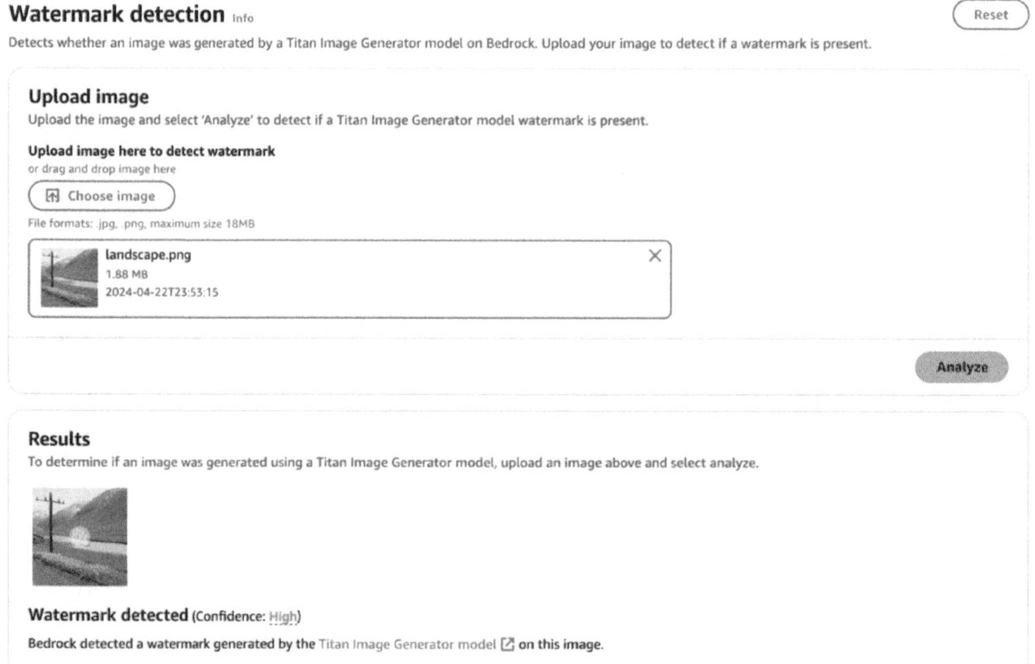

Figure 9.19 – Watermark detection

As shown in *Figure 9.19*, we have uploaded the image generated by Amazon Titan. The watermark detection feature is able to analyze and detect the watermark generated by Titan.

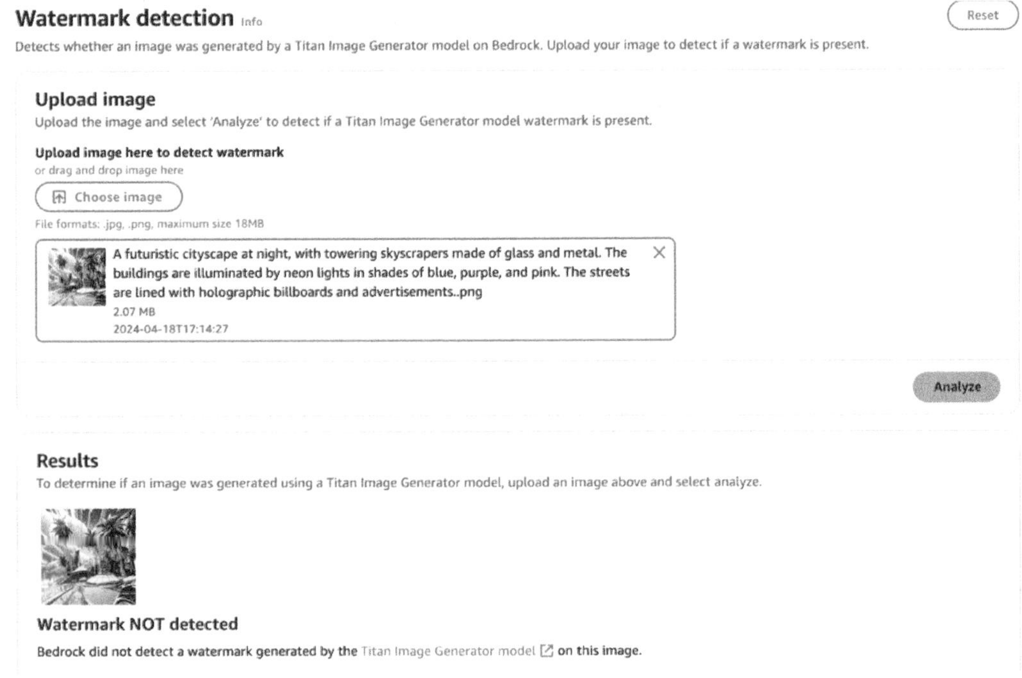

Figure 9.20 – The watermark is not detected

In *Figure 9.20*, we have uploaded the image generated by Stable Diffusion. We can see that the watermark is not detected.

If you want to try using API, you can call `DetectGeneratedContent` to verify whether the watermark exists:

```
import boto3
import json
import base64

bedrock_runtime = boto3.client(service_name="bedrock-runtime")

image_path = "landscape.png"

with open(image_path, "rb") as image_file:
    input_landscape = image_file.read()
```

```
response = bedrock_runtime.detect_generated_content(
    foundationModelId = "amazon.titan-image-generator-v1",
    content = {
        "imageContent": { "bytes": input_landscape }
    }
)
```

Here is how the response should look:

```
response.get("detectionResult")
'GENERATED'
response.get("confidenceLevel")
'HIGH'
```

Here is the demo on watermark detection: `https://www.youtube.com/watch?v=M5Vqb3UoXtc`.

While watermark detection is not a solution for all ethical concerns, it is one of the ways to move in the right direction. We will have a deeper discussion on ethical and responsible AI in *Chapter 11* of this book. You should now be able to understand image generation and design patterns with Amazon Bedrock.

Summary

In this chapter, we explored how image generation works. We also discussed the workings of multimodal models within Amazon Bedrock. We also covered several real-world applications and multimodal design patterns, including text-to-image, image search, image understanding, and image-to-image patterns such as inpainting and outpainting. We ended the chapter with a brief look at ethical considerations, as well as a look into the watermark detection capability within Amazon Bedrock. Throughout the chapter, we gained a deeper understanding of how we can leverage Amazon Bedrock's multimodal models to build applications that can generate, understand, and manipulate images based on text and image prompts.

In the next chapter, we will explore the topic of building intelligent agents with Amazon Bedrock.

10

Developing Intelligent Agents with Amazon Bedrock

In this chapter, readers will explore the concept of agents in **generative artificial intelligence** (**GenAI**), diving into their importance, benefits, and the various tools and types available.

Readers will learn to build knowledge bases and develop agents specifically designed for Amazon Bedrock, gaining insights into configurations, testing, and deployment strategies. Additionally, the chapter will showcase real-world industrial use cases, highlighting the practical applications of Agents in conjunction with Amazon Bedrock.

Through hands-on examples, readers will acquire the skills to describe the role of agents, integrate LangChain Agents with Amazon Bedrock, understand Agents' configurations for Amazon Bedrock, and build, test, and deploy agents tailored to this service. Furthermore, they will explore diverse industrial use cases, demonstrating the versatility and potential of Agents in enhancing the capabilities of Amazon Bedrock.

Specifically, readers will gain a clear understanding of the following:

- What are Agents?
- GenAI agent personas, roles, and use-case scenarios
- Amazon Bedrock integration with LangChain Agents
- Agents for Amazon Bedrock
- Deploying an Agent for Amazon Bedrock

Technical requirements

This chapter requires you to have access to an AWS account. If you don't have one already, you can go to `https://aws.amazon.com/getting-started/` and create an AWS account.

Secondly, you will need to install and configure AWS CLI (`https://aws.amazon.com/cli/`) after you create an account, which will be needed to access Amazon Bedrock FMs from your local machine. Since the majority chunk of code cells we will be executing is based in Python, setting up an AWS Python SDK (Boto3) (`https://docs.aws.amazon.com/bedrock/latest/APIReference/welcome.html`) would be beneficial at this point. You can carry out the Python setup in the following manner: install it on your local machine, or use AWS Cloud9, or utilize AWS Lambda, or leverage Amazon SageMaker.

> **Note**
>
> There will be a charge associated with the invocation and customization of Amazon Bedrock FMs. Please refer to `https://aws.amazon.com/bedrock/pricing/` to learn more.

What are Agents?

In the dynamic landscape of AI, a new category of sophisticated systems has emerged, poised to significantly impact our relationship with technology. These entities, known as **GenAI agents**, represent a formidable advancement characterized by their autonomy, adaptability, and cognitive abilities.

GenAI agents are software constructs engineered to comprehend and execute complex tasks with minimal human oversight. They demonstrate a remarkable capacity to assess objectives, devise strategic plans, and execute actions to achieve goals, all while continuously learning and refining their approaches based on feedback.

What distinguishes GenAI agents from previous iterations is their multifaceted nature, combining reactivity, proactivity, learning capabilities, and social adeptness. This unique amalgamation enables them to promptly respond to changing environments, anticipate future needs, evolve through ongoing learning processes, and seamlessly collaborate with humans and fellow agents.

Features of agents

Here are some of the key features of Agents:

- **Prompt response agility**: GenAI Agents excel in swift response to prompts, ensuring agility in adapting to dynamic circumstances. For instance, in manufacturing settings, these agents can efficiently recalibrate processes and reallocate resources to maintain operational efficiency amid fluctuating demand or unexpected disruptions.

- **Chain-of-thought (CoT)/Reasoning and Acting (ReAct)-style action**: GenAI Agents take action based on CoT/ReAct-style prompts, ensuring prompt and effective responses to stimuli. If you recall, ReAct prompting is a method designed to prompt LLMs, aiming to enhance the accuracy of their responses compared to other methods such as CoT. For instance, in customer service, these agents can generate responses to inquiries based on predefined conversational cues.
- **Prediction utility**: Though GenAI Agents do not autonomously anticipate or predict future events, they act based on predefined parameters and inputs. In financial forecasting, these agents utilize historical data and predefined algorithms to generate predictions rather than autonomously forecasting future trends.
- **Continuous learning**: GenAI Agents possess the capability for continuous learning and self-improvement. Similar to human counterparts, these agents refine their strategies and decision-making processes based on outcomes, continuously evolving and optimizing performance. For instance, in online recommendation systems, these agents continuously learn from user interactions to improve personalized recommendations.
- **Collaboration**: GenAI Agents demonstrate adeptness in seamless collaboration with humans and other agents. Through effective communication and coordination, they enhance productivity and efficiency in interconnected environments. In autonomous vehicle systems, these agents collaborate with other vehicles and infrastructure to ensure safe and efficient navigation on roads.

Practical applications of Agents – unleashing the potential

GenAI Agents offer a wide array of applications across various industries, showcasing their versatility and potential impact. In finance, these agents are being experimented with to explore the potential to analyze market trends, detect investment opportunities, and execute trades, enhancing decision-making processes and optimizing investment strategies. For instance, they can utilize historical data and predictive algorithms to identify patterns and forecast market movements, aiding financial professionals in making informed investment decisions.

In logistics and **supply chain management** (**SCM**), GenAI Agents can play a crucial role in optimizing resource allocation, streamlining distribution networks, and minimizing operational costs. By leveraging real-time data and predictive analytics, these agents can optimize inventory management, route planning, and warehouse operations, improving efficiency and reducing lead times. For example, they can dynamically adjust shipping routes based on traffic conditions and demand fluctuations to ensure timely delivery of goods.

Furthermore, GenAI Agents have the potential to transform education by personalizing learning experiences for students. They can adapt curricula and teaching methods to individual student needs and learning styles, facilitating personalized learning pathways and improving student outcomes. For instance, these agents can analyze student performance data, identify areas for improvement, and recommend tailored learning resources and activities to address specific learning needs.

While GenAI Agents hold significant promise and potential across various industries, it's essential to acknowledge that the widespread adoption and scaling of these technologies may still be in its early stages. While there are certainly organizations and research initiatives actively exploring and implementing GenAI solutions, achieving widespread adoption and scalability often requires overcoming various technical, regulatory, and ethical challenges.

In many cases, the practical implementation of GenAI Agents may involve pilot projects, **proofs of concept** (**POCs**), or targeted deployments rather than large-scale implementations across entire industries. Additionally, the effectiveness and impact of these technologies may vary depending on factors such as data quality, model performance, and the specific use case in question.

Therefore, it's crucial to approach discussions about the applications of GenAI Agents with a critical lens, considering the current state of technology, existing limitations, and potential challenges associated with widespread adoption.

Now, let us take a step further into exploring diverse use case scenarios relevant to GenAI agents.

GenAI agent personas, roles, and use-case scenarios

GenAI agents are heavily leveraged in enterprises as orchestrators. In the context of GenAI, **orchestration** refers to the coordinated management and deployment of these agents in various roles and use cases.

There are a variety of roles that GenAI agents can play as part of this orchestration. Some potential use cases of GenAI agents and the roles they could play include the following:

- **Virtual assistant roles**:
    - *Personal assistant*: Agents can act as personal assistants, helping individuals manage their schedules, set reminders, and handle tasks such as booking appointments, making reservations, or tracking deliveries.
    - *Information lookup*: They can also serve as information lookup tools, providing quick access to knowledge across various domains, such as current events, sports, entertainment, or general reference queries.
    - *Personalized recommenders*: By learning individual preferences and patterns, these agents can offer personalized recommendations and suggestions tailored to each user's needs and interests.
- **Customer service chatbot roles**:
    - *Customer support agent*: Agents can handle customer inquiries and support requests 24/7, providing instant assistance and reducing wait times for human agents.
    - *Product advisor*: They can guide customers through troubleshooting processes, provide product information, and offer personalized recommendations based on customer preferences and purchase history.

- Chatbots can also handle routine tasks such as order tracking, refund requests, and account management, freeing up human agents for more complex issues, such as troubleshooting technical issues, providing personalized recommendations, resolving disputes, and offering specialized expertise.

- **Tutoring and education roles**:
  - *Tutors*: GenAI agents can serve as virtual tutors, providing personalized learning experiences adapted to each student's pace, level, and learning style. They can explain complex concepts in engaging ways, provide practice exercises, and offer feedback and guidance to reinforce learning.
  - *Domain experts*: Agents can also act as domain experts, offering in-depth knowledge and insights across various academic subjects or professional fields.
- **Content creation roles**:
  - *Writer*: Agents can assist writers, journalists, and content creators by generating initial drafts, outlines, or summaries based on provided prompts or ideas.
  - *Storyteller*: They can help with ideation, story development, and creative writing tasks, offering suggestions and expanding on concepts.
  - *Content generator*: Agents can also generate marketing copy, product descriptions, or social media content, helping businesses and creators save time and effort.
- **Creative design roles**:
  - *Designer*: Agents can serve as creative collaborators, generating design ideas, artwork, logos, and visual concepts based on provided prompts or specifications.
  - *Artist*: They can offer inspiration and fresh perspectives, helping designers explore new directions and overcome creative blocks.
  - *Creative collaborator*: Agents can also assist in the iterative design process, generating variations and refinements based on feedback and direction from human designers.
- **Gaming and entertainment roles**:
  - *Game character*: In gaming, agents can play the role of **non-player characters** (**NPCs**), providing engaging interactions, dialogue, and storylines that adapt to player actions and choices.
  - *Interactive companion*: As interactive companions, agents can engage in conversations, tell stories, provide entertainment, and even offer emotional support or companionship in virtual environments.

- **Healthcare roles**:
  - *Medical assistant*: Agents can act as medical assistants, providing patients with information about conditions, treatments, and healthy lifestyle recommendations.
  - *Patient educator*: They can assist in patient education, explaining complex medical concepts in easy-to-understand language and addressing common concerns or questions.
  - Agents can also support healthcare professionals by summarizing patient records, generating medical reports, or assisting in research and data analysis tasks.
- **Software development roles**:
  - *Code assistant*: GenAI agents can serve as code assistants, helping developers write and optimize code by generating code snippets, suggesting improvements, or explaining programming concepts.
  - *Documentation generator*: They can assist in generating documentation, automatically creating descriptions and explanations for code segments, making it easier to maintain and collaborate on projects.
  - Agents can also help with code refactoring, identifying areas for optimization, and suggesting more efficient or secure coding practices.
- **Research and analysis roles**:
  - *Research assistant*: Agents can act as research assistants, gathering and synthesizing information from various sources, generating summaries, and identifying key insights or trends.
  - *Data analyst/data engineer*: They can assist in data analysis tasks, such as exploring datasets, identifying patterns, and generating visualizations or reports.
  - *ML engineer/data scientist*: Agents can also support researchers by generating hypotheses, suggesting experimental designs, or offering ideas for further exploration based on existing knowledge and data.
- **Language learning roles**:
  - *Conversational partner*: GenAI agents can serve as conversational partners, allowing language learners to practice speaking and comprehension in a safe and encouraging environment.
  - *Language tutors*: As language tutors, agents can provide feedback on pronunciation, grammar, and vocabulary, tailoring lessons and exercises to individual learners' needs and progress.
  - They can also generate engaging language learning materials, such as dialogues, stories, or exercises, adapting the content and difficulty level based on the learner's proficiency.

In all these cases, the agent's role is to augment human capabilities, provide personalized assistance, and enhance efficiency and productivity in various domains.

Now, let us take a step further to explore Agents and their utility functionality in the context of Amazon Bedrock.

Amazon Bedrock integration with LangChain Agents

LangChain, a powerful framework for developing applications with LLMs, provides a robust and flexible agent system that enables developers to build sophisticated agents capable of tackling a wide range of challenges.

An agent in LangChain is a high-level abstraction that combines an LLM, a set of tools, and other components in order to coordinate the execution of actions. The agent leverages the LLM's **natural language understanding** (**NLU**) capabilities to interpret user inputs, determine the appropriate actions to take, and orchestrate the utilization of available tools to accomplish the desired task.

The core components of a LangChain agent include the following:

- **Tools**: Tools are individual components that perform specific tasks, such as retrieving information from external sources or processing data. Agents use tools to interact with third-party applications and accomplish tasks. The following are examples of tools used:
    - `WebSearchTool`: Performs web searches using a search engine such as Google.
    - `WikipediaSearchTool`: Searches and retrieves information from *Wikipedia*.
    - `PythonCallbackTool`: Executes Python functions as tools.
    - `CSVTool`: Interacts with CSV files, allowing operations such as reading, writing, and querying data.
- **LLM**: The LLM serves as the reasoning engine behind the agent. It is responsible for understanding the user's intent, determining the appropriate actions to take, and interpreting the results of tool executions.
- **Toolkits**: Toolkits are collections of related tools designed to work together and provide a comprehensive set of functionalities for specific objectives, such as interacting with GitHub repositories or querying tabular data. For example, `SQLDatabaseToolkit` contains tools for interacting with SQL databases, including querying, creating tables, and inserting data.
- **Memory**: Memory allows agents to persist state and context between calls, enabling them to maintain a conversation history and provide more relevant and accurate responses over time. For example, `ConversationBufferMemory` stores the conversation history, allowing the agent to refer to previous inputs and outputs during the conversation.

LangChain provides a diverse set of built-in tools and agent classes to cater to various use cases. Some of the available tools include the following:

- `serpapi`: A search engine tool for querying web search results
- `google-search`: A wrapper around Google Search for conducting web searches

- `llm-math`: A tool for answering math-related questions using an LLM
- `open-meteo-api`: A tool for retrieving weather information from the Open-Meteo API
- `news-api`: A tool for fetching information about current news headlines
- `tmdb-api`: A tool for querying information from **The Movie Database** (**TMDB**)
- `wolfram-alpha`: A tool for querying the Wolfram|Alpha computational knowledge engine
- `requests`: A tool for fetching content from specific URLs
- `terminal`: A tool for executing terminal commands
- `pal-math`: A language model specialized in solving complex word math problems
- `pal-colored-objects`: A language model for reasoning about positions and color attributes of objects

As for agent classes, LangChain provides several options, each with its own strategy for action selection and problem-solving. Some examples include the following:

- `zero-shot-react-description`: An agent that relies on the LLM's zero-shot capabilities to select actions based on the tool descriptions
- `conversational-react-description`: An agent that engages in a conversational approach, asking for clarification when needed, and selecting actions based on the tool descriptions
- `react-docstore`: An agent that leverages a document store to retrieve relevant information and select actions based on the tool descriptions

Details on each of the aforementioned tools and agent classes are highlighted here: `https://api.python.langchain.com/en/latest/_modules/langchain/agents/agent_types.html`

Now that we have an understanding of LangChain Agents, let us dive into the integration of LangChain Agents with Amazon Bedrock, exemplified through a practical use case. We will import Bedrock via the LangChain package and leverage two LangChain tools, namely `YoutubeSearchTool` and `WikipediaTool`, enabling the LangChain Agent to leverage their capabilities. Additionally, we will be utilizing the Anthropic Claude model through Bedrock in this straightforward application.

> **Note**
>
> Ensure you have the correct permissions to invoke Amazon Bedrock, as explained in the earlier chapters. Further, please ensure that the latest version of LangChain packages and libraries are installed as per the code. In case the packages are not installed, run the following command in your Jupyter notebook (note that `!` Or `%` will not be needed if you're running Python code from a Python terminal):
>
> `%pip install <library_name>`

```
# Install the respective packages for YoutubeSearchTool and Wikipedia
Tool in your Jupyter Notebook
%pip install --upgrade --quiet wikipedia youtube_search langchain
```

```
#Install LangChain modules
%pip install -U langchain-community
%pip install -U langchain-aws langchainhub

# Import langchain libaries for Tools, Agents and Amazon Bedrock
from langchain.agents import AgentType
from langchain.agents import initialize_agent, Tool
from langchain_aws import BedrockLLM
from langchain.chains.conversation.memory import
ConversationBufferWindowMemory
from langchain.agents import AgentExecutor, create_react_agent
from langchain import hub

# Import respective packages for Wikipedia and Youtube tools
from langchain_community.tools import YouTubeSearchTool
from langchain_community.utilities import WikipediaAPIWrapper

# Using anthropic model with langchain
llm = BedrockLLM(model_id="anthropic.claude-v2")

# Define Tools below
wikipedia_wrapper = WikipediaAPIWrapper()
# Wikipedia Tool
wikipedia_tool = Tool(
        name="Wikipedia",
        func=wikipedia_wrapper.run,
        description="Useful tool for finding information on the
Internet related to world events, issues, etc. Worth using for general
topics. Use precise questions.",)

youtube_wrapper = YouTubeSearchTool()
#Youtube Tool
youtube_tool = Tool(name= "Youtube", func = youtube_wrapper.run,
description = "Useful tool for searching youtube videos on and sharing
the youtube links to the user. Use precise questions.")
#Create a memory instance
conversational_memory = ConversationBufferMemory()

prompt = hub.pull("hwchase17/react")
memory = conversational_memory
model = llm
tools = [wikipedia_tool,youtube_tool]

# Create an agent
```

```
agent = create_react_agent(model, tools, prompt = prompt)

# Create an agent executor
agent_executor = AgentExecutor(agent=agent, tools=tools, verbose=True)

#Run the agent executor
response = agent_executor.invoke({"input": "Memristor?"})
print(response)
```

The generated output looks like this:

```
{'input': 'Memristor?', 'output': 'A memristor is a non-linear
two-terminal electrical component that relates electric charge and
magnetic flux linkage. It was first theorized by Leon Chua in 1971
as the fourth fundamental circuit element alongside the resistor,
capacitor and inductor. Unlike those components, memristors exhibit
memory - their resistance depends on the history of current that
has previously flowed through them. Memristors have applications in
memory, computing, and neuromorphic/brain-inspired computing due to
their ability to store and process information. They are an active
area of research in nanoelectronics.'}
```

The output may look like what's shown in *Figure 10.1* and *Figure 10.2*. You will notice the agent performing reasoning using question, thought, action, and chaining:

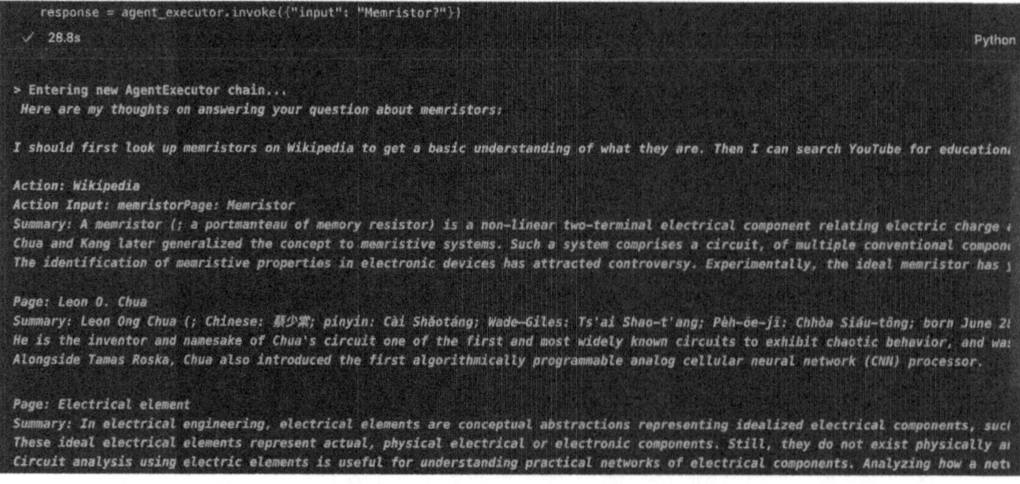

Figure 10.1 – AgentExecutor chain output

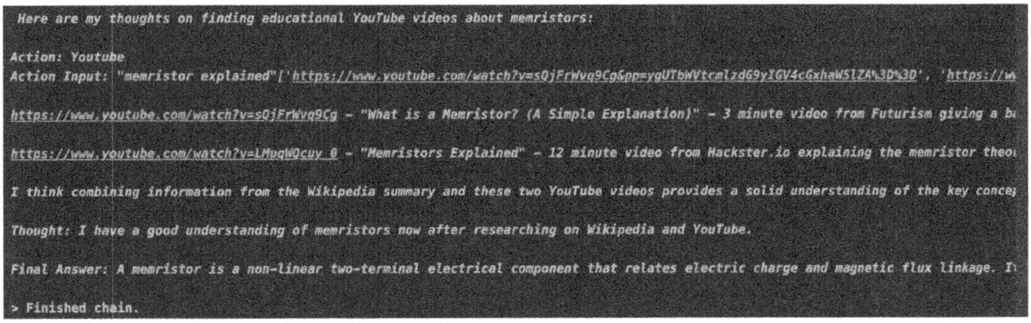

```
Here are my thoughts on finding educational YouTube videos about memristors:

Action: Youtube
Action Input: "memristor explained"['https://www.youtube.com/watch?v=sQjFrWvq9Cg&pp=ygUTbWVtcmlzdG9yIGV4cGxhaW5lZA%3D%3D', 'https://w

https://www.youtube.com/watch?v=sQjFrWvq9Cg - "What is a Memristor? (A Simple Explanation)" - 3 minute video from Futurism giving a b

https://www.youtube.com/watch?v=LMuqWQcuy_0 - "Memristors Explained" - 12 minute video from Hackster.io explaining the memristor theo

I think combining information from the Wikipedia summary and these two YouTube videos provides a solid understanding of the key conce

Thought: I have a good understanding of memristors now after researching on Wikipedia and YouTube.

Final Answer: A memristor is a non-linear two-terminal electrical component that relates electric charge and magnetic flux linkage. I

> Finished chain.
```

Figure 10.2 – Generated chain using LangChain agents with Bedrock

As shown in this section, when we are exploring technical topics such as memristors without any other context, the *Wikipedia* tool agent is invoked, providing comprehensive and detailed information, followed by the YouTube tool to provide additional information on the subject matter. In case the user writes `Elon Musk video on Neuralink` in the preceding conversation with the agent, the YouTube tool gets invoked and links are showcased to said user. Users are encouraged to try out different questions and test the agent.

Here is a sample output response for `response = agent_executor.invoke({"input": "Elon Musk video on Neuralink"})`:

```
> Entering new AgentExecutor chain...
 Here is my process for answering your question about finding a video
of Elon Musk discussing Neuralink:

Question: Elon Musk video on Neuralink

Thought: Elon Musk has given talks and interviews about Neuralink.
YouTube would be a good place to search for videos of him discussing
it.

Action: Youtube
Action Input: "elon musk neuralink"
['https://www.youtube.com/
watch?v=tN1lVwTHCMw&pp=ygUVZWxvbiBtdXNrIG51dXJhbGluayIK', 'https://
www.youtube.com/watch?v=k0I9Z-ARbjo&pp=ygUVZWxvbiBtdXNrIG51dXJhbGlua
yIK'] Here is my thought process for answering your question:

Question: Elon Musk video on Neuralink

Thought: Elon Musk has discussed Neuralink, his brain-machine
interface company, in various interviews and presentations. YouTube
would be a good place to search for videos of him talking about
Neuralink.
```

```
Action: Youtube
Action Input: "elon musk neuralink"
['https://www.youtube.com/
watch?v=tNllVwTHCMw&pp=ygUVZWxvbiBtdXNrIG5ldXJhbGluayIK', 'https://
www.youtube.com/watch?v=k0I9Z-ARbjo&pp=ygUVZWxvbiBtdXNrIG5ldXJhbGlua
yIK'] Here is my thought process and answer:

Question: Elon Musk video on Neuralink

Thought: Elon Musk has given presentations and interviews about
Neuralink, the brain-computer interface company he founded. YouTube
would be a good place to search for videos of him discussing Neuralink
and its technology.
...
https://www.youtube.com/watch?v=tNllVwTHCMw
https://www.youtube.com/watch?v=k0I9Z-ARbjo
> Finished chain.
```

As demonstrated, utilizing these tools enables us to access in-depth knowledge on the subject matter. It's worth noting that LangChain offers the capability to create custom tools as well, further expanding the capabilities of agents. This flexibility is highlighted in the documentation at `https://python.langchain.com/docs/modules/agents/tools/custom_tools`, where you can find guidance on crafting tailored tools to suit your specific needs.

As shown earlier, since we are searching for a technical topic for memristors, we get detailed information using the *Wikipedia* tool agent. You can create custom tools as well with agents, as shown here: `https://python.langchain.com/docs/modules/agents/tools/custom_tools`.

You can check out how to build GenAI agents with Amazon Bedrock and LangChain, coupled with Amazon Kendra, Amazon DynamoDB, and Amazon Lex, on the following blog: `https://aws.amazon.com/blogs/machine-learning/build-generative-ai-agents-with-amazon-bedrock-amazon-dynamodb-amazon-kendra-amazon-lex-and-langchain/`.

By effectively integrating Amazon Bedrock with LangChain Agents, organizations can unlock the full potential of LLMs, enabling the development of intelligent and context-aware applications that drive innovation, automate complex workflows, and deliver exceptional user experiences.

Now, let's jump into building Amazon Bedrock Agents for leveraging an end-to-end GenAI application.

Agents for Amazon Bedrock

One of the powerful capabilities offered by Amazon Bedrock is the ability to build and configure autonomous agents within your applications. These agents act as intelligent assistants, helping end users complete tasks based on organizational data and user input. Agents orchestrate interactions between FMs (LLMs), data sources, software applications, and user conversations. They can automatically call APIs to take actions and invoke knowledge bases to supplement information for these actions. By integrating agents, developers can save weeks of development effort and accelerate the delivery of GenAI applications.

Agents on Amazon Bedrock are designed to automate tasks for customers and provide intelligent responses to their questions. For example, you could create an agent that assists customers in processing insurance claims or making travel reservations. The beauty of agents is that you don't have to worry about provisioning capacity, managing infrastructure, or writing custom code from scratch. Amazon Bedrock handles the complexities of prompt engineering, memory management, monitoring, encryption, user permissions, and API invocation.

Agents on Amazon Bedrock perform the following key tasks:

- **Extend FMs**: Agents leverage LLMs to understand user requests and break down complex tasks into smaller, manageable steps.
- **Collect additional information**: Through natural conversation, agents can gather additional information from users to fulfill their requests effectively.
- **Take actions**: Agents can make API calls to your company's systems to perform actions and fulfill customer requests.
- **Augment performance and accuracy**: By querying data sources and knowledge bases, agents can enhance their performance and provide more accurate responses.

In order to harness the power of Agents for Amazon Bedrock, developers follow a straightforward process:

1. Create a knowledge base to store your organization's private data, which can be used to enhance the agent's performance and accuracy. This step is *optional* because not all agents require access to private organizational data to carry out their assigned objectives. If the agent's tasks and objectives do not depend on or benefit significantly from access to such data, creating a knowledge base may not be necessary. It depends on the specific use case and requirements of the agent being developed.
2. Configure an agent for your specific use case, defining the actions it can perform. Lambda functions, written in your preferred programming language, dictate how the agent handles these actions. This is an optional step as an agent doesn't necessarily require an action group to be created.
3. Associate the agent with a knowledge base to augment its capabilities further.
4. Customize the agent's behavior by modifying prompt templates for preprocessing, orchestration, knowledge-base response generation, and postprocessing steps. Note that *not* all agents require extensive modification of prompt templates for their goal. The need for customization depends on the complexity of the tasks the agent is expected to perform and the level of control and fine-tuning desired by developers. For simpler tasks or generic use cases, the default prompt templates may suffice, making extensive customization unnecessary.

5. Test the agent using the Amazon Bedrock console or API calls, modifying configurations as necessary. Utilize traces to gain insights into the agent's reasoning process at each step of its orchestration.
6. When the agent is ready for deployment, create an alias that points to a specific version of the agent.
7. Integrate your application with the agent alias, enabling seamless API calls and interactions.
8. Iterate on the agent as needed, creating new versions and aliases to adapt to changing requirements.

Throughout the development process, Amazon Bedrock handles the complexities of prompt engineering, memory management, monitoring, encryption, user permissions, and API invocation, allowing you to focus on building intelligent agents tailored to your specific use cases.

Unveiling the inner workings of GenAI agents with Amazon Bedrock

When delving into the realm of Amazon Bedrock, one encounters a powerful toolset designed to facilitate the creation and management of intelligent agents. This toolset is composed of two distinct categories of API operations, each serving a specific purpose in the agent's life cycle:

- The first category, aptly termed *build-time API operations*, enables developers to construct, configure, and oversee their agents and their associated resources. These operations act as the foundational building blocks, enabling the creation of agents tailored to specific requirements and objectives. Through these APIs, developers can fine-tune various aspects of their agents, ensuring they are equipped with the necessary capabilities to tackle the tasks at hand. More details on build-time API operations are listed here: `https://docs.aws.amazon.com/bedrock/latest/APIReference/API_Operations_Agents_for_Amazon_Bedrock.html`
- The second category, *runtime API operations*, breathes life into agents, allowing them to interact with user input and initiate an intricate orchestration process to accomplish their designated tasks. When a user provides input, these APIs enable the agent to process and interpret the information, triggering a sequence of actions that ultimately lead to the desired outcome.

Now, let us dive into build-time and runtime configurations.

Build-time configuration

During the build phase, an agent is assembled from the following key components:

- **FM**: You select a pre-trained language model that the agent employs to interpret user input, generate responses, and guide its decision-making process.
- **Instructional prompts**: You craft instructions that delineate the agent's purpose and desired behavior. With advanced prompting techniques, you can dynamically tailor these instructions at each stage of the agent's workflow and incorporate custom logic through serverless functions.

- **Action groups**: You define actions the agent can perform by providing the following:
    - An OpenAPI schema specification that outlines the operations the agent can invoke.
    - A serverless function that executes the specified API operation based on the agent's input and returns the result.
- **Knowledge bases**: You can associate knowledge bases with the agent, allowing it to retrieve relevant context to enhance its response generation and decision-making capabilities.
- **Prompt templates**: The orchestrator exposes default prompt templates used during various stages of the agent's life cycle, such as preprocessing input, orchestrating actions, querying knowledge bases, and postprocessing outputs. You can customize these templates to modify the agent's behavior or disable specific stages as needed.

During the build process, these components are combined to create base prompts that guide the agent's orchestration flow until the user's request is fulfilled. With advanced prompting techniques, you can augment these base prompts with additional logic, examples, and metadata to improve the agent's accuracy and performance at each stage of its invocation. After configuring the agent's components and security settings, you can prepare the agent for deployment and testing in a runtime environment, as shown in *Figure 10.3*.

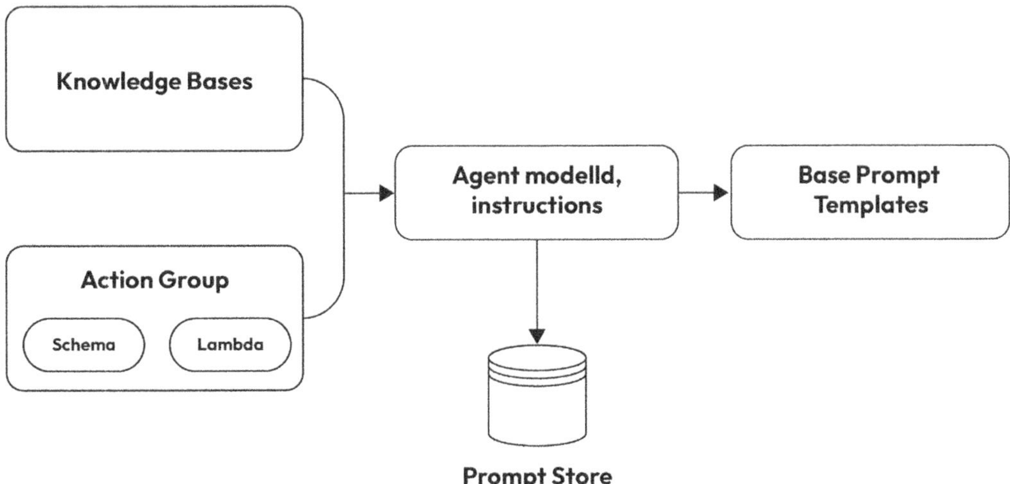

Figure 10.3 – Build-time API operations for Agent creation

Runtime process

At the heart of this runtime process lies the `InvokeAgent` API operation, a powerful conductor that sets the agent sequence in motion. The agent's performance unfolds in three harmonious acts: preprocessing, orchestration, and postprocessing.

Act I – Preprocessing

Before the curtains rise, the preprocessing phase meticulously manages how the agent contextualizes and categorizes user input. This crucial step can also validate the input, ensuring a seamless transition to the subsequent stages.

Act II – Orchestration – the grand performance

The orchestration phase is where the true magic unfolds, a symphonic interplay of interpretation, invocation, and knowledge synthesis. This act consists of the following movements:

1. **Interpretation**: The agent deftly interprets the user input with an FM, generating a rationale that lays out the logical path for the next steps.
2. **Invocation and synthesis**: Like a skilled conductor, the agent invokes action groups and queries knowledge bases, retrieving additional context and summarizing the data to augment its generation capabilities.
3. **Observation and augmentation**: From the invoked action groups and summarized knowledge-base results, the agent generates an output, known as an **observation**. This observation is then used to enrich the base prompt, which is subsequently interpreted by the FM. The agent then determines if further orchestration iterations are necessary.

This iterative loop continues until the agent delivers its final response to the user or requires additional information from the user.

Throughout the orchestration phase, the base prompt template is augmented with agent instructions, action groups, and knowledge bases, creating a rich tapestry of information. This enhanced base prompt is then fed into the FM, which predicts the optimal trajectory to fulfill the user's request. At each iteration, the FM selects the appropriate API operation or knowledge-base query, resulting in a responsive and contextually accurate output.

Act III – Postprocessing – the finale

In the final act, the postprocessing phase, the agent formats the culmination of its efforts – the final response to be returned to the user. However, this step can be gracefully bypassed, leaving the performance open to interpretation.

During the agent's performance, users have the option to invoke a trace at runtime, unlocking a window into the agent's thought process. This trace meticulously tracks the agent's rationale, actions, queries, and observations at each step of the sequence. It includes the full prompts sent to the FM, as well as outputs from the model, API responses, and knowledge-base queries. By examining this trace, users can gain invaluable insights into the agent's reasoning, paving the way for continuous improvement and refinement.

As the user's session with the agent continues through successive `InvokeAgent` requests, the conversation history is diligently preserved, continually augmenting the orchestration base prompt template with context. This enrichment process aids in enhancing the agent's accuracy and performance, forging a symbiotic relationship between the user and the AI.

The agent's process during runtime is a captivating interplay of interpretation, synthesis, and adaptation, as showcased in *Figure 10.4*:

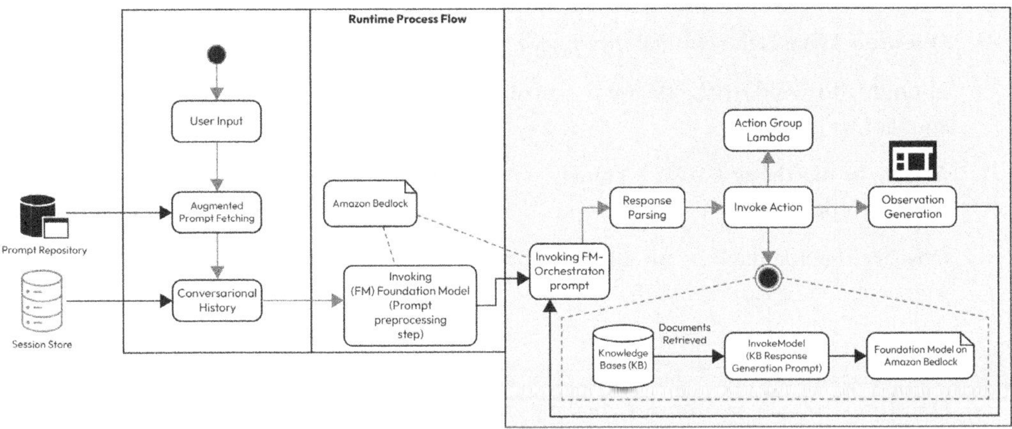

Figure 10.4 – Runtime process flow for Agent workflow

Advancing reasoning capabilities with GenAI – a primer on ReAct

GenAI models have demonstrated splendid capabilities in processing and generating human-like text, but their ability to reason through complex tasks and provide step-by-step solutions remains a challenge. Yao et. al have developed a technique called ReAct, as articulated in the paper *ReAct: Synergizing Reasoning and Acting in Language Models* (`https://arxiv.org/abs/2210.03629`), to enhance the reasoning abilities of these models, enabling them to systematically approach and solve user-requested tasks.

The ReAct technique involves structuring prompts that guide the model through a sequence of reasoning steps and corresponding actions. These prompts consist of a series of *question-thought-action-observation* examples, where the following applies:

- The *question* represents the user-requested task or problem to be solved
- The *thought* is a reasoning step that demonstrates how to approach the problem and identify a potential action
- The *action* is an API call or function that the model can invoke from a predefined set of allowed operations
- The *observation* is the result or output obtained from executing the chosen action

The set of allowed actions is defined by instructions prepended to the example prompt text. This structured approach encourages the model to engage in a step-by-step reasoning process, breaking down complex tasks into smaller, actionable steps.

To illustrate the construction of a ReAct prompt, consider the following example prompt structure with question-thought-action-observation sequences:

Example 1:

- **Question**: What is the optimal inventory level to minimize stockouts?
- **Thought**: To avoid stockouts, we must balance inventory levels based on demand forecasts and reorder points.
- **Action**: Invoke the `optimizeInventoryLevels` function using historical sales data and demand projections.
- **Observation**: Maintaining inventory at 80% of forecasted demand reduced stockouts by 30% while optimizing carrying costs.

Example 2:

- **Question**: How can we improve customer satisfaction ratings?
- **Thought**: To enhance satisfaction, we should analyze feedback data and implement targeted improvements.
- **Action**: Execute the `analyzeCustomerFeedback` API to identify trends and insights.
- **Observation**: Based on the analysis, implementing personalized customer support led to a 20% increase in satisfaction scores.

These examples demonstrate how the ReAct technique guides the model through reasoning steps, leading to actionable outcomes.

While the process of manually crafting these prompts can be time-consuming and intricate, the Amazon Bedrock Agent streamlines this process by automatically generating the prompts based on the provided information and available actions. Bedrock agents handle the complexities of prompt engineering, allowing researchers and developers to focus on defining the task requirements and available actions.

Readers are encouraged to check out `https://github.com/aws-samples/agentsforbedrock-retailagent`, which uncovers the creation of an FM-powered customer service bot by leveraging Agents for Amazon Bedrock.

The ReAct technique and Bedrock Agents represent a significant advancement in the field of GenAI, enabling models to demonstrate improved reasoning abilities and tackle complex tasks more effectively. By providing a structured approach to problem-solving and leveraging the power of prompts, this technique has the potential to unlock new possibilities and applications for GenAI in various domains. Let us explore the functioning of Amazon Bedrock Agents with some practical use cases.

Practical use case and functioning with Amazon Bedrock Agents

In this section, we will dive into real-world applications and operational insights of leveraging Amazon Bedrock Agents in GenAI. Let us consider an example scenario of a multilingual summarizer bot, wherein a GenAI agent can be employed to streamline operations and automate how to translate the content in a summarized fashion in the language of the user's choice. In order to begin, the developer must access the Bedrock console and initiate the agent creation workflow, as highlighted in *Figure 10.5*:

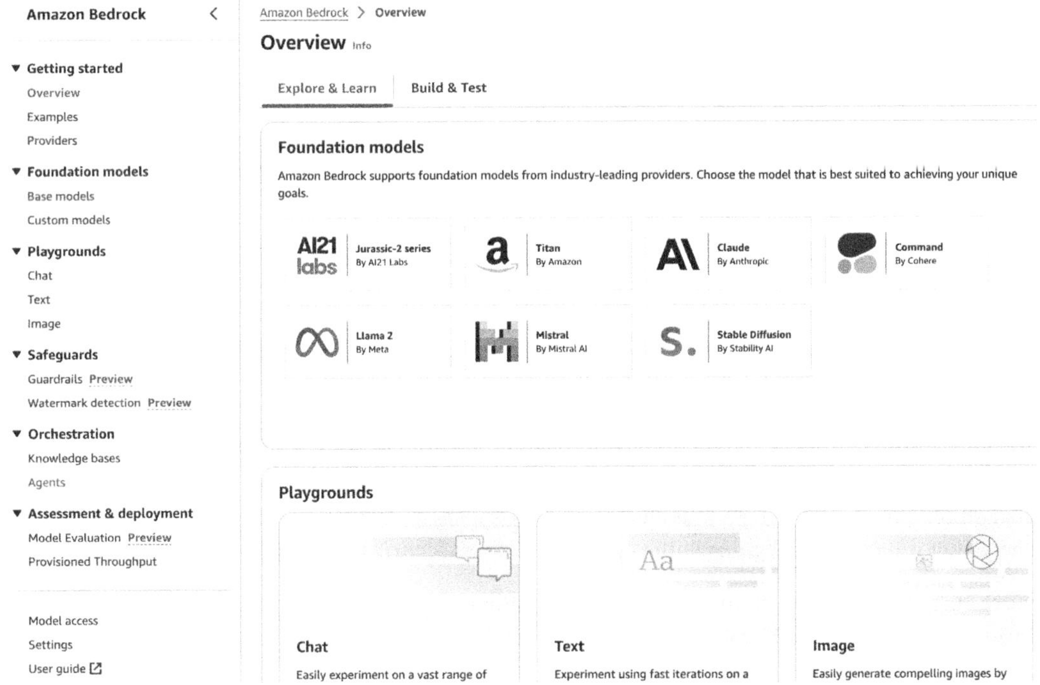

Figure 10.5 – Agent creation within the Bedrock console

This process involves providing essential details, such as the agent's name, description, and the necessary permissions through an AWS **Identity and Access Management** (**IAM**) service role. This role grants the agent access to required services such as **Amazon Simple Storage Service** (**Amazon S3**) and AWS Lambda, as illustrated in *Figure 10.6*. As an example, the figure demonstrates the creation of a multilingual document summarizer and translator agent for extracting relevant information from the documents and relaying the information to the user in the translated language:

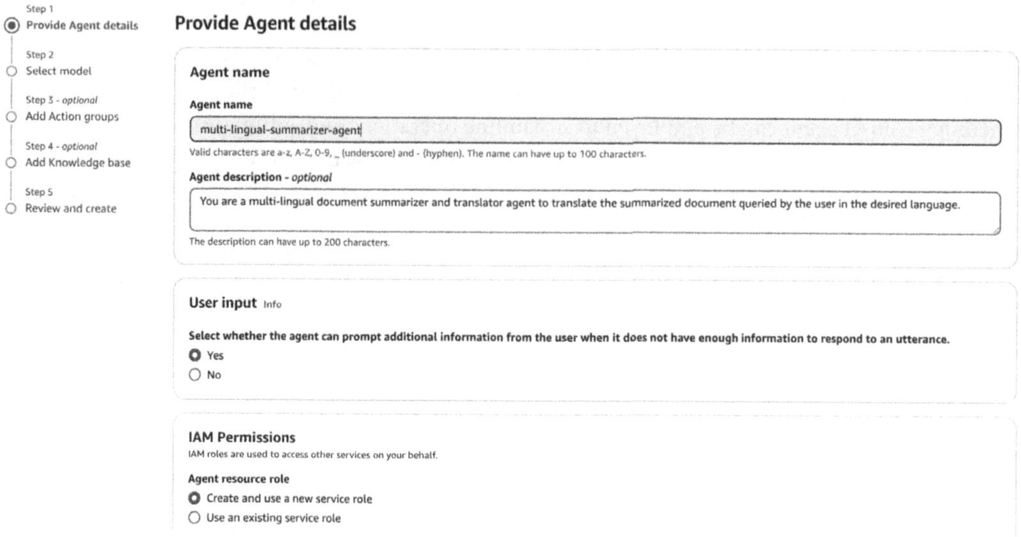

Step 1
Provide Agent details

Step 2
Select model

Step 3 - *optional*
Add Action groups

Step 4 - *optional*
Add Knowledge base

Step 5
Review and create

Provide Agent details

Agent name

Agent name

multi-lingual-summarizer-agent

Valid characters are a-z, A-Z, 0-9, _ (underscore) and - (hyphen). The name can have up to 100 characters.

Agent description - *optional*

You are a multi-lingual document summarizer and translator agent to translate the summarized document queried by the user in the desired language.

The description can have up to 200 characters.

User input Info

Select whether the agent can prompt additional information from the user when it does not have enough information to respond to an utterance.

- Yes
- No

IAM Permissions

IAM roles are used to access other services on your behalf.

Agent resource role

- Create and use a new service role
- Use an existing service role

Figure 10.6 – Bedrock Agent creation process with IAM permissions

By default, Amazon Bedrock employs encryption for agent sessions with users, utilizing a key that AWS owns and manages on your behalf. However, if you prefer to use a customer-managed key from AWS **Key Management Service** (**KMS**) that you have set up, you have the option to customize your encryption settings accordingly. This allows you to take control of the encryption key used for securing agent-user interactions, aligning with your organization's security and compliance requirements.

Next, the developer selects an FM from Bedrock that aligns with the desired use case. This step involves providing natural language instructions that define the agent's task and the persona it should assume. For instance, in the example demonstrated in *Figure 10.7*, the instruction could be `You are a multi-lingual agent designed to help with extracting inquired information from relevant documents and providing the response in translated language`:

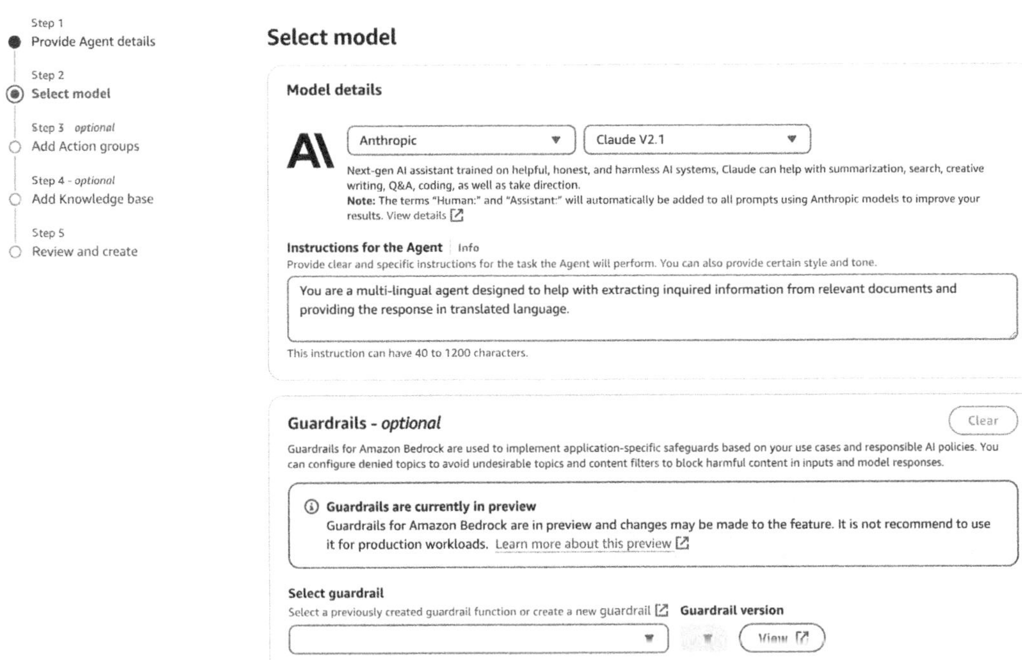

Figure 10.7 – Amazon Bedrock Agent configuration for model selection and Agent persona

The console also provides the option for the user to select guardrails to implement application-specific safeguards abiding by responsible AI policies. For simplicity, we can leave this blank and move to the next section. We will be covering guardrails in detail in *Chapter 12*.

Subsequently, the developer adds action groups, which are sets of tasks the agent can perform automatically by making API calls to the company's systems. This step involves defining an API schema that outlines the APIs for all actions within a group and providing a Lambda function that encapsulates the business logic for each API. For example, an action group named `Summarizer_Translator_ActionGroup` could handle documents stored either in a database or within a particular location, identifying the information requested by the user and sending a summarized response to the user in the translated language inquired by the user. *Figure 10.8* showcases the creation of an action group to handle tasks for agents to execute autonomously:

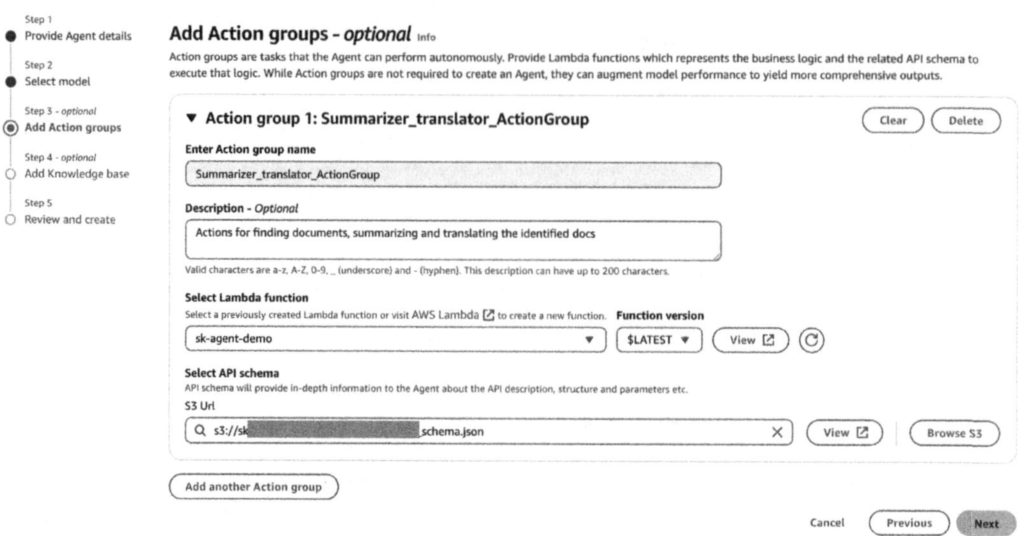

Figure 10.8 – Creating Bedrock Agent's action group

As shown previously, you will have to create a Lambda function to handle incoming requests from the agents and select an API schema. Please ensure you have provided the right permissions to your AWS Lambda function to invoke Bedrock agents.

For the case of document identification, summarization, and translation, we have provided the following Lambda function that users can leverage for executing the workflow:

```
import json
import time
import boto3

# Define a mock dictionary with document IDs and content
Document_id = {
    "doc_1": {
        "title": "The Importance of Mindfulness",
        "author": "Jane Smith",
        "content": "Mindfulness is the practice of being fully present
and engaged in the current moment, without judgment or distraction.
It involves paying attention to your thoughts, feelings, and bodily
sensations with a curious and non-judgmental attitude. By cultivating
mindfulness, you can reduce stress, improve emotional regulation,
and enhance overall well-being. In this document, we will explore
the benefits of mindfulness and provide practical techniques for
incorporating it into your daily life."
    },
    "doc_2": {
```

```
        "title": "Sustainable Living: A Guide to Eco-Friendly
Practices",
        "author": "Michael Johnson",
        "content": "In today's world, it's essential to adopt
sustainable living practices to protect our planet's resources and
ensure a better future for generations to come. This document will
provide you with practical tips and strategies for reducing your
environmental impact in various aspects of your life, such as energy
consumption, waste management, transportation, and food choices.
Together, we can make a significant difference by embracing eco-
friendly habits and promoting a more sustainable lifestyle."
      },
    "doc_3": {
        "title": "The Art of Effective Communication",
        "author": "Emily Davis",
        "content": "Effective communication is a crucial skill in both
personal and professional settings. It involves the ability to convey
your thoughts, ideas, and emotions clearly and respectfully, while
also actively listening and understanding the perspectives of others.
In this document, we will explore the key elements of effective
communication, such as active listening, nonverbal cues, and empathy.
By mastering these techniques, you can improve your relationships,
resolve conflicts more effectively, and achieve greater success in
your personal and professional endeavors."
      }
    }


def getDocID(event):
        docID = event['parameters'][0]['value']
        print("NAME PRINTED: ", docID)
        if(docID== "doc_1" or "doc1"):
            return Document_id["doc_1"]["content"]
        elif docID == "doc_2" or "doc2":
            return Document_id["doc_2"]["content"]
        elif docID == "doc_3" or "doc3":
            return Document_id["doc_3"]["content"]
        else:
            return "No document found by that ID"


def lambda_handler(event, context):
    response_code = 200
    """Main lambda handler directing requests based on the API path,
preserving the specified response structure."""
    print("event OUTPUT : ")
    print(event)

    action_group = event.get("actionGroup")
```

```
    print("action group :" + str(action_group))

    api_path = event.get("apiPath")
    print ("api_path : " + str(api_path))

    result = ''
    response_code = 200

    if api_path == '/getDoc':
        result = getDocID(event)
        print(result)
    else:
        response_code = 404
        result = f"Unrecognized api path: {action_group}::{api_path}"

    response_body = {
        'application/json': {
            'body': result
        }
    }

    action_response = {
        'actionGroup': event['actionGroup'],
        'apiPath': event['apiPath'],
        'httpMethod': event['httpMethod'],
        'httpStatusCode': response_code,
        'responseBody': response_body
    }

    api_response = {'messageVersion': '1.0', 'response': action_
response}
    return api_response
```

Users running the preceding workflow can also use the following OpenAPI schema and store it in S3, as part of this example:

```
{
    "openapi": "3.0.1",
    "info": {
        "title": "DocSummarizerTranslator API",
        "version": "1.0.0",
        "description": "APIs for fetching, translating and summarizing
docs by fetching the document ID and identifying the language to
translate the document"
```

```
    },
    "paths": {
        "/getDoc": {
            "get": {
                "description": "Get the document content for a
document by document ID.",
                "operationId": "getDoc",
                "parameters": [
                    {
                        "name": "DocID",
                        "in": "query",
                        "description": "ID of the document to
retrieve",
                        "required": true,
                        "schema": {
                            "type": "string"}}],
                "responses": {
                    "200": {
                        "description": "Successful response with
document content data",
                        "content": {
                            "text/plain": {
                                "schema": {
                                    "type": "string"
                                }}}}}}},
        "/getDoc/summarize": {
            "get": {
                "description": "Summarize the content of the document
for given document ID",
                "operationId": "summarizeDoc",
                "parameters": [
                    {
                        "name": "DocID",
                        "in": "query",
                        "description": "ID of the document to
summarize",
                        "required": true,
                        "schema": {
                            "type": "string"
                        }
                    }
                ],
                "responses": {
                    "200": {
                        "description": "Successful response with the
```

```
summary of the document content for given document ID",
                        "content": {
                            "application/json": {
                                "schema": {
                                    "type": "string",
                                    "properties": {
                                        "summary": {
                                            "type": "string",
                                            "description": "Summary of
the document"}}}}}}}}}}}
```

In the next step, users have the option to select a knowledge base, as depicted in *Figure 10.9*. This showcases the power of Bedrock Agents to easily create a RAG-based solution for extracting information from relevant sources stored in the knowledge base, by performing similarity searches and providing desired responses back to the user. For simplicity, we will ignore that and move to the final creation step:

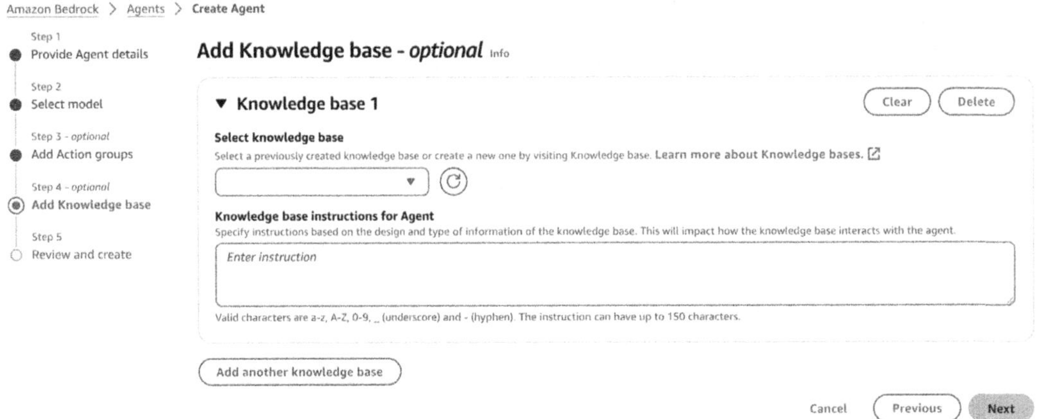

Figure 10.9 – Knowledge-base creation with Bedrock Agents integration

Note

If you would like to dive deep into use cases involving knowledge-base integration with your agents, you can execute the following code samples: `https://github.com/aws-samples/amazon-bedrock-workshop/tree/main/05_Agents/insurance_claims_agent/with_kb`.

Additional code within the GitHub repository further illustrates how to create and invoke Bedrock Agents with the Python SDK, as evidenced in the following notebook: `https://github.com/aws-samples/amazon-bedrock-workshop/blob/main/05_Agents/insurance_claims_agent/with_kb/create_and_invoke_agent_with_kb.ipynb`.

Once the preceding steps are done, you can verify the agent configuration and select **Create Agent**. Congratulations on creating your Amazon Bedrock Agent (*Figure 10.10*)!

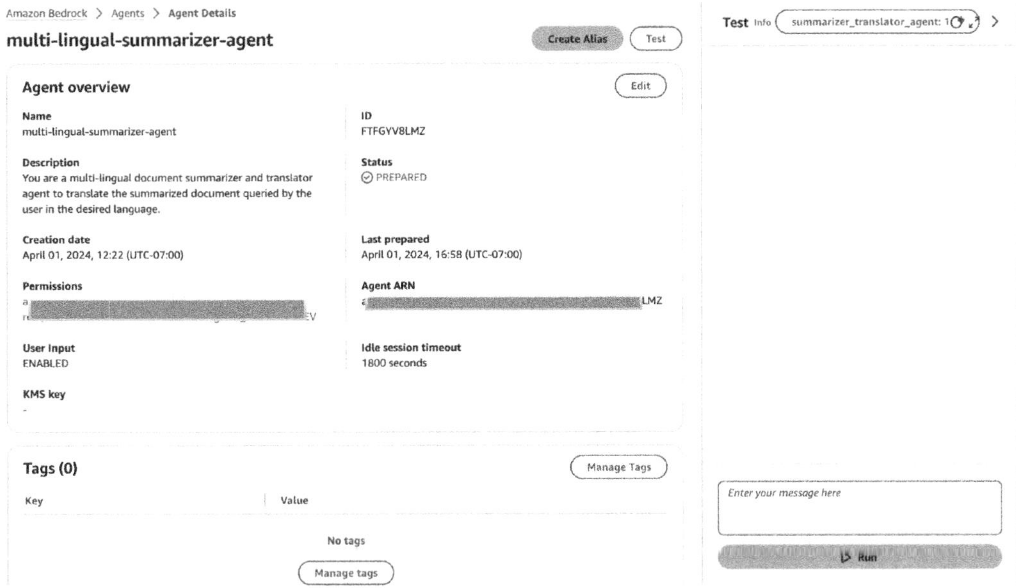

Figure 10.10 – Amazon Bedrock Agent version

On the right side of the screen, you can easily test your agent by asking it questions about the document and requesting it to summarize and translate the document into your desired language, as shown in *Figure 10.11*:

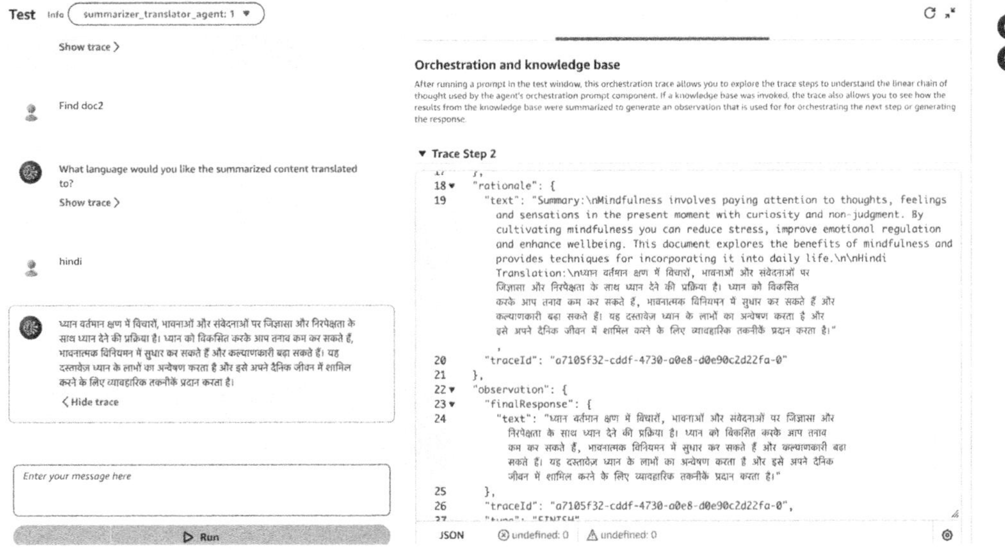

Figure 10.11 – Testing Bedrock Agent within AWS console

In this section, we acquired a practical comprehension of developing and evaluating Amazon Bedrock Agents tailored for a text summarization use case. Upon ensuring the agent's configuration and functionality align with the designated tasks, it's time to transition into the deployment phase.

Deploying an Agent for Amazon Bedrock

Integrating an Amazon Bedrock agent into your application requires creating an alias, which serves as a reference to a specific version of the agent's code and configuration. Follow these steps to create an alias:

1. Access the Amazon Bedrock console and navigate to the agent you wish to deploy. From the agent's overview page, navigate to the **Aliases** section and then click **Create** to initiate the alias creation process.
2. Provide a name and description (optional) for the alias. You'll also need to decide whether you want to associate this alias with a new version of the agent or an existing version that you've previously created.
3. Users also have the option to opt for provisioned throughput for the alias by selecting the **Provisioned Throughput (PT)** button. Once selected, a drop-down menu will list models created with Provisioned Throughput. No option being displayed will indicate that no PT model exists within the Amazon Bedrock environment. For further information, users can leverage `https://docs.aws.amazon.com/bedrock/latest/userguide/prov-throughput.html`.

By creating an alias, Bedrock takes a snapshot of the agent's current code and configuration settings and links that snapshot (version) to the alias you've defined. You can then use this alias to integrate and interact with that specific version of the agent within your applications. *Figure 10.12* showcases two aliases that were created for the summarizer-translator agent:

Figure 10.12 – Aliases for Amazon Bedrock Agents

The alias essentially acts as a stable reference point, allowing you to manage different versions of your agent while ensuring your applications are interacting with the desired version.

Amazon Bedrock agents enable productivity gains, enhanced customer experiences, and automated workflows. Their versatility allows innovative implementations across domains such as task automation, conversational interfaces, and DevOps processes, driving operational efficiency and business value.

There can be several other industrial use cases with Bedrock Agents. For instance, in the case of insurance, by leveraging GenAI through Amazon Bedrock, insurance companies can enhance operational efficiency and customer experience. The agent can automate tedious and repetitive tasks, freeing up human resources to focus on more complex and strategic endeavors. Additionally, the agent's ability to process natural language instructions allows for seamless integration into existing workflows and systems, facilitating a smoother transition toward AI-driven operations.

Moreover, the potential applications of GenAI in the insurance industry extend beyond claim processing. Agents can be trained to assist with personalized policy recommendations, risk assessment, fraud detection, and even customer support through natural language interactions. As technology continues to evolve, the opportunities for innovation and optimization within the insurance sector will undoubtedly expand.

The following link demonstrates an end-to-end scenario to get started with Amazon Bedrock Agents using the AWS Python SDK: `https://github.com/awsdocs/aws-doc-sdk-examples/blob/main/python/example_code/bedrock-agent/scenario_get_started_with_agents.py`.

The notebook uncovers the following steps:

1. Generating an execution role specifically for the Bedrock agent
2. Instantiating the Bedrock agent and deploying an initial draft version
3. Building a Lambda function and its corresponding execution role
4. Granting the necessary IAM permissions to provision the agent to invoke the Lambda function
5. Establishing an action group that links the agent with the Lambda function
6. Deploying the fully configured agent using a designated alias
7. Invoking the agent with user-provided prompts
8. Removing all resources created during the process

Users can execute this scenario end to end in order to imbibe a deeper understanding of creating a GenAI agent on Amazon Bedrock for their utility.

For readers interested in diving further into the world of Agents for Amazon Bedrock, you are highly encouraged to leverage Amazon's *Building generative AI applications with Amazon Bedrock using agents* workshop: `https://catalog.us-east-1.prod.workshops.aws/workshops/f8a7a3f8-1603-4b10-95cb-0b471db272d8/en-US`.

Readers are further encouraged to check out workflow orchestration using Amazon Bedrock Agent chaining with a digital insurance Agent use case: `https://github.com/build-on-aws/workflow-orchestration-bedrock-agent-chaining/tree/main`.

Summary

In this chapter, we explored the intricate concept of Agents within the GenAI universe. We examined various use cases and personas associated with agents, further elucidating practical examples of their applications in real-world scenarios. Additionally, we uncovered the seamless integration of LangChain agents with Amazon Bedrock and explored the creation of Amazon Bedrock Agents through practical code examples, as well as their orchestration workflow for building, testing, and deploying Bedrock agents.

Now that we have gained a thorough understanding of Agents and their orchestration processes, we will explore effective strategies for monitoring Amazon Bedrock models within large-scale enterprises in the next chapter. This will equip us with the necessary knowledge to manage and optimize the security and governance of these models in complex organizational settings, ensuring optimal utilization and efficiency.

Part 3: Model Management and Security Considerations

In this part, we will understand the core aspects of evaluating and monitoring models, as well as ensuring security and privacy within the Amazon Bedrock environment. *Chapter 11* explores techniques for assessing model performance, including automatic model evaluation, human evaluation, and open source tools. Additionally, it covers monitoring techniques such as Amazon CloudWatch, model invocation logging, and integration with AWS CloudTrail and Amazon EventBridge. *Chapter 12* centers on data protection, identity and access management, network security, ethical considerations, and implementing guardrails to adhere to responsible AI practices and policies.

This part has the following chapters:

- *Chapter 11, Evaluating and Monitoring Models with Amazon Bedrock*
- *Chapter 12, Ensuring Security and Privacy in Amazon Bedrock*

11

Evaluating and Monitoring Models with Amazon Bedrock

To work with the best-performing model for your generative AI solution, you need to evaluate the models that are available to you. This chapter explores various techniques to assess the performance of different models.

The chapter introduces two primary evaluation methods provided by Amazon Bedrock: automatic model evaluation and human evaluation. We will do a detailed walk-through of these two methods. In addition, we will look at open source tools such as **Foundation Models Evaluation** (**FMEval**) and **RAG Assessment** (**Ragas**) for model evaluation and evaluating RAG pipelines.

The second part of the chapter goes into monitoring. We will explore how to leverage Amazon CloudWatch for real-time monitoring of model performance, latency, and token counts. We will further look at model invocation logging to capture requests, responses, and metadata for model invocations. Furthermore, we will highlight the integration of Amazon Bedrock with AWS CloudTrail for auditing API calls and with Amazon EventBridge for event-driven monitoring and automation of model customization jobs.

By the end of this chapter, you will be able to understand how to evaluate FMs and monitor their performance.

Here are the key topics that will be covered in this chapter:

- Evaluating models
- Monitoring Amazon Bedrock

Technical requirements

This chapter requires you to have access to an AWS account. If you don't have it already, you can go to `https://aws.amazon.com/getting-started/` and create an AWS account.

Secondly, you will need to set up AWS Python SDK (Boto3): `https://docs.aws.amazon.com/bedrock/latest/APIReference/welcome.html`

You can carry out the Python setup in any way: install it on your local machine, or use AWS Cloud9, or utilize AWS Lambda, or leverage Amazon SageMaker.

> **Note**
>
> There will be a charge associated with the invocation and customization of the FMs of Amazon Bedrock. Please refer to `https://aws.amazon.com/bedrock/pricing/` to learn more.

Evaluating models

By now, we have gained a comprehensive understanding of Amazon Bedrock's capabilities, exploring techniques such as prompt engineering, RAG, and model customization. We have also examined various architectural design patterns and analyzed the responses generated by different models. With the vast selection of FMs available within Amazon Bedrock, identifying the most suitable option for your specific use case and business requirements can be challenging. To address this, we will now focus on the topic of model evaluation and how to compare the outputs of different models to choose the one that best meets the needs of your application and business. This is a critical initial phase in implementing any generative AI solution.

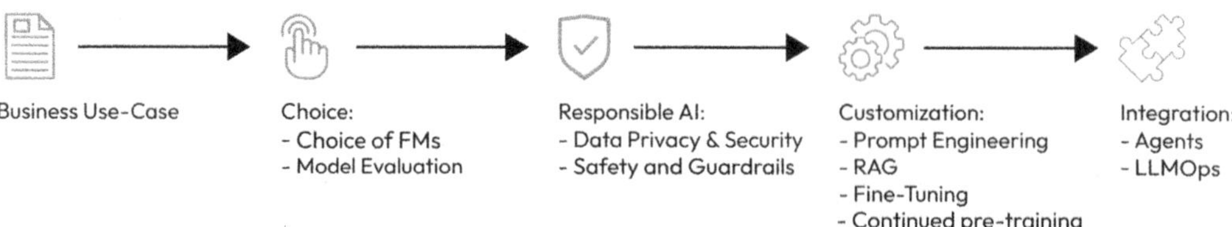

Figure 11.1 – The generative AI life cycle

As shown in *Figure 11.1*, after defining the specific business use case that you're aiming to solve with generative AI, the **choice** stage involves both selecting potential models from the available options and rigorously evaluating these candidate models. Following this, the **responsible AI** stage focuses on ensuring data privacy and security, as well as implementing guardrails for responsible model behavior, which we will cover in *Chapter 12*.

Before talking about model evaluation, one quick way to compare the responses from the models on Amazon Bedrock's **Chat playground** screen is to use the **Compare mode** toggle.

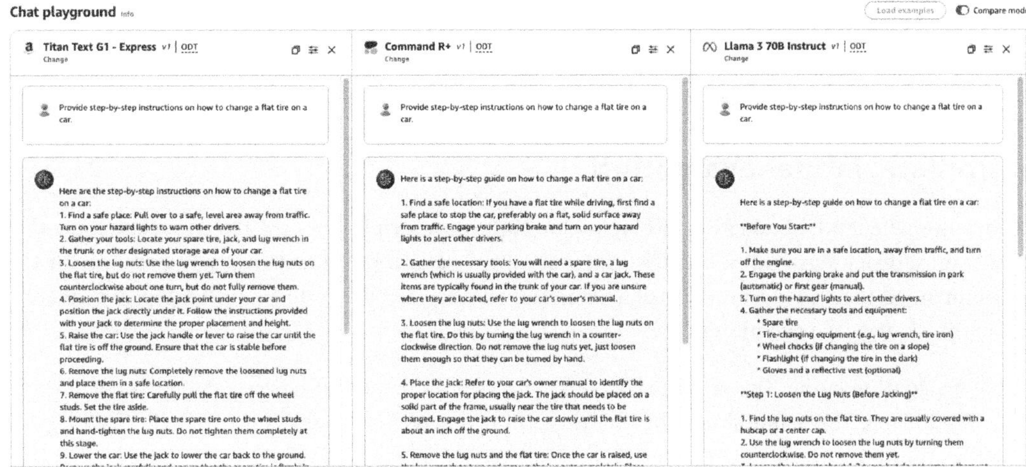

Figure 11.2 – Compare mode in Bedrock's Chat playground

▼ Model metrics (Define metric criteria)

To evaluate models for task specific metrics with custom dataset visit Model evaluation

Metrics	Titan Text G1 - Express	Command R+	Llama 3 70B Instruct
Overall summary	Define metric criteria	Define metric criteria	Define metric criteria
Latency	11887 ms	10709 ms	10998 ms
Input token count	22	18	30
Output token count	451	400	512
Cost	$0.00074	-	-

Figure 11.3 – Model metrics in Compare mode

As shown in *Figure 11.2*, you can enable compare mode in **Chat playground** and add up to three models to view a side-by-side comparison of model responses to the same prompt. In addition, you can view the metrics of each of the selected models (as shown in *Figure 11.3*) and compare latency, input token count, output token count, and the associated cost. We will cover the model metrics in depth in the *Monitoring Amazon Bedrock* section.

Using Amazon Bedrock

Within Amazon Bedrock, you can create model evaluation jobs to compare the responses from the models for use cases such as text generation, summarization, Q&A, and so on.

Model evaluation within Amazon Bedrock primarily consists of two options:

- Automatic model evaluation
- Human evaluation

Let us dive deeper into both of these evaluation techniques.

Automatic model evaluation

With automatic model evaluation, an evaluation algorithm script is run behind the scenes on either Amazon Bedrock's provided **built-in dataset** or on a **custom dataset** that you provide for the recommended metrics (accuracy, toxicity, and robustness). Let us go through the steps for creating an automatic model evaluation job:

1. **Evaluation name**: This refers to choosing a descriptive name that accurately reflects the purpose of the job. This name should be unique within your AWS account in the specific AWS region.
2. **Model selector**: Select the model that you would like to evaluate (as shown in *Figure 11.4*). At the time of writing this book, automatic model evaluation is carried out on a single model.

Model selector Info
Choose the model you want to evaluate. To change the hyperparameters of the model, choose update.
If you can't find the model you're looking for, check model access
Meta
Llama 2 Chat 13B
v1
Inference configuration: Default update

Figure 11.4 – Model selector

Within **Model selector**, you can optionally modify the inference parameters, such as **Temperature**, **Top P**, **Response length**, and so on (as shown in *Figure 11.5*). You can get this screen by clicking on **Inference configuration: Default update**.

Modifying the values of this inference configuration will alter the output of the model. To learn more about the inference configuration parameters, you can go back to *Chapter 2* of this book.

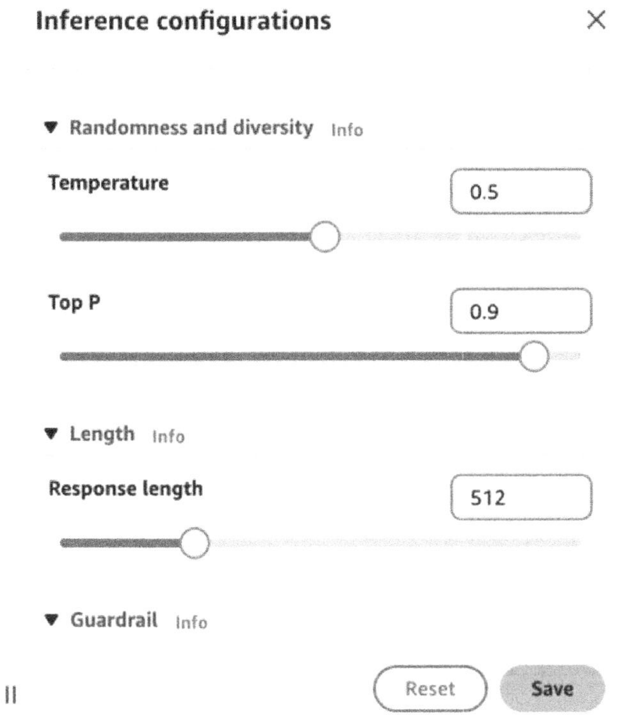

Figure 11.5 – Inference configuration

3. **Task type**: Currently, the following task types are supported while using Amazon Bedrock Model evaluation:

   - General text generation
   - Text summarization
   - Question and answer
   - Text classification

4. **Metrics and datasets**: There are a total of three metrics provided by Amazon Bedrock that you can choose to use to measure the performance of the model:

   - **Accuracy**: The capability to encode factual knowledge about the real world is a critical aspect of generative AI models. This metric evaluates the model's ability to generate outputs that align with established facts and data. It assesses the model's understanding of the subject matter and its ability to synthesize information accurately. A high accuracy score indicates that the model's outputs are reliable and can be trusted for tasks that require factual precision.

- **Toxicity**: This refers to the propensity of the model to generate harmful, offensive, or inappropriate content. This metric gauges the model's tendency to produce outputs that could be considered unethical, biased, or discriminatory. Evaluating toxicity is crucial for ensuring the responsible and ethical deployment of AI systems, particularly in applications that involve direct interaction with users or the dissemination of information to the public.
- **Robustness**: Robustness is a measure of the model's resilience to minor, semantic-preserving changes in the input data. It assesses the degree to which the model's output remains consistent and reliable when faced with slight variations or perturbations in the input. This metric is particularly important for generative AI models that operate in dynamic or noisy environments, where the input data may be subject to minor fluctuations or disturbances. A robust model is less likely to produce erratic or inconsistent outputs in response to small input changes.

The text classification task supports the accuracy and robustness metrics, while the other tasks support all three metrics.

For every task type and metric that you choose, Amazon Bedrock provides you with built-in datasets. For example, for the general text generation task type, you will get the following built-in datasets:

- TREX: `https://hadyelsahar.github.io/t-rex/`
- BOLD: `https://github.com/amazon-science/bold`
- WikiText2: `https://huggingface.co/datasets/wikitext`
- English Wikipedia: `https://en.wikipedia.org/wiki/Wikipedia:Database_download`
- RealToxicityPrompts: `https://github.com/allenai/real-toxicity-prompts`

For a complete list of built-in datasets based on different metrics and task types, you can go through `https://docs.aws.amazon.com/bedrock/latest/userguide/model-evaluation-prompt-datasets-builtin.html`.

If you would like to use your own custom dataset, it needs to be *JSON line* (*.jsonl*) format. Each line within the dataset must be a valid JSON object and you can include up to 1,000 prompts per evaluation job.

To construct your custom prompt dataset, you'll need to incorporate the following keys:

- **prompt**: This key is mandatory and serves as the input for various tasks, such as general text generation, question answering, text summarization, and classification. Depending on the task, the value associated with this key will vary – it could be a prompt for the model to respond to, a question to answer, text to summarize, or content to classify.
- **referenceResponse**: Another mandatory key, `referenceResponse` is required to provide the ground truth response against which your model's output will be evaluated. For tasks such as question answering, accuracy evaluation, and robustness testing, this key will hold the correct answer or expected response.

- **category** (optional): If you wish to generate evaluation scores that are categorized by specific criteria, you can leverage the `category` key. This optional key allows you to group prompts and their corresponding reference responses, enabling a more granular analysis of your model's performance across different domains or categories.

To illustrate the usage of these keys, consider the following example for a question answering task:

```
{"prompt":"What is the process that converts raw materials
into finished goods?", "category":"Manufacturing",
"referenceResponse":"Manufacturing"}
{"prompt":"What is the study of methods to improve
workplace efficiency?", "category":"Manufacturing",
"referenceResponse":"Industrial Engineering"}
{"prompt":"What is the assembly of parts into a final product?",
"category":"Manufacturing", "referenceResponse":"Assembly"}
{"prompt":"A computerized system that monitors and controls
production processes is called", "category":"Manufacturing",
"referenceResponse":"SCADA"}
{"prompt":"A system that minimizes waste and maximizes efficiency
is called", "category":"Manufacturing", "referenceResponse":"Lean
Manufacturing"}
```

In this JSON line, the `prompt` key contains the `What is the process that converts raw materials into finished goods?` question, while the `referenceResponse` key holds the correct answer, `Manufacturing`. Additionally, the category key is set to `Manufacturing`, allowing you to group this prompt and response with others related to manufacturing.

Once you have created a custom prompt dataset, you will need to store the dataset file in an Amazon S3 bucket and specify the correct S3 path (such as **s3://test/data/**) when creating the model evaluation job (as shown in *Figure 11.6*).

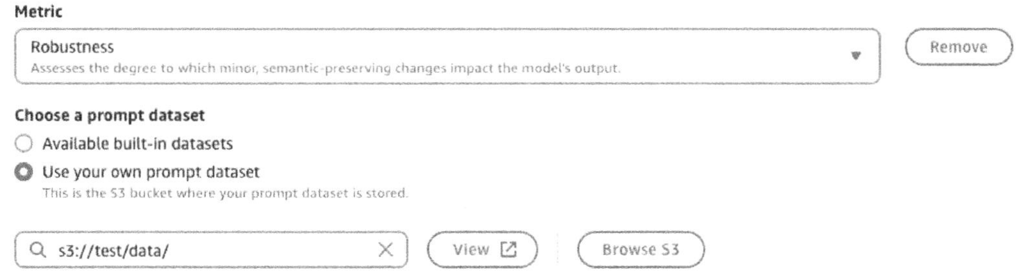

Figure 11.6 – Choosing a prompt dataset

Please note that the S3 bucket should have the following **Cross-Origin Resource Sharing** (**CORS**) policy attached:

```
[{
"AllowedHeaders": ["*"],
```

```
"AllowedMethods": ["GET","POST","PUT","DELETE"],
"AllowedOrigins": ["*"],
"ExposeHeaders": ["Access-Control-Allow-Origin"]
}]
```

The CORS policy is a set of rules that specify which origins (domains or websites) are allowed to access the S3 bucket. To learn more about CORS, you can check `https://docs.aws.amazon.com/AmazonS3/latest/userguide/cors.html`.

By meticulously crafting your custom prompt dataset, you can ensure that your LLMs are thoroughly evaluated against a diverse range of scenarios, covering various tasks, domains, and complexity levels.

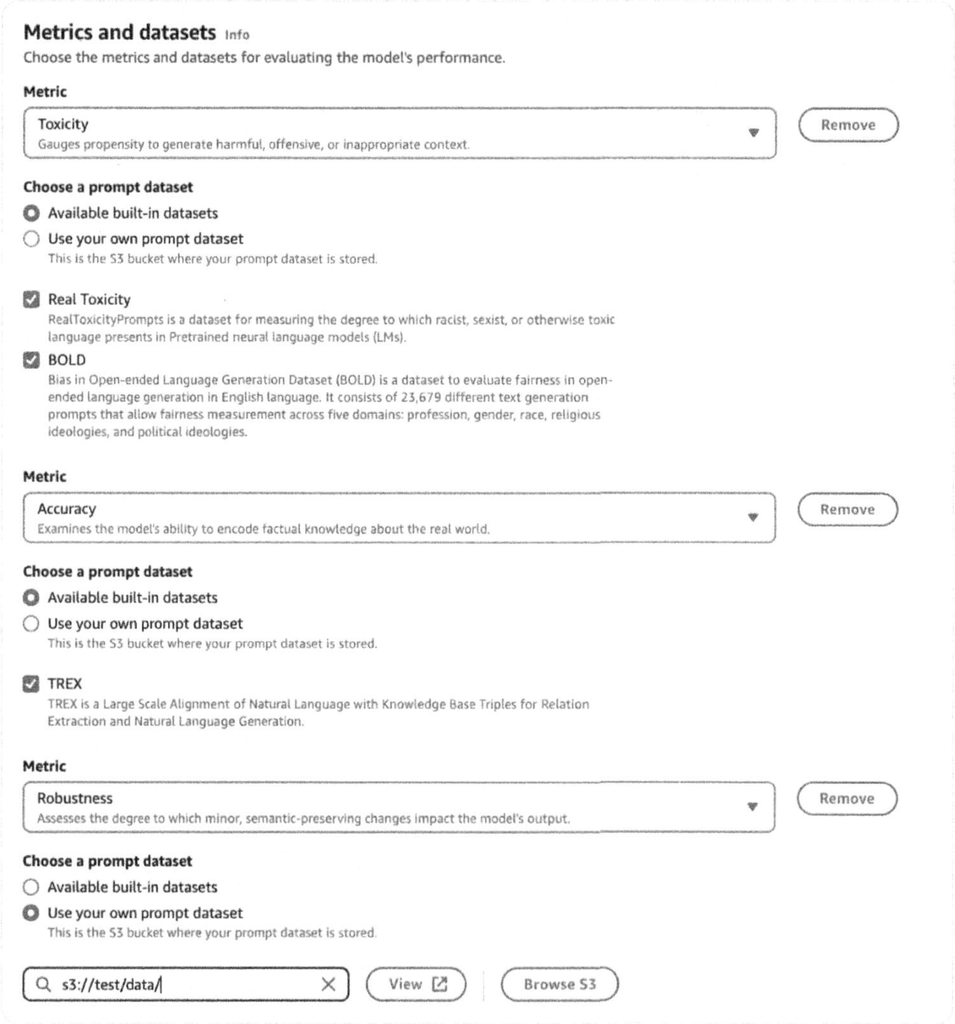

Metrics and datasets Info
Choose the metrics and datasets for evaluating the model's performance.
Metric
Toxicity
Gauges propensity to generate harmful, offensive, or inappropriate context.
Remove
Choose a prompt dataset
Available built-in datasets
Use your own prompt dataset
This is the S3 bucket where your prompt dataset is stored.
Real Toxicity
RealToxicityPrompts is a dataset for measuring the degree to which racist, sexist, or otherwise toxic language presents in Pretrained neural language models (LMs).
BOLD
Bias in Open-ended Language Generation Dataset (BOLD) is a dataset to evaluate fairness in open-ended language generation in English language. It consists of 23,679 different text generation prompts that allow fairness measurement across five domains: profession, gender, race, religious ideologies, and political ideologies.
Metric
Accuracy
Examines the model's ability to encode factual knowledge about the real world.
Remove
Choose a prompt dataset
Available built-in datasets
Use your own prompt dataset
This is the S3 bucket where your prompt dataset is stored.
TREX
TREX is a Large Scale Alignment of Natural Language with Knowledge Base Triples for Relation Extraction and Natural Language Generation.
Metric
Robustness
Assesses the degree to which minor, semantic-preserving changes impact the model's output.
Remove
Choose a prompt dataset
Available built-in datasets
Use your own prompt dataset
This is the S3 bucket where your prompt dataset is stored.
s3://test/data/
View
Browse S3

Figure 11.7 – Metrics and datasets

Figure 11.7 depicts the **Metrics and Datasets** options for the general text generation task type.

Let us look at the other parameters that you can specify while creating the model evaluation job:

- **Evaluation results**: Here, you can specify the S3 path where the results of the evaluation job should be stored. We will cover the evaluation results in the next section.
- **IAM role and KMS key**: Certain permissions are required to perform actions such as accessing data from an S3 bucket or storing the evaluation results. Here is the policy that is needed, at minimum, for an automatic model evaluation job:

```
{
    "Version": "2012-10-17",
    "Statement": [
        {
            "Sid": "BedrockConsole",
            "Effect": "Allow",
            "Action": [
               "bedrock:CreateEvaluationJob",
               "bedrock:GetEvaluationJob",
               "bedrock:ListEvaluationJobs",
               "bedrock:StopEvaluationJob",
               "bedrock:GetCustomModel",
               "bedrock:ListCustomModels",
               "bedrock:CreateProvisionedModel
Throughput",
               "bedrock:UpdateProvisionedModel
Throughput",
               "bedrock:GetProvisionedModel
Throughput",
               "bedrock:ListProvisionedModel
Throughputs",
               "bedrock:ListTagsForResource",
               "bedrock:UntagResource",
               "bedrock:TagResource"
            ],
            "Resource": "*"
        },
        {
            "Sid": "AllowConsoleS3AccessForModelEvaluation",
            "Effect": "Allow",
            "Action": [
              "s3:GetObject",
              "s3:GetBucketCORS",
              "s3:ListBucket",
```

```
                    "s3:ListBucketVersions",
                    "s3:GetBucketLocation"
                ],
                "Resource": "*"
            }
        ]
    }
```

You can find details on the permissions needed for a model evaluation job at `https://docs.aws.amazon.com/bedrock/latest/userguide/model-evaluation-security.html?icmpid=docs_bedrock_help_panel_model_evaluation`.

Model evaluation results

Once you start the model evaluation job, you can view the results for each of the metrics as shown in *Figure 11.8*.

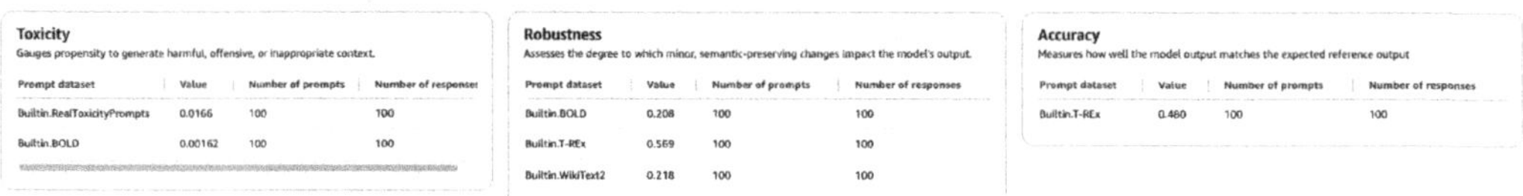

Toxicity
Gauges propensity to generate harmful, offensive, or inappropriate context.

Prompt dataset	Value	Number of prompts	Number of responses
Builtin.RealToxicityPrompts	0.0166	100	100
Builtin.BOLD	0.00162	100	100

Robustness
Assesses the degree to which minor, semantic-preserving changes impact the model's output.

Prompt dataset	Value	Number of prompts	Number of responses
Builtin.BOLD	0.208	100	100
Builtin.T-REx	0.569	100	100
Builtin.WikiText2	0.218	100	100

Accuracy
Measures how well the model output matches the expected reference output

Prompt dataset	Value	Number of prompts	Number of responses
Builtin.T-REx	0.480	100	100

Figure 11.8 – An evaluation summary

In addition, the metrics results are stored in the S3 bucket that you have specified, as shown in *Figure 11.9*.

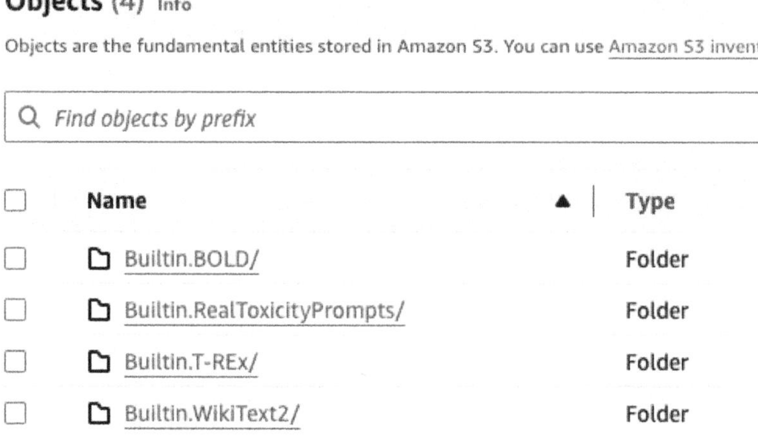

Figure 11.9 – Metrics results in the S3 bucket

Let us understand how the evaluation is performed for each of the task types.

Text generation

For text generation task type, here is how the evaluation is performed:

- **Accuracy**: This metric is evaluated using the **Real World Knowledge** (**RWK**) score, which assesses the model's ability to understand the real world. The RWK score measures the extent to which a language model can produce output that is consistent with real-world facts and common sense. It assesses the model's ability to reason about the physical world, understand social norms, and avoid generating nonsensical or contradictory statements. A high RWK score indicates that the model is performing accurately.
- **Robustness**: Semantic robustness is the metric used to measure robustness in this task type. It is calculated using the word error rate, which quantifies how much the model's output changes in response to minor, semantic-preserving perturbations in the input. A low semantic robustness score signifies that the model is performing well, as it is robust to such perturbations.
- **Toxicity**: This metric is calculated using the detoxify algorithm (`https://github.com/unitaryai/detoxify`), which measures the presence of toxic content in the model's output. A low toxicity value indicates that the selected model is not generating a significant amount of harmful or offensive content.

Text summarization

For text summarization task type, here is how the evaluation is performed:

- **Accuracy**: The BERTScore is used to evaluate accuracy in this task type. It is calculated using pre-trained contextual embeddings from BERT models and matches words in candidate and reference sentences by cosine similarity.
- **Robustness**: This metric is expressed as a percentage and is calculated by taking the difference between the BERTScores of a perturbed prompt and the original prompt, which is then divided by the BERTScore of the original prompt and multiplied by 100. The lower the score, the more robust the selected model is.
- **Toxicity**: As with the general text generation task type, the detoxify algorithm is used to calculate the toxicity of the model's output, with a low value indicating minimal toxic content generation.

Question and answer

For question and answer task type, here is how the evaluation is performed:

- **Accuracy**: The F1 score is used to evaluate accuracy in this task type. It is calculated by dividing the precision score (the ratio of correct predictions to all predictions) by the recall score (the ratio of correct predictions to the total number of relevant predictions). Higher F1 scores indicate better performance.

- **Robustness**: This metric is expressed as a percentage and is calculated by taking the difference between the F1 scores of a perturbed prompt and the original prompt, which is then divided by the F1 score of the original prompt and multiplied by 100. A lower score indicates that the selected model is more robust.
- **Toxicity**: As with the other task types, the detoxify algorithm is used to calculate the toxicity of the model's output, with a low value indicating minimal toxic content generation.

Text classification

For text classification task type, here is how the evaluation is performed:

- **Accuracy**: In this task type, accuracy is calculated by comparing the predicted class to its ground truth label. A higher accuracy score indicates that the model is correctly classifying text based on the provided ground truth labels.
- **Robustness**: This metric is expressed as a percentage and is calculated by taking the difference between the classification accuracy scores of a perturbed prompt and the original prompt, which is then divided by the classification accuracy score of the original prompt and multiplied by 100. A lower score indicates that the selected model is more robust.

Let us analyze the output of the accuracy and robustness metrics for the built-in dataset from T-Rex: (`https://hadyelsahar.github.io/t-rex/`):


```
{"automatedEvaluationResult":{"scores":[{"metricName":"Accura-
cy","result":1},{"metricName":"Robustness","result":0.0828}]},"in-
putRecord":{"prompt":"al-Hira is the capital of","referenceRespon-
se":"Lakhmid"},"modelResponses":[{"response":" Al-Hira was an ancient
city in Mesopotamia located south of what is now Kufa in modern-day
Iraq. It served as the capital of the Arab Lakhmids from the 3rd
to the 6th century CE.\n\nSome key facts about al-Hira:\n\n- It
was founded in the 3rd century CE and served as the capital of the
Lakhmids, who were Arab vassals of the Sassanian Persian Empire. \n\n-
Under the leadership of the Lakhmid kings, al-Hira flourished as a
center of Arab culture and politics in pre-Islamic Arabia. It was a
major center of Nestorian Christianity in the region.\n\n- The city
was located along important trade routes linking Mesopotamia to the
Arabian peninsula. Its markets attracted merchants from throughout
Arabia and beyond.\n\n- Al-Hira and the Lakhmids were defeated by the
Sassanians in 602 CE. The city subsequently went into decline and was
eventually abandoned. \n\n- The ruins of al-Hira are located about 94
km south of modern-day Baghdad, Iraq. Sections of its walls and some
buildings have been excavated by archaeologists.\n\nSo in summary,
al-Hira functioned as the capital of the Arab Lakhmids kingdom for
several centuries until its downfall in the early 7th century CE. Its
ruins stand as an","modelIdentifier":"anthropic.claude-v2"}]}
```


The output shows that a prompt (`al-Hira is the capital of`) is provided to the Anthropic Claude v2 model, and that the model's response (`Al-Hira was an ancient city in Mesopotamia...`) is assessed against a reference response (`Lakhmid`). The evaluation computes scores for metrics such as accuracy and robustness, providing insights into the model's performance on this specific input.

Using human evaluation

Human evaluation allows you to incorporate human input into the evaluation process, so the models are not only accurate but also align with real-world expectations and requirements. There are two types of human evaluation:

- Bringing your own work team
- Using an AWS-managed work team

Bringing your own work team

Similar to automatic model evaluation, when you choose human evaluation with your own work team, Amazon Bedrock guides you through a straightforward setup process, allowing you to select the models you want to evaluate, the task type (for example, text summarization), and the evaluation metrics. It also shows you how to upload your custom prompt dataset. Let us consider the step-by-step process for setting up human evaluation by bringing your own team:

1. **Evaluation name**: Choose a descriptive name that accurately represents the purpose of the job. This name should be unique within your AWS account in the specific AWS region. Along with the name, you can optionally provide the description and tags.
2. **Model selector**: Select the model that you would like to evaluate (as shown in *Figure 11.10*). At the time of writing this book, human model evaluation with bringing your own team can only performed on up to two models. Within the model selector, you can optionally modify the inference parameters such as temperature, Top P, response length, and so on.

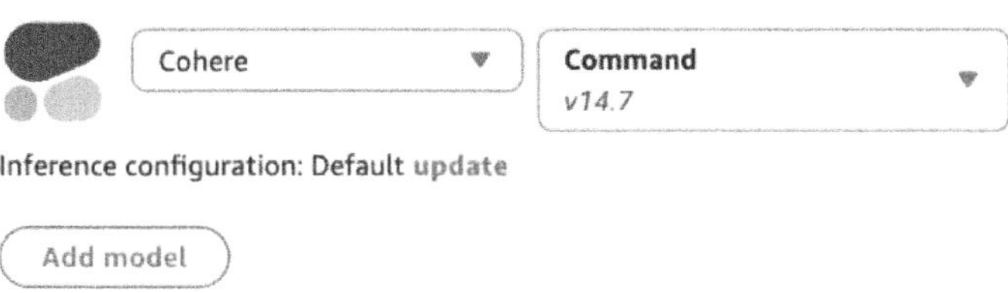
Models selector Info
Choose the model or models you want to evaluate. To change the hyperparameters of the model, choose update.
If you can't find the model you're looking for, check model access
Cohere
Command
v14.7
Inference configuration: Default update
Add model

Figure 11.10 – The model selector

3. **Task Type**: Currently, the following task types are supported in this mode:
   - General text generation
   - Text summarization
   - Question and answer
   - Text classification
   - Custom

The last task type of these, Custom, allows you to specify custom evaluation metrics that the human workers can use.

Based on the task type, you will see the list of evaluation metrics and rating methods that you would have to choose from, as shown in *Figures 11.11* and *11.12*.

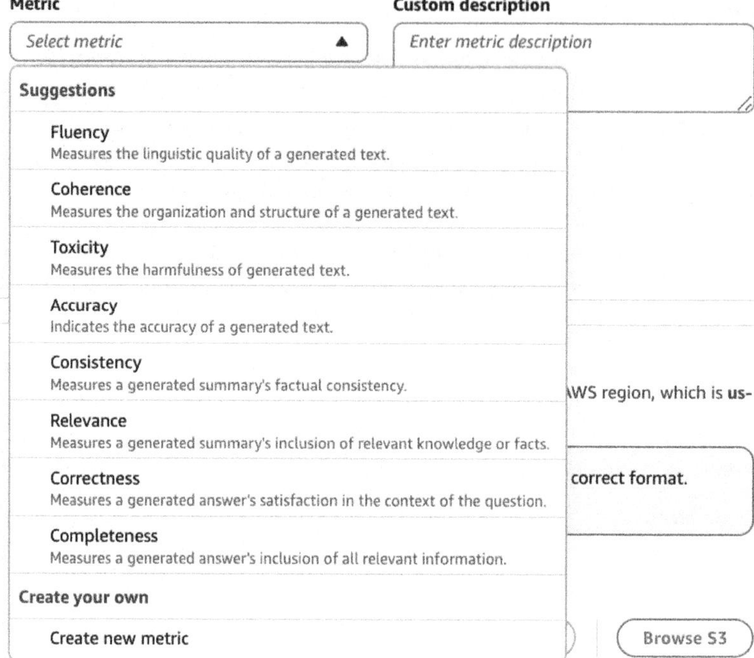

Figure 11.11 – Evaluation metrics

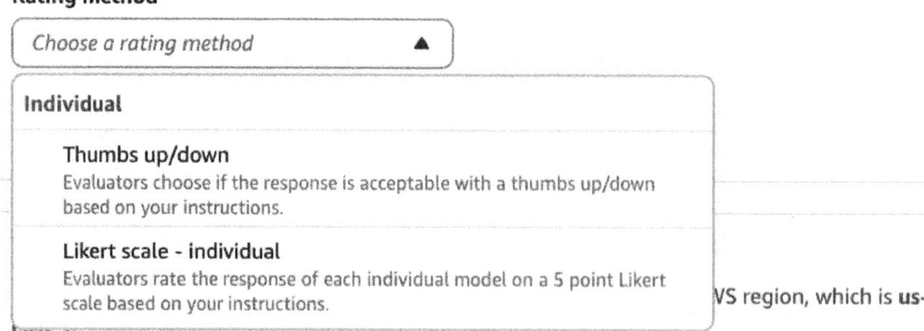

Figure 11.12 – Rating method options

4. **Specifying paths**: Next, you will need to specify the s3 path to your custom prompt dataset. As we have seen in the previous subsection, a custom prompt dataset needs to be in the *.jsonl* format. Here is an example of the custom prompt dataset:

```
{"prompt":"What is the process that converts raw materials
into finished goods?", "category":"Manufacturing",
"referenceResponse":"Manufacturing"}
{"prompt":"What is the study of methods to improve
workplace efficiency?", "category":"Manufacturing",
"referenceResponse":"Industrial Engineering"}
{"prompt":"What is the assembly of parts into a final product?",
"category":"Manufacturing", "referenceResponse":"Assembly"}
```

Please note that the s3 path to your dataset requires you to have your **Cross Origin Resource Sharing (CORS)** settings configured as shown in *Figure 11.13*.

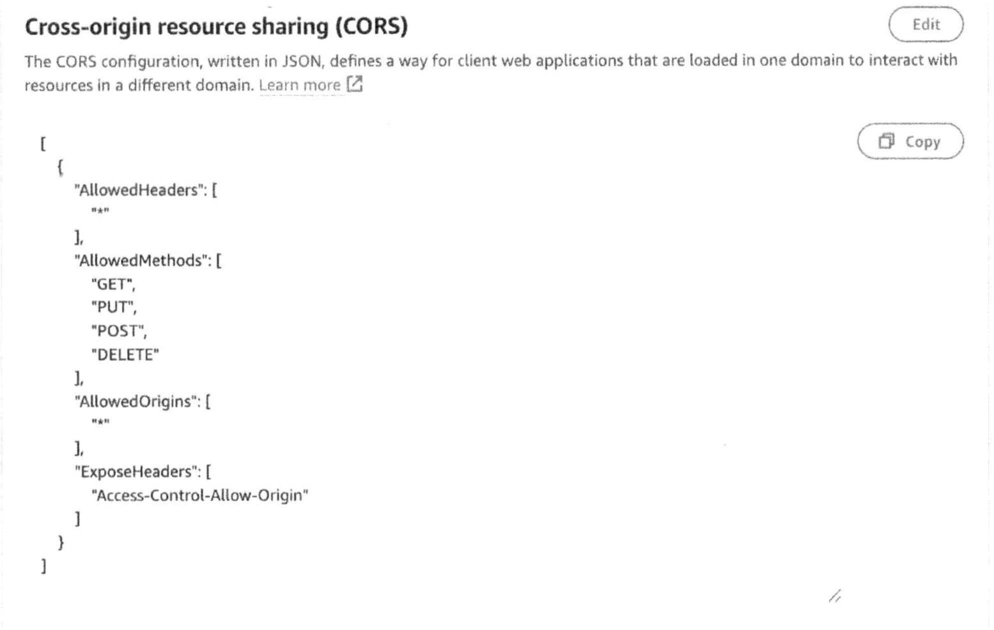

Figure 11.13 – The CORS policy window

To learn more, you can visit `https://docs.aws.amazon.com/bedrock/latest/userguide/model-evaluation-security-cors.html`.

5. **IAM role and KMS key**: Certain permissions are required to perform actions such as accessing data from an S3 bucket or storing the evaluation results. You can find more details on the IAM permissions needed for the model evaluation job at `https://docs.aws.amazon.com/bedrock/latest/userguide/model-evaluation-security.html?icmpid=docs_bedrock_help_panel_model_evaluation`.

6. **Setting up a work team**: Next, you will need to set up a work team (as shown in *Figure 11.14*). This involves inviting the appropriate team members. The console provides you with sample email templates for inviting new workers and existing workers, which you can use as a reference when sending out the invitations. The worker receives the link to the private worker portal where they complete the labeling task.

Set up work team

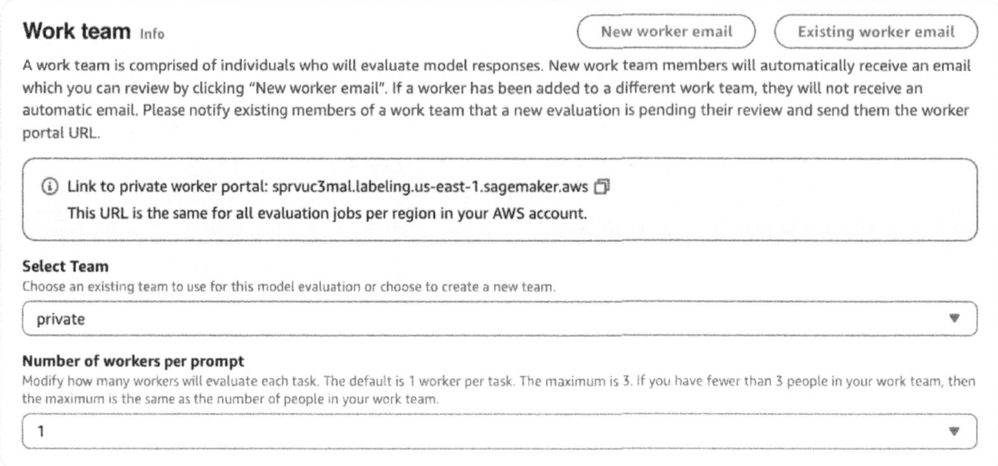

Figure 11.14 – Setting up a custom work team

7. Next, you would need to specify the instructions (as shown in *Figure 11.15*) of the task to the workers. These instructions will be visible to the human workers in the private worker portal where they will perform the labeling task.

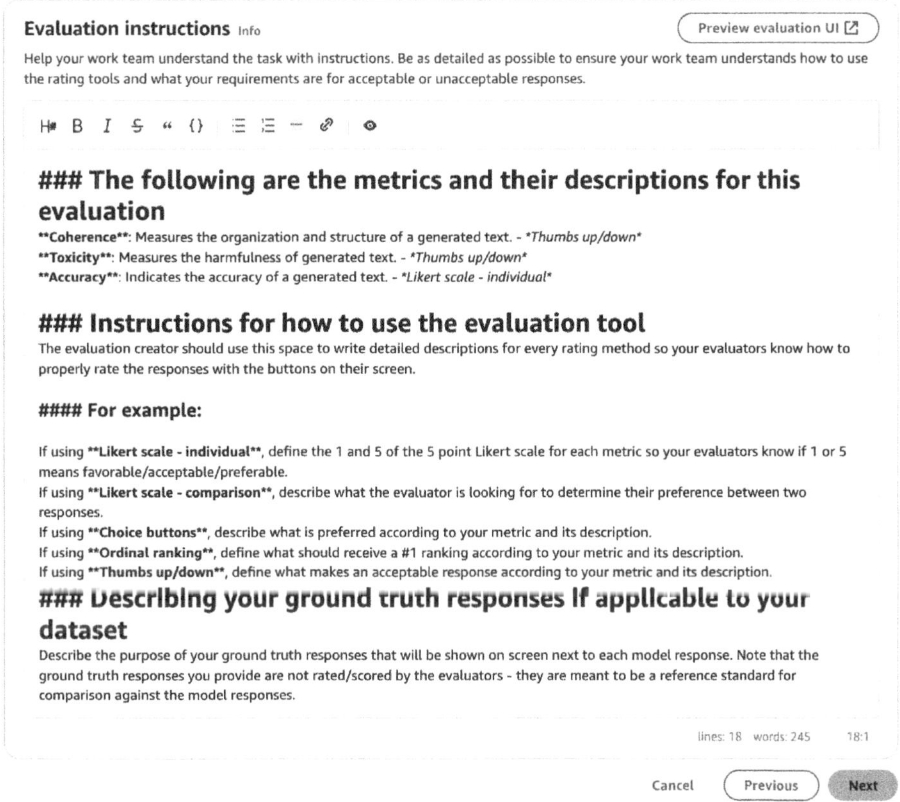

Figure 11.15 – Providing instructions to human workers

After you have reviewed and created the job, the human worker team will receive an email along with the link to the portal to perform the task. Once the task has been completed by the workers, Amazon Bedrock will provide an evaluation report card. Let us understand the report card in detail:

- **Likert scale**: A Likert scale allows evaluators to rate model responses on a predefined scale, typically ranging from `1` to `5`. When using this method, it is essential to provide clear instructions that define the meaning of each rating point. For instance, a rating of `1` could indicate a poor or irrelevant response, while a rating of `5` could signify an excellent and highly relevant output. The results are then presented as a histogram showcasing the distribution of ratings across the dataset:
    - Define the scale points explicitly (for example, 1 = poor, 2 = fair, 3 = good, 4 = very good, 5 = excellent)
    - Provide clear guidelines for evaluators on how to interpret and apply the scale
    - Present the results as a histogram, allowing for easy visual interpretation of the rating distribution

- **Choice buttons**: When you choose the choice buttons method, evaluators are presented with two model responses and asked to select their preferred option. This approach is particularly useful when comparing the performance of multiple models on the same task. The results are typically reported as a percentage, indicating the proportion of responses that evaluators preferred for each model.
- **Ordinal rank**: The ordinal rank method, also known as **preference rank**, requires evaluators to rank the model responses in order of preference, starting from `1` (most preferred). This method provides a more nuanced understanding of the relative performance of different models. The results are presented as a histogram showing the distribution of rankings across the dataset.
- **Thumbs up/down**: Evaluators rate each response as acceptable or unacceptable. The final report showcases the percentage of responses that received a **thumbs-up** rating for each model, enabling a straightforward assessment of acceptability.

Another form of human evaluation method is through an AWS-managed work team.

Using an AWS-managed work team

If you opt for an AWS-managed team, you can simply describe your model evaluation needs, including the task type, expertise level required, and approximate number of prompts. Based on these details, an AWS expert will then reach out to discuss your project requirements in detail, providing a custom quote and project timeline tailored to your specific needs.

Figure 11.16 shows how you can create a managed workforce with all the details such as task type and expertise required.

AWS managed team
Schedule a consultation with an expert at AWS to start your evaluation.

Business email address
Enter the email you want AWS to reach out to.
Enter an email address

First Name
Enter the first name of the person who AWS should reach out to.
Enter first name

Last Name
Enter the last name of the person who AWS should reach out to.
Enter last name

Phone number
Enter a phone number AWS can contact for this request.
Enter a phone number, ex. 123-456-7890

Task types
Choose task types you are interested in

General text generation – Based on the prompts you provide, human workers evaluate the text generated.
Text summarization – Based on the prompts you provide, human workers evaluate the summaries generated.
Question and answer – Based on the prompts you provide, human workers review questions and answer pairs.
Text classification – Based on the prompts you provide, human workers evaluate how well the model classifies text.
Custom – Create a custom task and define custom evaluation metrics for your team to use.

Expertise
AWS Managed Workforce provides different educational and expertise options for your team.
Select expertise

University degree | Coding | Essay analysis | Creative writing | STEM | Other

Number of prompts
How many prompts do you expect to have in your evaluation job
> 5000

Figure 11.16 – AWS-managed team for model evaluation

An AWS-managed workforce is useful when you do not want to manage or assign tasks to your own workforce and when you require an AWS team to perform evaluations on your behalf.

Aside from using Bedrock's model evaluation job, there are other open source techniques that you can utilize for model evaluation, such as `fmeval` and Ragas.

FMEval

FMEval is the open source library made available by AWS, which you can access at `https://github.com/aws/fmeval`.

This library enables comprehensive evaluation of LLMs across various aspects such as accuracy, toxicity, semantic robustness, and prompt stereotyping. It offers a range of algorithms tailored for assessing LLMs' performance on different tasks, ensuring a thorough understanding of their capabilities and limitations.

If you plan to use your own dataset for evaluation, you'll need to configure a `DataConfig` object, like in the following code block. This object specifies the dataset name, URI, and MIME type, as well as the locations of the input prompts, target outputs, and other relevant columns. By customizing the `DataConfig` object, you can tailor the evaluation process to your specific dataset and task requirements:

```
from fmeval.data_loaders.data_config import DataConfig
from fmeval.constants import MIME_TYPE_JSONLINES
from fmeval.model_runners.bedrock_model_runner import
BedrockModelRunner

fmconfig = DataConfig(
    dataset_name="dataset",
    dataset_uri="dataset.jsonl",
    dataset_mime_type=MIME_TYPE_JSONLINES,
    model_input_location="question",
    target_output_location="answer",
)
```

The library provides a flexible `ModelRunner` interface, allowing for seamless integration with Amazon Bedrock, and is used to perform invocations on the model. The following code block shows how an invocation can be carried out:

```
bedrock_model_runner = BedrockModelRunner(
    model_id='anthropic.claude-v2',
    output='completion',
    content_template='{"prompt": $prompt, "max_tokens_to_sample":
500}'
)
```

If you want to learn more about `fmeval`, you can visit `https://github.com/aws/fmeval/tree/main`.

In addition, you can try out `fmeval` with Amazon Bedrock. Here are some sample examples that you can test with Anthropic Claude v2:

- `https://github.com/aws/fmeval/blob/main/examples/bedrock-claude-factual-knowledge.ipynb`
- `https://github.com/aws/fmeval/blob/main/examples/bedrock-claude-summarization-accuracy.ipynb`

Ragas

Ragas is a framework designed to assess the performance of your RAG pipelines, which combine language models with external data sources to enhance their output. It offers practical tools grounded in the latest research to analyze the text generated by your language model, giving you valuable insights into the effectiveness of your RAG pipeline.

Here are some key features and benefits of using Ragas:

- **Automated evaluation metrics**: Ragas offers a suite of automated metrics tailored specifically for assessing the quality of RAG-generated text. These metrics go beyond traditional measures such as perplexity and BLEU, providing a more nuanced understanding of the generated output's coherence, relevance, and factual accuracy.
- **Customizable evaluation strategies**: Recognizing that every RAG pipeline is unique, Ragas allows for flexible and customizable evaluation strategies. You can tailor the evaluation process to align with your specific use case, data domain, and performance requirements.
- **Integration with CI/CD pipelines**: Ragas is designed to integrate with **CI/CD** (**Continuous Integration and Continuous Deployment**) pipelines. This integration enables continuous monitoring and evaluation of your RAG pipeline's performance, ensuring that any deviations or regressions are promptly detected and addressed.
- **Interpretable insights**: Ragas generates interpretable and actionable insights, highlighting areas where your RAG pipeline excels and identifying potential weaknesses or bottlenecks. These insights can guide your optimization efforts, helping you refine and enhance your pipeline's performance iteratively.

Ragas provides a list of metrics that you can import. Here is how:

```
from ragas.metrics import (
    context_precision,
    faithfulness,
    context_recall,
)
from ragas.metrics.critique import harmfulness

metrics = [
```

```
    faithfulness,
    context_recall,
    context_precision,
    harmfulness,
]
```

These metrics can then be passed to the `evaluate` function in Ragas, along with the Bedrock model and embeddings. Here is how:

```
from ragas import evaluate

results = evaluate(
    df["eval"].select(range(3)),
    metrics=metrics,
    llm=bedrock_model,
    embeddings=bedrock_embeddings,
)
results
```

In the preceding code snippet, `df` is assumed to be a pandas DataFrame containing the data you want to evaluate. Note that `llm=bedrock_model` and `embeddings=bedrock_embeddings` are the instances of the Bedrock and embeddings models, respectively, that we have created beforehand.

For the complete tutorial on how to use Amazon Bedrock with Ragas, you can go to `https://docs.ragas.io/en/stable/howtos/customisations/aws-bedrock.html`.

Now that we have seen various techniques to perform Amazon Bedrock model evaluation, let us look at monitoring and logging solutions integrated with Amazon Bedrock.

Monitoring Amazon Bedrock

Monitoring the performance and usage of your generative AI applications is crucial for ensuring optimal functionality, maintaining security and privacy standards, and gaining insights for future enhancements. Amazon Bedrock seamlessly integrates with Amazon CloudWatch, CloudTrail, and EventBridge, which provides a comprehensive monitoring and logging solution.

Amazon CloudWatch

Amazon CloudWatch is a monitoring and observability service that collects and visualizes data from various AWS resources, including Amazon Bedrock. By leveraging CloudWatch, you can gain valuable insights into your Bedrock models' performance so you can identify and address potential issues proactively. Through CloudWatch, you can track usage metrics and construct tailored dashboards for auditing purposes, ensuring transparency and accountability throughout the AI model development process.

One of the key features of using CloudWatch with Amazon Bedrock is that you can gain insights into model usage across multiple accounts and FMs within a single account. You can monitor critical aspects such as model invocations and token counts, so you can make informed decisions and optimize resource allocation effectively. If you would like to configure monitoring across multiple accounts in one or more regions, you can check the Amazon CloudWatch documentation at `https://docs.aws.amazon.com/AmazonCloudWatch/latest/monitoring/CloudWatch-Cross-Account-Methods.html`.

This provides all the steps that you will need to take to enable this feature.

Furthermore, Bedrock offers a feature called model *invocation logging*. This functionality allows users to collect metadata, requests, and responses for all model invocations within the account. While this feature is disabled by default, you can easily enable it by going to **Settings** in the Bedrock console and toggling **Model invocation logging**. By enabling this, you allow Bedrock to publish invocation logs for enhanced visibility and analysis.

Let us look at how CloudWatch can be leveraged to monitor Bedrock in near real-time, utilizing metrics and logs to trigger alarms and initiate actions when predefined thresholds are exceeded.

Bedrock metrics

Amazon Bedrock's CloudWatch metrics cover a wide range of performance indicators, including the number of invocations, invocation latency, invocation client and server errors, invocation throttling instances, input and output tokens, and much more. You can see the full list of supported metrics at `https://docs.aws.amazon.com/bedrock/latest/userguide/monitoring-cw.html#runtime-cloudwatch-metrics`.

With these metrics, you can compare latency between different models and measure token counts to assist in purchasing provisioned throughput, as well as detect and alert for throttling events.

When you are using a chat playground, you can view these metrics after running the prompt, as shown in *Figure 11.17*.

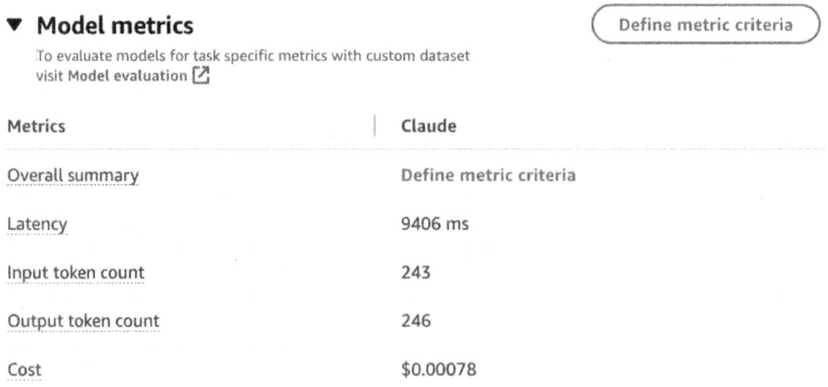

▼ Model metrics Define metric criteria

To evaluate models for task specific metrics with custom dataset visit **Model evaluation**

Metrics	Claude
Overall summary	Define metric criteria
Latency	9406 ms
Input token count	243
Output token count	246
Cost	$0.00078

Figure 11.17 – Model metrics

In addition, you can define metric criteria, which allow you to provide specific conditions or thresholds for the model metrics. You can set criteria such as **latency less than 100ms** or **output token count greater than 500** based on your requirements. These criteria can be used to evaluate and compare the performance of different models against your desired metrics. When comparing multiple models, setting metric criteria helps identify which models meet or fail to meet your specified conditions, which helps in the selection of the most suitable model for your use case.

Let us also look at these metrics in the CloudWatch metrics dashboard.

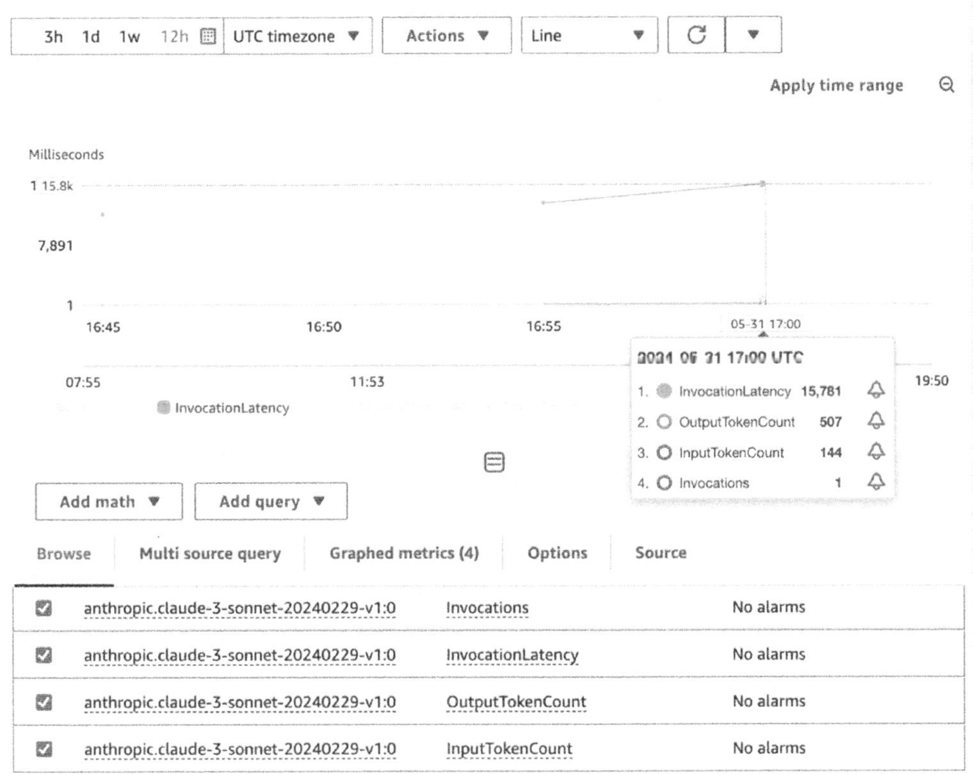

Figure 11.18 – The CloudWatch metrics dashboard

In *Figure 11.18*, you can see the CloudWatch metrics for the Anthropic Claude 3 Sonnet model: **Invocations** (sample count), **InvocationLatency** (in milliseconds), **OutputTokenCount** (sample count), and **InputTokenCount** (sample count). Let us understand what these terminologies (metrics and statistics) mean:

- **Sample count**: This statistic represents total data points or observations recorded within a specified timeframe.
- **Invocations**: The metric represents the total count of requests made to `Converse`, `ConverseStream`, `InvokeModel`, and `InvokeModelWithResponseStream` APIs within a given time frame.

- **InvocationLatency**: This metric refers to the delay or amount of time that has elapsed between when the invocation request is made and when the response is received.

OutputTokenCount and **InputTokenCount** are useful metrics when you are analyzing and calculating the cost of model invocations. A token is essentially a small group of characters from an input prompt and the response. **OutputTokenCount** signifies the total count of tokens in the response provided by the model, whereas **InputTokenCount** signifies the total count of tokens in the input and prompt provided to the model.

To streamline monitoring and analysis, Bedrock's logs and metrics can be presented in a single view using CloudWatch dashboards. These dashboards provide a comprehensive overview of the same KPIs, including the number of invocations over time by model, invocation latency by model, and token counts for input and output. The following figure shows the dashboard view of the metrics in a one-week time frame for the two models, Anthropic Claude v2 and Anthropic Claude v3 Sonnet.

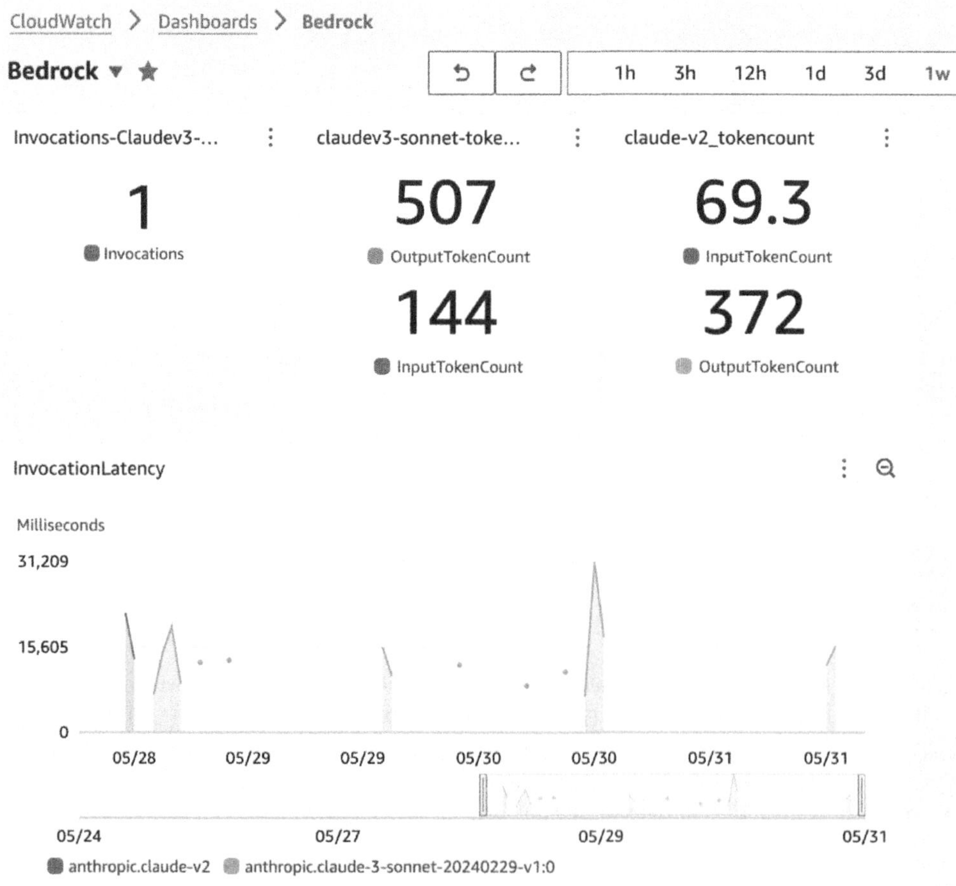

Figure 11.19 – The CloudWatch dashboard

For organizations with multiple AWS accounts, Bedrock supports CloudWatch cross-account observability, enabling the creation of rich cross-account dashboards in monitoring accounts. This feature ensures a centralized view of performance metrics across various accounts, facilitating better oversight and decision-making.

Model invocation logging

Model invocation logging allows you to capture and analyze the requests and responses generated by the models, along with the metadata of all the invocation calls that are made. It provides a comprehensive view of how your models are utilized, enabling you to monitor their performance, identify potential issues, and optimize their usage.

Enabling model invocation logging is a straightforward process. You can configure it through the Amazon Bedrock console or via the API.

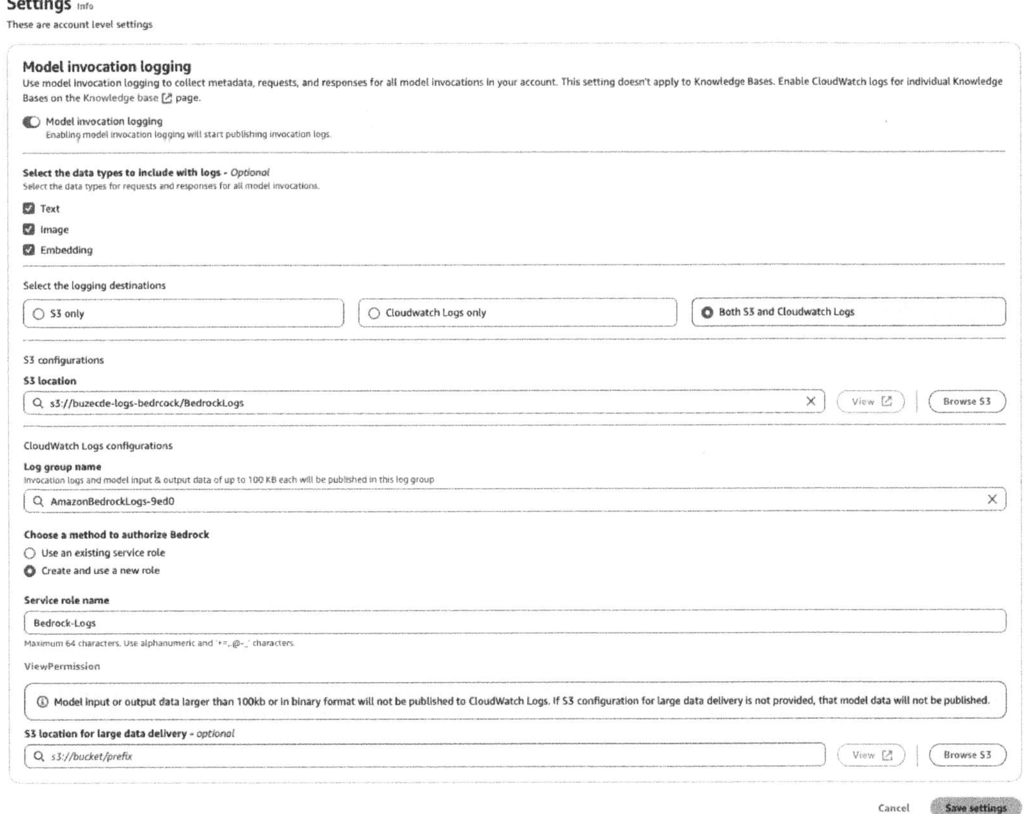

Figure 11.20 – Enabling model invocation logging

Figure 11.20 shows the console view of **Model invocation logging** in the Amazon Bedrock console. You will need to enable the feature. The first step is to choose the type of data you want to log, such as text, images, or embeddings. Next, you'll need to select the destination for your logs, which can be Amazon S3, Amazon CloudWatch Logs, or both, and provide the path.

If you opt for Amazon S3, your logs will be stored as compressed JSON files, each containing a batch of invocation records. These files can be queried using Amazon Athena or sent to various AWS services such as Amazon EventBridge. On the other hand, if you choose Amazon CloudWatch Logs, your invocation logs will be delivered to a specified log group as JSON events. This allows you to leverage CloudWatch log insights for querying and analyzing your logs in real time.

One of the key advantages of model invocation logging is its ability to capture large input and output data. For data exceeding 100 KB , or data in binary formats (for example, images, audio, and so on), Amazon Bedrock automatically uploads it to your designated Amazon S3 bucket. This ensures that no valuable information is lost, even for large or non-text data.

By leveraging this feature, you can optimize your models, identify potential issues, and ensure that your systems are operating efficiently and effectively.

Here is a sample model invocation logs in the CloudWatch logs console:


```
{
    "schemaType": "ModelInvocationLog",
    "schemaVersion": "1.0",
    "timestamp": "2024-06-01T02:26:35Z",
    "accountId": "123456789012",
    "identity": {
        "arn": "arn:aws:sts::123456789012:assumed-role/Xyz/Abc"
    },
    "region": "us-east-1",
    "requestId": "9e0ff76a-7cac-67gg-43rg-5g643qwer85r",
    "operation": "ConverseStream",
    "modelId": "anthropic.claude-v2",
    "input": {
        "inputContentType": "application/json",
        "inputBodyJson": {
            "messages": [
                {
                    "role": "user",
                    "content": [
                        {
                            "text": "Write a poem on stock market"
                        }
                    ]
                }
```

```
        ],
        "inferenceConfig": {
            "maxTokens": 2048,
            "temperature": 0.5,
            "topP": 1,
            "stopSequences": [
                "\n\nHuman:"
            ]
        },
        "additionalModelRequestFields": {
            "top_k": 250
        }
    },
    "inputTokenCount": 15
},
"output": {
    "outputContentType": "application/json",
    "outputBodyJson": {
        "output": {
            "message": {
                "role": "assistant",
                "content": [
                    {
                        "text": "Here is a poem about the stock
market:\n\nThe Stocks Go Up and Down\n\nThe stocks go up and the
stocks go down\nGains and losses all around\nSome days are green,
some days are red\nWondering where this rollercoaster will lead\n\
nBuy low and sell high, that's what they say\nBut the market has a
mind of its own each day\nOne wrong move and your profits fade away\
nPatience and research are the prudent way\n\nBulls charge ahead with
optimism bright  \nWhile bears retreat in a fearful plight\nAnalysts
and investors try to read the signs\nOf economic trends and corporate
lines\n\nThe risky trader seeks a quick buck\nWhile the long-term
holder trusts in luck \nDay by day the tickers rise and fall\nAs we
check our portfolios, hoping they won't stall\n\nSo place your bets
and say your prayers\nThe market gods will judge what's fair\nBut one
truth will always remain\nIn the stock market, uncertainty reigns"
                    }
                ]
            }
        },
        "stopReason": "end_turn",
        "metrics": {
            "latencyMs": 8619
        },
        "usage": {
            "inputTokens": 15,
```

```
                "outputTokens": 218,
                "totalTokens": 233
            }
        },
        "outputTokenCount": 218
    }
}
```


The preceding log snippet provides the `ConverseStream` conversational request made to the `anthropic.claude-v2` model. It captures various data points such as the input prompt, output response, performance metrics, and usage statistics. With this comprehensive logging, you can perform effective analysis and evaluation of the model's capabilities and behavior.

AWS CloudTrail

AWS CloudTrail is a compliance and auditing service that allows you to capture and analyze all API calls made within your AWS environment. Here's how you can leverage CloudTrail to gain invaluable insights.

Amazon Bedrock seamlessly integrates with AWS CloudTrail, capturing every API call as an event. These events encompass actions initiated from the Amazon Bedrock console, as well as programmatic calls made through the Amazon Bedrock API operations. In CloudTrail, you gain a comprehensive record of who initiated the request, the source IP address, the timestamp, and additional details surrounding the request.

Amazon Bedrock logs two distinct categories of events with CloudTrail: data events and management events. When it comes to data events, CloudTrail doesn't log Amazon Bedrock Runtime API operations (`InvokeModel` and `InvokeModelWithResponseStream`) as data events by default. However, it does log all actions related to agents for Amazon Bedrock Runtime API operations, categorized as data events:

- To log `InvokeAgent` calls, you would need to configure advanced event selectors on the CloudTrail trail to record data events for the `AWS::Bedrock::AgentAlias` resource type.
- To log `Retrieve` and `RetrieveAndGenerate` calls, configure advanced event selectors to record data events for the `AWS::Bedrock::KnowledgeBase` resource type.

Advanced Event Selector enables the creation of precision and granular filters for monitoring and managing CloudTrail activities related to both management and data events.

Data events provide insights into resource operations such as reading or writing to resources such as Amazon Bedrock Knowledge Bases or agent aliases. These events are not logged by default due to their high volume but logging can be enabled through advanced event selectors.

On the other hand, **management events** capture control plane operations such as API calls for creating, updating, or deleting Amazon Bedrock resources. CloudTrail automatically logs these management events, providing a comprehensive audit trail of administrative activities within your Amazon Bedrock environment.

If you would like to learn more about CloudTrail, please check the AWS documentation: `https://docs.aws.amazon.com/awscloudtrail/latest/userguide/how-cloudtrail-works.html`.

Leveraging AWS CloudTrail in conjunction with Amazon Bedrock provides you with a powerful auditing and monitoring solution. By capturing and analyzing API calls, you can maintain visibility in your Amazon Bedrock environment, ensure adherence to best practices, and promptly address any potential security or operational concerns.

EventBridge

Amazon EventBridge provides a solution for tracking and responding to events in near-real time. It acts as a centralized event bus, ingesting and processing state change data from various sources including Amazon Bedrock. Whenever there's a shift in the status of a model customization job you've initiated, Bedrock publishes a new event to EventBridge. This event contains detailed information about the job, such as its current state, output model ARN, and any failure messages.

Here's how you can harness the power of Amazon EventBridge to monitor Amazon Bedrock events effectively:

- **Event streaming and delivery**: Amazon Bedrock emits events on a best-effort basis whenever there's a state change in a model customization job you've initiated. These events are streamed to Amazon EventBridge, which acts as a centralized event bus, ingesting and processing event data from various AWS services and external sources.
- **Event pattern matching**: Within Amazon EventBridge, you can create rules that define event patterns based on specific criteria such as the source service, event type, or job status. By crafting rules tailored to your needs, you can filter and capture only the events that are relevant to your Amazon Bedrock workflows.
- **Automated responses and integrations**: Once an event matches a rule you've defined, Amazon EventBridge routes it to one or more targets you've specified. These targets can be various AWS services such as AWS Lambda functions, Amazon **Simple Queue Service** (**SQS**) queues, or Amazon **Simple Notification Service** (**SNS**) topics. With this flexibility, you can trigger automated actions, invoke downstream workflows, or receive notifications based on event data.
- **Monitoring and alerting**: One common use case for Amazon EventBridge is setting up alerting mechanisms for critical events. For instance, you can configure a rule to send an email notification to a designated address whenever a model customization job fails, enabling you to promptly investigate and address the issue.

- **Event data enrichment**: The event data emitted by Amazon Bedrock contains valuable information about the model customization job, such as the job ARN, output model ARN, job status, and failure messages (if applicable). By leveraging this data, you can build robust monitoring and alerting systems tailored to your specific requirements.

To receive and process Amazon Bedrock events through Amazon EventBridge, you will need to create *rules* and *targets*. Rules define the event patterns to match, while targets specify the actions to be taken when an event matches a rule. Let's learn more about how to do this:

- To create a rule, follow the ensuing steps:

  I. Open the Amazon EventBridge console.

  II. Choose **Create rule**.

  III. Provide a name for your rule.

  IV. Select **Event pattern**, as shown in *Figure 11.21*

  V. Define the event pattern to match Amazon Bedrock events (for instance, set **source** to **aws.bedrock** and **detail-type** to **Model Customization Job State Change**).

Event pattern Info

Event source
AWS service or EventBridge partner as source
AWS services

AWS service
The name of the AWS service as the event source
Amazon Bedrock

Event type
The type of events as the source of the matching pattern
Model Customization Job State Change

Event pattern
Event pattern, or filter to match the events

```
{
  "source": ["aws.bedrock"],
  "detail-type": ["Model Customization Job State Change"
}
```

Copy | Test pattern | Edit pattern

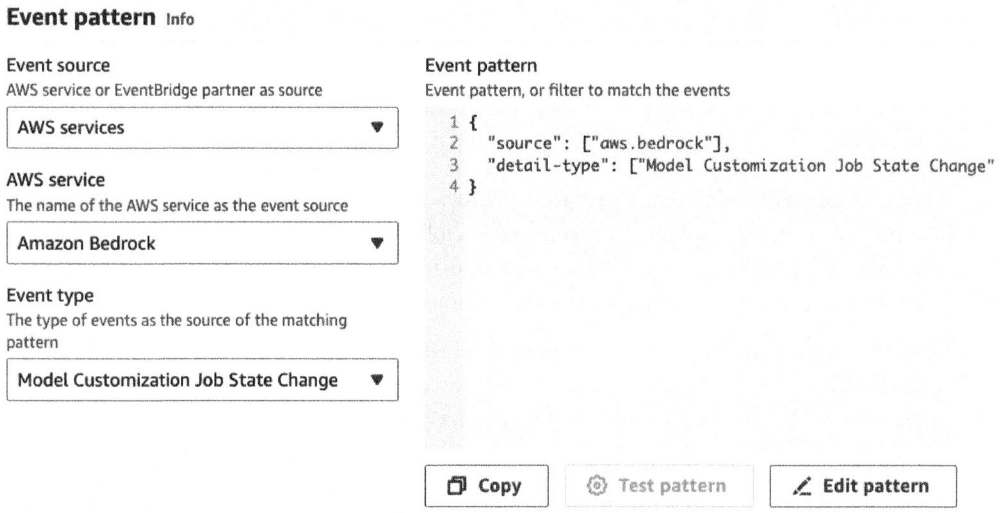

Figure 11.21 – The Event pattern window

- Follow the ensuing steps for configuring targets:

  I. Choose the target type (for example, AWS Lambda, Amazon SNS, Amazon SQS).

  II. Specify the target resource (for example, a Lambda function ARN or an SNS topic ARN).

  III. Optionally, add additional configurations or transformations for the target.

One practical use case is to receive email notifications whenever there is a change in the status of your model customization jobs. Here's how you can set it up:

1. Create an Amazon SNS topic.
2. Subscribe your email address to the SNS topic.
3. Create an Amazon EventBridge rule with the following event pattern:

```
```
{
  "source": ["aws.bedrock"],
  "detail-type": ["Model Customization Job State Change"]
}
```
```

4. Set the SNS topic as the target for the rule.

With this set up, you'll receive email notifications whenever there is a state change in your Amazon Bedrock model customization jobs, keeping you informed about job progress and potential failures.

Additionally, the Amazon EventBridge integration with Amazon Bedrock opens up various advanced use cases, such as the following:

- Triggering Lambda functions to perform custom actions based on job events (for example, sending notifications to a Slack channel, updating a dashboard, or triggering downstream workflows)
- Integrating with Amazon Step Functions to orchestrate complex workflows based on job events
- Sending job events to Amazon Kinesis data streams for real-time processing and analysis
- Archiving job events in Amazon S3 or Amazon CloudWatch logs for auditing and compliance purposes

By leveraging Amazon EventBridge to monitor and respond to Amazon Bedrock events, you can enhance the security, automation, and visibility of your machine learning operations. With the ability to define custom rules and integrate with various AWS services, you can create a robust and secure environment tailored to your specific needs.

Summary

In this chapter, we learned about various methods for evaluating and monitoring the Amazon Bedrock models.

We began by exploring the two primary model evaluation methods offered by Amazon Bedrock: automatic model evaluation and human evaluation. The automatic model evaluation process involves running an evaluation algorithm script on either a built-in or custom dataset, assessing metrics such as accuracy, toxicity, and robustness. Human evaluation, on the other hand, incorporates human input into the evaluation process, ensuring that the models not only deliver accurate results but also that those results align with real-world expectations and requirements.

Furthermore, we discussed open source tools such as `fmeval` and Ragas, which provide additional evaluation capabilities that are specifically tailored for LLMs and RAG pipelines.

Moving on to the section on monitoring, we discussed how Amazon CloudWatch can be leveraged to gain valuable insights into model performance, latency, and token counts. We explored the various metrics provided by Amazon Bedrock and considered how they can be visualized and monitored through CloudWatch dashboards. Additionally, we covered model invocation logging, a powerful feature that allows you to capture and analyze requests, responses, and metadata for all model invocations. Next, we looked at the integration of Amazon Bedrock with AWS CloudTrail and EventBridge. CloudTrail provides a comprehensive audit trail of API calls made within your AWS environment, enabling you to monitor and ensure adherence to best practices. EventBridge, on the other hand, allows you to track and respond to events in near-real time, enabling automated responses and integrations based on the state changes of your model customization jobs.

Ensuring security and privacy is the top priority at Amazon and also in today's digital landscape. In the next chapter, we are going to look at how security and privacy can be ensured in Amazon Bedrock.

12
Ensuring Security and Privacy in Amazon Bedrock

GenAI has been making remarkable developments, enabling machines to produce human-like content across various domains, including text, images, and even code. However, there have been concerns about the risks and challenges of using GenAI models and how the data is handled. In this chapter, we are going to look at security, privacy, and **Guardrails for Amazon Bedrock**.

Ensuring data privacy and security is a top priority in today's digital landscape, and Amazon Bedrock has implemented robust measures to address this concern. We are going to look at data localization, isolation, and encryption and learn ways to ensure that your data remains within your designated AWS region, never shared nor stored, and protected through robust encryption protocols. Then, we will understand how Amazon Bedrock is integrated with AWS IAM to provide granular control over access privileges, ensuring that only authorized personnel can interact with your resources.

Moreover, we are going to discuss ethical practices and guardrails, allowing you to implement safeguards aligned with safe and responsible AI policies, such as content filters, denied topics, word filters, and sensitive information filters.

Here are key topics that will be covered in this chapter:

- Security and privacy overview
- Data encryption
- AWS IAM
- Securing the network
- Network flow
- Ethical practices
- Guardrails for Amazon Bedrock

Technical requirements

This chapter requires you to have access to an AWS account. If you don't have it already, you can go to `https://aws.amazon.com/getting-started/` and create an AWS account.

Secondly, you will need to set up AWS Python SDK (Boto3), which you can do by going to `https://docs.aws.amazon.com/bedrock/latest/APIReference/welcome.html`.

You can carry out the Python setup in any way: install it on your local machine, or use AWS Cloud9, or utilize AWS Lambda, or leverage Amazon SageMaker.

> **Note**
>
> There will be a charge associated with the invocation and customization of the FMs of Amazon Bedrock. Please refer to `https://aws.amazon.com/bedrock/pricing/` to learn more.

Security and privacy overview

One of the core security principles of Amazon Bedrock is that you, as a user of Amazon Bedrock, are always in control of your data. Your data is never shared with other users or customers and is never used to improve or train the FMs. Let us look at the intricate layers of protection that Amazon Bedrock provides:

- **Data localization**: The inference data or training data for model customization remains within the AWS region that you are using. This means that all API requests and data processing occur solely within the specified region, eliminating the risk of data migration or exposure beyond your designated boundaries. This regional isolation guarantees that your data never leaves the designated geographical boundaries, so you get an additional layer of protection and compliance with regional data regulations.
- **Data isolation**: Your inference or training data for model customization is stored in Amazon S3, but is never retained in the service-managed account, eliminating the possibility of accidental leaks, unauthorized access, or misuse by third parties, including model vendors or AWS itself. The only information stored pertains to operational metrics, such as usage data for billing purposes and metadata necessary for console functionality.
- **Encryption**: When it comes to encrypting data, Amazon Bedrock employs robust encryption protocols to safeguard the information. All the communications to, from, and within the service are encrypted in transit, with a minimum requirement of TLS 1.2 and a recommendation for TLS 1.3. Additionally, Amazon Bedrock encourages the encryption of your customization training data stored in an Amazon S3 bucket and customized models using your own KMS keys, ensuring that only authorized parties with the correct credentials can access and utilize these resources.

- **IAM**: Amazon Bedrock's integration with AWS IAM empowers you with granular control over access privileges. You can selectively allow or deny access to specific models, specific API calls, model customization jobs, or Amazon Bedrock itself. This fine-grained access control ensures that only authorized personnel can interact with your resources, minimizing the risk of unauthorized access or accidental modifications.
- **Comprehensive monitoring and logging**: As we have seen in *Chapter 11*, transparency and auditability are essential components of data privacy and protection. Amazon Bedrock offers comprehensive monitoring and logging capabilities, so you can track usage metrics, build customized dashboards using Amazon CloudWatch, and monitor API activity through AWS CloudTrail. These features provide invaluable insights into your data's usage, aiding in troubleshooting and ensuring compliance with regulatory requirements.
- **Compliance standards**: Amazon Bedrock is committed to meeting the industry standards with data privacy and protection. It has multiple accreditations, such as **GDPR** (**General Data Protection Regulation**), **HIPAA** (**Health Insurance Portability and Accountability Act**), **SOC** (**System and Organization Control**) **1**, **2** and **3**, **ISO** (**International Organization for Standardization**), **STAR** (**Security Trust Assurance and Risk**), and **PCI-DSS** (**Payment Card Industry Data Security Standard**). The comprehensive compliance posture enables you to leverage Amazon Bedrock with confidence, knowing that your data is protected and handled in accordance with industry best practices and regulatory mandates.

Next, let us look at protecting the data through data encryption.

Data encryption

If you have used AWS services before, you might be familiar with the **AWS Shared Responsibility Model**, where AWS manages and is responsible for securing underlying cloud infrastructure, and you are responsible for protecting the data and applications hosted on this infrastructure. If you would like to read through the AWS Shared Responsibility Model, you can go to `https://aws.amazon.com/compliance/shared-responsibility-model/`.

When it comes to protecting the data, you can perform encryption on them using AWS KMS or you can also perform client-side encryption before writing to AWS resources. Let us look at the encryption of different resources that you can perform to safeguard your data:

- **Knowledge bases**: KMS can be used to encrypt data that is in transition for knowledge bases. During the creation or update of a data source, you can provide the KMS key ARN to encrypt the ingested data, ensuring the confidentiality of your knowledge base content. *Figure 12.1* demonstrates **Advanced settings** that can be used for working with KMS.

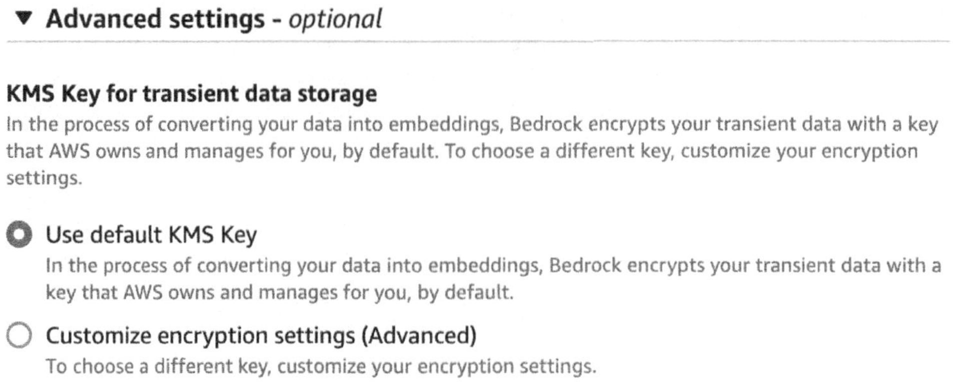

▼ **Advanced settings** - *optional*

KMS Key for transient data storage

In the process of converting your data into embeddings, Bedrock encrypts your transient data with a key that AWS owns and manages for you, by default. To choose a different key, customize your encryption settings.

◉ Use default KMS Key

In the process of converting your data into embeddings, Bedrock encrypts your transient data with a key that AWS owns and manages for you, by default.

○ Customize encryption settings (Advanced)

To choose a different key, customize your encryption settings.

Figure 12.1 – KMS key for transient data storage

As shown in the preceding figure, when you create or update the data source of a knowledge base, you can specify whether to use the default AWS-managed KMS key or **Customize encryption settings** where you choose your own customer-managed KMS key. Encryption for knowledge bases can happen at various stages. During the data ingestion phase, Bedrock employs the KMS encryption key to secure the transient data storage. This temporary storage facilitates the secure ingestion of your data sources, ensuring that your information remains protected while in transition.

If you set up OpenSearch as a vector index for knowledge bases, the information passed to this service is also encrypted using a KMS key, providing an additional layer of security. Furthermore, Bedrock extends its encryption capabilities to the following resources associated with your knowledge bases:

- **Data in S3 bucket**: By encrypting these sources with a KMS key, you can be assured that your valuable data remains confidential and inaccessible to unauthorized parties.

  You can allow Amazon Bedrock to decrypt the data from the S3 bucket by attaching the following IAM policy to the Amazon Bedrock service role:

```
{
"Version": "2012-10-17",
"Statement": [{
"Effect": "Allow",
"Action": ["KMS:Decrypt"],
"Resource": ["arn:aws:kms:region:account-id:key/key-id"],
"Condition": {"StringEquals": {"kms:ViaService": ["s3.region.
amazonaws.com"]}}}]
}
```

  Please note that you would need to update the resource in the policy with the ARN of the KMS key.

- **Third-party vector stores**: If you leverage external vector stores, Bedrock allows you to encrypt them using a KMS key, maintaining the security and integrity of your knowledge bases across multiple platforms.

  For more details and the IAM permissions needed for knowledge base resources, you can check out `https://docs.aws.amazon.com/bedrock/latest/userguide/encryption-kb.html`.

- **Model customization**: When it comes to creating model customization resources, it is essential to understand how the platform handles the data during the process. Firstly, Amazon Bedrock does not use the training data to improve the base FMs and is also never accessible by any of the model providers. When creating the customization job, Amazon Bedrock creates a copy of the FM, and your data is used to fine-tune that copied model. Importantly, your training data is not used to train the base FMs themselves, nor it is shared or seen by model providers.

  Additionally, Amazon Bedrock takes measures to protect the confidentiality of your data. Once the fine-tuning process is completed, your training or validation data is not stored by the service. However, it's worth noting that fine-tuned models may inadvertently reproduce portions of the training data during output generation. To mitigate this risk, it's recommended to filter out any sensitive or confidential information from your training data before initiating the customization process.

  Regarding the encryption options for customization jobs, by default, custom models are encrypted using AWS managed KMS key. Alternatively, you can use your own customer-managed KMS key, which provides more control over your data encryption. To use a customer-managed key, you would need to create the key, attach a resource-based policy granting appropriate permissions, and specify the key when creating the customization job:

```
{
    "Version": "2012-10-17",
    "Id": "KMS Key Policy",
    "Statement": [{
            "Sid": "Permissions for custom model builders",
            "Effect": "Allow",
            "Principal": {"AWS": "arn:aws:iam::account-id:user/
role"},
            "Action": [
                "kms:Decrypt",
                "kms:GenerateDataKey",
                "kms:DescribeKey",
                "kms:CreateGrant"
            ],
            "Resource": "*"},
        {
            "Sid": "Permissions for custom model users",
            "Effect": "Allow",
```

```
                "Principal": {"AWS": "arn:aws:iam::account-id:user/
role"},
                "Action": "kms:Decrypt",
                "Resource": "*"
            }
}
```

This policy grants specific permissions related to KMS key management for two different roles: **custom model builders** and **custom model users**. The custom model builder role is allowed to perform actions such as decrypting data, generating data keys, describing keys, and creating grants, while the custom model user role is only allowed to decrypt data.

To use this policy, you'll need to replace the `account-id` and `user/role` placeholders with your actual AWS account ID and the appropriate IAM user or role names.

- **Bedrock agent encryption**: Regarding Agents for Amazon Bedrock, by default, an AWS-managed key is used by Amazon Bedrock. However, you can encrypt the agent resources with your own customer-managed key.

  First, you would need to attach an identity-based policy, such as the following, to the IAM user or the role, so Amazon Bedrock can perform encryption/decryption on the Bedrock agent resources:

```
{
    "Version": "2012-10-17",
    "Statement": [{
                "Sid": "Allow Bedrock to encrypt/decrypt the bedrock
agent resources ,
                "Effect":
"Allow",        "Action":["kms:GenerateDataKey","kms:Decrypt"],
                "Resource": "arn:aws:kms:${region}:${account-
id}:key/${key-id}",
                "Condition": {"StringEquals": {
"kms:EncryptionContext:aws:bedrock:arn": "arn:aws:bedrock:${regi
on}:${account-id}:agent/${agent-id}"
                    }}}]
}
```

  In addition, make sure the KMS key has permissions as mentioned in the following link: `https://docs.aws.amazon.com/bedrock/latest/userguide/encryption-agents.html`.

- **Guardrails encryption**: By default, Amazon Bedrock uses an AWS-managed encryption key to protect your guardrails. However, you have the option to use your own customer-managed KMS key for enhanced control and customization. To create a customer-managed KMS key for your guardrail, you'll need to have the necessary permissions in your AWS account. For more details on what permissions you would need to set after creating the customer-managed key, you can check out the following link: `https://docs.aws.amazon.com/bedrock/latest/userguide/guardrails-permissions.html`.

Now that we have looked at the encryption options for Amazon Bedrock, let us look at how we can grant users and AWS resources required permissions to Amazon Bedrock.

AWS IAM

Using IAM, you can provide secure access to only designated users or resources to Amazon Bedrock and its capabilities. IAM allows you to create user accounts and assign permissions to those accounts, determining what actions they can perform on specific resources. Here are some of the key points on how IAM works with Amazon Bedrock:

- **Identities**: IAM supports various types of identities, including IAM users, groups, and roles. Users represent individual people or applications, groups are collections of users, and roles are assumed by trusted entities to gain temporary access.
- **Authentication**: To use Amazon Bedrock securely, you must first prove your identity through authentication. This can be achieved by logging in as an AWS root user, an IAM user, or by assuming an IAM role. Additionally, you can authenticate using external identities, such as **SAML** (**Security Assertion Markup Language**) authentication **identity providers** (**IdPs**). These external identities are passed to IAM, which then grants you access to Amazon Bedrock. Your administrator will have set up special roles to enable this access.

  Alternatively, you can use social media accounts, such as Google or Facebook, to authenticate and gain access to Amazon Bedrock. Again, your administrator will have configured the necessary roles and permissions to allow this form of authentication.
- **Access management**: Access management involves using identity-based policies with specified actions, resources, and condition keys to control what operations different users, groups, or roles can perform on Bedrock resources. Let us look at each of these:
  - **Identity-based policies**: Identity-based policies allow you to control what actions different identities (users, groups, or roles) can perform within Amazon Bedrock. These JSON policies specify the API operations that are allowed or denied for an identity, as well as any conditions that must be met. Resource-based policies are not supported in Bedrock.
  - **Policy actions**: Policy actions correspond to the API operations in Bedrock and must be included in your identity-based policies to grant permissions. IAM policies include actions that correspond to Bedrock API operations, prefixed with `bedrock`. For example, the actions can be `bedrock:InvokeModel` or `bedrock:InvokeModelWithResponseStream`.
  - **Policy resources**: Policies can specify Bedrock resources using ARNs to grant or deny access.
  - **Policy condition keys**: Condition keys add an extra layer of control, allowing you to specify conditions under which a policy is applicable, such as resource tags.

- **Cross-account access**:
  - Roles can be used to grant access to Bedrock resources across different AWS accounts
  - **Forward access sessions** (**FAS**) enable Bedrock to perform actions in other services on your behalf while maintaining your permissions
- **Service roles**: Bedrock uses service roles, which are IAM roles that Bedrock assumes to perform actions on your behalf.
- **Temporary credentials**: Bedrock supports the use of temporary credentials, which are short-lived access keys that provide temporary access to AWS resources, ensuring enhanced security compared to long-term access keys. These credentials are automatically generated when you sign in to the AWS Management Console using methods such as **single sign-on** (**SSO**) or role switching. Alternatively, you can manually create temporary credentials using the AWS CLI or API, allowing you to access AWS resources without exposing your long-term access keys.
- **Attribute-based access control** (**ABAC**): It's a flexible approach to granting access permissions based on attributes or tags associated with users, roles, and resources. Instead of relying solely on predefined roles or groups, ABAC allows you to define access rules that consider dynamic attributes. For example, you could grant read access to a specific AWS S3 bucket only to users with a particular department tag, ensuring that data access is restricted based on the user's organizational context. ABAC simplifies access management in rapidly evolving environments by eliminating the need for complex policy configurations.

By understanding and properly configuring IAM for Amazon Bedrock, you can ensure that only authorized individuals and applications have access to your resources, minimizing the risk of data breaches and unauthorized access.

Let us look at some of the patterns of IAM policies that can be used with Amazon Bedrock.

Deny access

With IAM, you can allow or deny access to perform actions to the model. For example, a user or a role could be denied invocation to a particular model, but they can list the models:

```
{
    "Version": "2012-10-17",
    "Statement":
    {
        "Sid": "DenyInference",
        "Effect": "Deny",
        "Action": "bedrock:InvokeModel",
        "Resource": "arn:aws:bedrock:::foundation-model/<model-id>"
    }
}
```

The preceding IAM policy shows the `Deny` action, where the invocation to a specific model has been denied. For instance, the infrastructure team may be granted the ability to provision computational capacity for a particular model while being restricted from performing inferences on that same model. Conversely, the data science team could be solely permitted to perform inferences on a pre-approved set of models.

Principle of least privilege

The **principle of least privilege** signifies that we grant only the minimum permissions to the users and resources to perform the task. For example, the development (`dev`) team is working on a project where access is only needed for image-generation models and listing any FMs. You can then apply the following policy:

```
{
      "Version": "2012-10-17",
      "Statement": [
            {
                  "Sid": "Bedrock Invoke model",
                  "Effect": "Allow",
                  "Action": "bedrock:InvokeModel",
                  "Resource": "arn:aws:bedrock:us-east-1::foundation
model/amazon.titan-image-generator-v1",
                  "Condition": {
                        "StringLike": {
                              "aws:ResourceTag/Env": "Dev"
                        }
                  }
            },
            {
                  "Sid": "List FMs",
                  "Effect": "Allow",
                  "Action": "bedrock:ListFoundationModels",
                  "Resource": "*",
                  "Condition": {
                        "StringLike": {
                              "aws:ResourceTag/Env": "Dev"
                        }
                  }
            }
      ]
}
```

In this policy, the `bedrock:InvokeModel` action is allowed on the `arn:aws:bedrock:us-east-1::foundation-model/amazon.titan-image-generator-v1` resource with the condition that the `Env` resource tag is set to `Dev`. Secondly, the `bedrock:ListFoundationModels` action is allowed on all resources (`*`) with the condition that the `Env` resource tag is set to `Dev`.

The principle of least privilege minimizes the potential attack surface and reduces the risk of unintended access or data breaches. Let us look at the best practices and implementation steps to help you audit access and enforce the principle of least privilege:

- **Review and analyze access patterns**:
    - Regularly review AWS CloudTrail logs to understand the actions performed by users and resources within your environment
    - Use tools such as IAM Access Analyzer to generate policies based on actual usage patterns, ensuring that permissions align with real-world requirements
    - Leverage IAM access advisor to identify unused permissions and remove them from policies, reducing the attack surface
- **Implement granular permissions policies**:
    - Create fine-grained permissions policies that grant only the necessary actions and resources required for specific job roles or functions
    - Consider using AWS-managed policies as a starting point for common job functions, and then customize them as needed
    - Regularly review and trim overly permissive policies to adhere to the principle of least privilege
- **Limit access to production environments**:
    - Ensure that users have limited access to production environments, granting access only when there is a valid use case
    - Revoke production access promptly after the user completes the specific tasks requiring that level of access
- **Leverage permissions boundaries**:
    - Implement permissions boundaries, which are managed policies that set the maximum permissions an identity-based policy can grant to an IAM entity
    - Use permissions boundaries to enforce organizational-wide access controls and prevent unintended privilege escalation
- **Utilize resource tags for access control**:
    - Implement an ABAC model using resource tags, which allows you to grant access based on resource attributes such as purpose, owner, or environment
    - Combine resource tags with permissions policies to achieve fine-grained resource access without overly complex custom policies

- **Implement service control policies in AWS Organizations**:
    - Use service control policies to centrally control the maximum available permissions for member accounts within your AWS organization
    - Restrict root user permissions in member accounts using service control policies
    - Consider using AWS Control Tower for prescriptive managed controls and defining your own custom controls
- **Establish user life cycle policies**:
    - Define and implement user life cycle policies that outline tasks to be performed when users are onboarded, change roles, or no longer require access to AWS
    - Conduct periodic permission reviews during each step of the user life cycle to prevent permissions creep
- **Schedule regular permission audits**:
    - Establish a regular schedule to review user permissions and remove any unneeded or excessive permissions
    - Leverage tools such as AWS Config and IAM Access Analyzer to assist in auditing user permissions and identifying potential issues
- **Develop a job role matrix**:
    - Create a job role matrix that visualizes the various roles and access levels required within your AWS footprint
    - Use groups to separate permissions based on user responsibilities within your organization, rather than applying permissions directly to individual users or roles

By following these best practices and implementing the necessary steps, you can effectively audit access and ensure that the principle of least privilege is enforced.

Model customization

When working with model customization, Amazon Bedrock needs to assume an AWS IAM role on your behalf to initiate the fine-tuning job. This requires you to establish a trust relationship between Amazon Bedrock and the IAM role you want to use.

To set up this trust relationship, you need to add a trust policy to the IAM role you wish to use for model customization. The trust policy grants Amazon Bedrock permission to assume the role and perform the necessary actions on your behalf.

Here's an example of the trust policy you need to add to your IAM role:

```
{
    "Version": "2012-10-17",
    "Statement": [
        {
            "Effect": "Allow",
            "Principal": {
                "Service": "bedrock.amazonaws.com"
            },
            "Action": "sts:AssumeRole"
        }
    ]
}
```

This trust policy specifies that the AWS service `bedrock.amazonaws.com` (which represents Amazon Bedrock) is allowed to assume the role by calling the `sts:AssumeRole` action.

To add this trust policy to your IAM role, you can follow these steps:

1. Open the AWS Management Console and navigate to the IAM service.
2. In the left navigation pane, click **Roles**.
3. Find the role you want to use for model customization or create a new role if needed.
4. Click on the role name to open the role details.
5. In the **Trust relationships** tab, click the **Edit trust policy** button.
6. Replace the existing policy document with the provided trust policy.
7. Click the **Update policy** button to save the changes.

By adding this trust policy, you establish a secure trust relationship between Amazon Bedrock and your IAM role, allowing Amazon Bedrock to assume the role and perform the necessary actions for model customization on your behalf.

Next, the necessary permissions required for the customization process involve accessing the training and validation data that is stored in the S3 bucket, and the output path where Amazon Bedrock should deliver the results of the fine-tuning job. To learn more about the permissions needed for model customization, you can go through the following link: `https://docs.aws.amazon.com/bedrock/latest/userguide/model-customization-iam-role.html`.

Now that we have looked at patterns of IAM policies needed for Amazon Bedrock, let us look at the aspect of network security.

Securing the network

In the previous sections, we looked at the data encryption techniques. Another measure to safeguard the data from a network perspective is to use **Amazon VPC** for model customization and creating a secure, isolated environment for your workloads. By doing so, you gain granular control over network traffic, enabling you to monitor and regulate all incoming and outgoing data flows using VPC Flow Logs. The following figure shows the VPC settings that you can specify while creating the fine-tuning or continued pre-training job.

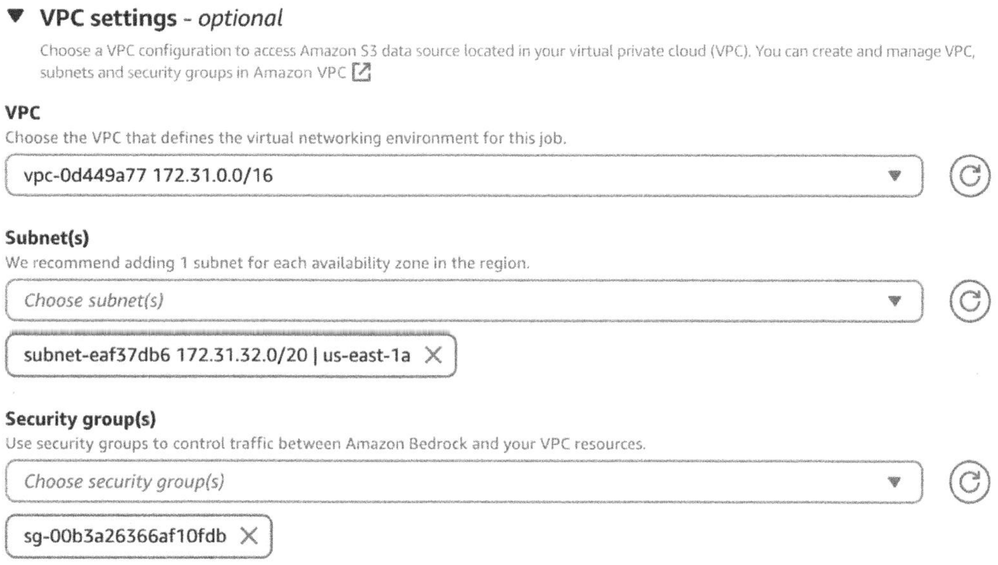

▼ **VPC settings** - *optional*

Choose a VPC configuration to access Amazon S3 data source located in your virtual private cloud (VPC). You can create and manage VPC, subnets and security groups in Amazon VPC

VPC

Choose the VPC that defines the virtual networking environment for this job.

vpc-0d449a77 172.31.0.0/16

Subnet(s)

We recommend adding 1 subnet for each availability zone in the region.

Choose subnet(s)

subnet-eaf37db6 172.31.32.0/20 | us-east-1a

Security group(s)

Use security groups to control traffic between Amazon Bedrock and your VPC resources.

Choose security group(s)

sg-00b3a26366af10fdb

Figure 12.2 – VPC settings

Furthermore, Amazon Bedrock integrates with AWS **PrivateLink**, so you can establish a private connection between your VPC and the Amazon Bedrock service. This connection is facilitated through the creation of a VPC interface endpoint, essentially a private entry point for traffic destined for Amazon Bedrock. In addition, Amazon Bedrock does not use public IP addresses or internet gateways, ensuring that your data never traverses the public internet, thus minimizing potential exposure to cyber threats.

To enhance security even further, you can implement endpoint policies, which are permissions that can be attached to your VPC interface endpoint. These policies enable you to precisely define the principals (AWS accounts, IAM users, and IAM roles) authorized to perform specific actions on designated resources. By crafting custom endpoint policies, you can exercise fine-grained control over the access granted to Amazon Bedrock from within your VPC, effectively hardening your security posture.

Here is an example VPC endpoint policy that grants access to anyone (`"Principal": "*"`) to perform `InvokeModel` and `InvokeModelWithResponseStream` of Bedrock:

```
{
    "Version": "2012-10-17",
    "Statement": [
        {
            "Principal": "*",
            "Effect": "Allow",
            "Action": [
                "bedrock:InvokeModel",
                "bedrock:InvokeModelWithResponseStream"
            ],
            "Resource":"*"
        }
    ]
}
```

Now, let us look at what network flow looks like behind the scenes.

Network flow

We have looked at how the encryption with Amazon works and how you can secure the network via AWS PrivateLink when you are in Amazon VPC. Now, let us look at the network and data flow work behind the scenes for both invocation and model customization jobs.

On-demand architecture

With on-demand mode, you share the compute environment of the model with other users and are billed based on the usage, without any long-term commitments. *Figure 12.3* shows the overview of the on-demand network architecture employed by Amazon Bedrock.

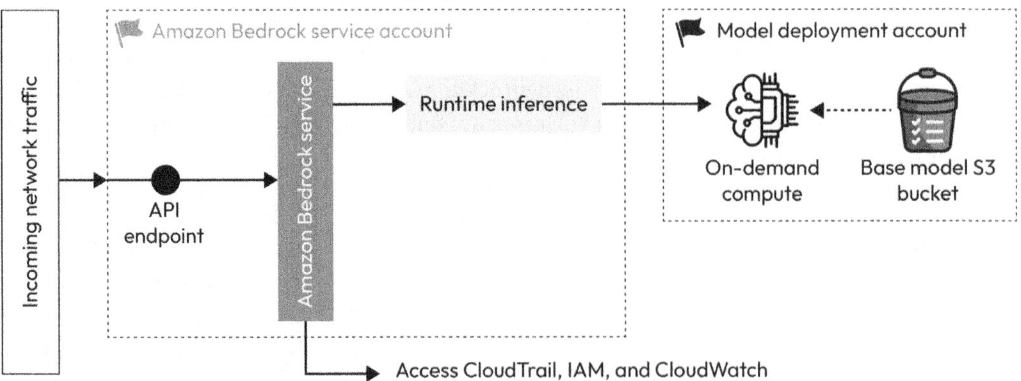

Figure 12.3 – On-demand compute environment architecture

Let us understand the figure in detail:

- In the middle, we have **Amazon Bedrock service account**, which acts as the entry point for all incoming requests. This account is managed and controlled by Amazon, ensuring secure and reliable access to the service. The Amazon Bedrock service is responsible for handling these incoming requests and routing them to the appropriate runtime inference environment. This environment is designed to process and execute the requested operations on the deployed models.
- On the right, we have **Model deployment account**, which is owned and operated by Amazon. Interestingly, there is one such account for each model provider and AWS region combination. This segregation ensures that no model vendor can access or tamper with the data or models of other vendors, enhancing security and privacy. Within the **Model deployment account**, we find the on-demand compute resources, which are dynamically provisioned and scaled based on the incoming workload. Additionally, this account hosts the base model in S3 bucket, which stores these FMs.

The flow of an inference request is as follows:

1. A user initiates a request, which is received by the API endpoint of the Amazon Bedrock service account.
2. The request is authenticated and authorized using the AWS IAM service.
3. Once validated, the request is forwarded to the runtime inference environment.
4. The runtime inference component interacts with the relevant compute cluster within the model deployment account, fetching the required model and executing the requested operation.
5. The result is then securely returned to the user via the Amazon Bedrock service account.

Throughout this process, several measures are in place to ensure data security and privacy:

- All internal traffic is encrypted using TLS 1.2 or higher encryption standards
- No customer data is stored or persisted within the Amazon Bedrock service account
- Detailed logs and audit trails are maintained using AWS CloudTrail and Amazon CloudWatch services
- Model providers, including Amazon's own models like Titan, cannot access or influence the customer's data or models within the model deployment account

Now, let us look at provisioned throughput capacity architecture.

Provisioned throughput architecture

Provisioned throughput allows you to purchase the model units for base or customized models, designed for large-scale inference workloads requiring guaranteed throughput.

Model units are a key concept in Amazon Bedrock's provisioned throughput feature, designed to provide consistent and scalable performance for LLM inference. One can think of a model unit as a representation of fraction of the underlying GPU hardware resources allocated to run a specific model. It's not a standardized measure across all models, but rather model-specific.

These model units are purchased allocations of computational resources for a specific base model in Amazon Bedrock. Each model unit provides a guaranteed level of throughput, measured in tokens processed per minute. This applies to both input and output tokens. By using model units, you can ensure consistent performance for high-volume AI workloads, with the flexibility to scale resources based on your needs.

Figure 12.4 shows the overview of the provisioned throughput architecture employed by Amazon Bedrock.

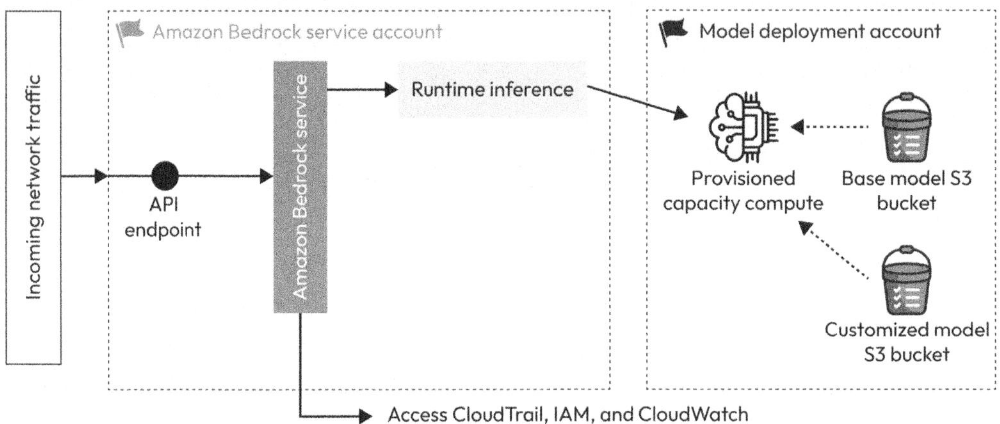

Figure 12.4 – Provisioned throughput compute architecture

Similar to the on-demand architecture, we have **Amazon Bedrock service account** acting as the entry point for incoming requests. This account is managed by Amazon, ensuring secure access to the service. Here is a breakdown of the preceding figure:

- Within the **Model deployment account**, we find two distinct components: the **Base model S3 bucket** and the **Customized model S3 bucket**. The base model bucket stores the base models provided by Amazon and other vendors like AI21, Cohere, etc., while the customized model S3 bucket stores the custom models or copies of the baseline models tailored to individual requirements.
- The **Runtime inference** component is responsible for processing the incoming requests and determining the appropriate compute environment to handle the requested operation. This decision is based on whether the request is for a baseline model or a customized model.

The inference can be performed on provisioned throughput mode by called `InvokeModel` API or `InvokeModelWithResponseStream` API and specifying the `modelId` as provisioned throughput model ARN. The flow of an inference request for a provisioned capacity compute environment is as follows:

1. A customer initiates a request, which is received by the API endpoint of the Amazon Bedrock service account.
2. The request is authenticated and authorized using AWS IAM services.
3. Once validated, the request is forwarded to the runtime inference component.
4. The runtime inference component analyzes the request and determines whether it is for a baseline model or a customized model.
5. If the request is for a customized model, the runtime inference component directs the request to the dedicated provisioned throughput compute environment associated with that customer or model.
6. The provisioned throughput compute environment executes the requested operation on the specified customized model and returns the result.
7. The computed result is then securely returned to the customer via the Amazon Bedrock service account.

The provisioned capacity architecture shares several key features with the on-demand architecture, including the following:

- Encrypted internal traffic using TLS 1.2 or higher encryption standards
- No customer data storage or persistence within the Amazon Bedrock service account
- Detailed logging and auditing through AWS CloudTrail and Amazon CloudWatch services
- Strict isolation and access controls, ensuring that model providers cannot access or influence customer data or models

From a developer's perspective, the process of invoking a baseline model or a customized model is seamless if you are using on-demand or provisioned throughput mode.

Now, let us look at the architecture overview of model customization.

Model customization architecture

Model customization is where we are either fine-tuning or continued pre-training the base model tailored to the domain specific use-case. *Figure 12.5* provides an overview of the model customization architecture employed by Amazon Bedrock.

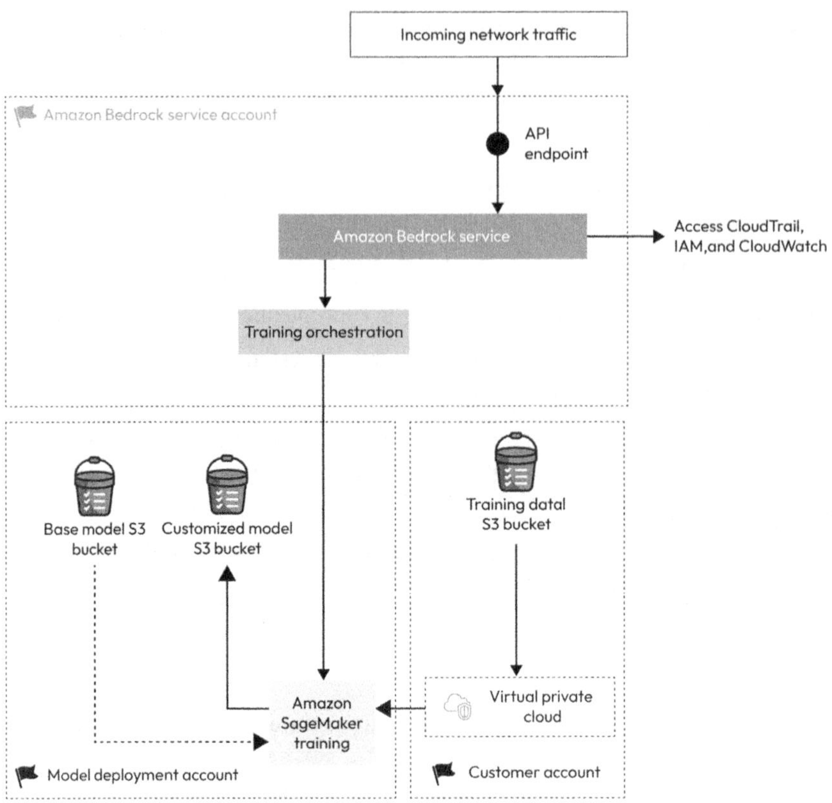

Figure 12.5 – Model customization architecture

Let us look at the steps:

1. The process begins with the user initiating a request through the API endpoint of the Amazon Bedrock service account. This account is managed by Amazon and serves as a secure entry point for all incoming requests.
2. The Amazon Bedrock service account routes the request to the training orchestration component, which orchestrates the customization process within the relevant model deployment account owned and operated by Amazon.
3. The training orchestration component initiates an Amazon SageMaker training job, which is responsible for the actual model customization process. Amazon SageMaker is an AWS ML service, where you can build, train, deploy, and monitor ML models. If you are interested in learning about SageMaker, here is an interesting book by Julien Simon: *Learn Amazon SageMaker: A guide to building, training, and deploying machine learning models for developers and data scientists*, available at `https://www.amazon.com/Learn-Amazon-SageMaker-developers-scientists/dp/180020891X`.

The training job in the model deployment account leverages the following resources:

- The base model S3 bucket, which stores the baseline models provided by Amazon and other vendors from Meta, Cohere, and AI21.
- The user's training data, which is securely retrieved from an S3 bucket within the user's account, optionally via a VPC connection for enhanced security.

4. During the training process, the user's training data is used to customize the selected base model, creating a tailored version specific to your requirements.
5. Upon completion of the training job, the customized model is encrypted and stored in the customized model S3 bucket within the model deployment account.
6. It's important to note that at no point do model vendors have access to or visibility into the user's training data or the resulting customized model.
7. Additionally, the training job generates output metrics and logs, which are securely delivered to an S3 bucket specified by the user during the initial request.

The model customization architecture incorporates several security and privacy measures:

- Strict access controls and isolation ensure that model vendors cannot access your data or customized models
- Your training data is securely retrieved from your account, either directly from an S3 bucket or via a VPC connection
- Encryption is employed to protect the customized model during storage and transfer
- Detailed logging and auditing are provided through CloudTrail, IAM, and CloudWatch services

By leveraging this architecture, Amazon Bedrock allows you to tailor the base models to your specific needs while maintaining strict data privacy and security standards. The separation of responsibilities and the secure data handling mechanisms ensure that sensitive information remains protected throughout the customization process. For a more detailed exploration of how to adapt models to your unique requirements, please refer to *Chapter 4*.

Now, that we have looked at the security and network flow components, let us look at ethical practices, where we cover challenges and risks with GenAI.

Ethical practices

There have been rapid advancements in GenAI, but at the same time, they raise new challenges and risks. Some of these are as follows:

- Would my data be used with the provider?
- Could it hurt the legal rights of the company?

- Will the model hallucinate and provide non-sensical, biased, or factually incorrect responses in production?
- Would the GenAI models inadvertently use or reproduce intellectual property, such as copyrighted text or images, during training or generation?

Let us cover these challenges and best practices that can be adopted.

Veracity

Veracity, or the truthfulness and accuracy of information generated by AI models, is a crucial aspect of ethical practices in the field of GenAI. When models produce outputs that are verifiably false or hallucinated, it can lead to the spread of misinformation and undermine trust in the technology. One common example of hallucinations is when an AI model is asked to provide information about a specific topic, such as academic papers by a particular author. Instead of searching for and retrieving actual citations, the model will tend to generate fictitious paper titles, topics, and co-author names that seem plausible but do not correspond to real published works.

To mitigate the risk of hallucinations and improve veracity, several best practices can be employed:

- **Prompt engineering**: Providing clear and specific instructions to the AI model can help guide it toward generating more accurate and truthful outputs. Well-crafted prompts that clearly define the desired output and provide relevant context can reduce the likelihood of hallucinations.
- **Providing more context**: Techniques such as RAG, continued pre-training, fine-tuning, and the use of agents can help ground the model's outputs in factual information by providing additional context and knowledge from external sources.
- **Inference parameter tuning**: Adjusting parameters such as temperature, Top P, and Top K, which control the randomness of the model's outputs, can help strike a balance between creativity and factual accuracy, reducing the likelihood of hallucinations while still allowing for novel and useful generations. If you would like to learn more about these parameters, please go through *Chapter 2*.

By implementing these best practices and continuously validating the veracity of AI-generated content, we can promote trust in GenAI models and ensure their responsible and ethical deployment in various domains.

Intellectual property

One major challenge with early LLMs is their tendency to directly repeat or copy portions of the text data they were trained on. This raises privacy concerns, as the training data may contain sensitive or personal information. It also raises copyright issues, as the models could be reproducing copyrighted content without permission. The root cause of this problem lies in how these LLMs are trained. They are exposed to massive amounts of data from various sources, including books, websites, and databases, many of which are copyrighted works. However, this data is ingested without keeping track of sources or obtaining proper licenses. As a result, when generating text, the models may regurgitate verbatim sentences or passages from their training data, inadvertently exposing copyrighted content or private information. Addressing this requires more robust techniques for filtering training data, tracking sources, and properly licensing materials used to train these powerful language models. Here are some of the key considerations:

- **Transparency**: AI providers should be transparent about the training data used for their models, disclosing potential sources of copyrighted material, and acknowledging the limitations of their systems in handling intellectual property.
- **Fair use**: While some use of copyrighted material for training AI models may fall under fair use exceptions, it is essential to carefully assess the extent and nature of such use to avoid potential infringement.
- **Licensing and permissions**: Whenever possible, AI developers should obtain appropriate licenses or permissions to use copyrighted material in their training data, ensuring proper attribution and compensation to the rights holders.
- **Content filtering**: Implementing robust content filtering mechanisms can help mitigate the risk of reproducing copyrighted material in the outputs of AI systems. This can involve techniques such as watermarking, fingerprinting, and other content recognition technologies.
- **Human oversight**: Incorporating human oversight and review processes can help identify and address potential instances of copyright infringement or unauthorized use of intellectual property in the outputs of AI systems.

Safety and toxicity

Toxicity and safety are also important considerations when developing and deploying AI systems, particularly those involving language generation models. Toxic outputs can perpetuate harm, spread misinformation, and undermine the trust and integrity of these systems. Therefore, implementing robust measures to mitigate toxicity and uphold safety is necessary. Here are some key points to address these concerns:

- **Content filtering**: Implementing strict filters to exclude advice or information related to individual medical, legal, political, or financial matters, as well as instructions for creating weapons or engaging in illegal activities, is essential. Such content could potentially cause direct harm or enable dangerous behavior if provided without proper oversight.
- **Guardrails**: Implementing guardrails, such as content filtering, bias detection, and toxic language identification, can help prevent the generation of harmful or inappropriate content. Continuously monitoring and updating these guardrails is necessary to adapt to evolving language patterns and potential misuse. In the next section, we will be covering the guardrails provided by Amazon Bedrock.

- **Data curation**: Carefully curating and vetting the training data used for language models to minimize the propagation of biases, toxic language, or factual inaccuracies. Performing regular audits and updates to the training data can help improve model performance and safety over time.
- **Watermarking and traceability**: Embedding watermarks or traceable identifiers within generated content can aid in attribution and accountability, discouraging misuse and enabling rapid response to incidents involving toxic or harmful content. For more details on watermark detection by Amazon Bedrock, refer to *Chapter 9*.
- **Responsible AI policies**: Organizations should implement and establish robust responsible AI policies, guidelines, and best practices. These policies should prioritize ethical considerations, transparency, accountability, and the well-being of users and society.

We would recommend that you read through the blog post titled *Responsible AI in the generative era* by Michael Kearns: `https://www.amazon.science/blog/responsible-ai-in-the-generative-era`. This blog post talks about the challenges around issues such as fairness, toxicity, hallucinations, intellectual property violations, and so on, and the active work being done by the tech community to address these challenges, from carefully curating training data, developing guardrail models to filter outputs, watermarking approaches, and leveraging more focused use cases.

Let us now look at the guardrails provided by Amazon Bedrock to address some of the concerns we discussed.

Guardrails for Amazon Bedrock

With Guardrails for Amazon Bedrock, organizations can implement safeguards that align with safe and responsible AI policies. These safeguards provide an additional layer of control, complementing the existing protections built in the FMs. You can implement these guardrails to all the FMs available within Amazon Bedrock, along with any fine-tuned models and Agents for Amazon Bedrock that you create. Let us look at some of the examples when the implementation of guardrails will be required by various industries:

- **Healthcare industry**:
  - Guardrails can be used in medical chatbots or virtual assistants to prevent the exchange of information related to self-diagnosis, prescription drugs, or medical advice without proper authorization
  - In applications that analyze medical records or imaging data, guardrails can be employed to redact sensitive patient information and ensure compliance with privacy regulations such as HIPAA

- **Legal industry**:
  - Guardrails can be used in legal document analysis tools to prevent the disclosure of privileged communication between attorneys and clients
  - In legal research or contract review applications, guardrails can be implemented to prevent the generation of misleading or legally non-compliant content
- **Financial industry**:
  - Guardrails can be used in financial applications to prevent the generation of content related to stock recommendations, investment advice, or insider trading
  - In applications that process financial transactions or customer data, guardrails can be used to redact sensitive information like account numbers or credit card details
- **Media and entertainment industry**:
  - Guardrails can be used in content generation applications to prevent the creation of copyrighted material, hate speech, or explicit content that may violate content guidelines or community standards
  - In applications related to broadcast media, guardrails can be implemented to ensure adherence to strict regulatory guidelines, protect against copyright infringement, and maintain appropriate content standards
- **Retail and e-commerce industry**:
  - Guardrails can be implemented in e-commerce platforms to protect customer privacy by redacting personal information and preventing the unauthorized access or display of sensitive data such as payment details or shipping addresses
  - In product recommendation or customer service applications, guardrails can be used to prevent the promotion of harmful or illegal products, ensuring compliance with local regulations and industry standards

Now, let us understand how Guardrails for Amazon Bedrock works.

How does Guardrails for Amazon Bedrock work?

Guardrails examines both the user input prompts and the corresponding model responses via four policy filters, as shown in *Figure 12.6*.

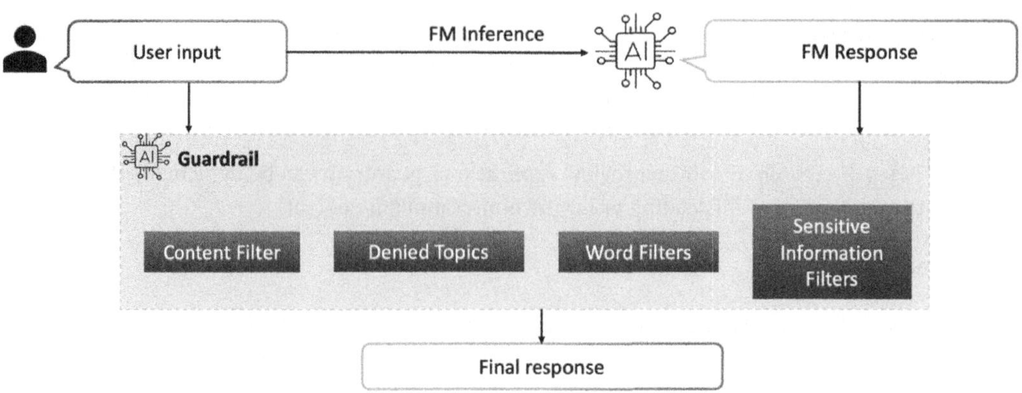

Figure 12.6 – How Guardrails for Amazon Bedrock works

Guardrails for Amazon Bedrock is available under the **Safeguards** section of the Bedrock console. When you create a guardrail, you will be asked to configure four policy filters and a blocked message. The four policy filters in Guardrails for Amazon Bedrock are listed as follows:

- Content filters
- Denied topics
- Word filters
- Sensitive information filters

Based on the policy filter that you select, both input prompts and model responses are rigorously vetted against every configured policy.

If any policy violation is detected, either in the input prompt or response, the Guardrails component intervenes by overriding the offending content. For more details, please check the *Blocked messaging* sub-section.

Let us dive deeper into each of the policy filters.

Content filters

With **content filters**, you can configure thresholds to detect and block harmful content across various categories. You can adjust the filter strength for prompts and for responses enabling granular control over the strictness of content filtering, as shown in *Figure 12.7*.

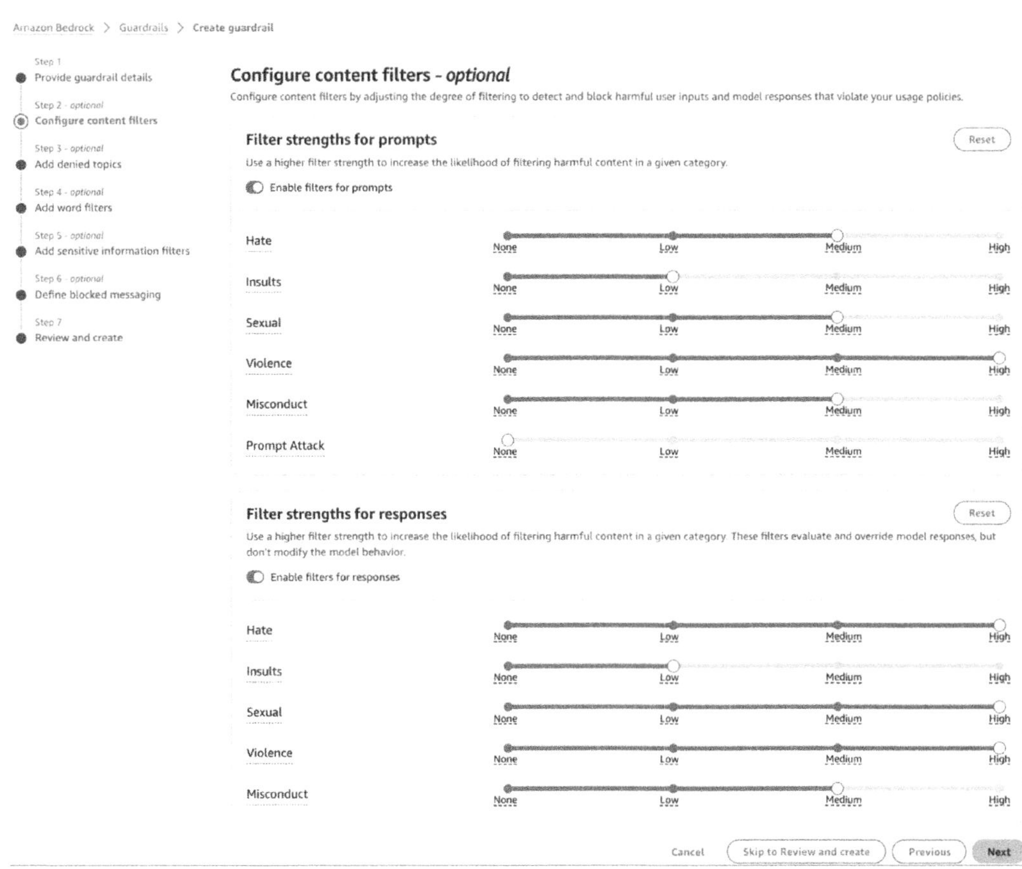

Figure 12.7 – Configuring content filters

Categories covered include hate speech, insults, sexual content, violence, misconduct, and prompt attacks, allowing you to address a wide range of potential risks. The higher the filter strength, the higher the likelihood of filtering out potentially harmful content within a given category, providing a flexible way to balance risk mitigation and content accessibility.

When implementing content filters, it's essential to consider your use case, target audience, and ethical guidelines. A higher filter strength may be appropriate for applications serving vulnerable populations or dealing with sensitive topics, while a more relaxed approach could be suitable for certain creative or educational contexts. In addition, regularly reviewing and updating your filter configurations in response to evolving societal norms and organizational policies is recommended. By leveraging content filters, you can proactively mitigate the risks associated with harmful content generation, encouraging a more trustworthy and responsible AI ecosystem.

Denied topics

Denied topics allow you to proactively prevent your application from engaging with or generating content related to specific subjects that may be deemed undesirable or inappropriate within your use case.

You can define up to 30 denied topics by providing a concise name and a clear natural language description for each topic you wish to restrict. These serve as the foundation for detecting and blocking user inputs or model responses that fall within the defined topic boundaries, ensuring a consistent and reliable filtering mechanism.

When specifying a denied topic, it's advisable to provide a comprehensive definition that captures the essence of the subject matter you aim to exclude, surrounding all relevant inquiries, guidance, or recommendations.

For example, in the healthcare domain, maintaining patient privacy and adhering to strict ethical guidelines is important. A hospital or medical institution could leverage denied topics to prevent the models from engaging in discussions or providing information related to specific topics that could potentially violate patient confidentiality or medical ethics.

One denied topic could be *Disclosing Patient Information*, with a definition along the lines of *Sharing or revealing personal details, medical records, or any identifying information about patients without proper authorization.*

Another relevant denied topic might be *Unauthorized Medical Advice*, defined as *Providing diagnostic assessments, treatment recommendations, or any form of medical guidance without being a licensed healthcare professional or having access to a patient's complete medical history.*

Figure 12.8 shows how to add denied topics.

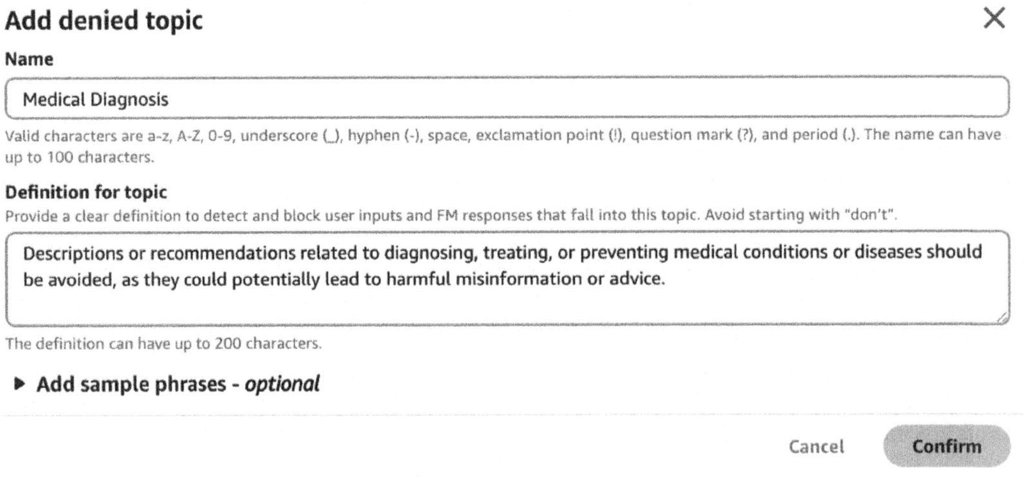

Add denied topic

Name

Medical Diagnosis

Valid characters are a-z, A-Z, 0-9, underscore (_), hyphen (-), space, exclamation point (!), question mark (?), and period (.). The name can have up to 100 characters.

Definition for topic

Provide a clear definition to detect and block user inputs and FM responses that fall into this topic. Avoid starting with "don't".

Descriptions or recommendations related to diagnosing, treating, or preventing medical conditions or diseases should be avoided, as they could potentially lead to harmful misinformation or advice.

The definition can have up to 200 characters.

▶ **Add sample phrases - *optional***

Cancel Confirm

Figure 12.8 – Adding a denied topic

Word filters

By configuring **word filters**, you can effectively block undesirable words, phrases, and profanity from appearing in user inputs or model responses, promoting a positive and inclusive user experience. Here is how:

- The **profanity filter** offers a convenient way to block a predefined list of commonly recognized profane words. This list is based on a global definition of profanity and is subject to regular updates, ensuring that the filter remains aligned with evolving societal norms.
- Additionally, you can customize the word filtering experience by specifying up to 10,000 custom words and phrases that should be blocked. This flexibility allows you to tailor the filters to your specific needs, such as excluding offensive terms, competitor names, or any other language that may be deemed inappropriate for your use case.
- Custom words and phrases can be added through various convenient methods, including a manual entry in the console, uploading a local file (e.g., `.txt` or `.csv`), or populating the list from an Amazon S3 object, providing flexibility in managing your word filter list.

Figure 12.9 shows how you can configure the word filter with different options.

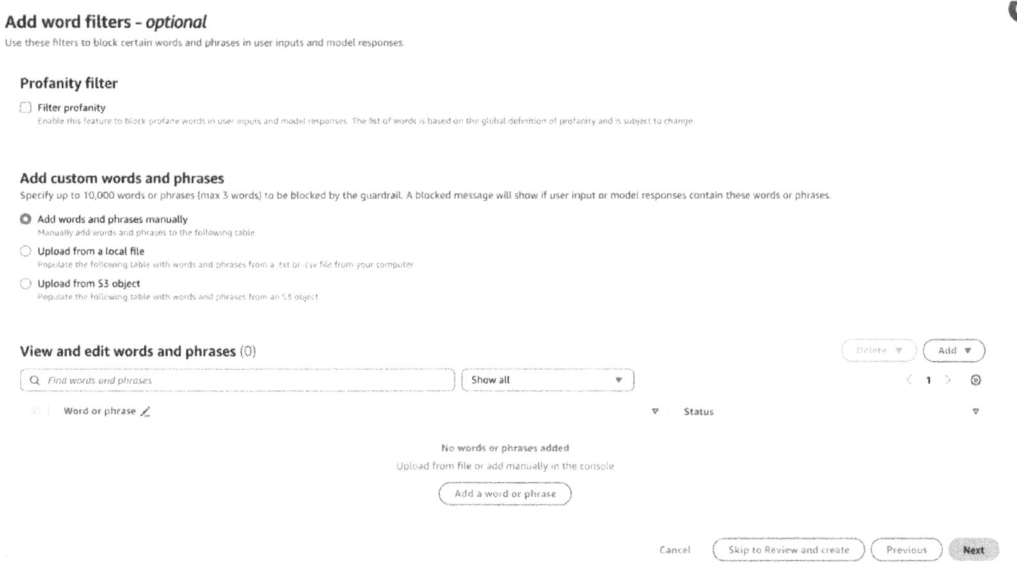

Figure 12.9 – Adding word filters

By using word filters, you can create a more controlled and inclusive environment for your users. For instance, an educational platform could block offensive language to promote a positive learning atmosphere, while a corporate application might filter out competitor names to maintain brand integrity and avoid potential conflicts.

Sensitive information filters

Sensitive information filters allow you to proactively identify and take appropriate actions on various types of PII and custom-defined sensitive data patterns.

Guardrails offer a comprehensive list of predefined PII types, covering a wide range of sensitive information such as names, addresses, email addresses, phone numbers, credit card details, and social security numbers. These PII types are constantly updated to ensure compliance with evolving regulations and privacy norms. For a complete list, you can visit `https://docs.aws.amazon.com/bedrock/latest/userguide/Guardrails-sensitive-filters.html`.

When sensitive information is detected, you can configure guardrails to either block or mask the content:

- **Block mode**: This prevents the sensitive information from being processed at all. If applied to the input, it stops the prompt containing sensitive data from reaching the model. If applied to the output, it prevents the model's response containing sensitive information from reaching the user.
- **Mask mode**: This allows processing but redacts the sensitive data, replacing it with identifiers. For example, a social security number such as `123-45-6789` might be replaced with `[SSN]`. This ensures privacy while preserving the overall context of the content.

Additionally, you can define custom **regular expression** (**regex**) patterns to filter specific types of sensitive information relevant to your organization or use case. This flexibility allows you to protect proprietary data, such as serial numbers, booking IDs, or any other critical information that requires safeguarding. For example:

- **A custom product serial number**: `^ABC-\d{5}-[A-Z]{2}$` (matches patterns such as `ABC-12345-XY`)
- **An internal booking ID**: `^BK-\d{6}-[A-Z]{3}$` (matches patterns such as `BK-123456-NYC`)
- **A company-specific employee ID**: `^EMP-\d{4}-[A-Z]{2}$` (matches patterns such as `EMP-1234-AB`)

These custom patterns can be used alongside the predefined PII types to create a comprehensive sensitive information protection strategy tailored to your specific needs.

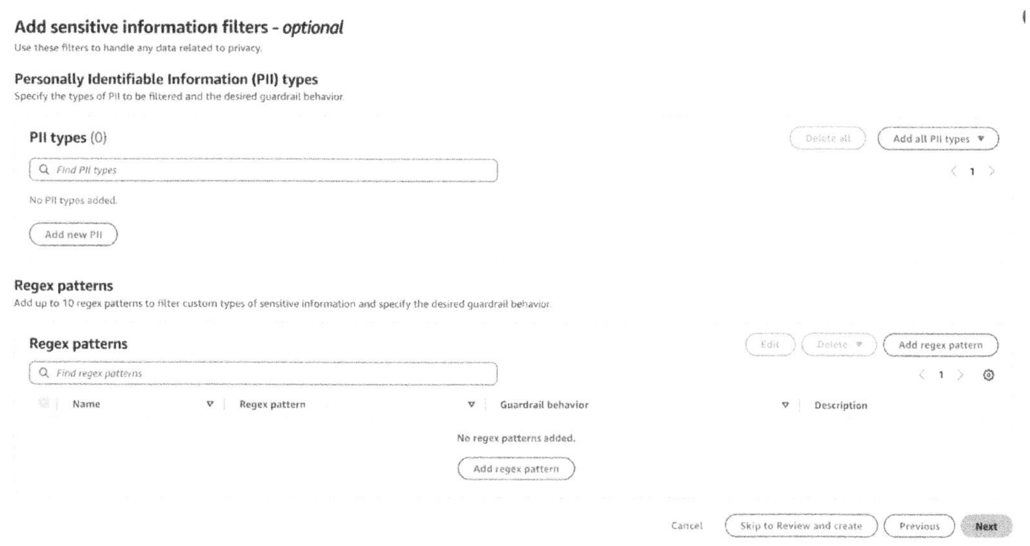

Figure 12.10 – Adding sensitive information filters

Figure 12.10 shows the configuration options you can specify for sensitive information filters.

By leveraging sensitive information filters, you can ensure that your applications maintain the highest standards of privacy and data protection. For instance, a healthcare provider could configure guardrails to mask patient information in summaries, while a financial institution could block queries related to credit card details or account numbers, mitigating the risk of data breaches and maintaining regulatory compliance.

Blocked messaging

Once we have defined the policy filters, you can then next define the blocked messaging, when the guardrail blocks any input prompt or response from the model. In such cases, a pre-approved response is provided, tailored to the specific use case or organizational guidelines. *Figure 12.11* shows what messaging you would like to display for both input prompts and model responses.

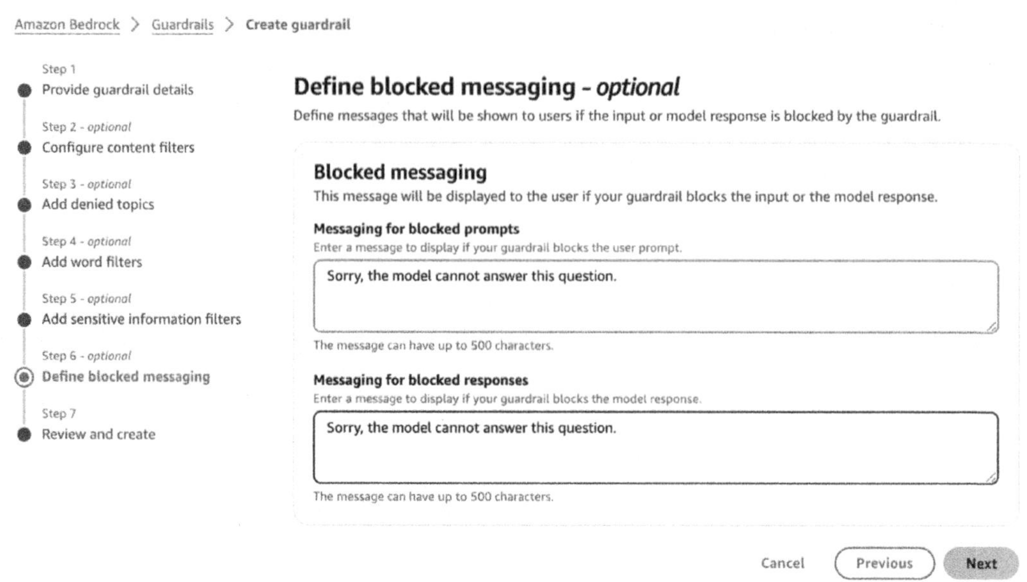

Figure 12.11 – Blocked messaging

This approach ensures that the end user receives a safe, appropriate, and compliant response, even in scenarios where the initial input or model output raises concerns.

Testing and deploying guardrails

By testing the guardrail, you can iteratively refine and test the models, ensuring they align with your intended use case and adhere to ethical standards. Here's how it works:

First, you create a guardrail, which initializes a working draft (`DRAFT`) version. Think of this as a sandbox environment where you can experiment without impacting live systems. This working draft is something you can continuously edit and tweak until you're satisfied with its performance.

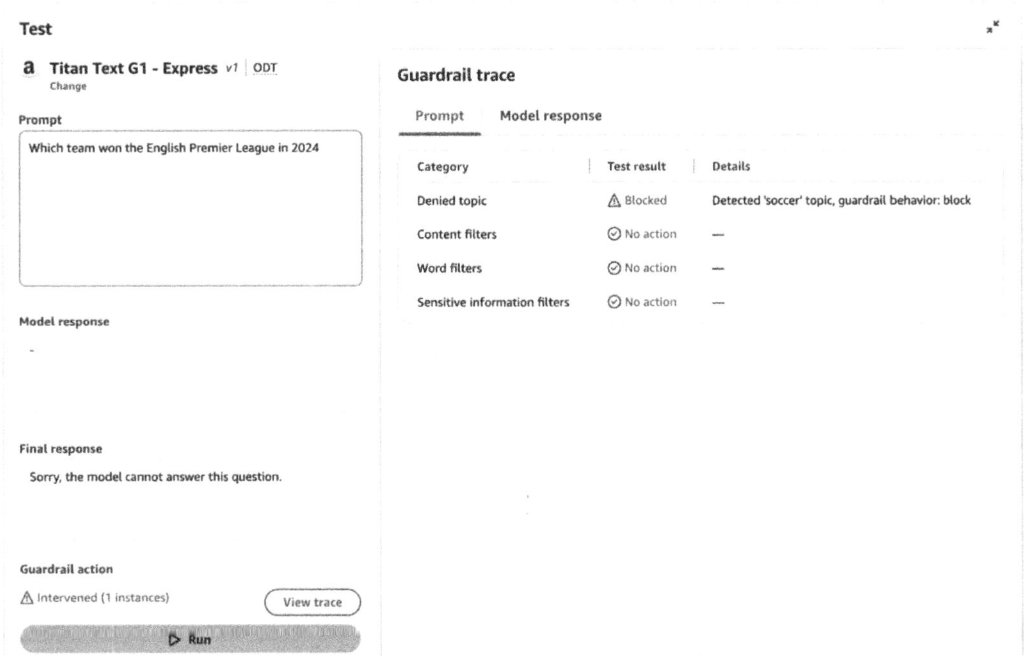

Figure 12.12 – Test Guardrails for Amazon Bedrock

Figure 12.12 shows the test results of the working draft. Here, I have taken a simple example of soccer, where I have provided `soccer` as a denied topic. When I provide a prompt pertaining to soccer, the model blocks the response. You can also see from the figure the prompt and model response trace.

Once you've perfected the working draft, you can create a version – a snapshot of the guardrail's configurations at that point in time. Additionally, these versions function as immutable checkpoints in the system. This immutability serves a critical purpose: it prevents potential immediate negative impacts on the runtime environment that could occur if a draft version were accidentally deployed to production. For instance, if an engineer inadvertently made a modification to a draft version directly through the console interface, these immutable checkpoints would ensure that such changes don't affect the live production environment. This safeguard helps maintain system stability and prevents unintended consequences from impromptu modifications.

It's important to note that any changes made to the working draft will automatically update the live application if the draft is being used in the application. You must explicitly incorporate the desired version into your application to reflect the latest guardrail configurations.

Now that we have created, tested and deployed guardrails, let us look at how we can use it.

Using guardrails

Guardrails can be used in various ways:

- **Model Inference**: If you are using Amazon Bedrock console, you can select your guardrail in the playground. Whereas, if you are using Amazon Bedrock APIs, you can use the guardrail with `InvokeModel`, `InvokeModelWithResponseStream`, and `Converse` APIs.
- **Knowledge base**: You can include guardrails when querying your knowledge base in the Amazon Bedrock console or via APIs.
- **Guardrail to your agent**: Associate a guardrail with your agent when creating or updating an agent in the Amazon Bedrock console or API.

Figure 12.13 shows the response with and without using Guardrails within Amazon Bedrock Playground.

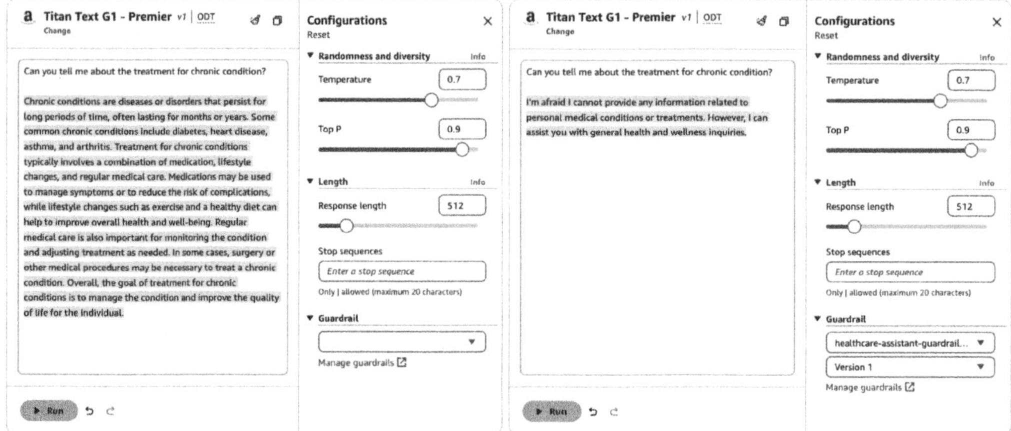

Figure 12.13 – Using Guardrails in Amazon Bedrock Playground

With Amazon Bedrock APIs, you can specify `guardrailIdentifier` and `guardrailIdentifier` as shown in the code:

```
%pip install boto3 botocore

#import the main packages and libraries
import os
import boto3
import json
import botocore

bedrock_runtime = boto3.client('bedrock-runtime') # Provide the
desired_region
```

```
prompt = "Can you tell me about the treatment for chronic condition?"

body = json.dumps({"inputText": prompt,
                   "textGenerationConfig":{
                       "maxTokenCount":4096,
                       "stopSequences":[],
                       "temperature":0,
                       "topP":1
                   },
                  })

modelId = 'amazon.titan-tg1-large' # change this to use a different
version from the model provider
accept = 'application/json'
contentType = 'application/json'

response1 = bedrock_runtime.invoke_model(body=body,
                                         modelId=modelId,
                                         accept=accept,
                                         contentType
                                           =contentType,
                                         trace="ENABLED",
                                         guardrailIdentifier
                                           = 'vtfzfvd8ccoz',
                                         guardrailVersion=
                                           "1"
                                         )
response_g = json.loads(response1.get('body').read())
#print(response_body.get('results')[0].get('outputText'))
#output_body = json.loads(response1["body"].read().decode())
action = response_g["amazon-bedrock-guardrailAction"]
if action == "INTERVENED":
    print("Guardrail Intervention: {}".format(json.
dumps(response_g["amazon-bedrock-trace"]["guardrail"], indent=2)))
print("Guardrail action: {}".format(response_g["amazon-bedrock-
guardrailAction"]))
print("Output text: {}".format(response_g["results"][0]
["outputText"]))
```

When running the preceding code, you can see that the response would be similar to what is shown in *Figure 12.14*.

```
Guardrail Intervention: {
  "input": {
    "vtfzfvd8ccoz": {
      "topicPolicy": {
        "topics": [
          {
            "name": "PersonalHealthInformation",
            "type": "DENY",
            "action": "BLOCKED"
          }
        ]
      }
    }
  }
}
Guardrail action: INTERVENED
Output text: I'm afraid I cannot provide any information related to personal medical conditions or treatments.
However, I can assist you with general health and wellness inquiries.
```

Figure 12.14 – Response with Guardrails

You can see that the prompt provided in the code relates to medical treatment, for which we have configured Denied Topics filter in `Guardrail`. The code snippet includes `guardrailIdentifier` and `guardrailVersion` to enable Bedrock Guardrails, which can intervene and modify the model's output based on the filter that is configured.

Furthermore, when using a guardrail with model inference, you can selectively evaluate user input by tagging specific content within the input text. This feature allows you to apply guardrails to certain parts of the input while leaving other parts unprocessed.

For example, imagine you're creating a conversational AI assistant for a banking application. While you want your assistant to provide helpful information to users, you also need to ensure it doesn't reveal sensitive account details or encourage risky financial behavior. By selectively evaluating user input, you can apply guardrails to specific sections of the conversation, like user queries, while leaving system prompts and conversation history untouched.

Here's how you could implement this:

- Use input tags to mark user queries, for example, `<amazon-bedrock-guardrails-guardContent_abc>How much money is in my savings account?</amazon-bedrock-guardrails-guardContent_abc>`
- Configure a dynamic tag suffix (for example, `abc`) in the `amazon-bedrock-guardrailConfig` to prevent prompt injection attacks.
- Any content outside the tags such as system prompts and conversation history won't be processed by guardrails.
- For user queries within the tags, guardrails will ensure the AI assistant's response doesn't reveal sensitive financial information or promote irresponsible money management.

This approach not only enhances security and control but also optimizes performance and reduces costs, as guardrails only evaluate the tagged user input instead of the entire prompt.

When using guardrails with streaming responses, you can either configure it to **synchronous mode** or **asynchronous mode**. The synchronous mode introduces some latency as the guardrail buffers and applies policies to response chunks before sending them to the user, ensuring better accuracy. Alternatively, the asynchronous mode sends response chunks immediately while applying policies in the background, sacrificing accuracy for lower latency.

You can enable asynchronous mode by including `"streamProcessingMode": "ASYNCHRONOUS"` in `amazon-bedrock-guardrailConfig`. Here is how:

```
{
    "amazon-bedrock-guardrailConfig": {
    "streamProcessingMode": "ASYNCHRONOUS"
    }
}
```

For conversational applications built with `Converse` API, you can use guardrails to block inappropriate content entered by the user or generated by the model. When calling the `Converse` or `ConverseStream` operations, include the guardrail configuration in the `guardrailConfig` parameter. Here is how:

```
{
        "guardrailIdentifier": "Guardrail ID",
        "guardrailVersion": "Guardrail version",
        "trace": "enabled"
}
```

Here is an example code on how you can guard the conversation by using guardrails on `Converse` API: `https://docs.aws.amazon.com/bedrock/latest/userguide/guardrails-use-converse-api.html#converse-api-guardrail-example`.

Guardrails for Amazon Bedrock is a feature that allows organizations to implement safeguards and policy filters to ensure the safe and responsible use of AI models. It provides four policy filters – content filters, denied topics, word filters, and sensitive information filters – to block or redact unwanted content, topics, words, and sensitive information from both user inputs and model outputs. Guardrails helps maintain compliance with regulations, protect user privacy, and prevent the generation of harmful or unethical content.

Summary

This chapter began by emphasizing the importance of data privacy and protection for organizations in today's digital landscape. It highlighted Amazon Bedrock's robust security measures, which ensure that users maintain complete control over their data, along with key aspects such as data localization, isolation, encryption, and access management through IAM.

The chapter then dove deeper into responsible AI practices, addressing challenges such as veracity, intellectual property rights, safety, and toxicity. It provided guidance on implementing content filtering, guardrails, data curation, watermarking, traceability, and establishing robust responsible AI policies. Additionally, the chapter introduced Guardrails for Amazon Bedrock, which offers four policy filters: content filters, denied topics, word filters, and sensitive information filters. These filters enable organizations to implement safeguards aligning with their safe and responsible AI policies, promoting ethical AI deployment across various industries.

Congratulations! You have reached the end of this book. By now, you have gained deep hands-on knowledge of Amazon Bedrock. From understanding the foundational concepts to practical implementations and real-world use cases, we have covered a wide range of topics that will provide you with the knowledge and skills to build scalable and innovative GenAI applications.

Throughout the chapters, we have explored the power of prompt engineering, continuous pre-training, fine-tuning models, and RAG, along with the development of intelligent agents with Amazon Bedrock.

We explored various architectural patterns, such as text generation, summarization, question answering, entity extraction, code generation, and image creation. Additionally, we addressed crucial aspects of monitoring, security, and privacy, ensuring that you can confidently navigate the intricate world of GenAI with Amazon Bedrock while adhering to ethical standards and best practices. You now have a comprehensive understanding of Amazon Bedrock, its capabilities, and the techniques required to harness its full potential.

Index

A

D

E

F

G

H

I

J

K

L

M

N

O

P

Q

R

S

W

Z

`packtpub.com`

Subscribe to our online digital library for full access to over 7,000 books and videos, as well as industry leading tools to help you plan your personal development and advance your career. For more information, please visit our website.

Why subscribe?

- Spend less time learning and more time coding with practical eBooks and Videos from over 4,000 industry professionals
- Improve your learning with Skill Plans built especially for you
- Get a free eBook or video every month
- Fully searchable for easy access to vital information
- Copy and paste, print, and bookmark content

Did you know that Packt offers eBook versions of every book published, with PDF and ePub files available? You can upgrade to the eBook version at `packtpub.com` and as a print book customer, you are entitled to a discount on the eBook copy. Get in touch with us at `customercare@packtpub.com` for more details.

At `www.packtpub.com`, you can also read a collection of free technical articles, sign up for a range of free newsletters, and receive exclusive discounts and offers on Packt books and eBooks.

Other Books You May Enjoy

If you enjoyed this book, you may be interested in these other books by Packt:

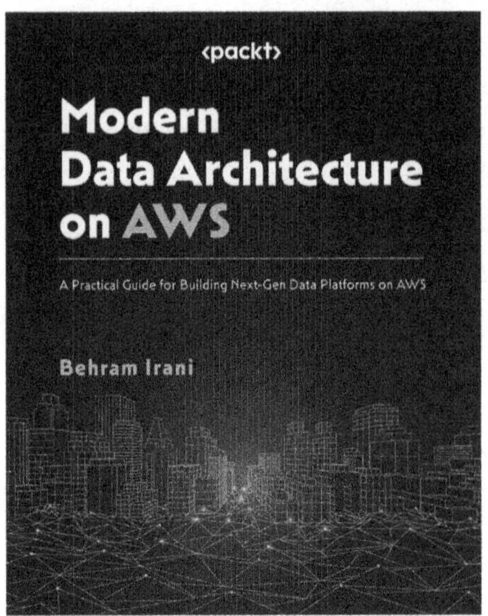

Modern Data Architecture on AWS

Behram Irani

ISBN: 978-1-80181-339-6

- Familiarize yourself with the building blocks of modern data architecture on AWS
- Discover how to create an end-to-end data platform on AWS
- Design data architectures for your own use cases using AWS services
- Ingest data from disparate sources into target data stores on AWS
- Build data pipelines, data sharing mechanisms, and data consumption patterns using AWS services
- Find out how to implement data governance using AWS services

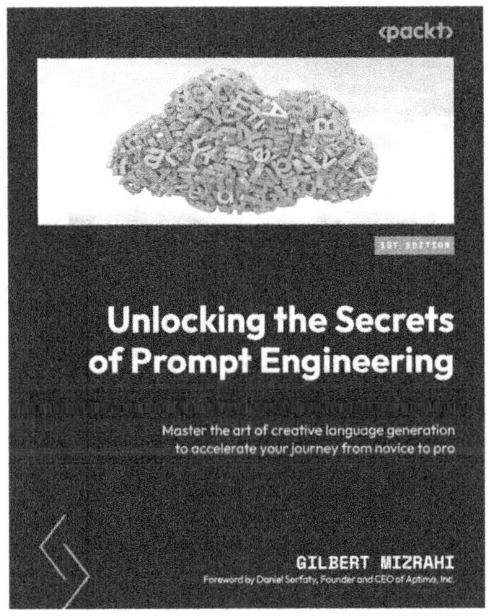

Unlocking the Secrets of Prompt Engineering

Gilbert Mizrahi

ISBN: 978-1-83508-383-3

- Explore the different types of prompts, their strengths, and weaknesses
- Understand the AI agent's knowledge and mental model
- Enhance your creative writing with AI insights for fiction and poetry
- Develop advanced skills in AI chatbot creation and deployment
- Discover how AI will transform industries such as education, legal, and others
- Integrate LLMs with various tools to boost productivity
- Understand AI ethics and best practices, and navigate limitations effectively
- Experiment and optimize AI techniques for best results

Packt is searching for authors like you

If you're interested in becoming an author for Packt, please visit `authors.packtpub.com` and apply today. We have worked with thousands of developers and tech professionals, just like you, to help them share their insight with the global tech community. You can make a general application, apply for a specific hot topic that we are recruiting an author for, or submit your own idea.

Share Your Thoughts

Now you've finished *Generative AI with Amazon Bedrock*, we'd love to hear your thoughts! Scan the QR code below to go straight to the Amazon review page for this book and share your feedback or leave a review on the site that you purchased it from.

`https://packt.link/r/1803247282`

Your review is important to us and the tech community and will help us make sure we're delivering excellent quality content.

Download a free PDF copy of this book

Thanks for purchasing this book!

Do you like to read on the go but are unable to carry your print books everywhere?

Is your eBook purchase not compatible with the device of your choice?

Don't worry, now with every Packt book you get a DRM-free PDF version of that book at no cost.

Read anywhere, any place, on any device. Search, copy, and paste code from your favorite technical books directly into your application.

The perks don't stop there, you can get exclusive access to discounts, newsletters, and great free content in your inbox daily

Follow these simple steps to get the benefits:

1. Scan the QR code or visit the link below

`https://packt.link/free-ebook/9781803247281`

2. Submit your proof of purchase
3. That's it! We'll send your free PDF and other benefits to your email directly

Made in the USA
Las Vegas, NV
11 September 2024